High

Long Canyon with full moon over the route *2 Plumb*

Introduction

Moab Climbs: High on Moab by Karl Kelley
©2017 Sharp End Publishing. All rights reserved. No part of this book may be used or reproduced in any manner without written permission of the publisher.

Published and distributed by
Sharp End Publishing, LLC
PO Box 1613
Boulder, CO 80306
t. 303.444.2698
www.sharpendbooks.com

ISBN: 978-1-892540-76-8
Library of Congress Control Number: 2014940047

Front cover: In the foreground, Jay Smith on the third pitch of his route *Clearlight* 5.11, belayed by his wife Kitty Calhoun. In the background, Telluride climber Sarah Szczech on the summit of Lighthouse Tower with Chris Johnson, Brandon Griep, and Ben Jefferies at the final belay.

Special Thanks: Charley Graham for editing; Joe Slansky for pre-press and photo corrections; Jason Keith for educating us all with his words of concern on an area loved by so many, and for fighting for our continued access.

Printed in South Korea.

READ THIS BEFORE USING THIS BOOK: WARNING!

Climbing is a very dangerous activity. Take all precautions and evaluate your ability carefully. Use judgment rather than the opinions represented in this book. The publishers and authors assume no responsibility for injury or death resulting from the use of this book. This book is based on opinions. Do not rely on information, descriptions, or difficulty ratings as these are entirely subjective. If you are unwilling to assume complete responsibility for your safety, do not use this guide book.

THE AUTHOR AND PUBLISHER EXPRESSLY DISCLAIM ALL REPRESENTATIONS AND WARRANTIES REGARDING THIS GUIDE, THE ACCURACY OF THE INFORMATION HEREIN, AND THE RESULTS OF YOUR USE HEREOF, INCLUDING WITHOUT LIMITATION, IMPLIED WARRANTIES OF MERCHANTABILITY AND FITNESS FOR A PARTICULAR PURPOSE. THE USER ASSUMES ALL RISK ASSOCIATED WITH THE USE OF THIS GUIDE.

It is your responsibility to take care of yourself while climbing. Seek a professional instructor or guide if you are unsure of your ability to handle any circumstances that may arise. This guide is not intended as an instructional manual.

Table of Contents

Introduction — 4

Highway 191 North — 23

313 Road — 31
- Along the 313 Road — 33
- Canyonlands — 45

Little Valley — 77

Arches National Park — 85

Potash Road — 101
- Wall Street — 105
- Culvert Canyon — 131
- Day Canyon — 135
- Long Canyon — 143

River Road — 179
- Roadside — 181
- Castle Valley — 205
- Onion Creek — 239
- Fisher Towers — 245

Kane Creek — 253

La Sal Mountains — 281

191 South — 295

Appendices & Index — 303

About the Author

Karl Kelley, a self-proclaimed adventurer, started visiting Moab in 1984 after moving west to pursue his lifelong dream of being a ski bum. He grew up in Franconia, NH where he started skiing at the age of three. He spent the late 80s and early 90s living and skiing at resorts throughout the West until settling in Salt Lake City in 1994. He and his wife Michelle fell in love with Utah, , especially the Moab valley—the mountains, the sunshine, the snow, the incredible beauty. It was in SLC that Karl started climbing. Though winters were filled with wonderful skiing, climbing soon became a passion. Frequent trips to Moab to climb, bike, hike and camp made Karl and Michelle realize that there was something very special about it.

They finally decided it was time to escape the hustle and bustle of the city and moved to Moab in 2001 where they opened a restaurant, the Desert Bistro. Karl is the chef and works a full-time schedule March – November, but still finds plenty of time quench his thirst for climbing and adventure by day, working by night. He has climbed well over 1000 desert routes and, with friends, has established over 250 new routes. Karl loves to travel and experience new sights and cultures all over the world. A new passion was also discovered during the creation of this book—being behind the lens—photographing skiing, climbing, landscapes, flowers and good food. Karl feels lucky to share some of his own photos alongside the great photographers in this book.

Introduction

Foreword

This book is a gift. It is Karl's gift to you. These pages, these words, came from his heart. They express a passion for the climbs, the landscape, the people, and the community of Moab. I've published nearly 40 books and penned a few of my own, and I've seen no author put so much thought or heart into a project the way Karl has. I've watched him pain over the presentation, not only with the writing, but more importantly, in the way in which he would capture the desert—in trying to provide you, the user, with a guide to his most special place.

I met the author nearly a decade ago, when without knowing me, he reached out to help with our Indian Creek book. He selflessly shared his profound knowledge, filling in the blanks, and allowing us to create a better, more complete book—one that provided visitors with a better experience. This is how Karl and I became friends.

The Moab desert represents, to me, adventure, discovery, and wildness. The red rock cliffs and spires are unique, as is the nascent climbing community. When I first climbed in the region, there were no guides. The new route book at Rim Cyclery (which served as a climbing shop) was the only real source of information in the pre-internet day. Local climbers, apart from Kyle Copeland, didn't exist. I travelled to Moab so much that I felt like a local. A profound shift occurred with the publication of Eric Bjørnstad's *Desert Rock*—a book that inspired so many. It exposed endless possibilities for adventure and discovery. Soon, armed with a "standard desert rack" climbers began migrating to Edward Abbey's desert (for climbers, it may have been Bjørnstad's desert).

I've watched the town grow over 30 years and a climbing community develop. Folks, like Karl, looking for year-round cragging in a profound setting, began to flock to this region of endless rock and untapped potential. When *Desert Rock* became extinct, I filled the void with a book (more of a pamphlet) that would later morph to *Classic Desert Climbs*. Other books followed, including more from Bjørnstad, which documented the endless supply of new lines or select visions of desert climbing.

Until *High on Moab*, however, there hasn't been a far-reaching guide authored by a true active local. This is an important caveat. The Moab community is unique, and by community I mean more than just the climbing community. I can't imagine what it's like for long-time residents who watched their town evolve from a ranching and mining village to a tourist hub for outdoor pursuits. I've seen it happen, but from afar. I've watched a diverse climbing community develop, with a Mill Creek crowd, an Indian Creek crowd, a Wall Street crowd…. It's a vocal, concerned, and deeply passionate confederacy—one for which Karl cares dearly. In our many conversations during this guidebook process, Karl's primary concern has been creating a tome that would represent locals while empowering visitors to create the climbing trip of their dreams.

Some locals may be distressed, but I promise them they were heard. Karl reached out to everyone, relied on all. Even more than an author, he is the spokesman for the clan. A local needed to create this guide, one who hears and addresses the concerns of residents. Karl is that local. Anyone who knows, or has even met him, knows there's no ego involved. He loves and respects everyone in the community. He doesn't judge other users and solicits respect for the off-roaders, the residents, the land managers, the others who enjoy the landscape in their own ways. There's no motivation for profit; from the get-go Karl pledged 100% of his royalties to charities, and after much debate decided on the Access Fund.

I find his emotional challenges very much in line with the sage of the Canyon Country—the late Edward Abbey. Cactus Ed empathized with the Catch-22 faced by the National Park Service, deeded with the responsibility to "protect and preserve for the enjoyment of all" —a mandate that is inherently conflicted. In more recent time, Richard Louv's book *Last Child in the Woods* posits that our nation's "Nature Deficit Disorder" stems from our inability to interact with nature—that we are too controlled, that children can no longer throw stones, dam a creek, build a dirt jump or a tree fort. Yes, these activities come with a marginal environmental cost (as does climbing), but the ensuing connection to nature outweighs the minor costs.

A century ago, a boy ran along a beach with his gun, handmade from a piece of lead pipe. From time to time, he would stop and shoot at a gull. Today, such activity would be cause for time spent in juvenile hall, but for young John Muir, it was another way to connect with nature. Muir went on to become one of the initiators of modern environmentalism.

Please, go out and have an adventure; explore lonely crags; summit a slender spire; enjoy our public lands; connect with the natural world. Yes, the desert—more than many other places—is fragile. I'm not a believer in harming the environment; we must protect our resources. I also believe the lands are for the enjoyment of all and that mindful exposure will lead to love, that will—in turn—cultivate a desire to protect and preserve.

Enjoy this gift.

-Fred Knapp
Publisher

Muir's story excerpted from *Last Child in the Woods*

High on Moab

My "High on Moab" began before I even knew how to climb. My fascination with the West started in 1984, shortly after getting out of high school in Franconia, NH. Skiing was my life and some of my fondest memories involved going to the high school auditorium as a youngster to watch the newest Warren Miller ski films. As the years went by, I set my sights on moving west to fulfill my dream of being in the "real" mountains. After high school I left for Colorado to become a full-fledged ski bum. Crested Butte was my destination and where my "high" began. When winter ended and mud season set in, I was asked by a friend "do you want to mountain bike in the desert?" I didn't even know where that was, but he told me about a place not too far away called Moab. So, we packed up the camping gear and bikes and took off.

As we drove down the River Road, I was totally blown away. Having grown up in the dense woods of New Hampshire, I couldn't believe my eyes—the vastness and open lands, the sheer red walls lining the river, the most incredible valley (Castle Valley) with towers in the foreground and white peaks in the background. It was Shangri-La. I fell in love with the area before rock climbing became a part of my life.

As a ski bum I moved all over the West, checking out the areas that impressed me from the Warren Miller films: Tahoe, Taos, Crystal Mountain, to name a few. However, one thing remained constant—I headed to Moab every spring and fall. Eventually, I moved to Salt Lake City to experience the greatest snow on earth. My first year in Alta featured a 900" winter. I was home and there was no going back! My visits to Moab became much more frequent—camping over long weekends, vacations, or any window of time. Skiing brought my wife and I to Utah, but the spring, summer and fall activities are what kept us there. We bought harnesses, a rope, a few carabiners and some books—and set out to learn how to climb! Slowly but surely, I gained the experience and confidence to start leading. I was hooked! Skiing and climbing merged to create a new balance.

After several years of bliss, our year-round employment in Alta became seasonal. With the Salt Lake Valley growing, we welcomed change and a reprieve from the crowds. We desired a home that offered world-class climbing, great weather AND mountains. Moab was the answer.

Shortly after making the move, we opened a restaurant. We serve dinners only, which allows us to climb until early afternoon just about every day. Business is slow enough in the winter months, that we close shop and depart for epic ski journeys. We often joke that we had to move to the desert to become true ski bums. That being said, we climb for 9+ months in this beautiful desert we call home and I'm as "high" as ever on this place.

While I might not climb the biggest, baddest and hardest lines, I truly enjoy the entire experience! I only wish I had started climbing earlier in my life.

Michelle enjoying the Moab high

Introduction

It has been six years since this guidebook was first envisioned. My friend Fred Knapp asked me if I would be interested in helping him revamp his *Classic Desert Climbs* guidebook. There was really no hesitation—of course I would help my friend. I was honored he asked and it also gave me the opportunity to explore reaches of the Moab Valley I had never been to or only visited briefly in past years. Since its start, the project has morphed from a rediscovery of the time-tested "select" classics of yesteryear into a more detailed book that would include the classics, but also introduce newly developed areas and offer comprehensive coverage to some of the more popular, well-established crags.

Over the years my friends have asked what the book would be titled. It was as stressful as coming up with a name for our restaurant over a dozen years ago...silly really, what's in a name? *High on Moab* to me is perfect. This book is built by people who are as high on this area as I am, people who live and love it here (at present or in the past), people who have spent many of their vacations or free time here. This is a tribute to all of them! Even those who chose not to contribute helped build this book with their silence. I consider their reserve a testament to their concern.

My wife and I have been fortunate enough to travel to some very special places—whether to ski, bike, climb, or just simply sightsee. We recently took a trip to the Dolomites in Italy where we picked up a souvenir coffee-table book *Dolomiti*. The first page offers a passage that struck me to the core, summing up exactly how I feel about the Moab area:

> The Dolomites: natural shapes, metaphors for "monuments," "cathedrals," and "buildings," capable of producing extraordinary feelings.
>
> They are objects that unite people and do not divide them. People who are constantly in search of beauty such as poets, painters and musicians, are moved by the very same emotions as common people. Social, cultural, ethnic and religious differences dissolve into awe in view of the Dolomites. A hymn to universality which extreme, almost absolute beauty can create and thus draw us closer to God.
>
> But not all humans allow themselves to be caught, almost lifted, by the strong emotions these mountains convey. Some people have the narcissist and racist belief to be the only ones to hold the key to interpreting the beauty of the Dolomites. If they could, they would build a huge fence around these mountains, and only few chosen ones—picked by those people themselves, of course—could gain access and enjoy these feelings.
>
> But the fact that UNESCO designated them a World Heritage site is a severe cultural punishment for all those who see the mountains only in their conservative-elitest meaning and not as a good to be enjoyed with wisdom and as widely as possible. All the world should have the right to be delighted by this geographical condition, not only a few arrogant and self-centered people."
>
> —Giovanni Campeol (the Secretary General of the Dolomites UNESCO foundation)

As I read this, I thought: "Wow, aside from being declared a world heritage site, if you replaced the word *dolomite* with *red rock cliffs and canyons*, this quote could be perfectly fitted to the Moab valley. Many artists, poets, and musicians have been moved by this place; movies have been filmed, books have been written, etc.

We have our own rich history here, including our climbing history, with the likes of Layton Kor, Huntley Ingalls, Harvey Carter, Fred Beckey, Jim Donini and our own, late Eric Bjørnstad. Many of the greats have rolled through the Moab valley to experience the many splitters, corners, and wild summits the valley has to offer. Some have even stayed and made it their home: Jay Smith, Kitty Calhoun, Gregg Child, Lyle Dean, Tom Gilji, Steph Davis to name a few. Indeed we climb in the shadows of many *greats*.

Moab is not like our neighboring Indian Creek. Certainly not as "craggy" or as easily accessible. Instead the climbing here is more spread out with a "you gotta want it" feel! There is a lifetime of great climbing in the Moab area. Stacks of towers to summit, two different national parks, many adventurous drives and approaches, and so much solitude and beauty, Moab offers all sorts of varied climbing and *High on Moab* gives you a taste. When you come here for the first time you are blown away by the eye candy. Camping on a clear night unveils a blanket of stars over the open desert; sunsets and moonrises are paramount; and the rock—well, get on it! In the words of Giovanni, "all the world should have the right to be delighted by this geographical condition." I couldn't agree more, which is why I want to share it with you.

Be safe, and respectful!

Enjoy,
Karl

Influences and Mentors

There are so many people to whom I owe a thank-you! Where to start? A huge thank you to an old friend, Scott Oda, who got me into climbing as well as brought me on my first multi-pitch route and summit—Castleton Tower. Words of wisdom from Scott years ago will forever stick in my head. I was new to climbing, living in S.L.C., cragging in the Wasatch, and moving through the grades, ascending every 5.6 I could find, then every 5.7, and then on to 5.8. While in the 5.8 range, I remember struggling on *Satan's Corner* in Little Cottonwood. I was stubborn and didn't want to move on to 5.9 without completing this dihedral clean. Had I plateaued at 5.8? I confided in Scott who was an excellent climber ticking much harder grades. He asked me why I climb. I told him it was because I love it. He said, "Then why do you care about the grades? If you have plateaued at 5.8 and you will never climb any harder and you love climbing, then travel the world and climb every 5.8 you can!" Though over the years I have certainly challenged myself to climb as hard as I can, I have never really worried too much about where I am within the grading system. Thanks to Scott, I STILL CLIMB TO HAVE FUN. To reiterate something another climbing mentor, Jim Donini, once said, "As long as I can get out of bed, I will continue to climb."

Another influence is Scott Carson, a working owner of International Mountain Equipment in Salt Lake City. Scott is one of the most humble and nicest climbers/human beings I ever had the pleasure of meeting! While living in SLC, I bought most of my gear/supplies at his shop. I would make my purchase and always ended up staying and talking local beta and lore with Scott. At first, I had no idea he owned the place, nor did I know of his climbing history. Here was a man who could climb 5.13, and he is sharing beta with me about 5.6 climbs—not only sharing beta, but actually excited about the routes! I always found a great deal of pleasure in our conversations.

As the years went by, I started traveling to Moab and Indian Creek. I found that Scott had a lot of history down there and quickly learned how bad-ass he really is. He put up many quality and difficult lines. At this point, I would go into IME and talk about cracks and technique with him. He had so much to offer, not only teaching me different things about climbing, but more importantly—without knowing—making me strive to be a better human being. One of the greatest days climbing in the desert for me was when Scott came down for a visit. I brought him to The Wall at Indian Creek, a crag that I and Dylan Warren had started to develop. What a great day—climbing with a man that I admired for so many reasons. He enjoyed the new lines we had discovered and reminisced about the old days in The Creek, discovering and putting up his own new routes. And so many classics: *Puzzle Factory, Tube Steaks Tomorrow*, and the Eastwood Crag, to name few. Thank you Scott, for all of your great routes, beta, and the wonderful conversations about yesteryear, and for the many future chats to come.

Charley "Flash" Graham is one of those guys that the minute you meet him you know you're in the company of an awesome human being! For a long time I have called Charley my *moral mentor*. Charley is kind, smart, humble, and incredibly motivated. He brings all of these characteristics to the climbing arena. His endurance is unbelievable with

Introduction

crazy link-ups like Castleton Tower, The Rectory, and The Priest—yes, done many times before, but maybe not after working until midnight and being back to work the next day by 3:30! I could fill pages with his amazing feats! His motivation is second to none.

After becoming a new father and working at a full-time job, often not getting off until midnight, he would talk some of us into full-moon outings in Kane Creek or car-headlight missions on Wall Street. He is a graceful climber with smart movements, finding rests when he can, placing pro efficiently and intelligently, and he is capable of some very bold climbing.

Jay Smith, some have referred to as the "Secret Weapon." Since meeting and climbing with him, I choose to call him *The Schoolmaster*. What to say…Jay is the real deal. He has climbed since I was one-year-old (I'm now 50). He has climbed all over the world, in all methods—rock, ice, alpine, and high altitude! If you want a day of some interesting reading, just Google him. I first got to know Jay through his visits to the Bistro where we engaged in some short, tableside conversations. Those conversations always started with, "How's the food?" then ended with the topic of climbing. He was always vague about WHERE he had been climbing—I assumed because he could sense a familiar thirst for first ascents. He often mentioned that we should get out climbing. I thought to myself, "I can't go climbing with the Jay Smith of Latok, Everest, and Thaley Sagar!" One night he was in for dinner, and I must have had too much vino (courage in a bottle) because before I knew what I was doing, I agreed. Oh shit, what have I gotten myself into this time! Damn wine! We met the next morning and started by asking each other where we wanted to go. I inquired if he'd like to put up a new route. I swear I saw a twinkle in his eye. He countered if I had one in mind. I brought him to Long Canyon to a gigantic forming arch. He asked what size it was and I admitted that it offered some hard sizes for me, looks like off-fingers. He was in, so I said, "my gift to you." And so it began that day. The route: *Stingray* 5.11+, a great addition to Long Canyon climbing. I honestly think the first dozen times climbing together we didn't climb an established route. While writing this book, Jay gave us the gift of his hand-drawn topos for Castle Valley and Big Bend Butte—amazing drawings that I consider one of the highlights of this guide. Going through his binders, I noticed topos of Patagonia, Nepal, Antarctica, and so many other cool places. I asked if there's a country he has visited where he did not put up a new route. "Nope."

Watching Jay climb has been inspirational to say the least, but what I admire most is his care for the way things are done. I wished I had met him before I ever put up my first first ascent! He has taught me much and I hope that will continue! You will be hard pressed to get on a Jay Smith route that is not a fantastic, well-thought-out line! I, like all others, have made mistakes over the years—unfortunately, some in the realm of climbing ethics and etiquette that I wish I could undo. That being said, all I can do is strive to be more like my mentors. Climbing, like life, seems to present a learning curve and I am still learning!

The Schoolmaster

Introduction

Help with the Book

A very long list indeed:

My biggest thank you goes to Sharp End Publishing—most notably to my good friend, Fred Knapp. Without Fred this never would have happened. He has shown me the patience equivalent to what most parents have for their children! I'm sure I am the farthest thing from a scholar that he or the staff at Sharp End has ever worked with! My grammar? Not so good. My spelling? Atrocious! My organizational skills? Yeah, right! Thank you Sharp End (Fred) for your patience, hard work, and dedication! Also at Sharp End, thank you Steve (Crusher) Bartlett for all the time spent with me on edits and the wonderful maps/topos. Sharp End is unquestionably the right publisher for this book. They, too, have a love affair with the desert as well as a true "High on Moab."

To my wife, Michelle, for all those belays, all of the "Hey, how do you spell...," for all the sacrifices made for me and my obsession with this project.

To Dylan Warren and his amazing memory of details and specifics about routes we climbed so long ago that my faded memory could not recall! Thank you for the best climbing partnership I have ever had and most likely ever will have. All of those trips down to Indian Creek, the trips to France, the Bugaboos, the Sierras...countless tent-bound evenings, buzzes, craziness, and general debauchery! Will we be those old retired folks going back to dirt bagging, climbing, whatever and whenever we can? Man, I hope so!

To all of my staff at the Desert Bistro...dealing with me and my computer on the line while cooking, in-putting beta, and covering my ass when I came in late from *research*!

To the photographers, all of whom are amazing with their craft: Andrew Burr, Eric Odenthal, Whit Richardson, Jimmy Chin, Joe Auer, Tom Gwinn, Jay Smith, Todd Bogan, Crusher Bartlett.

Also thank you to Chris Noble for his knowledge and pointers for shooting from a heli as well as his great nature with giving advice to a rookie.

Thank you to Ben at Pinnacle Helicopters for flying doorless and allowing Chris Noble and me to shoot Jay and Kitty on the Big Bend Butte and giving us a very special hour in the sky.

A big thanks to Lisa Hathaway who nearly authored the bouldering sections of this book; she provided many lost or mis-reported route names and history.

Thank you Scott, Scott, Charley, and Jay for being you!

To so many climbers from the past and present that answered emails and phone calls with all sorts of beta and topos:

Jay Smith for stacks of beta and topos, in particular Castle Valley and Big Bend.
Bret Ruckman recalling his time-tested classics!
Eric Bjørnstad
Sam Lightner (Theatre, and much more)
Josh Gross (Cinema, as well as others)
Noah Bigwood (Big Bend Boulders)
Dave Medara (all over)
Jimmy Dunn (Long Canyon)
Tom Perkins (Long Canyon, Kane Creek, Potash)
Topher Donahue (Long Canyon)
Brad Barlage (Castle Valley)
Charley Graham (all over)
Herb Crimp (Long Canyon)
Pamela Pack (offwidths)
Luke Malatesta (aid climbing topos and beta, Wall Street)
Jason "Froto" Matz

James Webster (Kane Creek)
Zack Smith (Brumley, Ninja Training Center)
Tom Gilji (Brumley, Kane Creek)
Lisa Hathaway (Day Canyon)
Jake Warren (Hell Roaring, all over)
Steven Lucarelli (Trail of the Navajo)
Ben Riley (Day Canyon)
Steph Davis (Tombstones, Concepcion)
Linus Platt (all over)
Tim "The Prez" Noonan (Wall Street)
Dave Sadoff (Little Valley, North Dakota)
Paul Irby (Kane Creek, Culvert Canyon)
Bob "Round Head" Novellino (Culvert Canyon, Town Wall)
Paul Ross (Lost World, Dubinky Well Road)
Marco Cornacchione
Trish Ortiz (for help with Arches)

GearHeads
OUTDOOR STORE

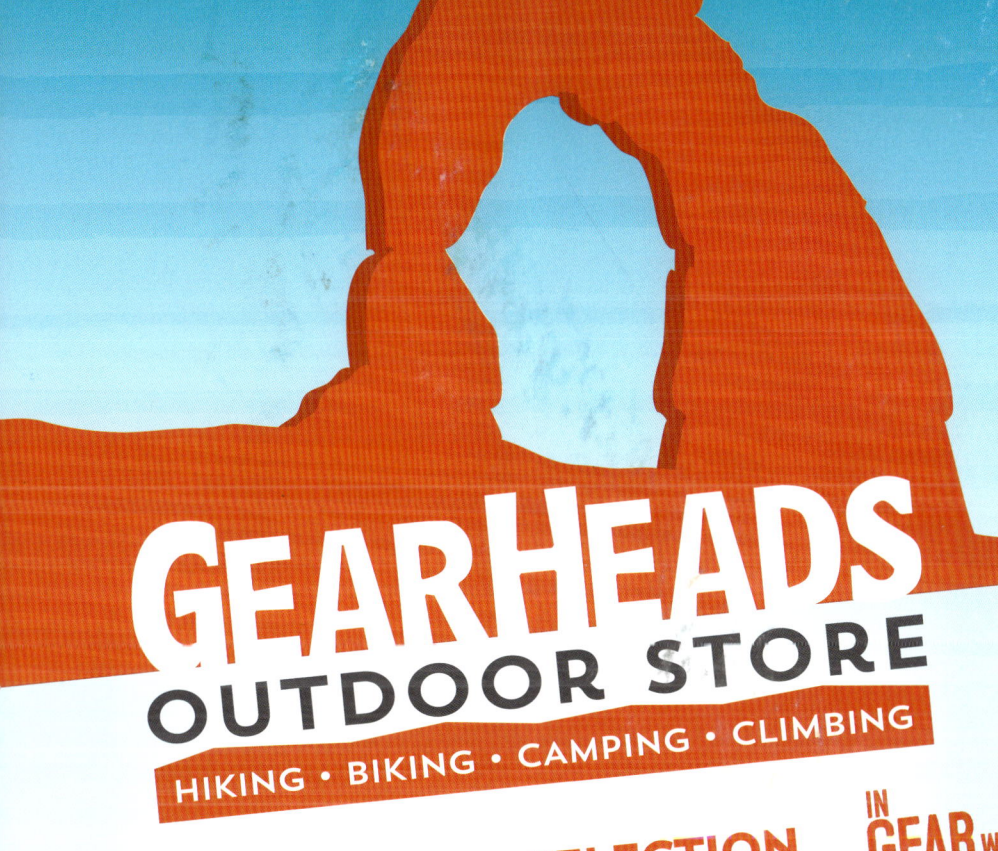

HIKING • BIKING • CAMPING • CLIMBING

WORLD'S LARGEST SELECTION OF CLIMBING GEAR!

IN Gear WE TRUST
20th ANNIVERSARY

AND MOAB'S LARGEST SELECTION OF
Gear | Clothing | Footwear | Camping Equipment | Camp Fuel

💧 FREE FILTERED WATER

IN GEAR WE TRUST — 20th ANNIVERSARY

Established in 1998, Gearheads has been serving outdoor enthusiasts in beautiful Moab for over twenty years.

WWW.MOABGEARHEADS.COM
435-259-4327 | 471 S. Main St. #1 | Moab, UT 84532
Open 8a-9p Mar-Nov | 9a-6p Dec-Feb

Introduction

Climbing Partners

Certainly this would never have happened without climbing partners! I have had so many in the 6 years of working on this book, and have enjoyed so many partnerships!

My wife Michelle deserves the world for all the time spent holding the rope for me, along with countless wonderful days and adventures in this desert we call home.

Dylan Warren. Man, we spent a lot of time together. We climbed so many routes, were late to work so many times. We have had so many epics! Those were some good times—times I will never forget.

Kiefer Kelley. Climb on little man! Remember Elephants Perch? The best of times with a whole lifetime more to come!

Jay Ackerman
Mirek Hladik
June Ray
Jenny Badewitz
Chris (L-dub) Willie
Nick Mirhashemi
Charley Graham
Tom Gwinn
Joe Slansky
Tim Naylor
Jenna Gardineer

Jeanine Saia
Sarafina Gerard
Julie Zaranik
Jay Smith
Anne Merchandise
Steven Lucarelli
Carrie Finn
Adeline Guay
Emily Klarer
Paul Irby
Rusty Rigg

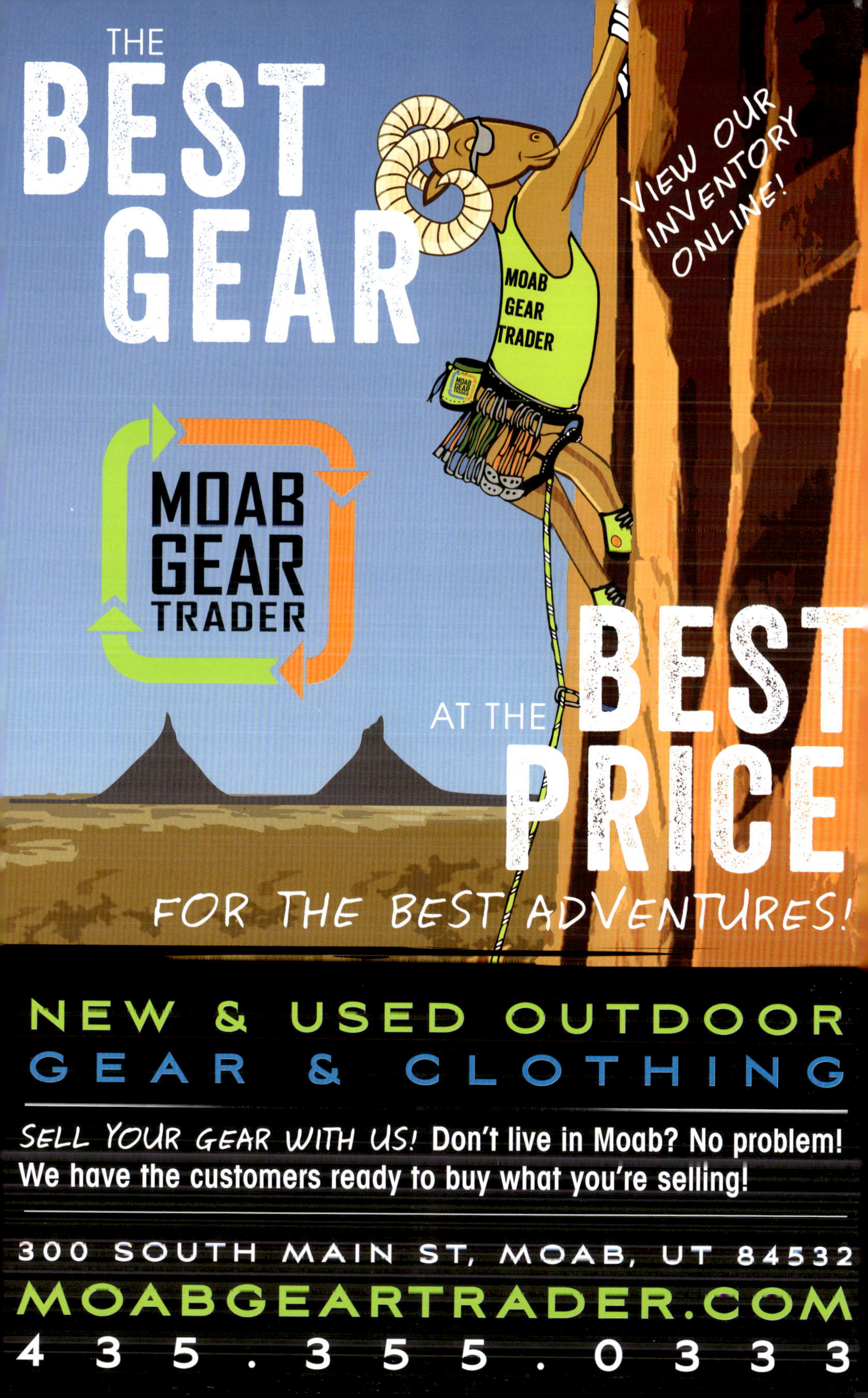

Introduction

The Scope of this Book...
To sum it up.... a COMPREHENSIVE, SELECT, ADVENTURE CLIMBING book.

Truly there are stacks of established climbs in Moab, so to get them all under one cover, a book would weigh more than a *standard desert rack*. This is meant to be a single book that highlights both classic and new areas, as well as high-volume and off-the-beaten path areas of high quality. If you are a purist, rest assured, this guide leaves plenty of room for your own adventures.

For crags, descriptions are as comprehensive and up-to-date as possible. Individual climbs that are not at crags are often marked as select and are never under three stars in quality. I have also included adventure climbs—these may be a scramble or a bolt ladder to a cool summit or maybe just an adventurous approach via river or bike.

This book doesn't really cover aid climbing, with exceptions of a select few that go clean or have fixed gear.

I have a great respect for the climbing in Moab and the people in this community (past and present) who have made the climbing what it is! Some locals have expressed their concerns over a new book, saying it brings the crowds and the issues that come with them. I, too, see the logic in that. However, word-of-mouth and the ever-growing online world also bring the masses. That being said, part of the responsibility in putting out this book, includes expressing the genuine concerns of locals and providing up-to-date information on access issues and impact concerns, as well as route information.

I have added a *Local's Choice* section, too. In a nutshell, I was always curious how guidebook authors determined star ratings. Is it just the author and select friends sitting around drinking beer going, "Yeah man, that thing is five stars" or an ego thing where only the harder grades get five stars? So, I started thinking why not take a bunch of local climbers who have been climbing in Moab for a decade or more and ask them. The question is worded: "If you moved away and came back for vacation, or if you had a good friend coming to town, which five do-not-miss routes would you choose?" The only parameters were to not pick towers, mostly because every local knows not to miss the towers. It was fascinating to see what people chose as their favorites. One of the best examples and funniest circumstances came from Charley Graham and Joe Slansky. I was getting some beta from Charley Graham on *Frenchies Nightmare*, and he aid, "I'm not sure you should include it in the book." Not even a day later, Joe emailed me his Top 5, with *Frenchies* at the top of the list. Both are terrific climbers who climbed for a long time in the desert and both, obviously, have completely different tastes for climbing.

An important note: If you are the type of guidebook user that likes crux beta, gear counts, and exact pitch lengths, THIS BOOK MAY NOT BE FOR YOU! For me, climbing in the desert has always been on the epic side of the spectrum. One of many things that keeps me in love with this special place is always being on the edge of the unknown. This guide is meant to help you in the most basic way. It is meant to give you the means to find the climbs, a range of the gear size needed for the climb, and the length of rope you will need to get up and down safely. When it is imperative to have a certain length rope or even two ropes, rest assured this beta is included.

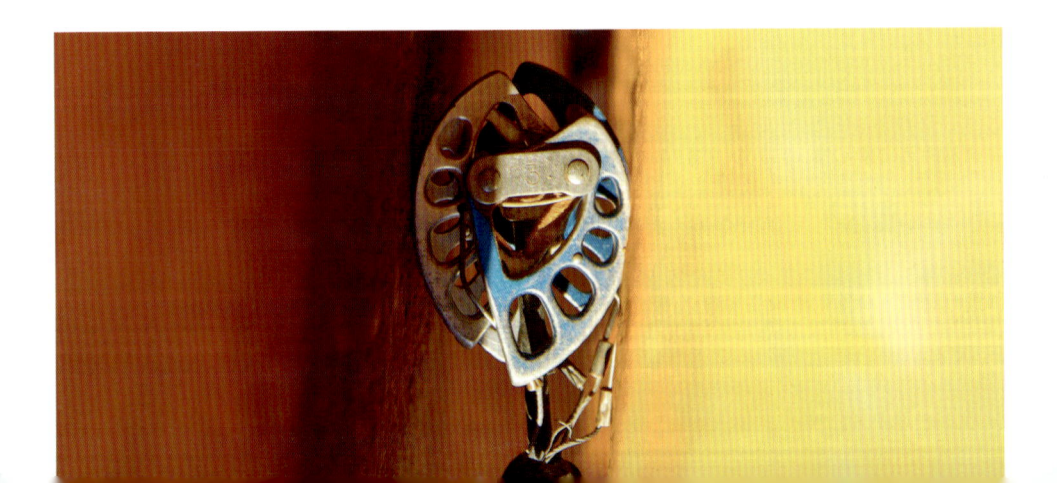

Gear

The gear selection is a hint of the sizes you may need for safe travels. Climbing in the desert requires an abnormal amount of the same-size protection, therefore I did not suggest a number of the specific sizes needed. For example, *Program Director* in Long Canyon uses from 0.75–3.0, heavy on the 3.0s—I may climb it using four 3.0s, but my wife has smaller hands and may want a half dozen or more. The amount of gear is left up to you when you arrive at the bottom, look up, and determine your needs. An exception to this is Castle Valley, where the approach is long and climbers generally plan on a specific multi-pitch route. The idea, proffered by the quintessential developer Jay Smith, is that unlike a crag which requires an arsenal of cams which, at the base, are sorted for particular single pitches, the distant towers and long approaches can be best enjoyed by taking exactly what's needed. Still, extra gear has its place, and should the route you choose be occupied, additional gear could be beneficial.

In the gear descriptions, Camalot sizes are used when referencing cam sizes. TCU sizes reference Metolius. While many great cam manufacturers provide a plethora of choices, these brands seem to be the common reference point for most desert climbers. The conversion chart below will also help you to convert to other cams, as well as provide a consensus for the different sizes based on tips through ow.

GEAR CONVERSION CHART

Body Part	Inches	Black Diamond Old	Black Diamond New	Wild Country	Wired Bliss	Metolius	Aliens	Big Bro
<Tips	< 0.5			"zeros"	0.40	.00	0.33	
Tips	.5/.65	0.2 / 0.3	0.2 / 0.3	0.00 / 0.5	0.50	.0 / 1.0	0.38 / 0.50	
Fingers	.65/1.0	0.4	0.4	1.0	0.75 / 1.0	2.0 / 3.0	0.75 / 1.0	
Off-fingers	1.0/1.3	0.75	0.75	1.5	1.5	4.0	1.5	
Thin hands	1.3/1.7	1.0	1.0	2.0	2.0	5.0 / 6.0	2.0	
Hands	1.5/2.5	2.0	2.0	2.5 / 3.0	2.5 / 3.0	7.0	2.5	
Big hands	2.0/3.0	3.0	3.0 / 2.1"/2.8"	3.5	3.5	8.0		
Fist	2.5/4.0	3.5	4.0 / 2.7"/3.6"	4.0	4.0	9.0		
Off-fist	3.0/4.5	4.0	5.0 / 3.6"/4.8"			10.0		Big Bro #1
Small OW	3.5/5.5	4.5		5.0				Big Bro #2
Big OW	5.0/7.0	5.0		6.0				Big Bro #3
> Big OW	> 7.0							Big Bro #4

Stars

Star ratings are an ever-difficult, open-to-interpretation, crux in writing a guide. I talked with friends, publishers, authors and climbing shops about what 5-star means to them and I must say there are many different opinions. Should it include: length, quality of rock, aesthetics, the style in which it was established, the movement, etc. Should it be compared to a Yosemite 5-star? Should we decide what is the very best climb in the desert and compare all the rest to it? It seems to me just politics—everyone believes what they believe, and most climbers are very passionate about their beliefs. There is no correct answer, no right opinion.

So, the star ratings in this book are very loose. If you truly love to climb, then you probably, at some point, would love to climb every route! Therefore stars wouldn't, shouldn't, mean a pisshole in the snow anyways!

So the star ratings for this book defined:
- ★★★★★ Moab classic. A must-do while you're in Moab. A local favorite.
- ★★★★   Crag classic. Route not to be missed at that particular crag.
- ★★★   Worth driving to Moab for. You won't be disappointed.
- ★★   Killer climbing anywhere else in the world!
- ★   Worth your time while you're here.
- No star Another tick if you live here.

Cliff or Route Aspect ✹ W

Throughout this book, I have tried to include a compass bearing woth a compass symbol (pictured above) to indicate the direction the cliff faces.

Color Coding & Grade Conversion

This guide employs a color-coded system for fast reference—you can look over a cliff photo or the tick boxes preceding the route name to get a quick overview of the difficulty range at each crag. The following chart shows the color-coding scheme and the American to French conversions.

Roped Grades		Bouldering Grades	
YDS	**FRENCH**	**VERMIN**	**FONTAINBLEAU**
5.6	4		
5.7	4+	V0	
5.8	5a	V1	5c
5.9	5b	V2	
5.10a	6a	V3	6a
5.10b	6a+	V4	6b
5.10c	6b	V5	6c/6c+
5.10d	6b+		
5.11a	6c	V6	7a
5.11b		V7	7a+/7b
5.11c	6c+	V8	7b+
5.11d	7a	V9	7c
5.12a	7a+	V10	7c+
5.12b	7b	V11	8a
5.12c	7b+	V12	8a+
5.12d	7c	V13	8b
5.13a	7c+	V14	8b+
5.13b	8a	V15	8c
5.13c	8a+		
5.13d	8b		
5.14a	8b+		
Clean Aid			

paganmountaineering.com
ORN AGAIN PAGAN
MOAB-UTAH
PAGAN
Mountaineering
Pagan Mountaineering - 59 So. Main St. #2 - Moab, Utah - 435.259.1117
E-mail us at pagan@paganmountaineering.com - Support local business

Weather

Moab—a place where you can depend on a dry climate. Getting rained out? Likely just for a few hours! When I visit my home state, New Hampshire, I always bring my rack and hardly ever get to use it. If it's not raining, it most likely will be wet from a previous rain. The granite there is so sweet, but if you're on vacation for a week, odds are you may get only one day on the rock. It's quite the opposite here; you will surely tire before the sun does—days and days of cloudless skies. There is something to be said for making plans three weeks out when there's a 99% chance you won't get rained out.

That being said, we do get some impressive rain storms and every climber should show some concern—they can come in quickly and violently. Recent huge rains, for example, completely washed out the Mineral Bottom Road—the access down to the White Rim trail and the Green River. Moses, Charlie Horse Needle, and a bunch of cragging was no longer easily accessible until the 2.5 million dollar repairs were finished. Many other areas in this book were also affected by this storm. Due to rains and flash floods like this, approaches (by foot and vehicle) change! It can't hurt to go into one of the local shops and ask about recent changes. Doing a tower? Lightning should be a genuine concern. Flash floods are real and can come with little warning; make sure your vehicle is running well and that you have plenty of water in case you have to walk out. Some areas mentioned in this book are not visited very often and you cannot rely on a passerby to help you! Ahhh, I love it!

Introduction

Season to Season

It is possible to climb comfortably in Moab (weather permitting) during any month of the year, but spring and fall are the most desirable times.

February 15–May 15:
An excellent time to visit: the days are getting longer and the desert is in bloom. However, there can be stretches of stormy weather and the wind is often a factor. Daytime temperatures range from the low 50s to high 70s.

May 15–September 15:
Summer in the desert is not everyone's cup of tea. You will be climbing exclusively in the shade, limiting which walls you visit. An early start is advised to avoid heat stroke on the approach, and one gallon of water per person is advised. Daytime temperatures range from the upper 80s to about 100.

September 15–November 15:
The days are getting shorter, but generally high pressure can stay in place for weeks at a time. A primo time to be in Moab. Daytime temperatures from the 50s to the 70s. October is statistically the wettest month in the Moab area.

November 15–February 15:
Winter is hit-or-miss and long, cold nights are guaranteed. Storms can last for days at a time, or beautiful sunny days can remain for a while. Daytime temperatures in the 30s to 50s.

Concerns Other than the Weather

Besides the obvious weather concerns: lightning, flash floods, etc., there are other concerns to consider:

TRASH Though it's nice to have a celebratory beverage after your day of ascents, consider cans instead of glass so as to avoid accidental breakage. As with everywhere on the planet, pack it in, pack it out, and please recycle.

ROCK/ANCHORS The sandstone is soft! If establishing a new route, if possible, place the anchors so that pulling ropes creates the least amount of wear on the rock. Paint your anchors the color of the rock. Consider using rap or ring hangers instead of webbing. While toproping, use draws instead of running your rope through the anchors. Consider rappelling instead of lowering, as a rope used in the desert accumulates grains of sand that act as sandpaper on the anchors.

CAMPING Fires can be just as dangerous in the desert as in the forest. If you wish to have a fire, try to choose a site with an existing pit/ring. Check to make sure no permit is needed and that you're not on private property. Gain good karma by showing your honesty and paying the fee at self-service sites. As always leave the site cleaner than when you arrived.

SNAKES, SPIDERS AND SCORPIONS Yup, we have 'em all. Hiking without your headphones in is a good idea for discerning the warning rattle. It's always wise to check your shoes, packs, and sleeping bags for the stray scorpion and black widow.

GOATS & BIRDS Most areas described in this guide enjoy the presence of goats and birds. Often such areas are subject to seasonal wildlife closures. Again work on the karma—if you show up to an area where there are goats, consider going somewhere else for the day and let them have their space. If you see a bird's nest and that area is not closed, do the right thing and go elsewhere.

CHILDREN AT THE CRAG I love seeing kids at the crag getting exposed to the climbing lifestyle. Please, however, refrain from allowing them to draw on the cliffs with chalk or sketch on the walls with stones.

FIRST ASCENT CONCERNS Do your homework! Make sure the route you intend to put hardware on has not already been ascended! Just because you don't see anchors, it does not mean the route has not already been ascended. Case in point—the very first route in this book is a victim of such a misunderstanding. The route had been published as *Digital Stimulous*—a route that was originally climbed without a midway anchor. The route was originally led by Ralph Ferarra and John Rzeczycki. It was led to the top as 5.11,A1 and named *Tragedy of the Commons*. Perhaps start with online research or visit the local climbing shops.

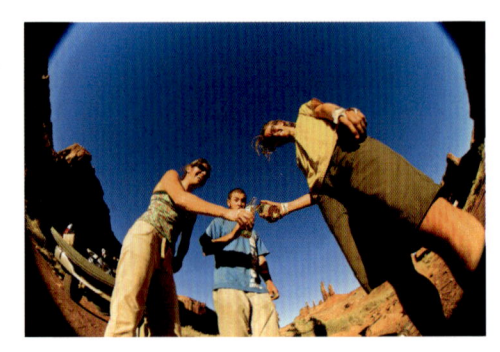

Introduction 21

Concerns...continued

DOGS I am a dog lover! I very much enjoy seeing them at the crag. However there are people that do not. Consider keeping them on a leash. If you know they are super vocal dogs, consider leaving them home. Always pick up your dog's poop!

THE ANCIENTS We have a lot of native american writings, petroglyphs, and ruins (as well as dinosaur tracks). Please climb well away from these historic areas and leave them undisturbed. Also there is a fair amount of petrified wood around the Moab area; please leave it in place for others to enjoy.

TRAIL MAINTENANCE Trail maintenance is always time well spent. We ask everyone, including the guide services, to please consider putting aside some time to work on trail maintenance.

THE ALL IMPORTANT POOPING It's something we all do, and don't really like to discuss. Certainly many options to *take care of business* exist:

A. Find the nearest bathroom, toilet, or outhouse.
B. Wag bag.
C. Dig a hole at least 10" deep and bury your waste, well away from any waterway including dry washes. Lots of people burn their paper. Well accepted, maybe, but not the best for the environment, especially if an ember flies away and starts a fire. Personally, I feel there are only two ways to deal with paper. Pack it out, or don't use it. Consider wiping with a rock or stick—maybe not the most comfortable but you will live.

Thank you from the Moab community for your participation in these matters.

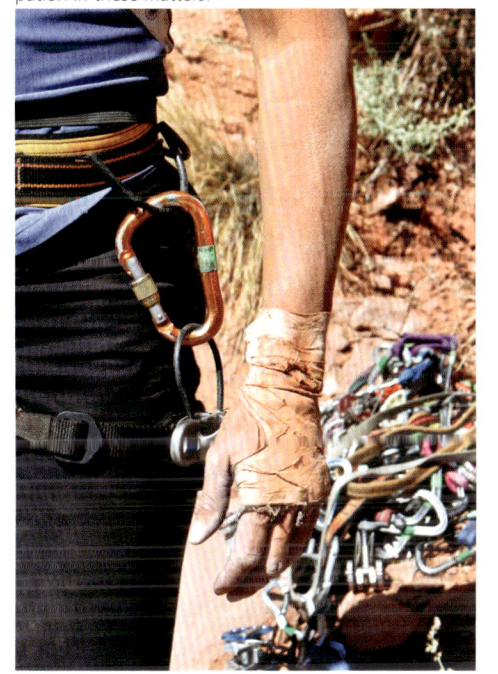

Getting There

FROM THE NORTH:
I-15 south to Provo, southeast on Highway 6 past Price to I-70, east to Highway 191, south to the town of Moab.

FROM THE NORTHWEST:
I-70 east to Highway 191, south to the town of Moab.

FROM THE NORTHEAST:
I-70 west to Highway 128, south at the Cisco exit (River Road), to Moab. The Danish Flats exit also works (and eliminates a couple miles of back-tracking) but the road is unmaintained.

FROM THE EAST:
Highway 145 from Telluride to Naturita, then Highway 90 west through Bedrock and the Paradox Valley, which becomes Highway 46 west at the Utah border, to Highway 191 South, then north to Moab.

FROM THE SOUTHEAST:
Highway 160 west from Durango to Cortez, then Highway 491 from Cortez to Monticello Utah, north on Highway 191 to Moab.

FROM THE SOUTH:
Highway 191 north to Monticello, Utah, and then continue to Moab.

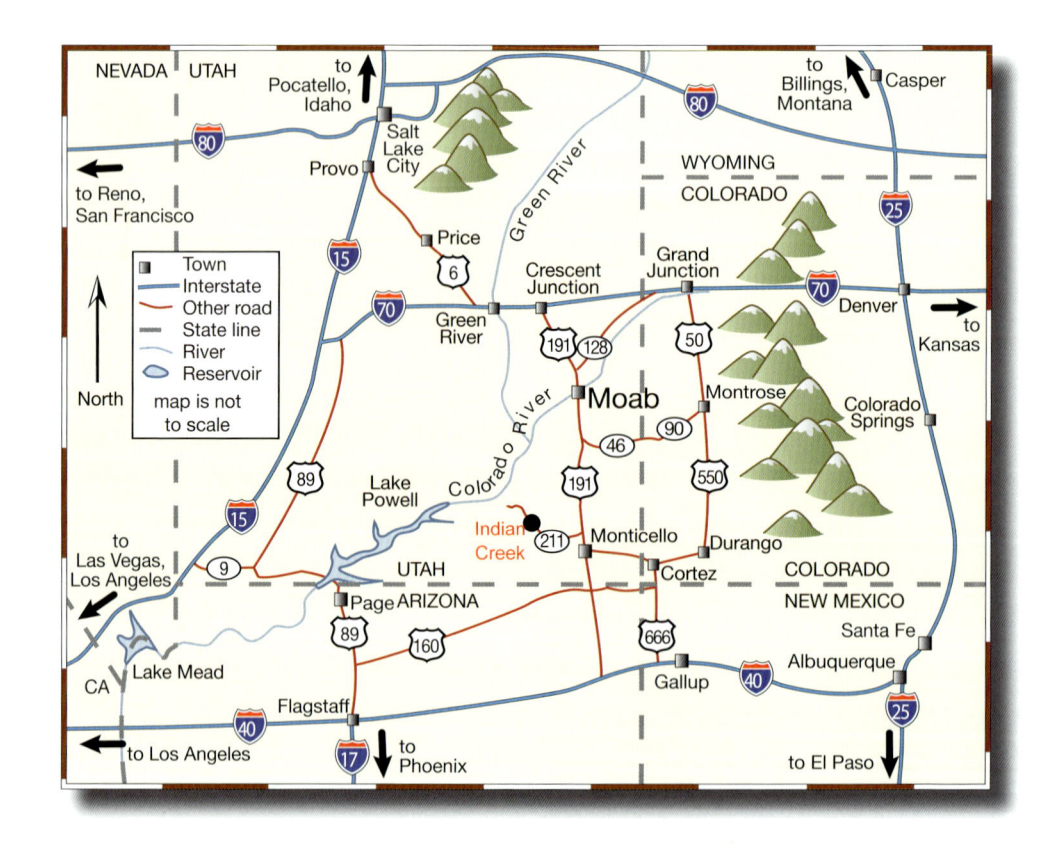

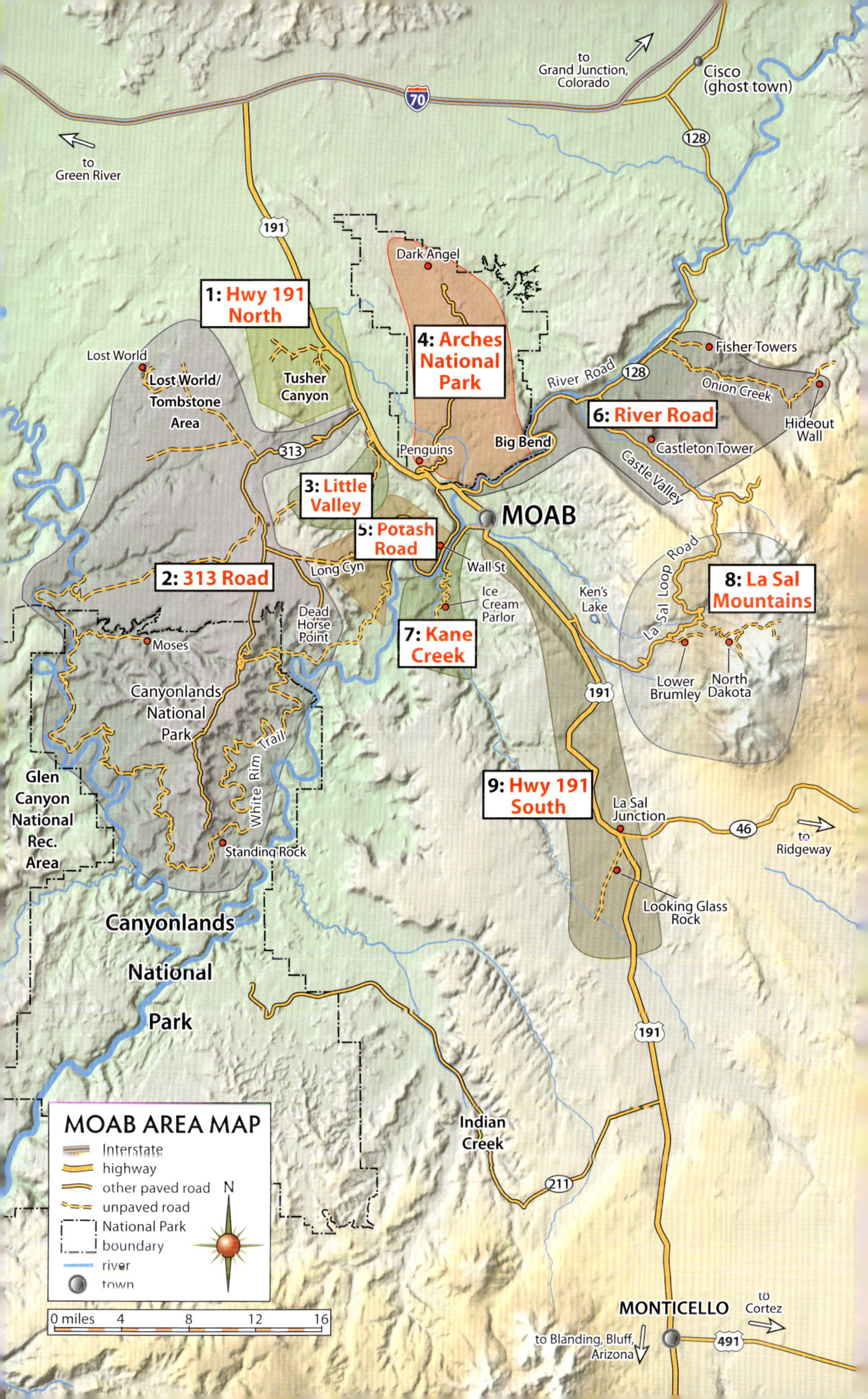

MOAB AREA MAP
Interstate
highway
other paved road
unpaved road
National Park boundary
river
town
N
0 miles 4 8 12 16
to Grand Junction, Colorado
Cisco (ghost town)
70
128
to Green River
191
1: Hwy 191 North
Tusher Canyon
Lost World
Lost World/ Tombstone Area
313
Dark Angel
4: Arches National Park
Penguins
Big Bend
River Road
Fisher Towers
Onion Creek
Hideout Wall
6: River Road
Castleton Tower
Castle Valley
3: Little Valley
5: Potash Road
MOAB
Wall St
Long Cyn
2: 313 Road
Dead Horse Point
Moses
Ice Cream Parlor
7: Kane Creek
Ken's Lake
La Sal Loop Road
8: La Sal Mountains
Lower Brumley
North Dakota
Canyonlands National Park
White Rim Trail
Glen Canyon National Rec. Area
Standing Rock
9: Hwy 191 South
La Sal Junction
46
to Ridgeway
Looking Glass Rock
Canyonlands National Park
Indian Creek
211
MONTICELLO
to Cortez
491
to Blanding, Bluff, Arizona

FRIENDS OF INDIAN CREEK
PRESERVING ITS FUTURE

The Friends of Indian Creek Need You!
(or, "Wow, that oil well wasn't here last time!")

What was your first desert climb? Why did you first come to Moab and why do you keep coming back? What do you want this place to look like 20 or 40 years from now?

My first Moab climb was in 1983 when my fledgling partners and I blundered off route on Castleton's Kor-Ingalls route and epic-ed trying to climb Black Sun with our one cam and a few Hexes. Despite the beatdown, our retreat, and demoralizing descent down Castleton's talus cone, that day the desert became part of me and I pledged that eventually I would live in this beautiful place full of wonder and adventure. The next year I returned, sketched my way up the 5.9 chimney, and celebrated on what would be the first of many desert summits. I'm now a proud member of the "chossmasters"—a nutty group of crusty desert rats who have ticked 100+ desert summits. Even though this arbitrary project is downright silly and requires scaling a lot of crappy routes, there is a benefit in that the 100+ summits goal took me all over the Colorado Plateau to a diversity of amazing desert climbing areas, from Indian Creek, the Fishers and Castle Valley, to more remote locations like Hell Roaring Canyon, Lockhart Basin and Lost World Butte. What's even more remarkable is that there are now a few dedicated climbers that have ticked over 200 summits—we're talking serious choss when you get to that level! What motivates such wacky behavior? It's not just the world-class crack climbing ('cuz, truth be told, there's lots of choss out here), it's also the spectacular and unique quality of the breathtaking landscape in southern Utah. This place inspires people.

Yet there's trouble in paradise. We're on the cusp of the Moab area potentially transforming into an industrial center with dramatic increases in oil, gas and potash development that could significantly degrade our climbing experiences. The Lower 48's biggest-producing oil well is located right near the top of Long Canyon (with plans nearby for more), and as this book goes to print the BLM is considering oil, gas and potash leasing on nearly 1 million acres at locations covered in this book. Right now Congress is considering massive public lands legislation that could establish everything from resource extraction zones, new wilderness designations, state land trades, and recreation management areas. And as usual, the BLM issues quarterly leases for oil and gas (yep, those new wells you see on the way into Indian Creek and at the doorstep of Canyonlands's Island in the Sky district). There is also talk of oil refineries and experimental tar sands development in the area, and even a nuclear plant near Green River. In short, over the next few years long-term decisions will be made that will affect the experiences of the readers of this book.

Think about that first climb you did in Moab and whether you want a similar experience preserved for others. Perhaps you want more protections for this landscape—or maybe you want more resource extraction (if you checked this second box, let's dispense with the falsity that because you drive to the crags you can't have an opinion on where to drill. The industrialization of Moab has nothing to do with the country's oil and gas supply and demand, but it does have something to do with whether Moab's recreation assets and conservation values will be protected). Most people say some version of "I like it the way it is/was"—but it's too late for that as change has already occurred and momentum is building.

The good news is that there's someone minding the store. If you feel compelled to help protect our climbing experiences you can get involved by supporting the Friends of Indian Creek (friendsofindiancreek.wordpress.com or find us on Facebook), a group started by a few local climbers to work on Indian Creek issues. We've since expanded our focus beyond Indian Creek to regional issues of access, conservation, and community. We now work on projects at Castleton, Arches, Potash Road, Kane Creek, the La Sals, and several other places to make sure climbing is protected and enhanced across southeastern Utah. So if you want to stay connected to what's happening and have a voice in the future of climbing in the Moab area, join FOIC and support the many organizations and businesses (Access Fund, AAC, Petzl, Pagan, BD, Gear Heads, Camp USA) that help us protect the many world-class climbing experiences around Moab.

Access is obviously important, but it's the unique quality of Moab's climbing environment that is essential to the desert experiences we all love. Twenty years from now we'll look back at this period as one of transformation. The Friends of Indian Creek need you to help us shape the future of desert climbing.

Jason Keith
Moab, Utah

Chapter 1

Highway 191 North

Katie Brown on *Window Route* 5.10+, Whit Richardson photo

TUSHER CANYON MAP

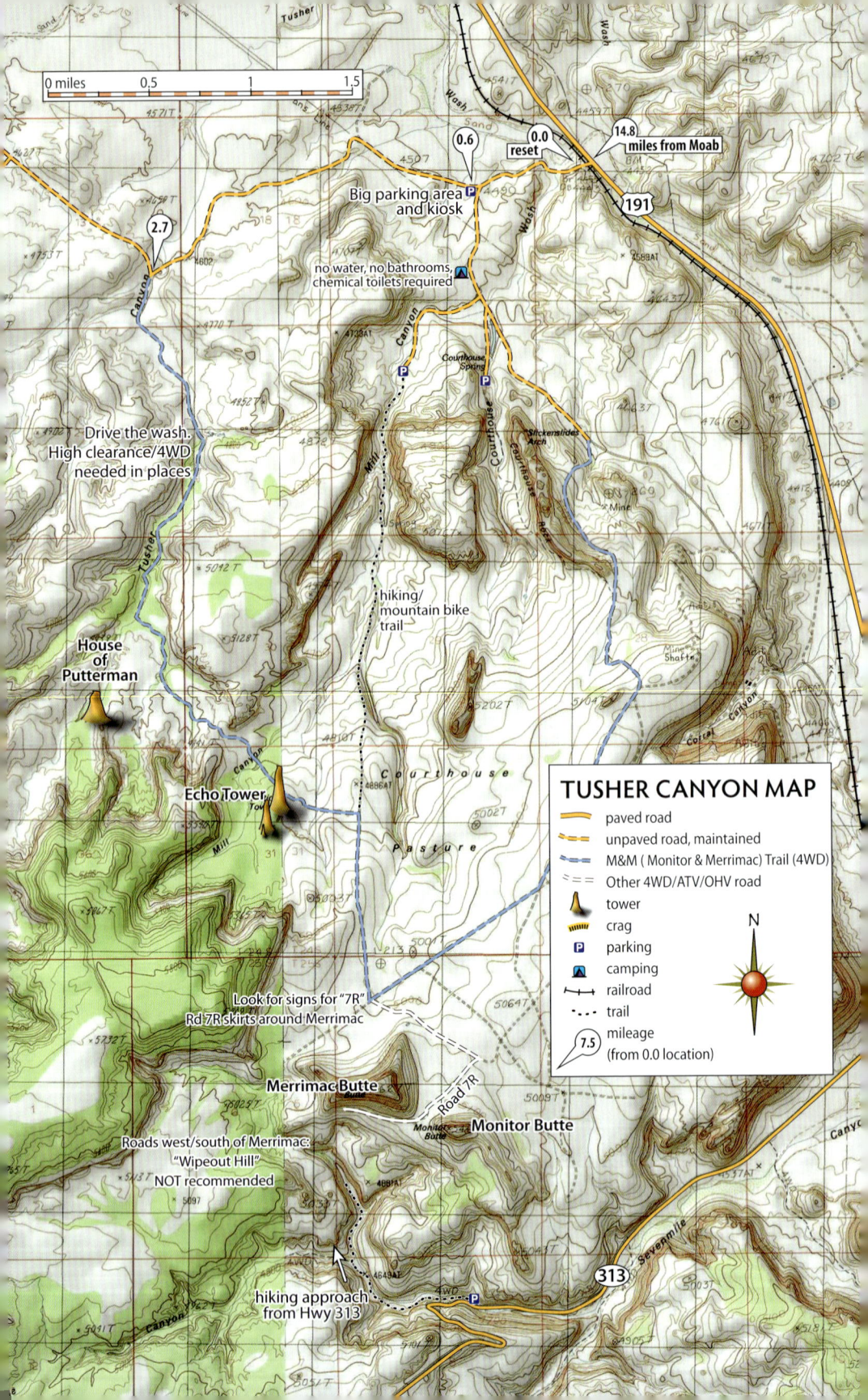

- paved road
- unpaved road, maintained
- M&M (Monitor & Merrimac) Trail (4WD)
- Other 4WD/ATV/OHV road
- tower
- crag
- parking
- camping
- railroad
- trail
- mileage (from 0.0 location)

N

0.0 reset
0.6
2.7
14.8 miles from Moab
7.5

Big parking area and kiosk

no water, no bathrooms, chemical toilets required

Drive the wash. High clearance/4WD needed in places

House of Putterman

Echo Tower

hiking/mountain bike trail

Courthouse Pasture

Look for signs for "7R" Rd 7R skirts around Merrimac

Road 7R

Merrimac Butte

Monitor Butte

Roads west/south of Merrimac: "Wipeout Hill" NOT recommended

hiking approach from Hwy 313

191

313

191 North

TUSHER WASH AREA

Tusher Wash is a beautiful area, filled with cool formations. It's a Moab multi-use area in all its glory, complete with ATV, dirt bike, and Jeep trails. It's also a gateway for mountain bike excursions in the Tusher and Bartlett washes. The region has a fair bit of climbing, but lacks the peace and tranquility of other areas. The proximity to the Moab airport means you might get buzzed by small aircraft when on the summit of Echo Pinnacle.

Drive north out of town for 14.8 miles, turning left onto Mill Canyon Road. Follow this road for 0.6 mile to a fork in the road with a kiosk. Take a right, follow this until another fork at 2.7 miles—signed to indicate Monitor and Merrimac to the left and Tusher Tunnel to the right. Go left, driving in the wash. Follow the wash for 4.6 miles to yet another fork. This one indicates Monitor and Merrimac are reached via the left. A dead-end is reached by continuing straight.

The House of Putterman, Neighbor of Putterman, and some various pitches of good quality are reached by going towards the dead end. If you take a left at the fork, you can access the Echo Pinnacle, Aeolian Tower, and the Monitor and Merrimac buttes.

DEAD END AREA
THE HOUSE OF PUTTERMAN FORMATION

The House of Putterman hosts a variety of Entrada climbs, but only two classics are described here. The *Walden's Room* route on the south face is a meandering but enjoyable summit line. It's also worth doing *The Tragedy of the Commons* on the north face (visible from the car).

From the dead-end road, the House of Putterman will be obvious on your left. Park at a small pullout. A short walk leads to the saddle between the House of Putterman and Neighbor of Putterman.

The routes are listed from right to left.

North Face

☐ 1. **THE TRAGEDY OF THE COMMONS** 5.11, A1 ★★★
A good line. The goods can be reached by two methods, neither of which is particularly good:
Approach 1: Traverse in from the right along a shallow bench (5.easy).
Approach 2: Climb broken rock left of the route (5.9 with tricky gear, nuts helpful). Set up a belay at a cave at the start of the corner.
The free portion climbs a finger crack to the main left-facing corner, then powers up mostly off-fingers to the bolted anchor. From the new, retrobolted anchor, anyone wishing to go to the top faces just a couple of clean aid moves up to a ledge and belay, then a 5.10 pitch to the summit.
Gear for free section: A few smaller TCUs to 2.0 (heavy on the off-fingers)
FA: Ralph Ferrara, John Rzeczycki

South Face

☐ 2. **WALDEN'S ROOM** 5.10 ★★★
This is a bit of a meandering line with some good climbing.
P1: Climb the less-than-vertical left-facing corner handcrack. Pass an old belay, gunning for the ledge with a bolted belay.
P2: Directly above the ledge is an ow protected by a fixed piece. Fortunately, enough toeholds exist to diminish the grunt factor. Above the ow, you'll see the anchor up and left. A final boulder problem with a hidden sequence awaits (5.10).
P3: A 4th class walk to just below the summit.
P4: A rough little crux! A devious sequential finger crack leads to bolt-protected face climbing (friable 5.10+).
Gear: Single set from 0.3–1.0, doubles on hands and big hands, optional 6.0, many shoulder-length slings.
Rap: Three raps with a single 70m.

☐ 3. **DIRECT START** 5.11
This is the left-facing corner just right of the original start. Begin in nut-protected pin scars and continue up the ever-widening crack to a chimney (good rest), then pop out over a roof and continue to the ledge via fingers.
Gear: Small to medium nuts, double set of TCUs, and a big hands piece for entering the chimney.
FA: Cameron Burns & Brian Takei

Neighbor of Putterman

Park as for House of Putterman. The Neighbor is just right and the two routes described are on the north-facing side.

☐ 1. PUTTERMAN'S BIG TOE 5.9 40'
A short low-angle left-facing corner featuring cool stemming at the halfway mark.
Gear: Tips and a few hand pieces
FA: Brian Shelton

☐ 2. AFTER THE RAIN 5.10+ ★★★
Located on the right side of the north face. Approach as for *Big Toe* and traverse the cliff to the base—look for a big boulder on the bench at the bottom of the right-facing corner.
P1: Climb the short right-facing thin corner to a rightward ledge traverse. Belay behind the huge boulder.
P2: Start with really good hands/big hands to a low-angle corner/flake system. As the corner gets steeper it gets wider! Layback or grunt up to a sloping bolted ledge belay (5.10).
P3: A short big hands splitter leads to some bulging ow climbing with some trickery that makes it doable. A final mantel move leads to a bolted belay. A short scramble left brings you to the summit.
Gear: a few tips pieces for the start; double 2.0–3.0, triple 3.5–5.0
Descent: Reverse the final scramble, double 60m rope rappel leads to the ground.
FA: Brian Shelton, Dan Russell

The next route is on the righthand side of a north-facing wall halfway between the House of Putterman and Echo Pinnacle (at 5.1 miles).

☐ 3. PUTTERMANS PINKIES 5.10 70' ★★★
Left-facing corner that starts with fingers and then goes up through the sizes to thin hands. Sweet Entrada line. Steep!
Gear: 0.3–1.0
FA: Cameron Burns

ECHO TOWER

☐ 1. FREE WINDOW ROUTE 5.10+ ★★★★★ ✺ W
Oh man, what a crazy route! When you arrive at the bottom, look at the first pitch and go, "Whoa-yuk." Pitches 2 & 3 can be linked by bringing extra draws and endurance.
P1: Pleasantly surprising. It takes pretty solid pro (some nuts may be helpful) and the climbing is fun. Climb the obvious weakness to the spacious belay ledge with an impressive window that you can literally walk through to the other side. Belay from hand-size gear, cordelette helpful.
P2: Climb over the window to a sweet hand crack that tightens up to off-fingers before reaching the belay. Great rock!
P3: I'm not even sure how to accurately describe this pitch, but one word could probably sum it up—bizarre! Climb an uncomfortable window (especially for the boys, if you know what I mean), clipping mostly fixed gear, then bust some wide hands to a stance and scramble to the huge belay ledge (the anchors are on the far side of that ledge just below the actual summit). The actual summit is gained by an easy boulder move that must be reversed for the descent.
Gear: 0.5–3.0 (heaviest on tight hands and off-fingers) optional set of nuts
FA: Eric Bjørnstad, Ken Wyrick, Terry McKenna (with a different first pitch on the east side)

☐ 2. ROUND-ABOUT 5.11 ★★★
The boyz were pretty creative with this first ascent. In a nutshell, climb the first pitch of the *Window Route* then girdle clockwise around the circumference and continue up the *Window Route* to the summit. Six pitches.
FA: Dave Medara, Jay Smith

MONITOR

☐ 1. THE PLUNGE 5.12 ★★★★★
The late Earl Wiggins called this "One of the best climbs in the desert."
P1: A stellar pitch by itself! A boulder-problem start, traversing left to right, leads to a weird high-step that gains a right-facing corner. Some hard thin moves lead to a short left-facing corner. Past this, even harder and thinner moves see you over a small roof and into a right-facing corner (tips and fingers). Off-fingers climbing on lower-angle rock cruises up through more comfy hand sizes. It gets steep again as the crack widens to big hands. One more hard move leads to the belay pod (5.12, 120').
P2: Oh man, you really gotta want the summit! The crack goes up to a #6 Camalot. Climb out the pod via fists and soon work to the dreaded 4.0 size. Continue ow through the sizes, passing some pitons along the way (5.11, 70').
Gear: nuts, 0.0–6.0, extra #2 Friends, doubles on big sizes
Rap: One double 70m rope rappel to the ground or two single rope raps with a 70m
FA: Ron Olevsky, Dave Mondeau
FFA: Earl Wiggins, Katy Cassidy, Peter Gallagher

MERRIMAC

☐ 1. ALBATROSS 5.11 ★★★★ ✺ SW
P1: Climb a tight hand crack that curves left near the end as it pinches down to off-fingers before reaching the belay ledge.
P2: Climb the obvious chimney, protected in the crack on the right side.
Gear: 0.4–3.5, two ropes
Rap: Two rap stations on climber's left
FA: Stuart and Bret Ruckman

☐ 2. HYPERCRACK ON THE ANCHOR CHAIN
5.11 ★★★★
Sorry, I only describe the first pitch, as I couldn't "sack up" for the second (way wide+way runout=no desire+no sack).
P1: Climb a short section of hands before beginning the ever-widening journey of fat splitterness. She gets steep just before the chains! If you choose to man-up and go to the top, two fixed drilled pitons will offer pro. From the top, you must walk the mesa top and choose rappels from the other routes.
Gear: 3.0–5.0 (heavy on the 4.0 5.0), 4 draws
FA: Jeff Widen, Jim Dunn

Michelle Kelley on pitch 1 of *The Plunge* 5.12

Chapter 2

313 Road

Monster Tower and Washer Woman

ROAD 313
OVERVIEW MAP
paved road
unpaved road
railroad
tower
crag
parking
Canyonlands NP border
camping
bathroom
trail
mileage
(from 0.0 location)
7.5
N
0 miles 1 2 4 6
To I-70
191
Lost World Butte
Pearly Gates
Road not Taken
Tombstone
6.3
8.1
Moab's Super Crack
Monitor
Merrimac
Sunset Tower
Rest/View Area
0.0
Class Act (1.5)
The Cove (1.4)
313 Slabs (2.0)
4.2
313
reset 0.0
1.4
8.0
Spring Canyon
Roaring Canyon
Hell
The Warlock
The Witch
no!
3.8
8.3
7.0
reset 0.0
11.5
11.8
Horsethief CG
0.0 reset
Cowboy CG
14.0
Dead Horse Point Rd
To Long Canyon
15.2
Mineral Canyon
Mineral Bottom Road
reset 0.0
12.8
Charlie Horse Needle
3.2
Trad Wall
5.1
6.4
Taylor Cyn
12.8
Zeus
Moses
Island in the Sky Visitor Center
17.7
reset 0.0
5.1
Bird's Eye Butte
Dead Horse Pt
To Moab
Washer Woman
Monster Tower
~18
32.6
Standing Rock

Along the 313 Road

313 ROAD

While most climbers may think of the 313 Road as a gateway to the major climbs and tourism of Canyonlands National Park and Dead Horse Point, the roadside cragging areas along 313 house some surprisingly good lines and some of the Moab area's most coveted ticks!

Getting there:

From Main and Center, drive north for 10.6 miles and turn left. Shortly after you turn left onto 313 you will cross a railroad track. RESET YOUR ODOMETER HERE!

Roadside Crag E

To approach the unnamed 5.10 splitter, drive 0.3 mile and take a right to the kiosk. Pass the kiosk and drive a short distance down the road. Look up at the east-facing cliff band and locate talus that skirts through the lower cliff bands. Once at the base of the cliff, walk a little left until you see the beautiful second-pitch hands splitter.

1. MOAB'S SUPER CRACK 5.10
P1: A broken start leads to a right-facing corner. Climb the corner and traverse over to the base of the splitter and set a belay (5.8, 50').
P2: ★★★★ Like Indian Creek's *Super Crack*, it starts with a bit of a gate keeper. Begin up splitter ow for a short distance and cruise the big hands and hands splitter. This would, for sure, receive more stars if not for the start.
Rap the route with a double 60m
Gear: 0.75–3.0 (heavy on 2.0s) optional 5.0 for the ow start on pitch 2

1. SUNSET TOWER 5.8 C3 or 5.13 S
Drive 1.4 miles and park off the side of the highway. A short approach up the talus brings you to the base.
P1: Awkward 5.10- to a wide ledge, then follow thin cracks with face moves for 5 meters to a decent finger lock (V6/7 R ish - a little sandy/soft with a bit of a flare). From there it's another 20m of splitter mostly fingers and wide fingers to the original double bolt belay stance (5.13- overall).
P2: Good varied finger crack climbing featuring footholds to an awkward groove at finish (5.12-).
These two pitches could easily be combined with a big rack and a good stance rest at the 1st anchor.
Gear: TCUs to #2 Friend for pitch 1; up to 3.5 for entire route
FA: Mike Baker, Leslie Henderson
FFA: Marco Cornacchione

☐ 1. **CLASS ACT** 5.11 ★★★★★ ✹ S-SW

To access, drive 1.5 miles and park on the right side of the road or a pull out on the left. The climb is the obvious right-facing corner on the right side of the road. Go under the fence and walk towards the right side of the talus cone and follow a faint trail to the base.

Class Act is a cherry paella climb! The first pitch is way sweet on its own if you don't feel inclined to climb the wide stuff above.

P1: Begin via the right-facing crack with a boulder move onto a ledge where the corner begins; ascend with tight hands passing a small slot to off-fingers around the steep bulge to anchors via fingers.

P2: A sustained right-facing offwidth corner.
Gear: P1: 0.3–1.0; P2: 4.0–6.0 (doubles of each), Carhartts, and tape
Rappel the route with a single 70m
FA: Earl Wiggins, Charlie Fowler, Katy Cassidy

Dylan Warren on *Class Act* 5.11

Along the 313 Road

THE COVE

The Cove SE

While you are in the Class Act area, check out four more routes inside the cove behind (lookers left & a short walk) the Class Act formation. Enter The Cove and these routes are on the left wall (listed left to right) as you walk in. There's also a huge boulder in the cove that from 313 looks tower-esque.

1. LEANIE MEANIE OF THE DESERT
5.11 120' ★★★
As you walk into The Cove, just before the huge boulder, is a right-facing corner that leans from left to right. Starts with tips and fingers and works up the sizes to big hands. The higher you get the steeper it gets.
Gear: 0.0–3.5
FA: Jason Keith, Scott Cole

2. UNNAMED 5.11+ 55' ★★
Start just right of *L.M.* up a small pedestal into the shallow left-facing fingers and tips corner. The corner changes aspects and stays fingers to tips to the anchor on the ledge. Shares anchors with *Jag*.
Gear: 00–1 (heavy on fingers and tips)

3. JAG 5.10+ ★★★
A sharp right-facing flake. Start with hands and quickly work your way through the sizes up to hand stacks. Punch it to the ledge.
Gear: 2.0–4.5
FA: Sonja Paspal

4. UNNAMED 5.10 55' ★★
A shallow left-facing corner that starts wide with some feet. Goes to hands before a final section of fingers.
Gear: 0.4–4.5

Elvis Memorial

A lone route just off the right side of the road at odometer 1.8 requires virtually no approach.

1. ELVIS MEMORIAL 5.12
Elvis Memorial is a right-facing corner in a forming arch.
P1: Four bolts of hard stemming to double overhanging thin hands corner.
P2: More thin hands, offwidth, with a bonus off-fingers roof traverse. The best way to climb the second pitch is to extend the first pitch above the bolted anchor to the large ledge 10 feet above. Begin pitch two from there (5.11).
RAP: From the top of the second pitch use two 60m ropes to get to the ground in one rappel.
FA: P1: Rob Slater, Jim Bodenhamer. P2: Charley Graham, Herb Crimp

ELVIS MEMORIAL

313 Slabs

Get your slab on! When the back of your hands feel like hamburger and it's too cold in the mountains, this south-facing wall is a perfect alternative. The routes do feel pretty runout, but I could be the world's worst slab climber. You can also toprope the left-side routes by walking to the anchors via a slabby shelf. This crag is located at 2.0 miles—just off the right side of the road. Park on either side. Routes are listed from left to right.

Dylan Warren on Friction 5.11c

❏ 1. **KOR ROUTE** 5.6
This route is easy to identify by its huge machine bolts with nuts on them.
FA: Layton Kor

❏ 2. **BEYER FRICTION** 5.9
Five pins to the anchor.
FA: Jim Beyer

❏ 3. **SHAKE AND BAKE** 5.11
Starts off a boulder and follows seven bolts to the anchor.
A: Kyle Copeland, Charlie Fowler

❏ 4. **FRICTION** 5.11 90'
Slab up the crux at the second bolt; pass four more and a pin to the anchor.

❏ 5. **PIGASUS** 5.10
About six feet from the previous route. Delicate climbing passing four pins to the anchor.
FA: Kyle Copeland

❏ 6. **BUY OR FLY** 5.12
Eight bolts.
FA: Jim Beyer

❏ 7. **BEACH PARTY** 5.11
Begin on the left edge of a forming half-arch. Follow fixed gear (four pins) to a seam and the anchor.
FA: Jim Beyer

An alternate approach for the Monitor and Merrimac buttes is to drive 2.8 miles to just below the first switchback before the road ascends. Park on the side of the road in a small pull out. Hike the main wash. At the first fork go right. Continue until you come upon yet another fork and continue left. Once you are in this left fork, look for a "path of least resistance" to your right. Once you are above the wash it is easy to see the formations. Hike directly while being careful not to bust the crust! 30–45 min.

Camping is available at 4.2 miles at the Monitor-Merrimac lookout which has a bathroom.

Additional camping can be found at 7.0 miles.

Tombstone

A cool-looking Entrada formation that, from the 313 Road, really does look like a giant tombstone. There are quite a few lines on the formation (mostly requiring aid) but only two (on the east face) are described here: *Epitaph* on the right horizon, and *Family Plot* just left of that in the shaded area. Doing both routes while you're there makes for a fun outing in a remote area—a sweet adventure!

☐ 1. **EPITAPH** 5.10+ ★★★★
✦ N

Epitaph, just shy of 300 feet, is the only free route on the formation. Start by making your way up to the saddle on the looker's right of the formation (either by heading right via the sand dune just past the cattle fence or left with a few short scrambles).
P1: The first few moves are pretty rough and exposed (the far side of the saddle drops away before good gear is had) on some soft rock. The rest of the pitch, however, is really fun. Mostly hands through some steep rock to a poor bolted belay out left on a sloping shelf—back it up with cams. (5.10+, 100').
P2: Follow good hands up the ever-widening corner. Make some awkward moves through steep slot/chimney to a sloping bolted belay (5.10, 100').
P3: Easy 5th class to the summit.
To descend scramble down the fifth class and rap the route with (2) 70m ropes from the top of the second pitch.
Gear: 0.2–4.0 (extra hands & big hands) (2) 4.0s would be nice. Many shoulder slings and draws are helpful.
FA: Smoot brothers

☐ 2. **FAMILY PLOT** 5.9 C1 ★★★★
✦ NE

A worthy route with clean aid that will most likely go free. Two pitches of thin cracks share the last easy 5th class pitch of *Epitaph*.
Gear: lots of small cams and double set up to an old 4.0
FA: Paul & Andy Ross

The Lost World Butte
Road not Taken, Mirage Crack & Pearly Gates

An aesthetic butte offering a mixed bag of climbing, largely the work of the legendary Paul Ross. While it houses quality lines, be aware that entrada sandstone can be loose and can provide some gripping climbing. There are more routes here than what is listed and it's well worth your time to explore this area.

Drive past the Tombstone and take an immediate right, past the west face of the Tombstone. Continue driving, and at the fork go left (straight) and follow it all the way to the white slickrock and park. The butte is straight ahead. Walk directly to the butte—about 10 minutes. Routes are listed left to right.

DUBINKY WELL AREA
Tombstone & Lost World Butte

These climbing areas are remote and in a beautiful desert setting (with some great camping). As such, it is popular with the motorhead crews. Be prepared to encounter some noise pollution and to co-exist! As in Arches, the rock here is Entrada, so be cautious of your gear placements. Running it out should be left for your Wingate adventures. This stone is soft!

Getting there: at 8.0 miles take a right on a dirt road (Spring Canyon) just after a Rest/View area on the left. RESET YOUR ODOMETER. Not far down the road on the right is the Lone Mesa group-camping area. An intersection at 1.4 miles reads Spring Bottom to the left and Dubinky Well to the right. Go right, pass over a cattle guard at 6.0 miles. At 6.3 there is a left turn called Dripping Springs just before the windmill. Take that to the Tombstone parking area at 8.1 miles.

TOMBSTONE

Along the 313 Road

THE LOST WORLD BUTTE E-SE

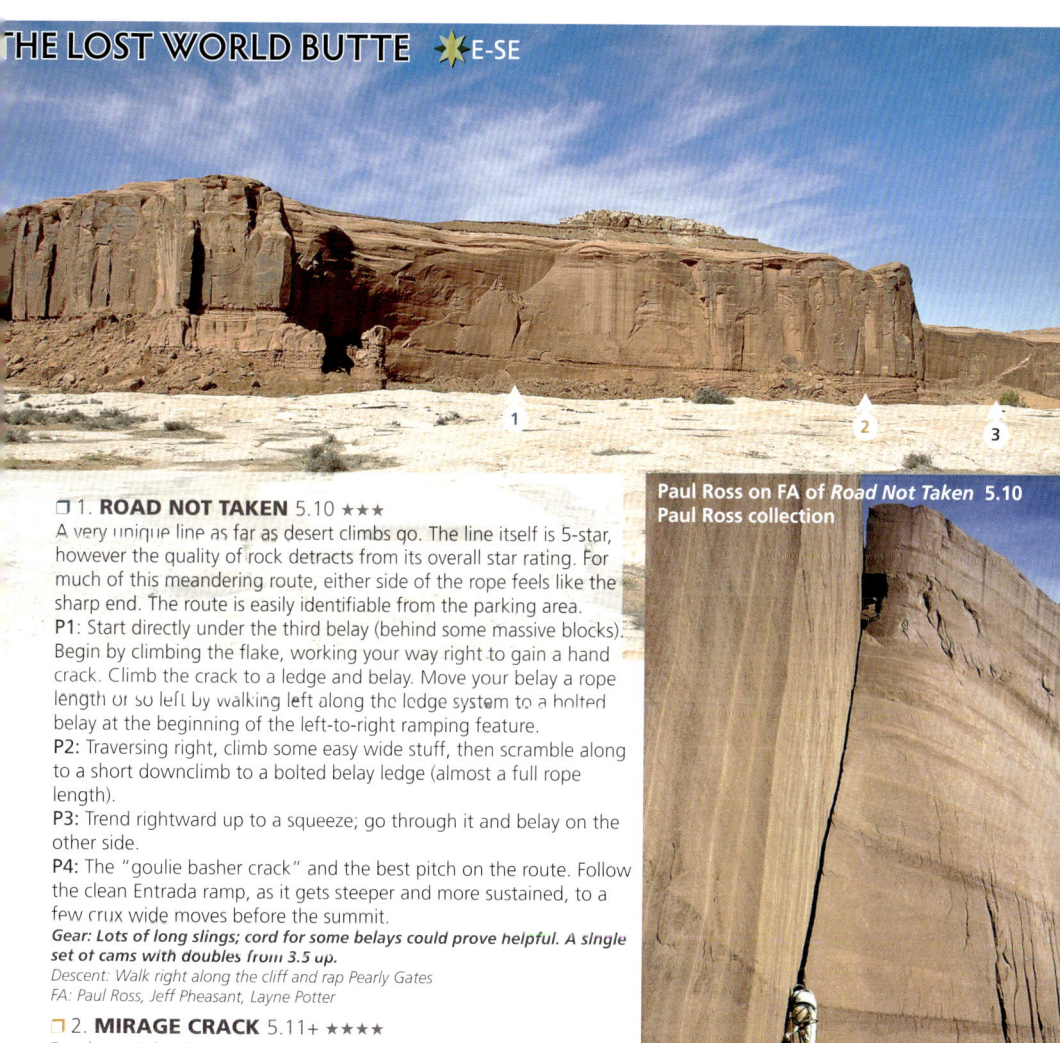

Paul Ross on FA of Road Not Taken 5.10
Paul Ross collection

❏ 1. **ROAD NOT TAKEN** 5.10 ★★★
A very unique line as far as desert climbs go. The line itself is 5-star, however the quality of rock detracts from its overall star rating. For much of this meandering route, either side of the rope feels like the sharp end. The route is easily identifiable from the parking area.
P1: Start directly under the third belay (behind some massive blocks). Begin by climbing the flake, working your way right to gain a hand crack. Climb the crack to a ledge and belay. Move your belay a rope length or so left by walking left along the ledge system to a bolted belay at the beginning of the left-to-right ramping feature.
P2: Traversing right, climb some easy wide stuff, then scramble along to a short downclimb to a bolted belay ledge (almost a full rope length).
P3: Trend rightward up to a squeeze; go through it and belay on the other side.
P4: The "goulie basher crack" and the best pitch on the route. Follow the clean Entrada ramp, as it gets steeper and more sustained, to a few crux wide moves before the summit.
Gear: Lots of long slings; cord for some belays could prove helpful. A single set of cams with doubles from 3.5 up.
Descent: Walk right along the cliff and rap Pearly Gates
FA: Paul Ross, Jeff Pheasant, Layne Potter

❏ 2. **MIRAGE CRACK** 5.11+ ★★★★
For those sickos looking for wide Entrada splitters, here you go!
P1: The full hand to fist spectrum (5.10, 60').
P2: Four inches to ever-widening (5.11+, 100').
FA: P1: Paul Ross, Andy Ross, *FA:* P2 Matt Lisenby

❏ 3. **PEARLY GATES** 5.5 A0
The perfect full moon or meteor shower route—easy climbing to a short bolt ladder and a summit that feels in the middle of nowhere.
P1: Climb the left-to-right ramping feature for 130' or so and build an anchor when you hit the twin ow cracks (5.4).
P2: Climb the double cracks to a ledge and belay (5.5, 65').
P3: Bolt ladder up a steep section of the wall and over the top to a bolted belay. (We did this in our sneakers at night and it felt spooky frictioning from the last bolt to the anchor—maybe save the beers for the top instead of the base of the climb).
Gear: A single rack of Camalots up to a 3.0 (though you could place a bigger piece), shoulder length sling, six draws for the bolt ladder.
Descent: DON'T RAP OFF THE ROUTE ANCHORS, instead, look for a rap station about 100' to the climbers left. One double 60m rope rappel leads down to the ramp and walk off. The longer your ropes, the further down the ramp you will go.
FA: Paul Ross, Jeff Pheasant

▲ Horsethief Campground, at 11.5 miles offers 58 campsites multiple bathrooms, dumpsters, picnic tables, and fire pits. The cost is $12 per site per night (two vehicles, four tents/trailors, and ten people per site). Quiet time is from 10pm-6am. Generators are allowed from 8am-8pm. Pets must be leashed.

HELL ROARING CANYON

A magical and obscure canyon that requires effort to experience!

Tom Gwinn and Heather Hillier on The Cauldrons. The Witch is on the left, The Warlock on the right.

The access can be summed up as adventurous and involved. Have fun!

Quickest approach: Once on the 313 Road, drive to the Mineral Point road (not to be confused with the Mineral Bottom just down the road). Turn right at the Horsethief Campground sign at about 11.4 miles. RESET YOUR ODOMETER.

At 3.8 miles go left at a fork in the road. At another fork at 7.0 miles (just before the end of the buttress on your right) go left. After about 8.3 miles there is another buttress off to your right. Turn right, continue around the buttress and drive straight for the rim. The road will end at a campsite. Park here. Hike down to the rim where you will be able to see the towers down and a bit left. Basically you need to drop down a couple of tiers with the intention of eventually working to the downstream side of the towers. Look for a small tree and scramble down to an alcove keeping your eyes peeled for a couple of bolts on a light-colored section of rock. Fix a line into the canyon.

Heather Hillier jugging out

Along the 313 Road

The Witch ✶ S

☐ 1. **MIDNIGHT RIDER** 5.11+ R ★★★★
P1: Begin on the south face. Easy face climbing past a drilled angle gains a crack. Some awkward moves on decent but silty rock leads to another short stretch of face climbing which ends at a comfortable belay ledge with a bolted anchor (5.10).
P2: Follow the left-facing corner that begins with fingers before gradually tapering to tips. There has been some warning in regards to the pro on this pitch, as apparently the crack flares inward. The pro seemed good to me, but we never got the chance to test it. Enduro climbing with small stances between sections of liebacking. The pitch ends at another decent belay ledge with modern anchors (5.11+).
P3: Move left of the belay into a brief section of loose rock. Follow the deep left-facing dihedral, clipping several drilled pitons intermixed with clean pro. At the top of the pitch is a huge flake with a hand crack on its underside. Exit onto lower-angled terrain and a belay ledge (5.10-).
P4: Face climb on friable-seeming but decent holds past several drilled angles to reach the top (5.9).
Descent: 3 double-rope rappels (60m ropes) Summit to top of P3, P3 to top of P1, P1 to the ground.
Gear: 0.0–3.0 (heavy on tips and fingers), set of nuts, shoulder length slings, 6 quick draws
FA: Ron Olevsky

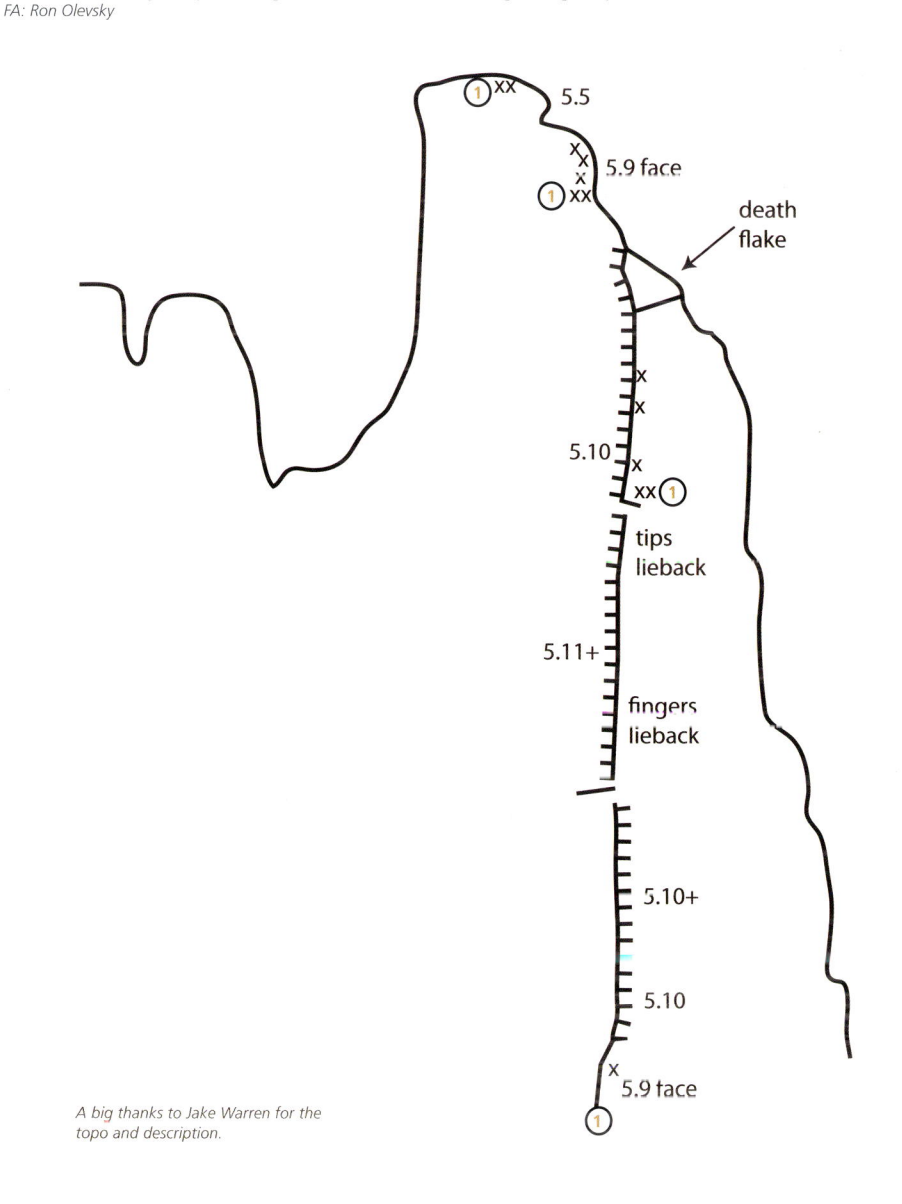

A big thanks to Jake Warren for the topo and description.

AN EVIL SPELL
An Account from Sam Lightner

Once a year Aimee and I try to celebrate 28 years of climbing together (and yet never making the mistake of dating) by doing a tower-adventure. 2008 was the year of The Witch via the Olevsky route, *Midnight Rider*.

A previous half-assed attempt to find the "rim approach" came up empty, so we piled into "Sherman" and drove the long way via Mineral Bottom. A 1.5 hour hike up canyon put us at the base, and another 45 minutes had us at the ledge-belay below pitch two. The delicate liebacking that is the business of pitch two looked to go on for a good 50 feet of darkly varnished Wingate. Sadly, only a few moves into the dihedral I skated off a smear and that was that—it was no longer going to be a flash attempt. As such, and as the day was short, we decided to just push on and go French-free so we could tag the top and make it home by happy hour.

I pulled on a 0.5 Friend, then placed a green Alien and clipped it. Pulled on the Alien, removed the Friend and pressed it into crack as high as I could. I reefed on the cam, then placed another friend high and clipped it. I continued clipping and skipping for about 35 feet, interchanging green Aliens, 0.5 Friends, and blue Metolius TCUs. They all had to be totally retracted at the lip of the crack, but then nearly tipped out once inside. Sadly, nothing larger would fit past the crack's opening, so I settled for the uninspiring placements. High in the dihedral the piece I was pulling on skated and then popped from deep in the crack. I took to the air and heard a "pop — pop — pop."

Aimee, not expecting to catch a 40-foot fall, let out a scream as she was yanked into the air. I was holding onto my ankle when I came to a stop. Just to add insult to injury a TCU, Friend, and Alien all slid down the rope and smacked me in the jewels. No matter, as I barely noticed it through the pain in my ankle.

"Do you have some powerful pain killers in your pack?" I asked while clutching my right foot.
"No," she replied, "Is it broken?"

"I can't tell, but I know I'm in for a long walk out," I said through a cringe. Aimee lowered me as I grabbed what remaining pieces there were. Ten minutes later I was on the ground. Aimee got the gear together while I taped my ankle into a field splint. She took the pack, and I set a goal of simply making it to the car by dark. It was intensely painful and I had to retape from the swelling, but we made it to the car and were at the hospital getting X-rays by 10 pm.

I returned to The Witch with Josh Gross a year later and managed to tag to the top. Her evil spell, however, has gotten the best of me. Two surgeries and three years later I am still dealing with swelling and intense pain after exercise. Twisting my right foot into a crack is very uncomfortable, and I'd rather walk through fire than 100 feet of scree. To say the least, it was a life-altering fall. One moment you're pulling through, the next you are reformatting your goals in climbing. So watch your placements, and remember that if they don't look too good, they probably aren't.

The Cauldrons ✦ S

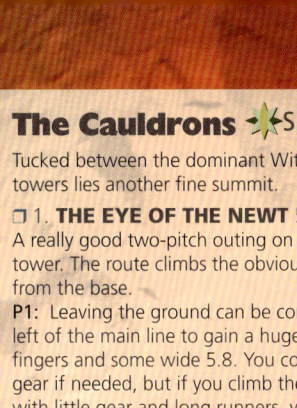

Tucked between the dominant Witch and Warlock towers lies another fine summit.

☐ 1. **THE EYE OF THE NEWT** 5.10+ ★★★
A really good two-pitch outing on the SW side of the tower. The route climbs the obvious weakness visible from the base.
P1: Leaving the ground can be confusing. We started left of the main line to gain a huge ledge with some fingers and some wide 5.8. You could belay here with gear if needed, but if you climb the bottom section with little gear and long runners, you can continue. Once on the ledge, walk a touch right to the base of the route. Climb the super-cool stembox with tips through hands. Continue via a wedge to a tight hands flake protected with a pin. More hand jams bring you to an awkward move out right around a small roof with some off-fingers & tight hands to a bolted belay ledge (5.10, 150').
P2: The huge roof pitch. Climb up the large wedge under the gigantic roof (use double length runners on any and all gear through this section). Thank the rock gods for that roof: A) It offers really good hand jams, and B) some good stems. Again slings are your savior for alleviating rope drag in this section. Once through the roof, climb some thin hands and varied climbing to a belay ledge between the twin summits (5.10+, 80'). An easy scramble brings you to the climber's right summit.
Gear: 0.4–3.0 (heaviest on all hand-size units)
Rap: Rap the route with 2 double ropes (60m)
FA: Davin Lindy, Mike Wood, James Funsten

Peter Vintoniv, *Eye of the Newt* 5.10
Andrew Burr photo.
Michelle Kelley on same route.

The Warlock

☐ 1. WINGS OF LEATHER 5.11 PG-13 350' ★★★

P1: Climb across or below the huge leaning block on the south side of the tower. Gain the deep squeeze chimney and top out on a spacious belay ledge with modern anchors. There's little to no pro on this pitch unless you sling some chockstones in the chimney or carry a #5 BigBro—not that you need it, though, for if you fall you won't go anywhere (5.8).

P2: Follow the gradually thinning crack on the left side of the dihedral until it pinches down, transforming into a wide silty crack to the right. Stack or layback until the crack narrows and you get a few fist/hand jams before it closes up at the bottom of a loose chimney. Stem through easy terrain with little pro. The rock gets better higher up and a thin crack with pods appears on the left wall, offering good pro. The chimney ends at a roof with an 8-inch crack on the right side. Stem to the outside of the chimney to clip a good bolt and grovel or aid into the offwidth. The offwidth gradually tapers down and the angle eases, leading to a good belay and modern anchors (5.11-/C0 or 5.11).

P3: Trend up and right to the outside corner of the tower. Easy crack and face climbing leads to a sloping ledge; trend left gaining an incipient crack and more slabby terrain. Trend left again, gaining a rotten corner that leads to the summit (5.9).

Gear: set of stoppers, 0.3–4.0 (double set) a couple of ow pieces, long slings
Rappel with double ropes (60m) from summit to top of pitch 2, again to the top of pitch 1, and one more to the ground.
FA: Matt Pickren, Sam Lightner and Brad Brandewine

☐ 2. DUDE, THAT'S NOT FUNNY 5.12b ✹ SW

This route follows the varnished splitter on the southwest face of the formation and is easily identified by a rectangular ow pod at about 160 feet. A bolt was added on the first pitch for the FFA, and there is a pin on the second pitch at the top of the chimney. No bolts were added at the belays.
P1: 5.12b, P2: 5.11, P3: 5.7
Rap the Wings of Leather route.
Gear: Nuts, triple set of Friends and TCUs
FA: Dave Medara, Mike Pennings FFA: Marco Cornacchione, Bret Ruckman

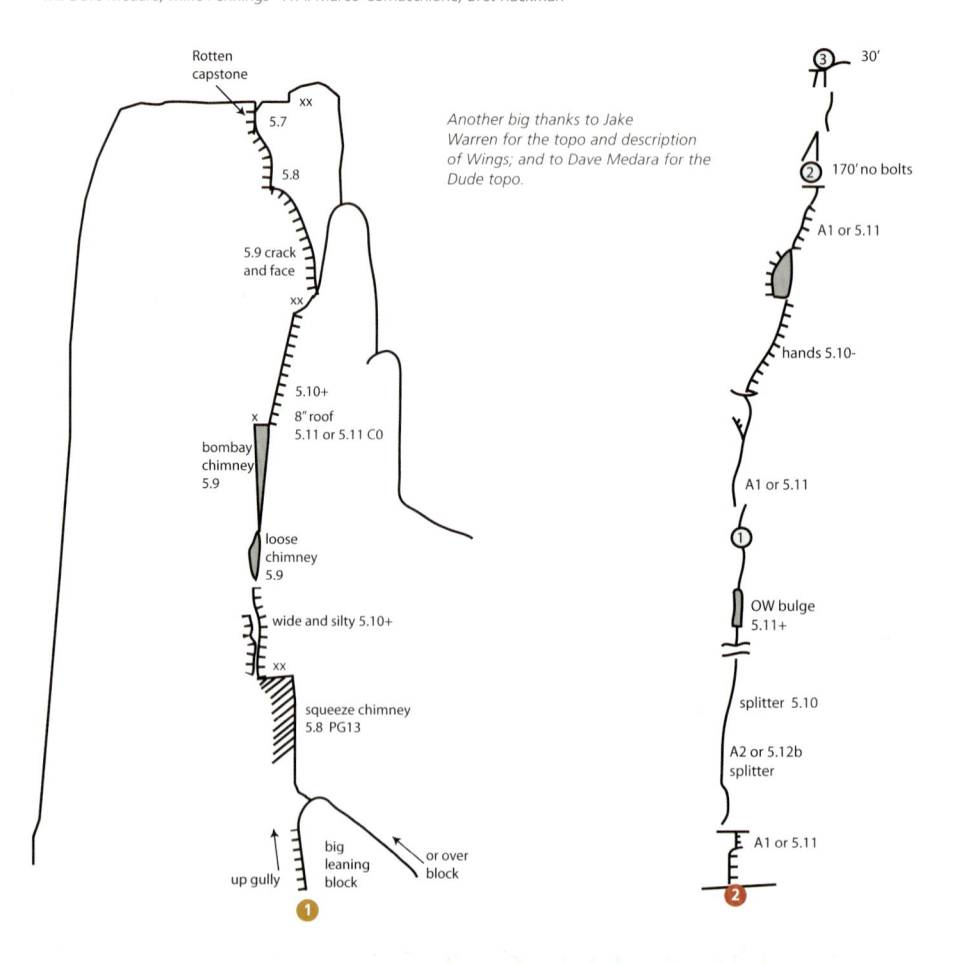

Another big thanks to Jake Warren for the topo and description of Wings; and to Dave Medara for the Dude topo.

Rotten capstone
xx
5.7
5.8
5.9 crack and face
xx
5.10+
8" roof
5.11 or 5.11 C0
x
bombay chimney 5.9
loose chimney 5.9
wide and silty 5.10+
xx
squeeze chimney 5.8 PG13
up gully
big leaning block
or over block
①

③ 30'
② 170' no bolts
A1 or 5.11
hands 5.10-
A1 or 5.11
①
OW bulge 5.11+
splitter 5.10
A2 or 5.12b splitter
A1 or 5.11
②

Canyonlands

Moses and Zeus Photo: Andrew Burr

CANYONLANDS NATIONAL PARK
paved road
unpaved road
tower
crag
parking
Canyonlands NP border
camping
bathroom
trail
viewpoint
mileage (from 0.0 location)
N
0 miles 1 2 4 6
The Warlock
The Witch
no!
3.8
no!
8.3
reset 0.0
11.5
11.8
Horsethief CG
reset 0.0
Gemini Bridges
12.5
Cowboy CG
14.0
Dead Horse Point Rd
15.2
131
Mineral Canyon
Mineral Road
reset 0.0
12.8
Horsethief Trail
No Boundaries
Word to the Bird
Bird's Eye Butte
3.2
Trad Wall
Charlie Horse Needle
5.1
6.4
Taylor Cyn
Zeus
Moses
12.8
Labyrinth CG
Hardscrabble CG
17.7
reset 0.0
Island in the Sky Visitor Center
Shafer Trail
5.1
Upheaval Dome
Potato Bottom CG
White Rim Trail
Candlestick Tower
Green River Overlook
Washerwoman
Monster Tower
Airport CG
White Rim Trail
~18
Candlestick CG
Gooseberry CG
Murphy CG
32.6
Grand Plan
Grandview Pt.
Grand Blast
Standing Rock
Junction Butte
Century Crack
White Crack CG

WHITE RIM-RIGHT
Trad Wall, Boundary Wall, Charlie Horse Needle, Taylor Canyon

The Mineral Bottom Road is home to stacks of great climbing, including many 5-star endurance routes. It is reached by traveling 11.8 miles down the 313 Road and turning right at the well-maintained road.

Follow the well-maintained road for about 12.8 miles. Here you will start to descend the steep switchbacks. At 14.2 miles, there is a fork in the road (right for swimming, left for climbing).

• Going right (swimming): There's a popular cliff-jumping rock off the left side of the road for those hot days, as well as a boat dock just down the road. After passing the boat dock you will reach the entrance to Mineral Canyon; past that is an alternate approach to Hell Roaring Canyon involving an hour-plus hike to the Witch and Warlock.

• Going left (climbing) at the fork is how you will access the climbing covered in this book.

Trad Wall aka Green River Buttress W-S

Take a left towards the park, at an intersection at the bottom of the switchbacks. At approximately 3.2 miles from the intersection, the Trad Wall will appear on the left. You can approach via the left (west face) of the cliff or via the right (southeast-facing) up a talus drainage. Hiking up the center would be difficult due to some lower cliff bands.

The first four routes are on the west-facing wall not far around the corner from the south face. Routes are listed left to right.

❏ 1. **ZIPPY** 5.10+ 60' ★★★
A shallow right-facing corner with off-fingers and tight hands. A few hand pods are much welcomed.
Gear: 0.75–1.0
FA: Tom Gwinn

❏ 2. **BENSON AND LEDGES** 5.10+ 70' ★★★
Starts just a few feet left of *Smokin Deal*. Start in a right-facing corner with off-fingers and hand pods. At half-height traverse right to a left-facing corner which changes directions again after a few body lengths.
Gear: 0.5–3.0 (heavy on off-fingers and tight hands)
FA: K3

❏ 3. **SMOKIN' DEAL** 5.10 60' ★★★
Offwidth to splitter tight hands. If it were longer it would receive more stars. The inconvenience of the short ow is worth the splitter above.
Gear: 0.75–6.0 (heavy on tight hands)
FA: Gary Olsen, Bret Ruckman

❏ 4. **MARLBORO CIG** 5.9+ 85' ★★★
A tighter-hands left-facing corner on the heavily-lichened left wall.
Gear: 1.0–3.0 (heavy on 1.0s)
FA: Bret Ruckman, Gary Olsen

The next five routes are on the south-facing wall and are in close proximity to each other.

☐ 5. **A3B** 5.10 50' ★★★
A perfect hands splitter that leans from left to right and eventually gains the right-facing corner. Finish with a short wide section.
FA: K3

☐ 6. **SEOUL GAMES** 5.10+ 160' ★★★★
Seoul Games starts behind a huge boulder that leans against the wall. Climb behind the boulder and out the hole to a stance on top. Climb the corner above via more off-fingers through some awesome link-ups. Further up offers some hand jams with siltier rock.
Gear: 0.4–3.5 (heavy on the off-fingers and tight hands)
Rappel with (2)60m ropes, tied for safety as they barely reach.
FA: Bret Ruckman, Gary Olsen

☐ 7. **B4WARNED** 5.11 100' ★★★
A sweet line with a hard size start. Splitter rattly fist on the left wall of a right-facing corner. Eventually the splitter merges with the corner and the size gets a bit friendlier passing through some wavy bulges.
Gear: 1.0–4.0 (heavy on the 4.0s)
FA: Joe Slansky

☐ 8. **SUPER NINJA CHIPMUNK** 5.11 65' ★★★★
A wild route. Begin up a shallow left-facing corner with tight hands and off-fingers. At some point, ninja movement will be required to reach the next left-facing corner to the left. Ascend that shallow corner via fingers and off-fingers to a bolted belay.
Gear: 0.3–1.0 (heavy on off–fingers and fingers)

☐ 9. **TRAD BADGER** 5.10+ 65' ★★★★
Begin as for *Super Ninja* but instead of the traverse left, continue up the main corner from hands to fingers.
FA: K3

☐ 10. **GLAD TO BE TRAD** 5.13 160' ★★★★★
An unbelievable line. I wish there was a set of lower anchors for mere humans to enjoy the really long section of steep off-finger/tight hands (#2 Friends) in a steep corner on killer rock. It then turns mutant, as splitter fingers lead to the anchor.
Gear: 0.3–2.0 Friends (lots)
FA: Steve Hong, Steve Carruthers

The next three routes are at the far right side of the wall.

☐ 11. **FUCK IF I KNOW** 5.11 90' ★★
Mostly fingers in a left-facing corner to tighter fingers in a flare.
Gear: 0.3–0.75
FA: Steven Lucarelli

☐ 12. **MIGHT AS WELL** 5.10- 50' ★
Start behind a leaning pillar on the far right side of the wall. Climb cupped hands and hands with stems from the pillar.
Gear: 1.0–3.0
FA: K3

☐ 13. **UNNAMED** 5.11+ 120' ★★★★
An easier version of the ultra classic *Glad to Be Trad*. Commence in a short (20') left-facing corner with off-fingers and tight hands, then switch aspects to a long (70') right-facing corner with more of the same. Eventually the corner ends and a short splitter with hand pods begins. Ascend the splitter (30') to the anchor.
Gear: 0.3–2.0 (heavy on off-fingers & tight hands)

Big Man Wall

The Big Man Wall—the buttress just right of the Trad Buttress—is most easily accessed by the right side talus approach for the Trad Wall. It is identified by two forming arches in whitish rock, and a pair of splitters beside each other in the black rock. *Little Big Man* is the left one.

☐ 1. **LITTLE BIG MAN** 5.12 100' ★★★
A sweet lonely route. Climb the tips and fingers splitter to "the flakes"— a little spooky. After the flakes, cruise the offset splitter via hands and big hands to the anchor.
Gear: 0.0–3.5

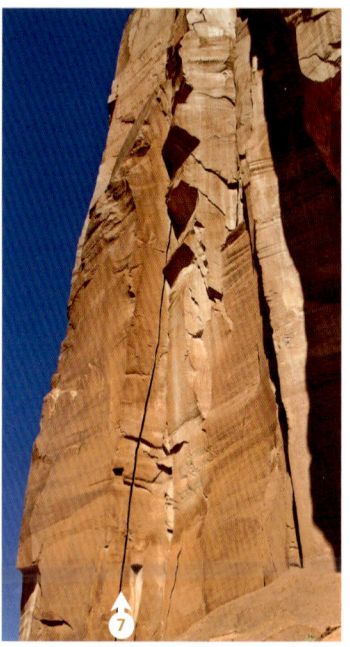

Canyonlands

Boundary Wall ☀ SW

The Boundary Wall is, literally, at the park boundary sign, 3.9 miles from where you take a left at the bottom of the switchbacks. The second wall right of the Trad Wall features some stellar Wingate lines. All the climbs are worthy of your time. This is a great après-Moses wall, even worth an extra night for a bonus day of climbing. You won't be disappointed! Routes are listed left to right.

BOUNDARY WALL

❏ 1. **KINDER AND GENTLER** 5.11- 65' ★★★
Great fingers/off-fingers climbing on good rock. Ascend the shallow right-facing corner varying from fingers to off-fingers. You'll wish it were longer.
Gear: fingers & off-fingers
FA: Bret Ruckman, Marco Cornacchione

❏ 2. **A CIRCLE OF QUIET** 5.11+ 155' ★★★★★
A super-sweet line of splitter cracks—a single splitter off the ground (featuring off-fingers and tight hands through a small bulge) leads to double cracks and a ledge (optional belay). Finish on the left splitter with tight hands, off-fingers and fingers.
Gear: 0.3–3.0 (heavy on off-fingers and tight hands)
FA: Bret Ruckman, Stuart Ruckman

❏ 3. **MARCO MY WORD** 5.10+ 100' ★★★★
An awesome big hands to fist splitter on good rock. Steeper than it appears!
Gear: 0.3–4.0 (heavy on fist)
FA: Marco Cornacchione, Bret Ruckman

The next route is around the corner to the right (around the tower) a couple hundred feet.

❏ 4. **SHADOW CHASER** 5.10+ 60' ★★★ ☀ S
A shallow right-facing corner. Starts with fingers and soon becomes off-fingers. At ¾-height, pass the pod and continue with off-fingers and tight hands.
Gear: 0.4–1.0
FA: Bret Ruckman

Jenna Gardineer on Might as Well 5.10, Trad Wall

The next route is at the far end of the south face of the Boundary Wall in a cove—just out of view from the road. It's easiest to hike from the drainage/wash just after the Boundary Wall. On the right side of the drainage lies an old mining road that can be followed to the back. Make sure to take the road left when you get in the back and follow big talus to the base of the climb (30 min).

5. 2 FRIENDS GETTING RED 5.11- 190' ★★★★★

I had done *Marco My Word* and *Circle of Quiet* years ago and recalled that there were a few more routes on either side of the buttress and I wanted to re-up the memory. That side of the White Rim has seen a bit of flood damage in the last few years and the White Rim has experienced frequent closures. A sign proclaimed road damage and a closure near Upheaval Dome. Undeterred, I went out on my motorcycle to re-visit the wall. I walked the south-facing wall that houses *Shadow Chaser*. The further I walked the fewer lines I saw and the chossier the wall became. Hiding from the sun beneath a boulder, I drank some water and put away my notebook and camera for the walk down the talus. While in the shade I took out the binocs and looked around. Further down, the wall became a cove with a partial crack visible past an obstruction. As I moved closer, it became evident that it was something special. The name refers both to the dirt-bike-rally approach and the dominant cam color.

Climb a short right-facing corner with off-fingers up to the first of two pods with thin hands in the back. Exit the first pod and enter the second not-as-friendly pod. A few off-width moves lead to a bolted belay. Clip the belay, keep going, and enter the beautiful tight-hands splitter that only gets tighter as it ascends. A final off-fingers bulge terminates at the bolted anchor.

Gear: 0.5–5.0 (heavy on the tight hands)
Descent : 2 raps with a 60m (keep the packs light)
FA: K3, Tom Gwinn

B.F.E.

Despite a bad case of seclusion, the following route is worth the effort of the approach. Drive into the park and after the park boundary, look for an old corral—you won't be able to see the cliff yet. Continue driving and looking back until the cliff comes in to view. Stop the car and take a good look—the line is super obvious and you'll be jonesing to climb it.

☐ 1. **BFE** 5.11 135' ★★★★★
Sweet! Super stellar offset splitter/shallow right-facing corner. Start by getting on top of the flake. Climb the shallow corner through a pod. Continue until you can traverse left to the next system. Follow the flake system to the anchor.
Gear: 0.4–3.0 (heavy on off-fingers)
Rappel with (2)60m ropes.
FA: Bret Ruckman, Gary Olsen

Bret Ruckman on the FA of *BFE* 5.11, Ruckman collection

Charlie Horse Needle

The Charlie Horse Needle is the largest in a row of spires on the left before reaching Taylor Canyon. The north-facing route makes for a great summer summit (and as an added bonus, some cragging routes are found along the way—albeit on the south side). From the intersection at the bottom of the switchbacks reset your odometer and drive 5.1 miles passing the Trad Wall, Boundary Wall, and BFE areas. Look for a small parking area on the left side of the road at the obvious box canyon, with the tower in view. Walk towards the tower in the box canyon; a short distance in, head diagonally up the left side and look for an easy scramble to the mesa. Continue toward the tower, avoiding the crypto. On reaching the talus, look for a faint trail (heading right) leading up to the cragging routes on the south face. The far right line is an unnamed 5.12 off-fingers splitter with a pod in the middle. As you continue to the prow—before you walk around to the north face—you will encounter a short 5.10 corner featuring angling hands.

1. CHARLIE HORSE NEEDLE 5.11 ★★★ N

A spectacular summit with great views! After walking around the prow, continue walking along the wall until you see the obvious window halfway up the tower. To reach the base scramble (fourth class) up the benches. A sizable bench/ledge allows for a great place to rack up at the base of the route. The route is on the opposite side of the tower from the photo.

P1: Commence via the *Simms-Hesse* variation up a fist splitter (5.10), just left of the obvious corner. An alternate start (5.12) begins just right of the corner in an arching fingers splitter. Either way, you will end up in the main corner headed towards the spectacular window with views through the tower to the Green River. Continue past the window utilizing some cool stems around a bulge. You can set a belay at the window or continue on via a finger crack on the left face. When the crack ends, move to the corner and up to a belay ledge with a bolted anchor.

P2: Up the left-facing corner through an off-fingers bulge.

Gear: 1 TCU–4.0, some long runners (optional big piece)
FA: Ron Olvevsky, Jay Ungritch FFA: Ken Simms, Mark Hesse, Maura Hanning-Simms

Carrie Finn on the summit of Charlie Horse Needle

Michelle Kelley passing the window on *Charlie Horse Needle* 5.11

Taylor Canyon

Taylor Canyon is perhaps the most profound setting for desert climbers—a remote canyon housing a row of slender spires. An awesome location and one of those places that is just a mind blow—a place people dream about after they've seen posters in the mall. As a climber, it's a place that should not be missed. Sitting on top, watching the sun go down, and reliving your day is magical!

The approach, besides the drive, is pretty easy. It's not unheard of to see a 2-wheel drive car out there. The hike itself is a pretty easy 10-minute walk. Follow the directions as for the Mineral Bottom climbs. Take a left at the fork in the road, at the bottom of the switchbacks. Follow the road (passing the Trad Wall) to the park boundary sign. About 2.5 miles after this there will be a fork in the road (6.4 miles on the odometer) Take a left here, this is Taylor Canyon and it is well signed. Drive for another 6.4 miles to reach the parking at the dead end.

Aphrodite, Zeus, Moses, and the Thracian Mare (left to right)

Moses

Park in the designated area at the end of the road and walk up the well-beaten path. When you are close to the base of the tower—heading right leads to the south-facing *Primrose Dihedrals*, while the left trail leads first to the *Dunn Route* and just beyond to *Pale Fire*. Only these three routes are described here, although others exist.

☐ 1. DUNN ROUTE 5.11 ★★★★ ☀ N

P1: The start is not that obvious. Locate the steep corner up near Moses's head and work your way down to the ground. A tricky bouldering start off the ground (over a bulge with some unique pockets here and there) brings you to a right-facing corner. Climb a wide bit to a bolted belay (5.9+).

P2: A fairly long chimney pitch. Continue up the corner and pass a pin (a variation out left involves 5.9 R face climbing). Continue with secure chimneying to a difficult squeeze. At the top of the squeeze work left to a fixed belay on a ledge (5.10+).

P3: Begin off the belay with a few easy but exposed slab moves (falling here would result in a fall directly on your belay). After the slab moves, climb the right-facing corner with some fingers and hands up to the belay ledge.

P4: Climb the right-facing corner with overhanging fists past a few drilled pins (strenuous 5.10+). When you can, tunnel inside the chimney and follow it to its top (bigger folks—if you don't fit you will need to climb the steep ow out right 5.11). Either way, you will land on Moses' shoulder and an optional belay. If you tunneled, it is possible to link it with the last pitch.

P5: Some 5.8 face climbing leads to the summit.
Gear: Carhartts, set of nuts, 0.4–4.0 (heavy on 3–4), optional big piece, shoulder slings and a few quick draws.
Descent: Rap Pale Fire or Primrose
FA: Jim Dunn, Stewart Greene, Doug Snivley, Kurt Rasmussen

☐ 2. PALE FIRE 5.12c ★★★ ☀ N

P1: A very long, very sustained pitch. Are you feeling strong? Climb some discontinuous cracks (5.12b) up to the main splitter. Follow the main splitter with, yikes, unrelenting off-finger jams (5.11+) passing the first belay and up an additional 50+ feet of handcrack to the next belay.

P2: Splitter hands and big hands bring you to the crack's terminus. Climb the face past some of Bjorny and Beckey's *incentive fixed protection* (incentive not to fall). Continue through the thin face up to a bolted hanging belay.

P3: Climb a bolted (relics) face near the arête and belay.

P4: Ascend the short face passing a couple of fixed pieces to the summit.
Gear: 1 TCU–3 triple set (heavier on off–fingers), bunch of quick draws (some bolts are hard to clip with modern biners, so bring some small-headed biners or tie-offs).
Rap the route with (2)60m
FA: Fred Beckey, Eric Bjørnstadt; *FFA:* Charlie Fowler & Chip Chace

Canyonlands

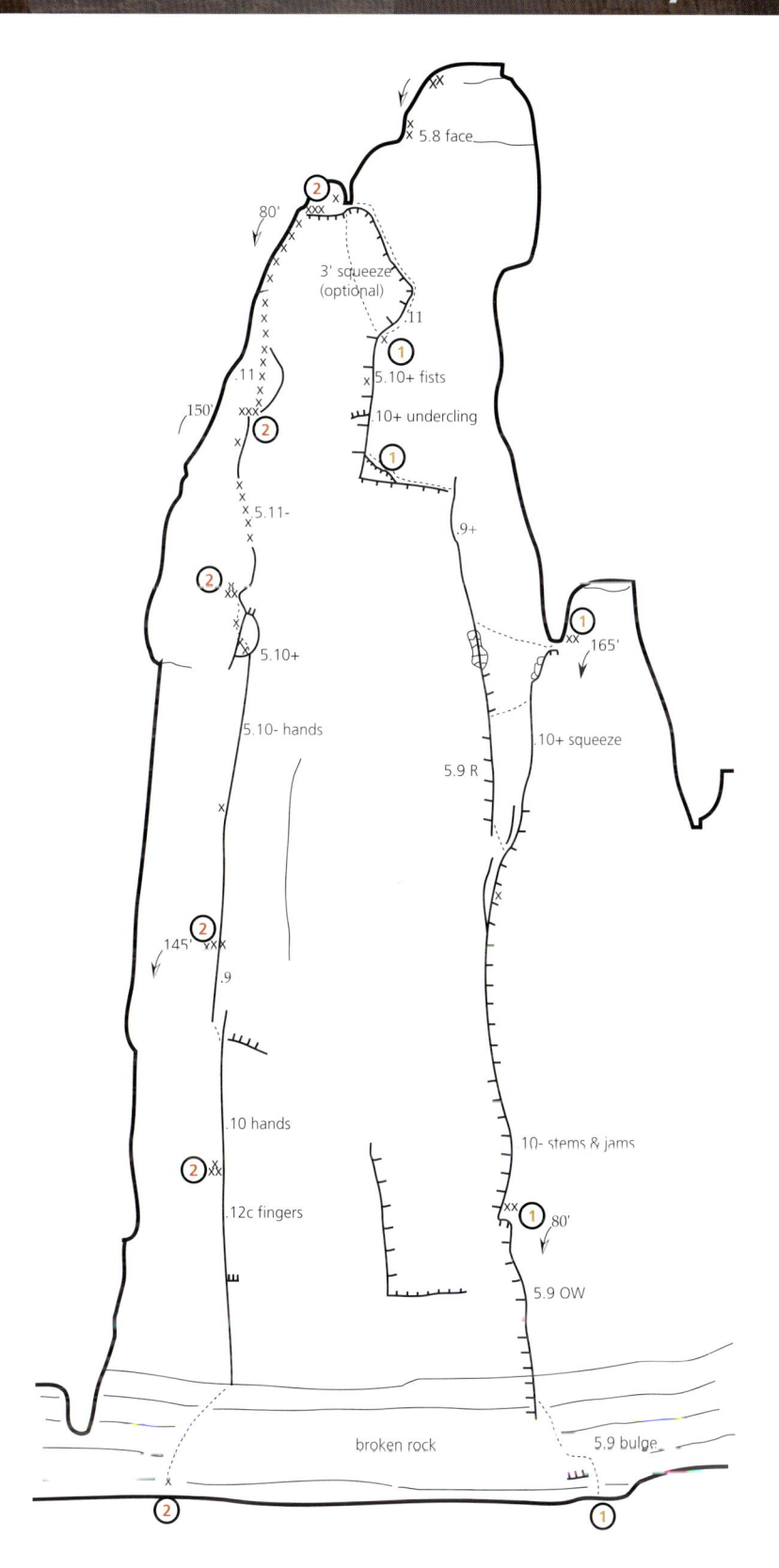

5.8 face
80'
3' squeeze (optional)
.11
5.10+ fists
10+ undercling
.11
150'
.9+
5.11-
5.10+
5.10- hands
165'
10+ squeeze
5.9 R
145'
.9
.10 hands
.12c fingers
10- stems & jams
80'
5.9 OW
broken rock
5.9 bulge

3. PRIMROSE DIHEDRALS 5.11+ ★★★★★

The route is described in five pitches but is often done in seven or eight.

P1: ORIGINAL START: Begin at the south face beneath a chimney/slot. The rock, despite its tiled appearance, is actually quite good. RPs and a large cam protect the bouldery 5.11d crux.

P1: VAR: From the notch between Moses and the small formation to the east, downclimb a bodylength and make a horizontal leftward traverse with good feet and face holds; continue around the corner (your belayer is blind to you now) to a bolted stance on a good ledge. (5.8, 50'—mostly horizontal)

P2: Climb up to a small roof via finger and off-finger jams in a left-facing corner. Pass the fixed pin and continue up the now right-facing corner with off-fingers to tight hands and back to some fingers. Here you must traverse left around a rounded arête. It is beneficial to sling your last several pieces with long runners. Once around the arête, lots of folks climb up the corner to a slung belay (backed up with 2.0 Camelots). It is best to forego the downclimb and head left to the section with stacked blocks and flakes (protecting with thin gear—your first several pieces should be clipped with long draws to alleviate rope drag). Climb the flakes to a bolted belay ledge (5.10+, 120').

P3: Great pitch! Start by climbing the right-facing corner, passing a small triangular roof with fingers—long draws here help with drag later in the pitch. Continue up to a small stance (fixed piece) just before a bulging (really good) big-hands corner. At the top of the corner it gets a bit wider but the climbing is a bit easier (an old 3.5 Camalot might be useful). Belay at a stance with bolts (5.10, 70').

P4: You are now at the famed "EAR" pitch. The first half of this pitch has been described in the past as the easiest section of the climb which may be true, but keep in mind it is also the most suspect section of rock on the route and should be climbed with that in mind. I recommend bringing larger stoppers. The last few moves of this section (just below the makeshift belay beneath the Ear) do feel hard/strenuous and maybe just a bit heady. Continue past the intermediate belay and clip a pin, continue past the Ear clipping six bolts and arrive at a stellar belay ledge equipped with good bolts (5.11, 120').

P5: Climb the chimney to its end. Pass the belay and face climb past two fixed pieces to the summit (5.8, 100').

Rap the route with two 60m ropes (70s add confidence). Two single raps lead to the top of the Ear. Two double-rope raps gain the ground. You can also rap Pale Fire (rumor has it that a single 70m works, but its up to you to do such a committing tower with only one cord).

Gear: Single 0.0 & 1.0 Metoliuos TCU, triples of 0.4–3.0, one set of nuts, plenty of shoulder and double shoulder length slings, 6 quick draws
FA: Ed Webster; FFA: Ed Webster, Steve Hong

Nik Berry at the Ear on *Primrose Dihedrals* 5.11+
Andrew Burr photo

Peter Vintoniv on *Pale Fire* 5.12b
Photo: Andrew Burr

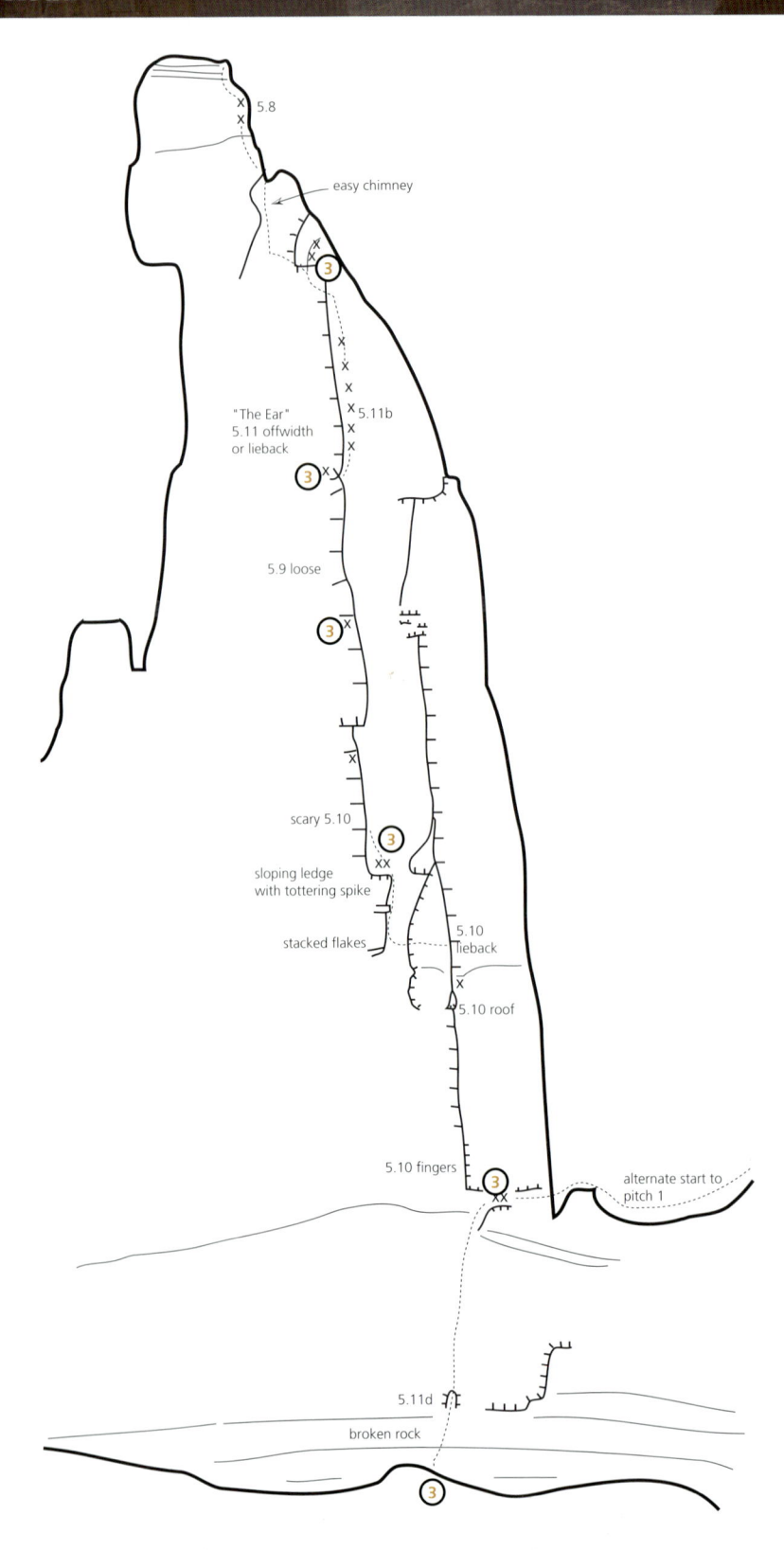

313 Road

5.8

easy chimney

"The Ear"
5.11 offwidth
or lieback

5.11b

5.9 loose

scary 5.10

sloping ledge
with tottering spike

stacked flakes

5.10 lieback

5.10 roof

5.10 fingers

alternate start to pitch 1

5.11d

broken rock

Nik Berry on *Sisyphus* 5.11 R   photo: Andrew Burr

Zeus ✳ s

Zeus is the sublime spire east of Moses. It has a reputation of stout climbing.

☐ 4. **SISYPHUS** 5.11+ R ★★★★
P1: Climb the left-facing corner with finger cracks and stemming past a few fixed pieces to a belay ledge. Belay with 0.75s. (5.10+).
P2: A thin (tips) strenuous lieback up the left-facing corner leads to an easier ow. Continue up and right over blocky terrain to a belay on a ledge just below an old bolt and hanger. At the time of this writing there was a single pin on the left wall or you can build a belay with 0.4 & 0.75.
P3: The "heady" R-rated pitch. Climb the left-facing corner past a fixed piece and continue with fingers to a ledge. Move right off the ledge and over the crux (with pro at your feet) to easier climbing passing two pins to the summit.
Gear: 0.3–3.5, (triple set) set of nuts, slings
Rappel the northeast side. Two 60m cords barely get you from summit to ground.
FA: Jimmy Dunn, Doug Snively; FFA: Jeff Achey, Chip Chace

DEAD HORSE POINT AREA
Rim Descent Wall, Crow's Head Spires, Bird's View Butte

This is a picturesque location with two towers, a butte, and a canyon rim wall. Who could want any more? Did I mention you can drive to the summit of a five-star route? You can arrive at your beer-filled cooler and enjoy a stellar sunset—the makings of a five-star day.

APPROACHES…
A few options exist and, yes, it is possible to avoid the nearly 400' rap/jug option, though that is my preferred method.

Option 1. THE RAP/JUG: From the railroad tracks on the 313 Road, drive for 15.2 miles and look for a dirt road on your left. Reset your odometer. Proceed to the first fork at 0.3 mile and go left. Continue to another fork at 1.8 miles; take the right road to its terminus at around 3.7 miles. (To reach *No Boundaries*, travel only 3.0 miles to a wishbone on the left). Follow this to its end. When you get out of the truck (you can drive most of this in a car but you would need to hike the last 0.75 mile if you don't have high clearance) walk west and soon you will see the Crow's Head Spires. On your first visit, it may take a few minutes to locate the rap anchors: as you walk towards the spires, look for a rectangular boulder tipped upward; scramble down below it. Once on a bench, again scramble to the next ledge and the anchors are visible.

Option 2. THE HIKE: From the railroad tracks on the 313 Road, reset your odometer. Drive for 17.7 miles, passing through the entrance of Canyonlands National Park. Take the first left onto the Shafer trail. Reset your odometer. Descend the harrowing switchbacks of the Shafer trail; at 5.1 miles there is an intersection. The right fork leads to the White Rim, while the left goes down to Potash Road. Take the left. Drive 1.8 miles to an obvious wash just before the park boundary and park here. Walk up the wash for 30 minutes. Here the wash forks; take the left fork and watch for some lower hoodoos (one has the appearance of an eagle's head). Shortly after these hoodoos, scramble up to a right-to-left leaning ramp that will put you on the next mesa level—this is important because if you keep going you will dead end at the wash's terminus. Once on the mesa, continue along the rim. Reaching the talus cone can be tricky due to three small cliff bands that have to be negotiated before arriving at the bottom of the climbs. A fairly straightforward route lies directly below the saddle between the Bird's View Butte and the Crow's Head Spires. The total approach time is 1:45 but if it were not for the cliff bands on the talus, this would be a preferred alternative to the rappels.

Bird's Eye, Don Juan, and Luminous Being

Rim Descent Wall

Routes are listed from right to left.

❒ 1. **WORD TO THE BIRD** 5.12- ★★★★ S

On the prow of the Rim Descent Wall.
P1: Begin behind the huge leaning pillar, exiting right onto the outside of the pillar finishing through rotten, easy 5th class to anchors.
P2: Climb the crack through hands to thin hands in a shallow left-facing corner pinching down to baggy fingers (0.5s), passing a small roof to anchors at a hanging belay.
P3: Move out and left past two bolts to the finger crack (0.5s), pass a small roof and continue through offset fingers (0.5 Camalots) which pinches down to tips in a left-facing corner, ending at a ledge with bolted anchors.
P4: Walk left 10m to a slot with a 0.5 Camalot crack in the back; climb to a big ledge. Follow an easy chimney to the left past soft rock to another ledge and crawl left 10m to a slot. Climb up the slot and exit at the top of the wall (no anchors).
FA: Jason "Froto" Matz, Jonathan Reckling

❒ 2. **TITANIC CORNER** 5.11 ★★★★ SW

A titanic climb that doesn't top out.
P1: Start up a pillar in a left-facing corner with big hands and hands past some wedged blocks to a spacious belay ledge with a belay bolt backed up with #2 Friends or 1.0 Camalots (5.9).
P2: Leave the belay and climb triple discontinuous cracks to the stellar left-facing corner. Climb the corner with tight hands to perfect hands, thinning back down to fingers, to a belay with a bolt and a fixed nut (5.11).
Gear: 0.4–3.0 (heavy on tight hands and hands)
Rap: Double 60s will get you to the ground.
FA: Drew Spaulding, Ty Hydrusko, Jed Workman, Dan Hackett

❒ 3. **LASER CRACK** 5.11 C1 ★★★ SW

P1: Start in a right-facing corner with hands up through a short offwidth section and back to hands to a two-bolt belay (5.10).
P2: Traverse right on a ledge and pass a bolt on your way to the "laser" splitter section. Climb the laser (from hands down to fingers) up to the roof, traverse right until you are able to climb around it to a great belay ledge with two bolts (5.11, C1).
P3: Climb past a bolt and a knife blade to a ramping corner that climbs fingers and tips to a ledge (5.10+).
P4: Work a bit left and follow the path of least resistance to a two-bolt anchor just under the main ledge.
Gear: 0.0–3.0 (heavy on the fingers) #4 optional for P1
FA: Drew Spaulding, Mark Minor

❒ 4. **THINK YA SHOULD** 5.11+ ★★★ SW

Rims out in three pitches. If you win the coin toss for pitches, go for the second.
P1: Start with a left-facing fist crack which leads eventually to a squeeze chimney. After the squeeze, a friendlier and easier chimney will bring you to a large ledge where the splitter of pitch 2 starts. Set a belay here. We used a few red Camalots but there are many options for setting the belay (5.10).
P2: ★★★★★ Climb the steep beautiful tight hands splitter to a short section of rightward-traversing hands and fingers to a belay ledge with a bolt and a drilled angle (5.11).
P3: From the belay, step left and locate a shallow left-facing corner. Climb the corner through a steep section to another splitter (big hands) until it ends. Face climb left to another ledge and ascend another left-facing corner (easy climbing but soft rock) up to the huge ledge just under the rim and belay from three bolts. From here, carefully walk left along the ledge; two moves up a left-facing corner lead to the ledge. Walk right to the car. Great route!
Gear: 0.5–3.0 (#2 Friends work best on pitch 2)
FA: Drew Spaulding, Mark Minor, Julie Peterson

Jason "Froto" Matz on pitch 2 of *Word to the Bird* 5.12- photo by Joe Auer

313 Road

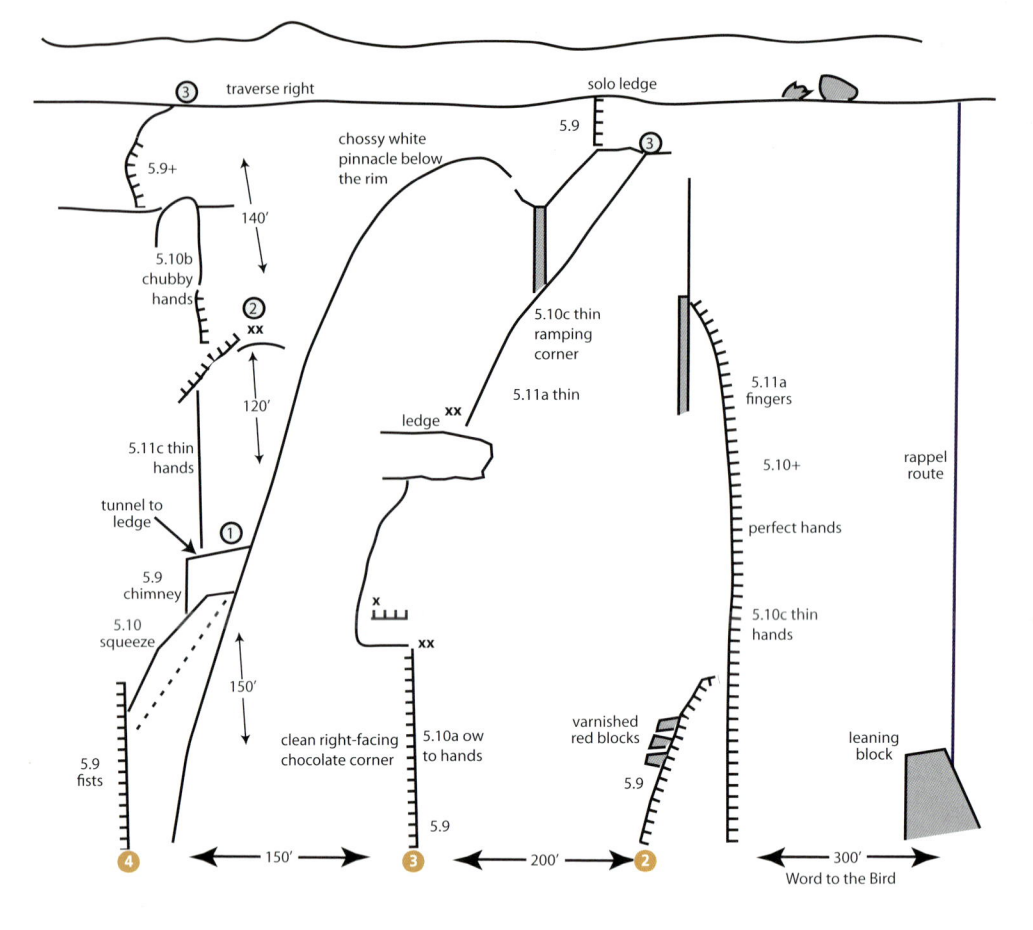

No Boundaries Wall

Located just within the boundry of Deadhorse Point, this is a rap in/climb out outing. See the approach description on page 60.

☐ 1. **NO BOUNDARIES** 5.11 330' ★★★★
✸ S

A spectacular route featuring a 165-foot big hand to fist crack splitter in an asthetic setting—looking out at Crow's Head spires and the White Rim.
P1: "The Man Crack" pitch. Broken blocks lead to a short offset off-fingers section which gains the start of the man crack. Climb the big hands and fist crack splitter to a short, stout, right-facing corner/seam with pods. Continue out left-leaning overhanging flake to a bolted belay (5.11).

P2: Climb fingers and off-fingers in a shallow left-facing corner/flake to just below a bolt on the left wall. Face climb out left passing a bolt (double shoulder-length sling) up and over a huge block to the base of the chimney (5.8 X) and follow it to its top. Once on top of the chimney, make sure to flick the rope out of the chimney to reduce drag. A short off-fingers boulder move to another ledge brings you to the first of three bolts protecting really fun rail climbing.
Rappel consideration: It's best to make two single-rope raps to the top of the Man Crack, to alleviate getting the ropes stuck on the big ledge. A double rope rappel to the ground is required for the final rappel from the top of the Man Crack.
Gear: (2 each) 0.4–1.0, (4 each) 2.0–3.0, (6) 4.0, double shoulder length slings
FA: K3, Michelle Kelley, Chris Willie

Jake Warren and Steven Lucarelli on pitch 2 of *No Boundaries* 5.11

313 Road

No Boundaries topo

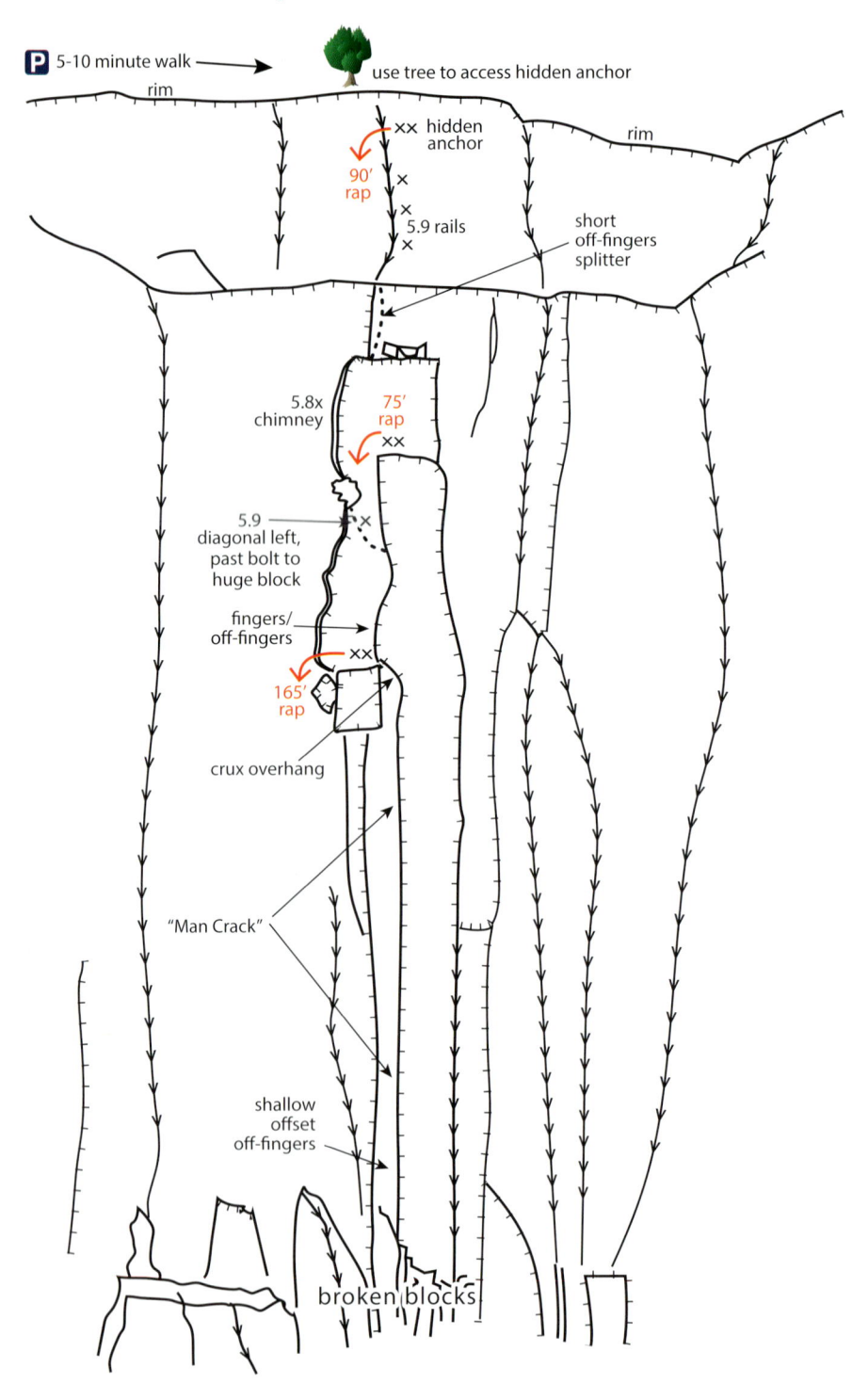

CROW'S HEAD SPIRE/BIRD'S VIEW BUTTE

Luminous Being Spire

The L.B.S is the closest spire to the Rim Descent Wall.

1. LIZARD ACTION 5.10+ N-NE
Several options exist for the first pitch (on the northern side).
P1: Take your pick—you'll see when you get there.
P2: Wrap around to the east side, climb around the bulge to the obvious crack, and follow it to the ledge. Move out to clip a fixed pin before moving to the arête to clip another; slab up to the anchor. Heady.
Gear: 0.4–4.0, a couple of quick draws and shoulder–length slings
Rappel to the notch and then to the ground with two 60m

FA: Robert Warren, Jeff Webb

Don Juan Spire

The D.J.S. is the second, or farthest, spire visible from the Rim Descent Wall.

1. DON JUAN 5.10 R NW
Coming from the Rim Descent Wall, *Don Juan* is located on the right side of the tower and closest to the notch.
P1: Ascend the triangular pillar, from the left or right, to some slung stones.
P2: Climb an awkward A-slot to broken cracks and reach the notch.
P3: Continue up and left to the chimney and proceed to its end. Move right and then ascend the slab (R) to the final corner and the summit.
Gear: 0.4–5.0 (at least doubles up to 4.0), slings
Rap: Two raps with two 60m

FA: Ken Trout

2. THE WORKING MAN 5.12- W
Pass *Don Juan* and head toward Bird's View Butte. Before the wall turns south-facing, you will notice a tips cracks and bolts. This marks the start of the climb. The FA party traversed in at the 20' height, above where the bolts were subsequently placed. The bolted variation is dubbed *The Way of Ignorance*.

FA: Mike Pennings, Jeff Hollenbaugh

3. YESTERDAY'S NEWS (FREE) 5.10 S
P1: Climb the south face up easy ground to a crack that is followed up to a belay ledge on the right.
P2: Move out left to some cracks that lead to a bulge. Go left over the bulge, then climb an offwidth to a ledge. Build a belay.
P3: An angling crack leads to the summit.
Gear 0.75–5.0, slings

FA: Jason Keith, Greg Bimesteffer

Don Juan Spire and Rim Descent Wall

Bird's View Butte

As seen from the Rim Descent Wall, Bird's View Butte is the butte behind the Crow's Head Spires. Rap the Rim Descent Wall, walk beneath and past the spires (we went right, around the spires), walk the saddle between the spires and the butte to the left (west-facing) and look on the southeast-facing side for a semi-detached spire (yes, there are routes on it—happy exploring). *Unemployment Line* lies just past the spire. Continue past *Unemployment Line* and wrap around to the south face to find *Happy Face* and *Great American Squiggler*. I climbed *Great American Squiggler* and found it to be worthy—because we were already there. That being said, the Rim Descent Wall is a better option if time and energy remain after *Unemployment Line*. Routes are listed right to left.

1. UNEMPLOYMENT LINE 5.11 ★★ SE
P1: Begin up a short left-facing easy corner to an overhanging 5.11 slot (a 5.0 helpful), pass a hard finger slot to some face moves. Move right to an obvious left-arching hand crack. At the top of the hand crack continue up the short right-facing corner via fingers to the base of the slot. Set a belay (0.5 & 0.75).
P2: Climb the wide slot (5.0s in the back) up to to what my partner aptly called "vertical talus" that can be bypassed by some face climbing on the right. We belayed out right on two rappel pins, though you could do as the first ascentionist did and continue left over a huge block and set a belay (0.75, 1.0, 3.0) around the corner under the final corner system.
P3: Climb the left-facing corner, with a short section of fingers through fists. Continue up the wide (old #4 Camalots and bigger). Placing gear on your left is advantageous. When some helpful rails on the left wall disappear, don't look back, as you're getting close to the ledge. Belay with cord around stones at the top.
P4: Climb onto the big leaning boulder at the base of the final short easy chimney (rope not needed).
Gear: 0.3–6.0
Descent: Two double-rope rappels are located climber's right of the route.
FA: Mike Pennings, Drew Spaulding

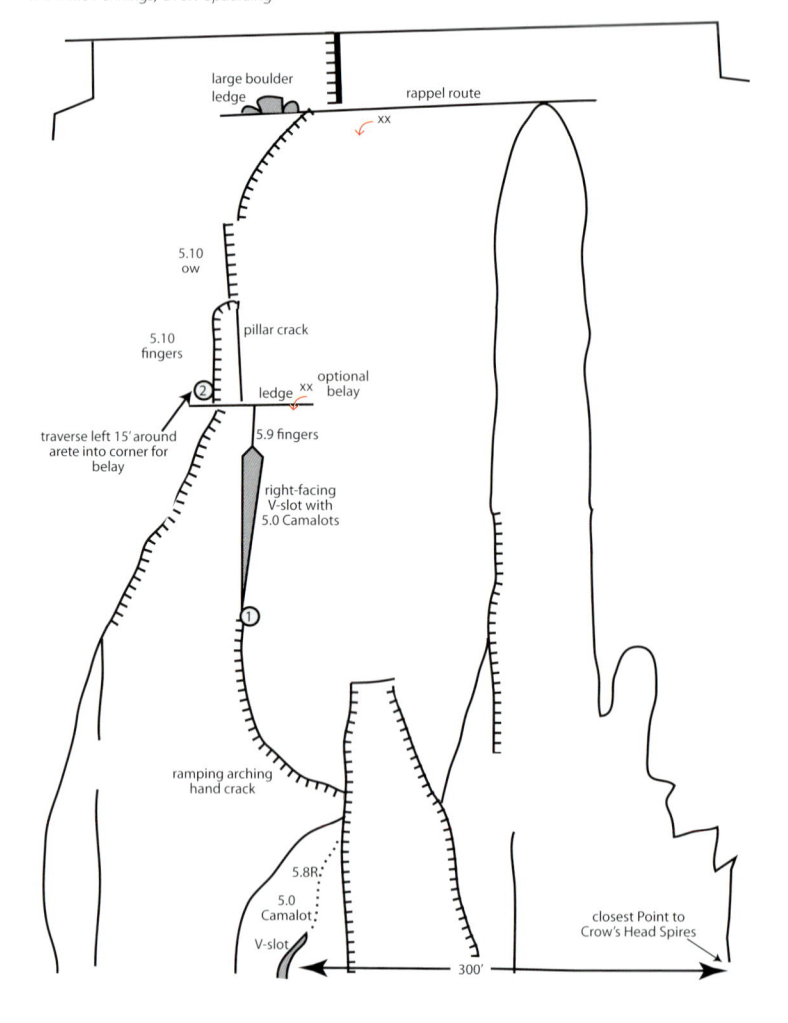

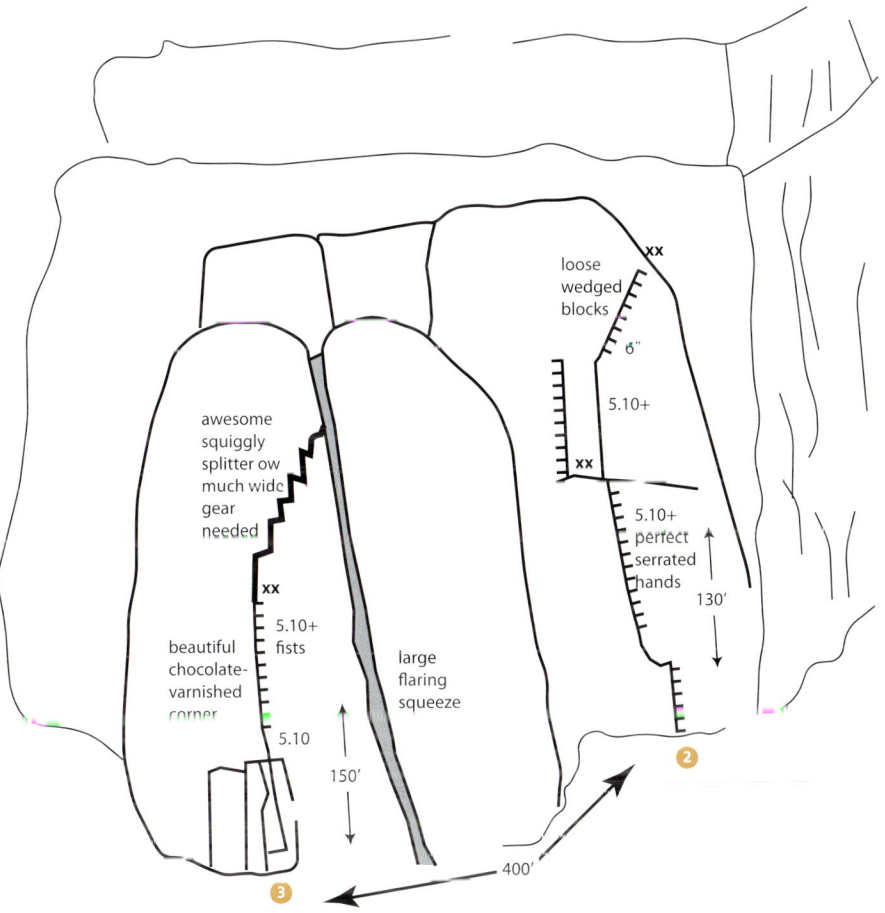

Canyonlands   67

☐ 2. **THE HAPPY FACE** 5.11
P1: Climb the left-facing corner to a steep slot. Once through the slot, cruise hands to the belay ledge.
P2: Offwidth.
FA: Drew Spaulding

☐ 3. **GREAT AMERICAN SQUIGGLER** 5.10+
Climb a wide crack to a ledge under the left-facing corner. Make some fun moves into a slot, then climb a left-facing fist and off-fist section. Finish on some spooky rock and make an awkward clip out right on a slopey ledge.
Gear: 1.0–4.0 (heavy on 3.5–4.0)
FA: Drew Spaulding

Nik Mirhashemi on pitch 3
Unemployment Line 5.11

loose wedged blocks
6"
5.10+
xx
5.10+ perfect serrated hands
130'

awesome squiggly splitter ow much wide gear needed

xx
5.10+ fists
beautiful chocolate-varnished corner
5.10
large flaring squeeze
150'

❸
400'
❷

CANYONLANDS/WHITE RIM LEFT
Monster Tower, Washer Woman, Standing Rock

WOW, what to say:
a. SPECTACULAR?
b. BEAUTIFUL?
c. MIND BLOWING?
d. ALL OF THE ABOVE!

A special place for climbing, mountain biking, jeeping, etc.—and it's right here in our back yard! The White Rim and the following climbs are inside Canyonlands National Park and you will need to pay a daily fee to enter. Camping requires a permit. In the spring and fall, a reservation is recommended. Check with the headquarters to see about any closures. No new fixed gear is permited in the park.

IF YOU PLAN ON DOING ANY NEW ROUTES OUT HERE YOU MUST CLIMB TO THE RIM AND LEAVE NO FIXED GEAR, THIS INCLUDES SLUNG CHOCKSTONES, THREADS, ETC….

That said, you should not miss the climbing here! Un-★★★★ing real summits with spectacular views in a mind-blowing setting. I have had some of the most special moments of my life out here!

To reach the Shafer trail, drive 17.7 miles from the railroad tracks, passing through the fee station. Immediately turn left on a dirt road—the beginning of the spectacular Shafer trail.

This section includes only selected climbs, but there's an abundance of routes out there for the adventurous to unravel. PLEASE, observe your surroundings, this place is pristine. Do more than your part to keep it this way. **Karma points are big in an area like this. If you see some trash take the time to pick it up. Pack everything out….**

If you must poo, try to do your thing in the bathrooms at the camping areas; if none are available, dig a hole at least 10" deep, away from any waterways (dry or wet); use a stick or a rock for your wipe and bury it with your waste. If you must use toilet paper, pack it out. Or, best yet, do as desert river runners have for years—pick up a wag bag at the outdoor store and bring it with you.

Washer Woman in front and Monster Tower on the right.
Photo: Andrew Burr

MONSTER & WASHER WOMAN TOWERS

These are the stunning towers featured in countless posters and postcards. Drive approximately 18ish miles from the start of the Shafer trail to the base of the southwest-facing talus slope. Park at a lefthand hairpin/switchback. Follow the well-traveled and cairned trail to the base of the towers.

Washer Woman Tower

❏ 1. **IN SEARCH OF SUDS** 5.10+ ★★★★ ☀ S-SW

A cool route with a few bonus features, including the "eye" where you can look out the other side of the tower and a wild free-hanging rappel over the archway off the deck! The route is a bit of a meandering line, but links awesome terrain. Gain the obvious saddle between Monster and Washer Woman with easy 5th, eventually working your way over to the corner under the "eye" (some folks rope up for this section).
P1: Start in the right-facing corner, climb steep hands and big hands. Continue over a few tricky (secure) chockstones, Continue with easier climbing to the belay stance and a fixed belay just under the "eye" (5.10).
P2: Climb up to the "eye," working your way into the corner that becomes wider the further you go. An few awkward moves put you on to the spacious bolted belay ledge (5.9+).
P3: Climb steep hands off the belay ledge, and as the crack gets smaller the angle eases up. A final steep headwall with some helpful face features brings you to the "washboard." Set a belay—a length of cord is nice to sling some boulders (5.10+).
P4: Fourth-class across the "washboard" and make a 5.9 move over a piton to a spacious bolted belay ledge (5.9).
P5: Climb some horizontal weaknesses (which, with imagination can be protected) up to some good face climbing past several fixed pieces (5.10+).
Descent: 1: Short rap down to the "washboard" (single 70m rope). 2: A ▲ ▲ ▲ ▲ ▲ rappel... locate the anchors that are above the arch. These anchors are a chore to set up. You may want someone to hold your legs. Lay down on your stomach and reach the chains; tie two 70m cords together and rap over the arch. There are some anchors near the bottom of the arch, but continue down to the next ones below. 3: Rap with double ropes to the ground. It has been suggested that you can rap the route with a single 70m but I have never done this. It would, for sure, make for a lighter pack on the approach.
Gear: *0.3–3.5 (doubles is enough for most folks) shoulder length slings*
FA: Charlie Fowler, Glenn Randall

Monster Tower

❏ 2. **NORTH FACE** 5.11 ★★★★

Start from the saddle between Washer Woman and Monster Tower by scrambling from the top of the approach trail from the southwest-facing side. Alternately, an optional 1st pitch 5.9 corner can be climbed from the opposite (northeast) side of the saddle.
P1: A sweet big hands/fist curving splitter. The splitter will spit you out at the base of a low-angle ow corner which can be frictioned off to the side or climbed via ow. You will land on a nice belay ledge with a bolted anchor (5.10).
P2: Move left off the belay to a shallow right-facing, off-fingers corner (punch it and be rewarded with a hand jam) to a rest. Eventually you will enter a little bit of ow. You can place some creative small gear in the ow but most folks will be happy they chose to bring along a wide piece. Belay on a ledge with a bolted anchor (5.11).
P3: Take your pick of the left or right options. Both are 5.9 and each have an element of choss. Left will bring you to the obscure bolted belay—the most direct. On both pitches you will encounter some wide sections. I personally have only done the right line, but many of my friends have done the left and both sound similar in quality and grade (5.9+).
P4: A bit of a meandering pitch with some difficult face moves. From the belay work right, up a corner, and over a bulge; follow weaknesses to a ledge. We did not climb the bolt ladder, but friends tell me it's spicy at the end. We followed the lefthand option, which I recall was gripping! Thin spicy climbing would sum it up (5.11b).
Gear: *Set of nuts, 0.4–4.0 (extras on 0.5, 0.75, 3, and 2 Friends,) a 4.5 would not go unused, plenty of shoulder length slings, quick draws, (optional helmet)*
Descent: Rap the route—a single 70m will work but two will get you down faster.

313 Road

WASHER WOMAN

gear belay

eye

optional belay

MONSTER TOWER

heady lead

roof

5.11 fingers crux

big hands and fist splitter

Canyonlands

Standing Rock

This is the tower made famous by its placement on the cover of Layton Kor's seminal work *Beyond the Vertical*. The tower is set in a Mars-scape beneath the White Rim Trail. No matter what you do, this is a long, time consuming venture. You can choose whether to drive down the Shafer or Mineral side on the White Rim, but it's pretty much sixes on which way is faster. Plan on several hours. A vehicle with clearance is necessary, and a cooler of beer a must. Once you have driven to the parking on the White Rim you still have more adventure ahead of you, as you must descend to the base of the tower. You have two choices: rappels or a one-hour hike.

To reach the tower via the hike, park at the first spot where the slickrock joins the road in Monument Basin. Follow the slickrock along the rim for about a mile, passing an arch and the Enigmatic Syringe (an obvious tower with a needle-like summit). A major gully system past this point affords a fairly moderate descent into the basin. Only one short section of rock slabs requires scrambling; the rest is a hike following cairns to the riverbed. Continue right and follow the wash to the tower.

While multiple rappel in/jug out options exist, climbers as of late have utilized a gully/semi-fixed rope option. This descent is located after passing an extended slickrock section where the road comes within 50 meters of the cliff edge. When a pretty arch comes into view, drive about a mile and cross a dry stream bed, parking in a small lefthand pullout. A short walk leads to the rim and a view of Standing Rock. Hike right along the rim for about five minutes keeping an eye out for the descent gully marked by a cairn—you should be able to see the fixed rope and a giant house-sized boulder. Some traversing through cliff bands leads to the dry creek bed and Standing Rock.

ALTERNATE APPROACH: Instead of driving down the White Rim, you can approach by parking at the end of Hwy 313 at the Grandview Point overlook. Look for a unmarked trail (Government Trail) down unobvious benches to the White Rim. Once at the bottom, walk right until you see a big hands and fist crack.

1. STANDING ROCK 5.11 ★★★★
P1: The pitch begins on the north side near large stacked boulders. Ascend a crack and right-facing corner and traverse right underneath the roof (5.10b) to a loose 5.7 crack (long slings). Continue up a small right-facing corner to a shallow belay ledge with bolts.
P2: Traverse right on the ledge and continue up a loosely-defined right-facing crack. Head for some tat at an optional hanging belay, passing two roofs (5.10) to a left angling crack. Continue past another bolt and several small roofs (5.10) to a bolted belay at a ledge.
P3: A mantel up and left leads to steep moves past bolts to a big left-facing flake. Gently move up and right to a comfortable belay ledge.
P4: Head up from the belay then right to an easy, but loose, passage to the summit.
Enjoy one of the finest summits anywhere on our planet!
Gear: Double set of cams, nuts, shoulder length runners.
FA: Layton Kor, Huntley Ingalls; FFA: Keith Reynolds, Walt Shipley

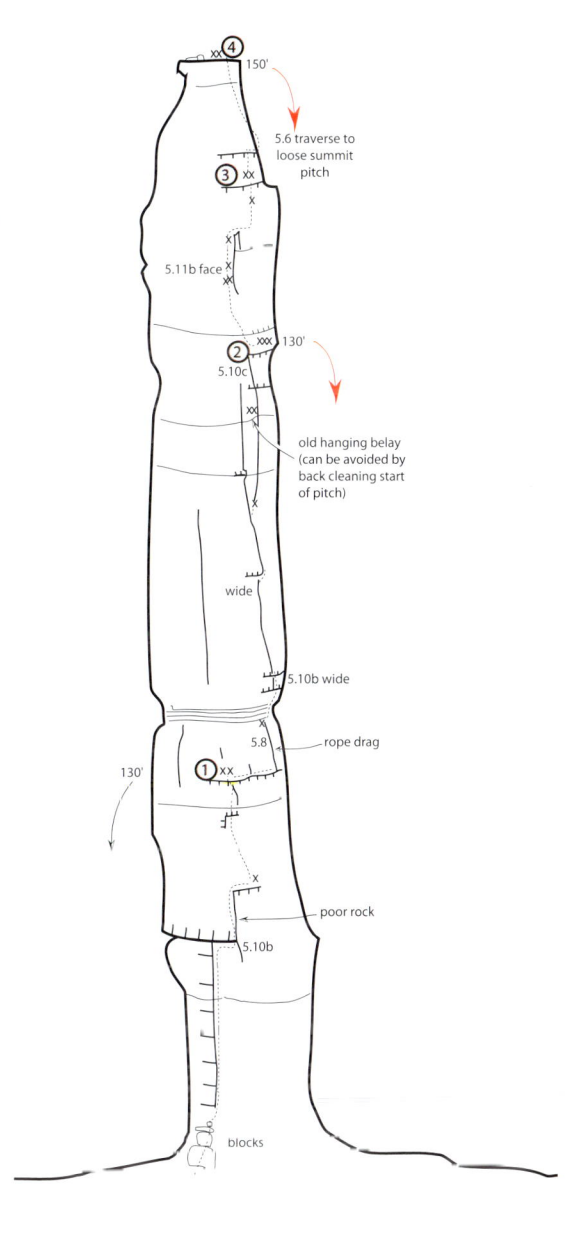

Cody Roth approaches Standing Rock, Monument Basin, photo by Andrew Burr

Steven Lucarelli on Standing Rock

Canyonlands 73

All photos of Pete Whittaker leading *Century Crack* 5.14b by Crusher Bartlett

Century Crack Area
On the White Rim Road about a mile past Monument Basin, look for an old road on the left. This is marked by a couple logs; it is closed to vehicles. Park and start hiking, first south, then northeast. After a mile, this skirts the rim with views across to Indian Creek. Follow the rim west for a few hundred yards to a gully where the talus slope below rises to within 70 feet of the rim. The lip is visible on the far side, emerging from a dark alcove/cave. Rappel into the gully (leave rope fixed), descend 400 feet and scramble up and into the alcove.

❏ CENTURY CRACK 5.14b ★★★★
To date, the longest roof-crack in the world to be climbed free. The free version of this 140-foot long crack is a surreal pitch of mind-blowing difficulty. Start in the righthand crack (hands/fists), enter the main roof-crack. This is a unique and grueling 4.5"–6" monster. Save some strength for the lip.
Gear: The start requires 2-3 sets of cams, hands upward. The rest takes as many (or as few) 5.0s (and occasional 6.0s) as comfort or fear allow.
FA: Crusher Bartlett; FFA: Tom Randall, Pete Whittaker

ISLAND IN THE SKY

The Grandview Point overlook—with Monument Basin and Standing Rock directly below—is a very popular tourist destination. From here you can see how the White Rim got its moniker.

To get to the Island, follow the 313 Road; at 14 miles the road forks left to Dead Horse Point (which is the continuation of 313). Continue straight, following signs to Canyonlands National Park. Drive on the main road for its entirety, 32.6 miles from the RR tracks.

For the two routes mentioned in this area, approach via a short walk (one minute) to the view area. Locate the Government Trail (an unmarked path) by looking right along the cliff line. Remain on the tourist rim hike—Grandveiw Trail—for five minutes or so and work your way to the cliff's edge looking for the Government Trail. Reach it via a 4th class scramble down the south-facing cliff side. There are no signs for the Government Trail and if you ask a park employee about it, they'll most likely remain mute. Rightly so, as this is not a place for any Tom, Dick, and Tourist to be messing around. Descend the trail, hike west (climbers left) towards Junction Butte. The hike meanders up and down over talus, as well as over a short, scary section of kitty litter just before the west face. When you have reached the prow (west face), *Grand Blast* will be obvious.

❏ 1. **GRAND BLAST** 5.11-
On the west face of the prow of Grandview Point.
P1: Climb the obvious rattly fist splitter to a huge flare with more rattly fist and belay at the top of the flare that forms a roof.
P2: Pull the roof and follow a splitter to another roof; the size gets friendlier above. Continue with hands to a slab. Ascend the slab and set a belay.
P3: Move left around the arête to a right-facing corner. Ascend the corner to the rim.
Gear: 0.75–4.0 heavy on big hands and fist
FA: Earl Wiggins, Katy Cassidy

Grand Plan (Author's Account)

Charley "Flash" Graham nailed it with this one! Years ago he told me of a stellar hand crack past *Grand Blast*. He then moved away but returned for the 2011 season armed with a wife and child. Charley is a man with overflowing motivation, so when his family is out of town, he explodes! One night at work, he mentioned, "I have to drop off the fam at the G.J. airport at 5:30am. You wanna meet at the 313 Road at 7:30 and go climb *Grand Blast*?" "Sound's great. I want to research that for the new guide anyway," I replied. I went to Google Earth to see what time the route would go into the sun. "Dude, no bueno! Goes into the sun around 10:30." (It was August 20th and the forecast predicted 103 degrees!)

He then reminded me of the handcrack he found on the north face. "I don't know, man, do you think we have time to do a new rim route and still get to work on time? The restaraunt had been quite busy—not a good time for both of us to be late. F#*K it, lets give it a shot."

The next morning we met in unison and cruised to Grandview Point, hiked down the Government Trail and arrived at the Wingate base. I was nervous that we wouldn't have enough time to pull it off. It was a beautiful day—warm, yes—but after stopping to take a closer look at *Grand Blast* and snap a few photos, we skirted to the north-facing and much-cooler side of the cliff.

This is my favorite part of climbing in the dez: not knowing what is around the next corner. My curiosity was piqued. I knew Flash recognized a great line when he saw one, and he assured me this would be one of the top splitter pitches either one of us had ever seen.

Holy shit! Are you kidding? What a gift from the climbing gods! I hiked stacks of cliff bases but this was a special sight. We were in a comfortable portion of the compass looking at a never-ending splitter. Though we couldn't see all the way to the rim, it was drawing us in. There would be no coin toss; this was Flash's find. "It's all you," I said, "Kill it!"

In typical style, Flash cruised 160' of mostly splitter reds (with a few golds thrown in) on absolutely stellar Wingate. He then continued through 40' of difficult steep wideness, carefully passing a few loose stones (the only choss thus far) to finish a full 60 meters. "Off," he yelled, "There's 50' of 5.9 to the rim."

Adrenaline was now flowing through me. As I cruised up this 5-star splitter, I took in my surroundings, wondering how many more of these days—with a great friend, perfect weather and killer scenery—I would have in my life, living here in the vast dez of Moab. There had already been so many. When we reached the summit, after congratulating each other, we just laughed. "What a day, time for work!"

I love the dez!

Charley Graham on the first ascent of *Grand Plan* 5.10+

313 Road

2. GRAND PLAN 5.10+ ★★★★★

Access *Grand Plan* by continuing past *Grand Blast*, staying high on the talus over to the north face. Once on the north face, walk climber's left for around five minutes. The route is the obvious, long, hand-size splitter just left of some broken pillars.

P1: ★★★★★ A good climb for a two-headed coin. You undoubtably will want to lead this amazing first pitch! Climb the hands splitter for 150' or so (optional hanging belay here with 2.0s & 3.0s) before entering the offwidth section which begins with big hands in the back, before tackling the grunt section. Arm bars to full-body wiggling bring you back to some big hands just before a natural stance at 200 feet. Bring a cordelette to tie off a large chockstone. A 70m rope will make things a bit easier, as this is a rope stretcher.

P2: Continue straight ahead off the ledge up a low-angle ledge to a 4.0-Camalot crack. Move right on the face (a bit soft, but easy) and continue up the chimney to the rim. There is a tree to sling just back a bit (5.9, 50').

Gear: (6)2.0, (4)3.0, (2)4.0 (2) old 4.5 or new 5.0, (2)old 4.0, (1)6.0
FA: Charley Graham, K3

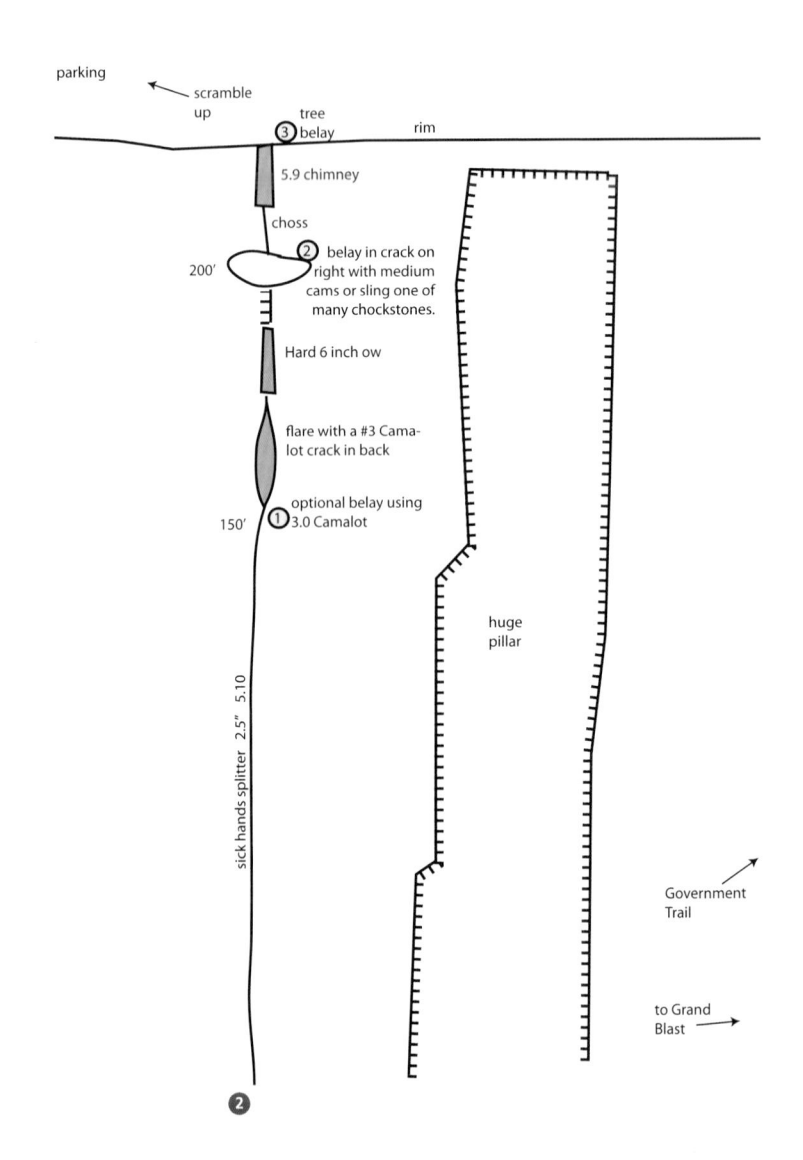

parking
scramble up
tree belay ③
rim
5.9 chimney
choss
200'
② belay in crack on right with medium cams or sling one of many chockstones.
Hard 6 inch ow
flare with a #3 Camalot crack in back
optional belay using ① 3.0 Camalot
150'
sick hands splitter 2.5" 5.10
huge pillar
Government Trail
to Grand Blast
②

Chapter 3
Little Valley

Joe Smith on *The Crack House* 5.13

LITTLE VALLEY

Little Valley, a hanging valley between Potash Road and the 313 Road, is likely best known as the gateway to the famed Gemini Bridges. Four destinations are covered in this guide: The Alcove, Pinky Tower, the Gooney Bird, and the Crack House.

To get there, drive 9.8 miles north from Center and Main. Turn left, set the odometer, and follow the dirt road. It initially heads back towards Moab but then leads up the hill, and heads west (right).

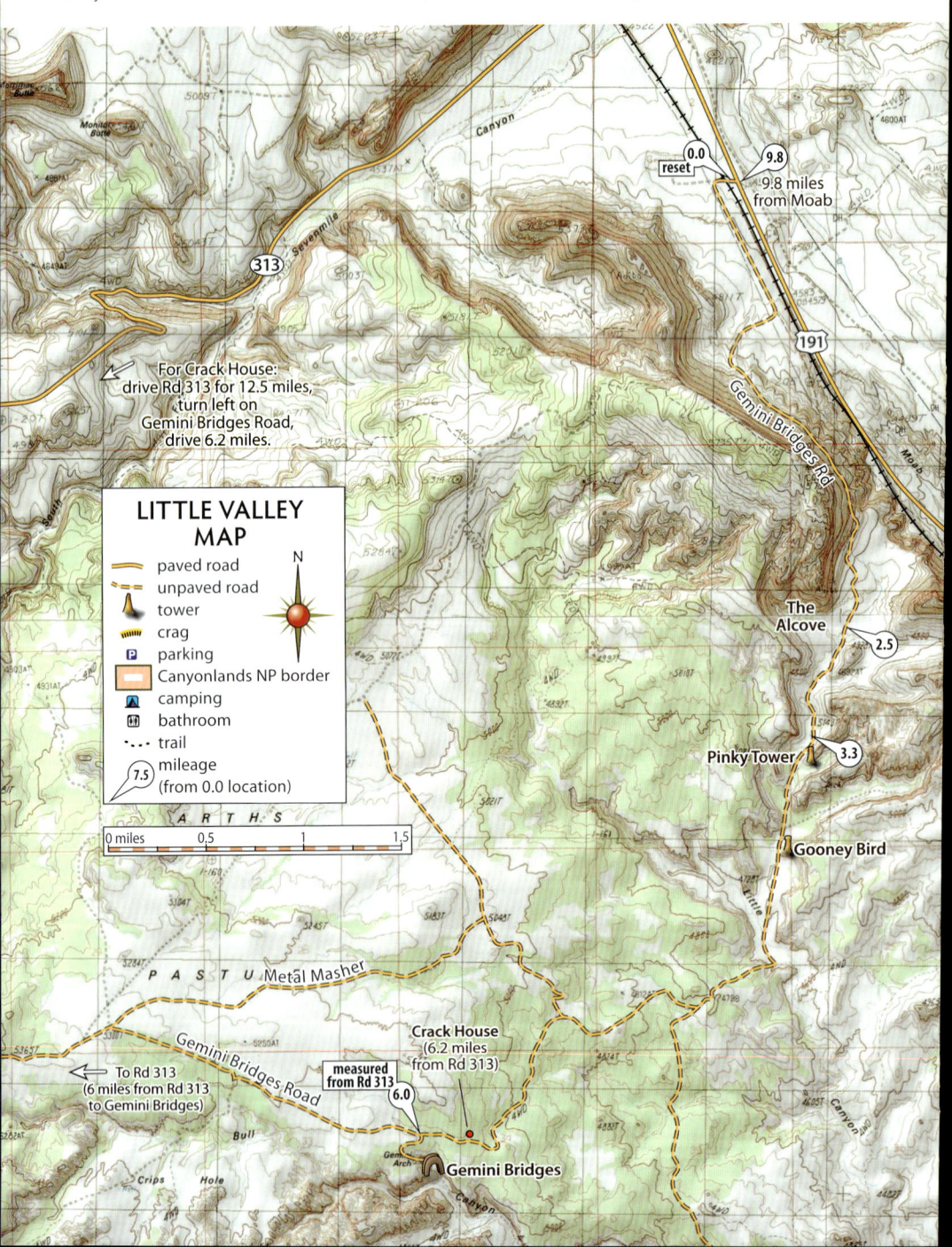

LITTLE VALLEY MAP

- paved road
- unpaved road
- tower
- crag
- parking
- Canyonlands NP border
- camping
- bathroom
- trail
- mileage (from 0.0 location)

Key locations:
- 9.8 miles from Moab (0.0 reset)
- The Alcove — 2.5
- Pinky Tower — 3.3
- Gooney Bird
- Metal Masher
- Crack House (6.2 miles from Rd 313)
- Gemini Bridges (6.0 measured from Rd 313)
- To Rd 313 (6 miles from Rd 313 to Gemini Bridges)

For Crack House: drive Rd 313 for 12.5 miles, turn left on Gemini Bridges Road, drive 6.2 miles.

Little Valley 79

The Alcove
At around 2.5 miles, park in the obvious pullout on the right. Beyond this, the old road from the parking is now closed to motorized vehicles. Routes are found on both the left and right side of the cove.

Cyclops
Poor Mota

Alcove Right ☀ E
The following pair of routes are located on the right side of The Alcove. Follow the road to the back of the cove and scramble to the base. *Premier* faces west and its counterpart faces southeast.

1. PREMIER 5.10 ★★★★
A left-facing corner starts with a short section of less-than-stellar rock to a stance. From here, climb fingers to a wedge and exit via tight hands. The crack slims down to a short section of off-fingers before connecting to a hands splitter on the right wall which leads to the anchors.
Gear: TCU–3.0

2. UNNAMED 5.11 110' ★★★★
A fun route! Start up broken rock to a short left-facing corner with fingers leading to the beautiful off-finger/tight hand splitter, then jog right through a pod and move past a block to the anchor.
Gear: 0.0 TCU, 3 long draws

Dylan Warren on *Unnamed #3* 5.10, following page

Little Valley

Alcove Left
These routes are on the left side of The Alcove. They are spread out along the entire cliff and listed right to left.

☐ 1. **POOR MOTA** 5.10 50' ★ ✹ NE
This right-facing corner route begins on the left wall in double cracks with the right crack thinning from hands to fingers; the left crack is an offwidth. Move into the sharp corner and continue with tight hands.
Gear: 0.75–2.0, 6.0 helpful
FA: Aaron Labelle

☐ 2. **CYCLOPS** 5.11 ✹ E
This semi-detached tower resides in the middle of the cliff that forms the Left Cove.
P1: Climb the right side of the formation from off-fingers to bigger than fists.
P2: Continue to a bolted anchor on top of the pillar.
P3: Pass a pair of bolts and grovel to a bolted ledge belay.
P4: Face climb past a single bolt to anchors on the rim.
FA: P1 Kevin Chase, Lisa Hathaway; Dave Sadoff, Aaron Labelle (to top)

☐ 3. **UNNAMED** 5.10 60' ★★ ✹ E
A left-facing corner (with a fingers splitter on the left wall and a dicey-looking flake with hands in the main corner) brings you to a small roof. Reach around with good fingers and climb a body-length of this size to a big block blob. Mantel onto the blob. Climb the left-facing corner with hands. Fun route.
Gear: 0.4–2.0

☐ 4. **ROUTE WITH A VIEW** 5.10 65' ★★ ✹ E
Start in a pod and continue with hands to fingers in a shallow left-facing corner.
Gear: 0.4–4.0, heavy on off-fingers
FA: Kevin Chase, Lisa Hathaway

☐ 5. **UNNAMED** 5.10 90' ★★★★ ✹ SE
A right-facing corner up some blocky terrain leads to hands moving to fingers, then passing a bolt to the painted hard-to-see anchors.
Gear 0.5–4.0
FA: Kevin Chase, Lisa Hathaway

Pinky Tower Buttress

The Pinky Tower Buttress is easily seen from The Alcove, as it lies just down the road on the opposite side. Please park well off the road, as it is popular with 4-wheelers.

Park at 3.3 miles and look for the obvious tower. Routes are listed from left to right.

❏ 1. **PRIVATE MYSTERY** 5.10 ★★★★
Begin up a low-angle right-facing corner and walk left on a ledge to the base of a shallow right-facing corner. Stem up to the beautiful splitter and ascend this to an anchor.
Gear: 0.0–2.0

❏ 2. **UNNAMED #1** 5.10+
P1: Share the start of *Private Mystery* and continue straight up the main corner. Follow a good chimney to a big-hands bulge and the belay anchor.
P2: Tight hands and hands lead to a steep ow bulge. Finish with more wideness to anchors.

❏ 3. **UNNAMED #2** 5.10- 25' ★
A might-as-well route that you wish was longer. A very short, shallow stem box with fingers.
Gear 0.0-0.4

❏ 4. **EWE WHAT** 5.10 50'
A left-facing corner that starts a little loose, passes a wide section, and finishes with fists.
Gear: 1.0–4.0, optional big cam

Pinky Tower NW

1. RING SIZER 5.10 ★★★★
This slender spire sits near the road and offers interesting face climbing to a horizontal crack, eventually finishing on an easy broken wide crack.

P1: Start in the right-facing corner (facing the road) and climb double cracks from thin hands to offwidth. Belay from gear at the notch (5.10). This pitch can be avoided by a 4th class pitch on the opposite side (50').
P2: Traverse left from the belay to the first bolt, back-cleaning any gear placed along the way. Continue up the line of bolts moving around the tower to a horizontal crack. Work left to an off-fingers crack that turns to a hand and fist crack. Belay at the top. Long slings will help eliminate rope drag (5.10+, 60').
A single 70-meter rope rappel reaches the ground.
Gear: 0.3–5.0 (doubles for hands and fists), 5 quickdraws, long runners
FA: Keith Reynolds, Matt Laggis, Bill Russell

2. PLANET CARAVAN 5.11d ★★★
 W-SW

A great sport climb addition to the Pinky Tower, but it doesn't top out. The route is obvious.
Gear: 7 draws
FA: Jake Warren, Brad Woodford

No Falls Paul on Ring Sizer 5.10

Gooney Bird ☀N-NW

This interesting tower sits directly on the popular jeep road. Park at 4.0 miles (enjoy the Wall Street-esque approach).

❏ 1. **TEA PARTY** 5.10+ ★★★
P1: Begin via slab climbing to a less-than-vertical left-facing corner with fingers and hands to a bolted belay (5.10, 100').
P2: Continue up the left-facing corner as it gets steeper and runs through all sizes. Continue as the angle eases and work right on face moves (often slick) to a bolted belay (5.10+).
P3: A meandering pitch with tricky slick moves on less-than-textbook gear. Essentially, you'll be circling the bird's head, climbing past a bolt up to a ledge, then moving back around to the right. Wide gear is helpful. Descent: Rap from the summit to the top of pich 2, then to the ground with two 60m ropes.
Gear: blue TCU–3.5, optional big piece, many slings, a set of nuts
FA: Keith Reynolds

❏ 2. **WEAPONS GRADE** 5.11 ★★★
☀N
A fun zig-zagging offset splitter located just after the Gooney Bird on the left. It faces the road.
Gear: 0.4–0.75
FA: Luke Malatesta

The Crack House

You've heard about it—one of the craziest inverted crack routes/boulder problems in the galaxy. The Crack House is most easily reached via the 313 Road.

Directions: The best approach is to take the 313 road toward the Island in the Sky visitor's center. At 12.5 miles from the Highway 191/313 Road intersection, look for a dirt road marked Gemini Bridges on the left. Reset your odometer, Follow the signs for Gemini Bridges. When you arrive at the bridges continue straight for another quarter of a mile and look for the cave entrance on your left. Park in the obvious parking spot 6.2 miles from the 313 Road turn-off.

1. THE CRACK HOUSE 5.13 ★★★★★
Approximately 85' of horizontal crack climbing, this classic runs through sizes, but is mostly hands. Begin on the far right (looker's right) of the formation. The original Crack House sit-starts at the back of bombay chimney (as per *The Birth Canal*) and traverses west through the entire cave and out the west exit (with the tiered, spotting steps).
Gear: Strong abs, several crash pads, spotter (some folks wear a harness and clip in to a toprope for the exit)
FA: Dean Potter

2. THE DEAN VARIATION 5.13
Start on face holds, outside the main cave (viewer's right), traverse into the cave at *The Birth Canal's* exit and finish as for *The Crack House*.
Gear: Same as for The Crack House
FA: Dean Potter

3. THE BIRTH CANAL 5.11+ ★★★★★
Start at the far right end of *The Crack House* in the back of the cave. At the junction, push on through the overhang to a vertical top-out. Often used as the start for *The Crack House* proper.

4. THE YUJI CRACK 5.12+/13-
Sit-start (pretty much lying down!) at the base of a finger-crack in the middle of the cave. Head straight out as for *The Crack House* finish, or head west at the crack confluence and finish as for *The Birth Canal*.
FA: Yuji Hirayama

5. FAT CRACK 5.12
Start at the back of the viewer's left side of the cave in an off-hands crack and head straight out.
Variation: As per *Yuji's Crack*, at confluence, head west and out *The Birth Canal* exit.

6. NO CRACKS IN MY HOUSE V4
If cracks aren't your thing or you're hamburgered from the above, get a good pump traversing right to left on the juggy face holds and exit as per *The Birth Canal*.

Chapter 4

Arches National Park

Tim Alexarder on *Be There or Be Talked About*
5.11 A0
Andrew Burr photo

ARCHES NATIONAL PARK

Arches National Park should be on every climber's must-visit list. The eye candy is amazing and the formations create a seeming rock-climbers paradise. There are, in fact, some exceptional climbing opportunities in Arches. Unfortunately, the predominant Entrada sandstone, despite appearances, rates low on the rock-quality spectrum, Therefore, despite the stacks of routes that have been established in the park, only a select few are described here. Stick to these, the best of the best, and you won't be disappointed.

In the not-so-distant past, climbing in the park was under serious scrutiny. At the time of this writing, climbing is allowed. Please adhere to all climbing regulations, policies and closures! If in doubt, ask at the visitor center for up-to-date infomation. Continued climbing access depends on climbers understanding and following both the letter and the spirit of park regulations.

Note:

We share this park with millions of others, please try to approach climbs in the most environmentally-friendly fashion. Use existing trails if they go in the right direction. If there is no trail, hike on *slickrock* (hard, exposed, rock surfaces) or use sandy washes. Avoid stepping anywhere else. In particular, DO NOT trample the fragile *cryptobiotic crust*, recognized by its dark, spongy, crusty appearance. If a trail seems to go the wrong way, consider alternatives; if it dead-ends, backtrack and find the proper path. Climbers are a recognized user group in Arches; we need to not only *follow* the rules, but show others that we will surpass expectations, leaving the park cleaner than before we arrived. Please pack out human waste, keep a low profile, and avoid climbing on any formation that shows signs of raptor nesting (whether posted or not).

Climbing Regulations, as of 2014:

Climbing registration is recommended. At the time of this writing, you can sign in at the kiosk located at the Visitor's Center (outside). In the near future you will be able to do this online. This is time well spent—when you register it allows the park to discuss where money will be allocated for additional parking, trail development, etc. It is the responsibility of all climbers to know and obey park regulations and route closures. The following closures, conditions, and restrictions apply to rock climbing or similar activities such as, but not limited to, technical rock climbing, free climbing, and clean aid climbing in Arches National Park:

Climbing Closures:

- Any arch or natural bridge named on the United States Geological Survey 7.5 minute topographical maps covering Arches National Park is closed to climbing year-round.
- Balanced Rock–Closed to climbing year-round.
- Bubo–Closed from January 1st to June 30th.
- *Industrial Disease* on the Devil Dog Spire is closed from January 1st to June 30th.

Restrictions

- Slacklining is prohibited anywhere within Arches National Park year-round.
- New routes and gear replacement are allowed with a permit. At the time of the writing you can apply at the Visitor's Center, but it will be available online in the future.
- No new equipment can be installed without a special use permit.
- Travel to and from routes must be in dry wash systems or on rock.
- Only hammerless aid climbing is allowed.
- If an existing software item (sling, runner etc.) is unsafe, it may be replaced with rock-colored webbing.
- Software (webbing, accessory cords, etc.) that is left in place shall match the rock surface in color.
- The intentional removal of lichen or plants from rock is prohibited.
- The physical altering of rock faces such as chiseling, glue reinforcement of existing holds, and gluing of new holds is prohibited.
- Motorized power drills are allowed outside the wilderness boundary but prohibited within the boundary.
- Fixed ropes may not be left in place for more than 24 hours. Fixed ropes left in place longer than 24 hours shall be considered "abandoned property" and removed.
- The use of chalk for climbing must be of a color that blends with the native rock. Not white!
- Rock climbing groups are limited to five people per group.

Definitions

- Technical Rock Climbing is defined as ascending or descending a rock formation utilizing rock climbing equipment.
- Free Climbing and Clean Aid Climbing are minimum impact approaches that employ chocks, stoppers, nuts, and camming devices, rather than pitons or bolts, for protection or direct support. These are climbing aids that are removable and do not damage the rock.
- Slacklining is defined as walking on a rope or other line that is anchored between rock formations, trees, or any other natural features. Height of the rope above the ground is immaterial.

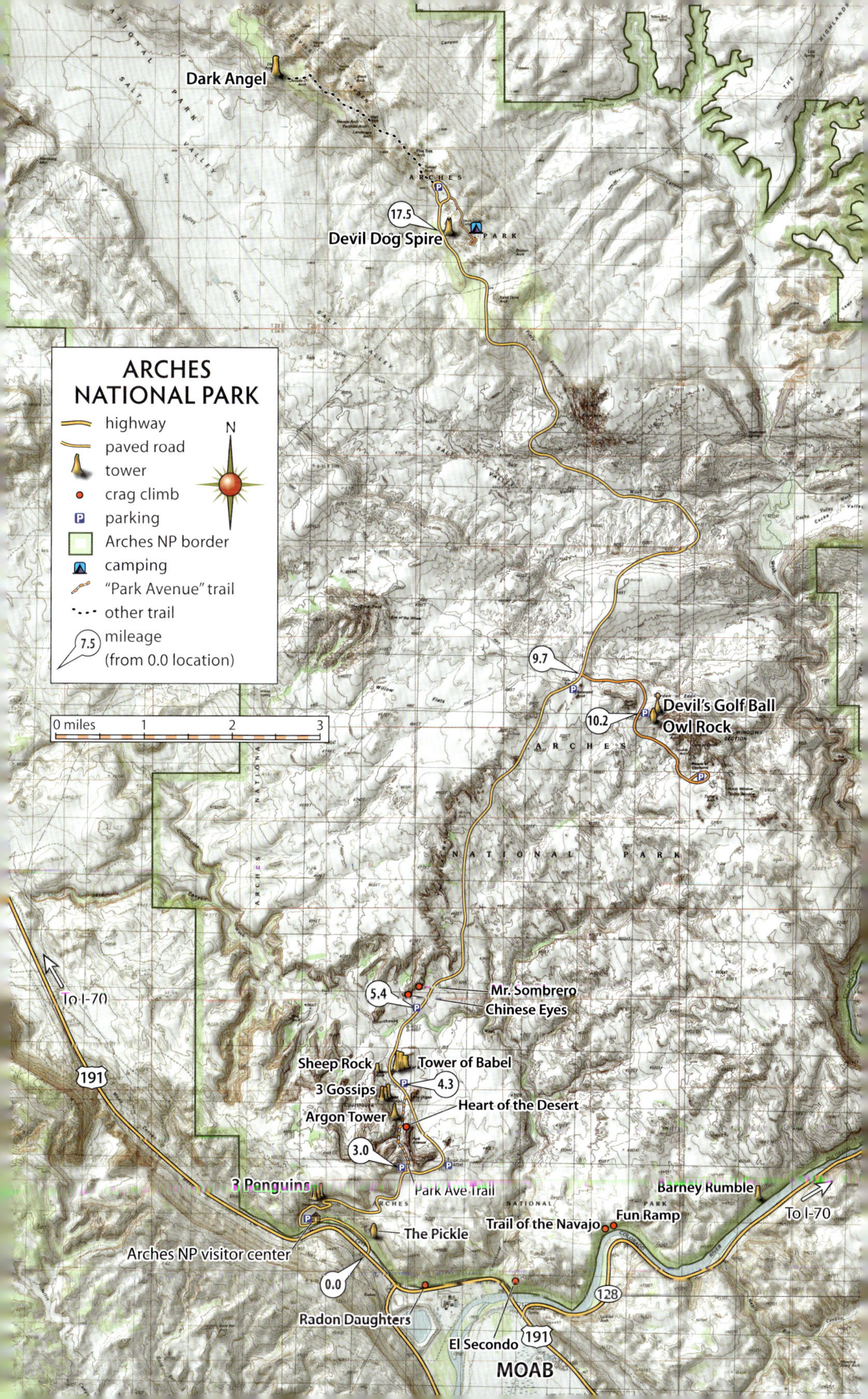

ARCHES NATIONAL PARK
highway
paved road
tower
crag climb
parking
Arches NP border
camping
"Park Avenue" trail
other trail
mileage (from 0.0 location)
7.5
N
0 miles
1
2
3
Dark Angel
17.5
Devil Dog Spire
9.7
10.2
Devil's Golf Ball
Owl Rock
5.4
Mr. Sombrero
Chinese Eyes
Sheep Rock
Tower of Babel
4.3
3 Gossips
Heart of the Desert
Argon Tower
3.0
3 Penguins
Park Ave Trail
Barney Rumble
To I-70
Fun Ramp
Trail of the Navajo
The Pickle
Arches NP visitor center
0.0
128
Radon Daughters
El Secondo
191
MOAB
To I-70
191
ARCHES
NATIONAL
PARK

Outlying Arches Climbs

The following routes are technically within the park boundaries (and thus subject to park regulations) but are accessed without driving through the park entrance.

1. EL SEGUNDO 5.9+ 90' ★★★ ✺ SW

This is the striking, obvious, right-facing corner seen while driving north across the Colorado River bridge from Moab toward Arches. After crossing the bridge, take an immediate right and head toward the footbridge, parking at a small pull-off on the left. The corner will be directly above you, but it starts on an inaccessible bench. Walk back and along the main highway (on the bike path) headed north to the entrance of Courthouse Wash; gain the ramping bench on the right and backtrack to the climb (passing some beautiful pictographs). Rope up at the end of the bench.
P1: Step down to a short 5th class traverse and gain a shelf with a belay. Please don't touch the pictograph left of the belay (25').
P2: Climb up the left-leaning flake to a less-than-vertical, right-facing corner with a section that appears loose but is quite secure. The hand crack will then steepen and tighten to the bolted belay (90').
Descent: Two rappels with a 70m rope will return you to just above where you parked.
Gear: 0.4–2.0
FA: Kyle Copeland

2. RADON DAUGHTERS 5.9

An obvious short splitter right off the road, a little beyond the Colorado River bridge, across from the UMTRA mine tailing cleanup project. Perhaps the closest and easiest climb to get to from downtown Moab.
FA: Tony Valdes, Bego Gerhart

Kiefer Kelley on *El Segundo* 5.9+

… Arches National Park   89

Climbs and Towers in Arches National Park

To reach Arches NP, drive north on Hwy 191 for 4.5 miles from the junction of Center and Main in Moab. There is a single paved road meandering northward from the entrance through the park, and climbs are described starting from the entrance. Reset your odometer at the turn-off into the park. The first route is located not far beyond the entrance station, just as the road begins to wind its way uphill.

The Pickle

This giant pickle-shaped boulder is easily seen just as you turn into the park, perched high on the hillside in front of you. Park at the visitor center then walk back along the road toward the entrance. Veer left into a major drainage, Bloody Mary Wash. Follow this wash until it is obvious to scramble left to the formation. The steep hike up the jumbled hillside is a quick test of your route-finding abilities. Staying to the north (left) of the formation may be a tad easier than stumbling up the rotten gullies to the south. Stay well away from the park administration buildings behind the visitor center and try to keep a low profile.

❒ **1. THE PICKLE** 5.7 A0 90' ★★
The route starts on the back side, as seen from the road. It's a ladder of bolts and drilled pitons almost the entire way, with a couple 5.7 slab moves at the top that can feel a bit gripping and sandy, especially after rain.
Rappel with a single 70m.
Gear: 20 or so draws, aiders or slings, jumars for the second (optional but faster)
FA: Benny Bach, Cameron Burns

Three Penguins

One of the all-time Moab classics. Park at a small pullout on the lefthand side of the road, 1.7 miles from Hwy 191, or else locate additional parking just past this on the right. The trail ascends a few small benches and continues up a short steep trail marked with cairns. At the top of the trail break left and walk along the obvious bench to the formation.
There are four routes on the Penguins, but only the *Right Chimney*, the best of these, is described here. Looking from the parking spot, this is the rightmost, right-facing dihedral.

❒ **1. RIGHT CHIMNEY** 5.10c 120' ★★★★★
☀ SE
A great route with a funny name: this isn't a chimney at all. Traditionally done as two pitches, it climbs quite well as one by clipping the midway anchor with a long sling. Great Entrada.
P1: Climb the right-facing corner, starting with a little off-fingers and moving to some steep big hands (5.10c).
P2: Some fun, steep hands widens to a few stacks which brings you to the notch between the climber's right and center tower. A few stem moves bring you to the center summit and chain anchors (5.10).
Descent: Rap the route. A single 70m rope just reaches. If using a shorter rope, do two raps via the intermediate anchor.
Gear: 0.75–4.5
FA Michael Kennedy, Molly Higgins, 1976

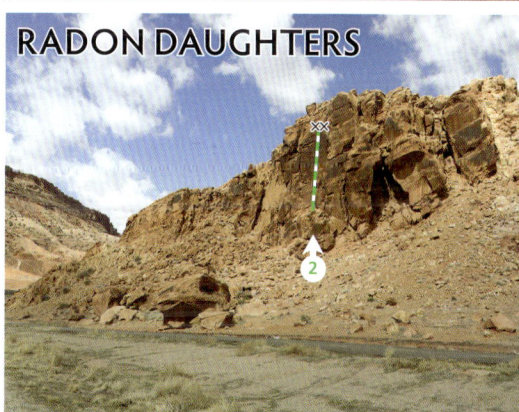

Jeanine Saia on *Right Chimney* 5.10, Three Penguins

Park Avenue ✳ NW

Park Avenue is a very popular one-mile-long trail that follows a winding wash through some spectacular scenery. The main, southern trailhead, located 3.0 miles from Hwy 191, can be used to approach the following routes, but a faster approach is from the north end, as described below.

Park at the Courthouse Towers parking area (at 4.3 miles) and walk across the road to a well-marked trail headed back up the wash towards Park Avenue. Follow the rock-lined trail.

☐ 1. HEART OF THE DESERT 5.10c 80'
★★★★ ✳ NW

Hiking south from Courthouse Towers, this climb is the obvious left-facing corner on the left, eastern bench. To get from the main trail to the bench, please ascend one of the rain-eroded drainages/gullies to avoid damaging the fragile landscape. Walk along the bench to the base of the corner.

Climb the left-facing corner with hands and fists, passing a few pods. Anchors on the right wall. Steep!
Gear: Couple sets, 2.0–4.0
FA: Jeff Widen, Dawn Burke, 1985

Ben Riley on *Heart of the Desert* 5.10

For the next three formations park at the Courthouse Towers parking lot. Note: park only in existing parking areas. Do not park on vegetation or block traffic.

Argon Tower

Slender and prominent in a Hollywood-Southwest setting, Argon Tower is a classic sandstone spire begging to be climbed. While pleasing to the eye, it can be rough on the ego. Both routes included here are known for a sandy, insecure feel.

Park at the Courthouse Towers parking area and walk across the road to the trail. Follow this to the wide wash; once there, head right until it becomes possible to follow another wash leading left to a terminus at some boulders. From here, work left onto the obvious ramp by using one of the main rain run-offs. Once on the ramp, scramble through rocks to the bench where the routes commence. Avoid the temptation to skirt the boulders for the easier walk on the fragile landscape.

❐ 1. WEST FACE 5.11c ★★★

P1: Start in a right-facing corner; climb with fingers and thin stemming to a ledge. Keep going up a fist crack which quickly widens to grueling offwidth (5.10+), finishing at the bolted belay (5.11c, 125′).
P2: The show-stopper, for some, despite its more modest rating, with rock that is dubious even by Arches standards. A brief chimney leads to some offwidth then some soft bulges. Belay at the big ledge (this ledge, and the next pitch, are shared by *Northeast Arête*) (5.10).
P3: A single pin protects face climbing on small, sandy holds to the summit (5.8 is mandatory, much harder without standing on the belay bolts, 30′).
Descent: Rap the route. A 30-foot rap from the summit gains the anchor at the big ledge. From here, a single rap with two 60m cords leads to terra firma. If you choose to do this tower with a single line, make sure it's a 70 (this will just make it down from atop pitch 1).
Gear: Triple sets of 0.3 through the new #5 Camalot, set of nuts
FA: John Pease, Steve Cheyney, 1972

❐ 2. NORTH-NORTHEAST ARÊTE 5.11 ★

Start on the huge ledge beneath the west face of the tower.
P1: Begin in a short, thin crack at the extreme left (north) end of the ledge. Insecure climbing leads to a ledge below the narrow north face (5.10, 30′).
P2: Climb the leftmost crack via hands and wide hands for 100 feet to an optional and undesirable bolted belay. Continue past this via a narrowing crack that pinches down from fingers to purple TCUs (crux) before landing on the big ledge beneath the summit pitch (5.11, 140′).
P3: Follow *West Face*'s last pitch to the summit.
Descent: Rap as for West Face.
FA: Todd Gordon, Dave Evans

Three Gossips

Another spectacular multi-summited landform that dishes out some challenging terrain.

Park at a pull-out at 4.5 miles on the right side of the road. Walk across the road to a beaten path leading to the wash. Take a right and follow the wash; go past the first (small) wash to the main (second) wash. Take a left here and follow this wash to the bottom of the obvious talus cone. Ascend this to the base of the climbs (on the back right as viewed from the parking).

❐ 1. WEST FACE 5.11 ★★★★★

Considered by many to be one of the park's finest routes, the *West Face* utilizes an arsenal of techniques including jams, stemming, offwidth, friction, and chimneying. The bolted belay ledges are comfy and the rock quality is great for Entrada.
P1: An excellent pitch. A steep bulging right-facing corner offers all sizes from fingers to offwidth (5.10, 100').
P2: Tight hands leads to a section of offwidth and then to the crux—fingers and stems—which gives way to an easy chimney.
P3: Some Entrada slabbing leads to an easy chimney and the summit.
Descent: You can rap the route but the ropes are hard to pull. Instead, rap from the summit to the saddle between the north and middle summits (one rope). From here, set a double-rope rappel between the summit heads and reach the ground. Walk away from the feature to pull the ropes, as this will decrease the drag.
Gear: Blue TCUs to 4.5, shoulder length slings, and a selection of nuts (inc. RPs). Two 70m ropes
FA: Alan Steck, Steve Roper, 1970

❐ 2. BE THERE OR BE TALKED ABOUT 5.11 C0 ★★★

This ascends the south summit, from the west side. The only aid is a short, final bolt ladder. Pitches 1 and 2 can easily be combined with careful use of long slings.
P1: Low-angle climbing, with sandy feet and a fingery flake (50').
P2: Start with a bit of chimneying off the belay; continue up a right-facing offwidth corner to a shallow chimney which leads to a nice belay ledge (70').
Variation: The 5.11+ left-facing fingers corner just right of the offwidth.
P3: Sweet! Start by stepping down and right off the belay into the righthand crack system. Work up an off-fingers crack in a flare (good feet) to a short wide section that you can reach through. Continue up the wedging right-facing corner (tight hands to hands). The hands get better and the wedge tighter as you get higher. A final exciting move leads to the belay ledge (110').
P4: You can leave your tag line and everything but draws. Walk right on flat ground until you see the road. Scramble up a block and clip awkwardly-located first bolt; follow the bolt-ladder to the top (40 feet, C0).
Descent: Rap with one rope from the summit to the top of pitch 3. From here, a double-rope (60m) rappel leads to the ground. It's helpful to walk towards the west face when pulling.
Gear: Double set from yellow TCUs to 0.75; triple sets of 1.0 to 2.0; two old #4 Camalots, one 5.0 and one 6.0, plus many long draws
FA: Peter Gallagher, Bego Gerhart; FA of P2 variation: Bret Ruckman

Arches National Park

Tower of Babel ✷ SW

☐ 1. **ZENYATTA ENTRADA** 5.8 C3- ★★★★
This is the destination aid climb of Arches—a magnificent steep line up the slender spine of the Tower of Babel. The route became controversial, as ugly pin scars soon developed, highly visible against the dark varnish and easily seen from the road. The first ascent party, believing that the route would attract no interest, removed many of the drilled placements, so even the bolt ladder sections became scarred. More recently the climb has been reestablished as a worthy clean aid challenge with ASCA-installed glue-in bolts.
P1: Just left of a massive leaning block, climb a thin crack to, and past the right end of a roof, to a wider section, then a ledge (C2, 115'). Variation: climb onto the large block and follow a crack, past loose blocks to the same ledge.
P2: A nice, shallow, left-facing dihedral leads to a splitter crack and a ledge on the left. Mostly good nuts (C1, 90').
P3: Follow the splitter for 30 feet to lower-angle terrain. Work up and left via bolts and seams until you can get into the obvious right-facing dihedral. Up this (easier) to a ledge (C2+, 130').
P4: Work into the big left-facing corner to the roof, then traverse right on some fixed pitons to the belay ledge (C3-, 80').
P5: Work up and right, past bolts and short seams to the big shoulder and a chain anchor (C2, 80').
P6: Walk back on the shoulder to a weakness with a couple bolts that lead to the summit (C1, 40').
Descent: Rap the route with two ropes.
Gear: Many nuts from small to large, including RPs and offsets. Set of Tricams. 2–3 sets of cams from smallest to 2-inch, 2 sets from 2-inch to 4-inch, hooks. Offset cams are very helpful.
FA: Charlie Fowler, 1986

The Lamb

Two flat-topped formations reside across the road from *Zenyatta*—the higher one is dubbed The Sheep and the shorter one is The Lamb. The Lamb has an obvious splitter up the middle with a pod at half-height.
Park on the left in a small pullout 4.8 miles from Hwy 191. Look for a culvert and follow its drain path down to the main wash. Follow the wash that looks like it will lead you to the base of the formation. Eventually you will need to leave this. Don't walk on the fragile dirt crust, stick to walking in whichever washes and drainage channels will get you to the base.

☐ 1. **SHEEP IN WOLF'S CLOTHING** 5.10 80' ★
Start up a left-trending, sandy ramp. Cut back right on the bench to the obvious splitter. Climb the crack, mostly hands, to a weird exit move to the left which brings you to a ledge with the belay. At the time of this writing the anchor was two drilled pins. There is no anchor on the true summit; you must climb a sandy chimney for 15 feet or so, then reverse it. It's kind of a grunt so keep your mouth closed or it will fill with Arches dirt!
Descent: Rap the route.
Gear: 0.0 TCU–4.5
FA: Charlie Fowler, 1986

TOWER OF BABEL

Dylan Warren on *Mr. Sombrero* 5.11+

The Great Wall ✸SE

This is a couple of miles beyond the Tower of Babel. As the name suggests, it is a large and mostly featureless wall, but a single feature—two leaning blocks that form a left-facing corner—provides a popular climb. Park at 5.4 miles, on the left side of the road, shortly after crossing over the Courthouse Wash bridge. At the west end of the pullout there is a trail that goes directly to *Chinese Eyes*.

❏ 1. **CHINESE EYES** 5.10 50' ★★★
Fun! Left-facing corner that goes through the sizes from fingers to offwidth.
Gear: 0.3–6.0
FA: Charlie Fowler, Clean Dan Grandusky, 1986.

❏ 2. **MR. SOMBRERO** 5.11+ 75' ★★★★★
This clean-cut left-facing dihedral offers great climbing on really good quality Entrada. The route is located at 5.7 miles, on the same wall as *Chinese Eyes* but several hundred feet farther along the cliff. The approach information here is rather important, as the Park Service doesn't want climbers to just punch it through the delicate soils. From the parking, please take the time to follow rain-runoff channels and washes to the base. The climb can also be accessed from *Chinese Eyes* by skirting rightwards along the cliff.
Start the dihedral with fingers that offer some feet, before a short challenging slot with hands. Punch it up to some steep tight hands, off-fingers, and even steeper off-finger before reaching the anchors.
Gear: 0.3–3.0 (heavy on off-fingers)
FA: Mark Lemmons, Rob Slater, Jim Bodenhamer, 1987

The Garden of Eden

It might not be total paradise, but the Garden of Eden is home to some excellent towers including, arguably, the best 5.8 tower climb in the desert—Owl Rock.

Approach: Drive 9.7 miles to the signed turnoff to "The Windows" area. Park shortly after the turnoff.

❐ 1. **OWL ROCK** 5.8 100' ★★★★★ W

Owl Rock is a singular spire in a majestic setting. It's just a minute or two from the car and surrounded by arches and wild hoodoos. What's more, the route features the best rock in the park and climbs more like a juggy sport route (albeit with gear protection) than a typical desert crack climb.
P1: Start on the the northwest side of the formation under the obvious steep crack. Crank to a ledge with anchors (5.8, 85').
P2: A few easy boulder moves on softer rock reach the summit. Please don't concoct a lower-off system, as this leaves ugly grooves in the soft rock; instead, downclimb back to the anchors (5.3, 15').
Descent: After downclimbing to the anchors, rappel. A single 70m rope will get you back to the ground.
Gear: Nuts, set of cams, a few shoulder–length slings
FA: Ron Olevsky

❐ 2. **EVE** AKA **DEVIL'S GOLF BALL** 5.10 C1 or 5.12 ★★ W

A striking tower deserving of its moniker. The spire rests just beyond Owl Rock and shares the parking. Climbing them in tandem is a great way to tick two cool summits. Commence beneath an obvious shallow corner. Climb the face, sans pro, to the corner's start. Fire in a few finger pieces and climb up and through the bulge with off-fingers and tight hands. The route will take you through all the sizes to a 4.0 before reaching a final bulge with a piton ladder. Seven clips bring you to an easy slab and the summit. Has recently been freed at 5.12.
Descent: Recently updated anchors are near the back of the tower. A single 70m cord is necessary to rap from the climber's-right side of the formation.
Gear: 0.3–4.0, a few shoulder-length slings, 7 draws, and aiders
FA: Unknown. FFA: Darren Knezek or Jimmy Dunn

Tim Alexander on *Owl Rock* 5.8. Photo: Andrew Burr

Arches National Park

Devil Dog Spire ✳N

The final two climbs are in the far north of the park. Devil Dog Spire is right off the road, on the righthand side, at 17.5 miles. Unfortunately, it is often closed for nesting raptors (generally from January 1st to June 30th). Be sure to confirm the status with the park before climbing it.

❏ 1. INDUSTRIAL DISEASE 5.11+ 200' ★★
Start on the north side, at the obvious crack.
P1: Physical climbing leads to burly offwidth moves past a fixed pin. Gain a ledge and belay (5.11+, 170').
P2: Gas through the roof splitter with great hands to an anchor on the ledge (25').
P3: Scramble to the summit (soft rock) and reverse the moves to the belay (15').
Descent: Rappel with double 60m ropes.
Gear: 2 sets, 0.5 to 6.0 with extras up to hand size; quickdraw, several shoulder–length slings. Sew it up—you're in Arches.
FA: Max Kendall, Scott Reynolds, 1986

Dark Angel ✳SW

This alluring tower sits by itself on what feels like the outskirts of the park, away from the roads and people—a remote and beautiful setting.
Park at the Landscape Arch trailhead in the Devils Garden area. The hike takes about 30–50 minutes. You pass Landscape Arch, and when you arrive at Double O Arch, Dark Angel is obvious, five minutes away.

❏ 1. WEST FACE 5.10+ 150' ★★★
P1: Commence on the west face, under a big flake with a finger crack above. Make your way up the flake by groveling up the left side (wide 5.7) or face climbing just a bit to the right to avoid the initial chimney. The right side of the flake goes at 5.8. Climb the finger crack to a tricky move left to the belay (5.9).
P2: Climb up and left from the belay to bolt-protected face and slab climbing on soft edges. When the bolts end, expect a 5.4 runout to the summit (5.10+).
Descent: One 70m rope gets you down. Pull from way back.
Gear: Singles, extra finger pieces, draws
FA: Dave Rearick, Bob Kamps, 1962

June Ray on Devil's Golf Ball

Arches Park with River Road Access

The Arches National Park boundary extends to the Colorado River for several miles upsteam of Moab. As such, several routes accessed from the River Road lie within the park and are subject to the Arches NP regulations and guidelines described at the start of the chapter.

To access the next two routes, drive north from town on Hwy 191. Just after the bridge that crosses the Colorado River take a right as for *El Segundo* (page 88). Follow the road to its end and park. Hike upriver for 10 minutes to reach *Trail of the Navajo*. Another five minutes will lead you to *The Fun Ramp*.
NOTE: Raptor nesting has prompted seasonal (typically springtime) closures on *Trail of the Navajo*. Please check with the park before climbing this.

❏ 1. TRAIL OF THE NAVAJO 5.11+ ★★★★★
✸ SE

This is an amazing climb, eight pitches in length, that the first ascensionist likens to Yosemite's *Astroman* (in a desert sort of way). Expect a wild ride.
The route follows a massive left-facing dihedral, easily viewed from the Goose Island campground about a mile up the river from Hwy 191 (the line begins in the obvious corner then face climbs up and left to the huge left-facing corner system).
P1: The left-facing corner. Clip the drilled piton left of the corner's start to keep your rope out of seasonal poison ivy. When you get to the bush just before the anchor, traverse low to the anchor (5.10, 170').
P2: Traverse directly left for 120 feet passing three bolts (5.4, 120').
P3: Climb up and right following nine bolts. A virtual sport pitch (5.10, 60').
P4: Climb the long left-facing dihedral. Protect with nuts, both offset and regular, and small cams (5.11a, 100').
P5: Continue up the corner as it pulls the first roof and into the wide crack. Eventually slither into the chimney and belay in a deep alcove (5.10+, 60').
P6: Begin climbing in the very back of the alcove into the bombay chimney and out the roof. Walk your cams to the lip to minimize drag. Continue up the corner to a small stance belay (5.11a, 100').
P7: Continue up the clean varnished corner to another deep alcove (5.10, 70').
P8: Begin deep in the back of the alcove, up into the bombay. Walk your cams to the lip again and pull the roof and continue to the anchors at the rim (5.11c, 30').
Descent: 4 raps down the route. Bring new cord (tan/brown) as the anchors get intense UV exposure. Stuck ropes are a real possibility—be careful. It is possible to walk off, but not recommended.
1: Rim to top of P7, 1 rope.
2: Top of P7, to top of P4, double 60m. Traverse 10 feet left to pull rope away from crack.
3: Top of P4 to top of P2, double 60m.
4: Top of P2 to ground, double 60m.
Gear: 2 sets of cams from green Alien–#3 Camalot, 1 set new 4.0–6.0 Camalots. Big selection of nuts including offsets. Extendable runners and quickdraws
FA: Leonard Coyne, Keith Reynolds

❏ 2. THE FUN RAMP 5.9+ ★★★★ ✸ SE
This is the obvious right-to-left trending ramp that runs almost the entire 300-foot height of the cliff, about 600 feet right of *Trail of the Navajo*.
FA: Layton Kor, Kyle Copeland, 1988

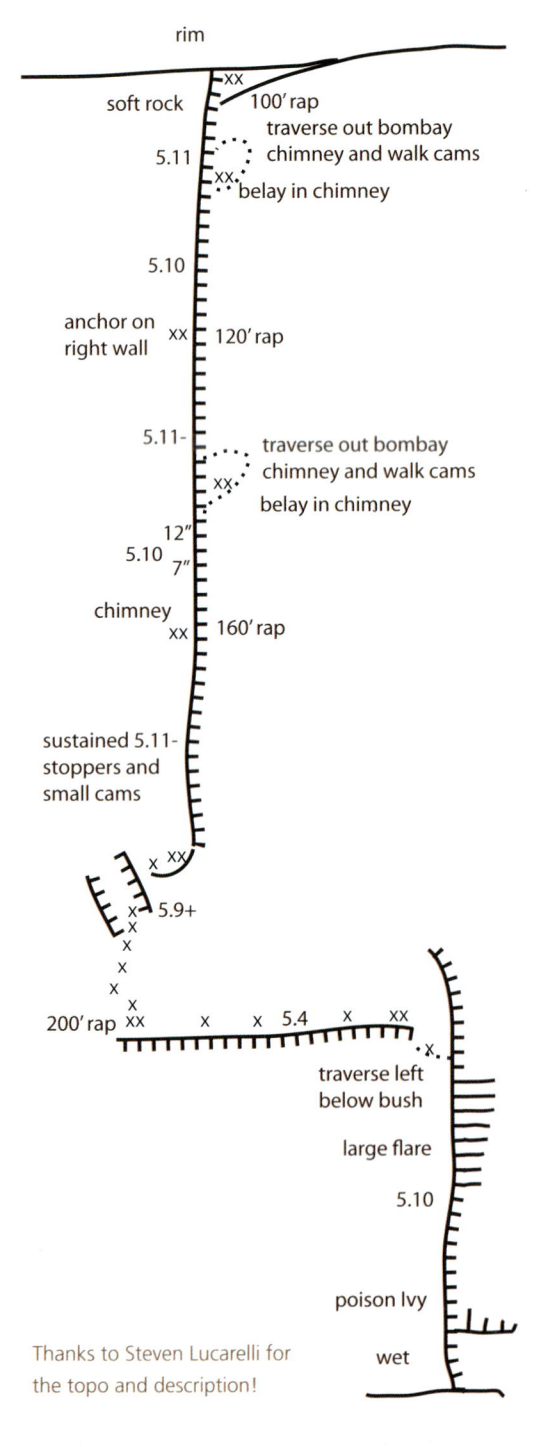

Thanks to Steven Lucarelli for the topo and description!

PROTECTING CLIMBING **ACCESS** SINCE 1991

Access Fund

| JOIN US |
WWW.ACCESSFUND.ORG

Jonathan Siegrist climbs the Third Millenium (14a) at the Monastery, Colorado. Photo by: Keith Ladzinski

Barney Rumble Tower

This is the obvious tower visible across the river 3.8 miles up the River Road from Hwy 191. Despite its over-the-river location the tower has become quite popular, as the climbing is quite good and at a modest grade. Park just after mile marker 4. The first crux is crossing the river; the second is finding a way onto the bench (this may require a short roped pitch) and gaining the base of the tower.

☐ 1. RAVEN'S DELIGHT
5.9+ 140' ★★★ E

P1: Climb the broken left-facing corner. Near its terminus, traverse left on slabby terrain to a right-facing corner and belay (5.9).

P2: A stiff pitch for the fledgling 5.9 climber. Follow the right-facing corner/crack to the summit (5.9+).

Descent: Rap anchors are located on the north face, just below the summit and might take a moment to locate. One double-rope (60m) rappel leads to the ground.

Gear: *2 sets, Blue TCU to 4.0, a few nuts*

FA: Bego Gerhart, Jeff Widen, Tony Valdes, Dawn Burke

Chapter 5

Potash Road

Amy Hinkey on *Flakes of Wrath* 5.9. Photo: Eric Odenthal

POTASH ROAD

Ahhh, Potash Road! A great place to study the cultures of many different outdoor users. Expect to mingle with curious sightseers and seekers of petroglyphs and arches. For mountain bikers, dirt bikers, Jeepers, and ATVers, Potash Road is a gateway to nearby trails such as Poison Spider and Golden Spike. The road itself is a popular road-bicycle ride. And yes, there is a working potash plant at the end of the road—watch out for large, fast, heavily-laden trucks roaring by.

For climbers, Potash Road is best known for the roadside access to Wall Street's multitude of short, sunny climbs. These are usually excellent quality and you can choose from vertical faces, cracks of all widths, overhangs, friction slabs, flares, sport, mixed, and trad routes.

Potash Road, however, encompasses more than just Wall Street and includes approaches that vary from easy to surprisingly adventurous, aspects that run from full sun to quiet and shady. There are a couple of towers, plenty of great bouldering, and even Moab's take on deepwater soloing at the boat launch.

The Wall Street area is the "workhorse" of Moab climbing, with zero approach and over 100 routes in less than a linear mile. The land belongs to the BLM, who are happy to let climbers play on the cliffs. Please take care to respect other users so as not to jeopardize this access.

A few concerns:

1. New routing: the etiquette here is, and has always been, that routes are established from the ground up. Following this ethic will help ensure that your route will not get chopped! Which brings us to the second issue:

2. Wall Street bolting wars. Enough already! You may feel you are doing the right thing but when it comes down to it you are just scarring the rock!

3. Never establish routes, climb, or even boulder near Native American cultural resources: petroglyphs, pictographs, dwellings, or any other signs of native history.

4. Desert routes usually involve some "breakable" rock. Here, the climbs are on softer Navajo sandstone right over the road, so If you pull off a rock it could hit a car and cause a serious accident. Use extra caution on new and multi-pitch climbs. Consider using a spotter on the road to let you know when cars are near. Clean up any fallen rocks immediately.

Wall Street, despite the noise and bustle, is an amazing resource for Moab climbing, a veritable outdoor gym for locals and visitors. Please take extra care to respect the multiple users of the Potash Road so as to ensure our continued right to play there.

There are several campgrounds with pit toilets and trash dumpsters that service this area with self-pay stations. Your honesty at the pay stations is appreciated; the money goes towards the cost of the operation and any area improvements.

Getting there

Potash Road follows the north bank of the Colorado River downstream from Moab. Drive north out of town on US 191, over the Colorado River bridge. Just over a mile past the bridge, turn left onto Potash Road (UT-279). Set your odometer to zero for locating the areas listed below.

COVERED IN THIS CHAPTER:

As one drives down Potash road from east to west:
1. Mars and The Scar sport crags
2. Wall Street area
3. Past Wall Street, select roadside climbs are described.
4. Culvert Canyon
5. Day Canyon
6. Long Canyon
7. Offwidth City
8. The Physics Department

POTASH ROAD MAP
highway
paved road
dirt road
tower
crag climb
camping
mileage
(from designated 0.0 spot)
N
0 miles
1
2
3
to Hwy 191, Moab, I-70
to I-70
into Arches NP
to Moab
to Moab
to Kane Creek
to Potash Plant, Canyonlands NP
to Dead Horse Point State Park
to Canyonlands NP
Dead Horse Point Rd
Gold Bar Tower
Culvert Canyon
Gold Bar Canyon
Block Tower
Gold Bar CG
Spur of the Moment
Day Canyon
Mission Tower
Long Canyon
Maverick Buttress
Warrior Tower
Offwidth City
Jaycee
Wall Street
Kane Springs
Williams Bottom
0.0
9.8
10.1
11.4
13.5
3.9
4.2
5.3
131
191
279

DRAGON
CAM

- TripleGrip cam lobes reduce walking and improve holding power
- Extendable sling saves on quickdraws
- Rated to 14kN from size one upwards

Designed, tested and manufactured in Wales, UK.

Alex Luger on *Monster Truck* (512), 4x4 Walls, Indian Creek, Utah. Photo: **Ray Demski**

DMM climb now work later

dmmwales.com

Wall Street

A young Canyon Knae on *Astrolad* 5.11 Photo: Eric Odenthal

Mars E

Mars has an easy approach and offers some really good sport climbing. The routes are long and of good quality. Park at 2.8 miles at a pullout on the left side of the road. Look for a cairn across and just up the road from the parking. A five-minute approach gets you to the base of the cliff. Routes are listed from left to right. Bolt counts may not be 100% accurate.

☐ 1. **ANDROIDS** 5.10b/c 40' ★★★
Fun warm-up. Right side of the leftmost forming arch.
Gear: 6 draws
FA: Andrea Cutter, Tom Perkins

☐ 2. **FREE BEER** 5.11c 50' ★★
Start between the forming arches, and trend up and left. Shares anchors with *Androids*.
Gear: 5 bolts
FA: Tom Perkins, Andrea Cutter

☐ 3. **ALIEN ABDUCTION** 5.12a 70' ★★
The left side of the second forming arch. Good, crimpy climbing!
Gear: 9 draws
FA: Tom Perkins, Shelley Malkin

☐ 4. **HUBBLE** 5.11d 95' ★★★★
A long pitch up the right side of the second forming arch. Great rock, probably the best pitch at Mars.
Gear: More than a dozen draws
FA: Josh Gross, Tom Perkins

☐ 5. **TAX FREE** 5.10c 95' ★★★
Right of the second forming arch are two chossy columns. *Tax Free* is just right of the first column. Fun, technical climbing. Lets up after the hard start.
Gear: More than a dozen draws
FA: Tom Perkins, Josh Gross

☐ 6. **CAMEO** 5.9+ 50' ★★
Just left of the second chossy column. Good warm-up.
Gear: 5 draws
FA: BJ Sbarra, Lynn Sanson, Josh Gross

The next three routes are located right of the second chossy column.

☐ 7. **SLAP CHOP** 5.11 90' ★★★
Nice stone. After bolt #5, climb up through the bulge. At bolt #7, traverse right, finish up with gear.
Gear: small to medium cams, 9 bolts
FA: Eric Schank, Anrea Cutter

☐ 8. **BIG HORNY SHEEP** 5.12a 85' ★★
Hard boulder problem. Some soft rock. After bolt #5 traverse right and bust through the bulge.
Gear: 11 draws
FA: Tom Perkins, Jamie Lynn Miller

☐ 9. **PUSS IN BOOTS** 5.11 60' ★★★
This is located on the main wall, just behind the tower. Good sustained climbing.
Gear: 7 draws
FA: Tom Perkins, Lisa Boose

The next two routes climb the obvious tower.

☐ 10. **DESERT GLOW** 5.11 60' ★★★
On the near side as you approach the tower. Climb through some heuco features.
Gear: 7 draws
FA: Josh Gross, Tom Perkins

☐ 11. **TWO THUMBS UP** 5.10 50' ★★
The easy way up the tower.
Gear: 0.5–0.75 Camalots, 3 draws
FA: Josh Gross, Tom Perkins

Wall Street

The Scar ✸ E

The Scar offers some shorter, pumpier sport climbs than its neighbor, Mars. Short and stout pretty much sums it up. The rock is of better quality than the appearance—and name—might suggest. Park as for Mars and access by using the same trail, but at its top break left instead of right. At the time of writing, all the climbs were plaqued.

Routes are listed right to left

❏ 1. **SUNKIST** 5.11d 80' ★★
Pumpy climbing and an airy crux. Not shown on topo.
Gear: 12 draws
FA: Tom Perkins, Shelley Malkin, Josh Gross

❏ 2. **SUB LUX** 5.12b 45' ★
Long arms are helpful on this one.
Gear: 8 draws
FA: Sam Lightner, Jason Keith

❏ 3. **POCKMARKS** 5.12a 45'
Anchor is shared with *Sub Lux*.
Gear: 8 draws
FA: Sam Lightner, Josh Gross

❏ 4. **EXTENDED CARE** 5.13a 70' ★★★
Climb past the first couple bolts of *Eviscerate* then head right. Crimpy crux, cool pinch feature up high. A few longer draws are nice.
Gear: 10 bolts
FA: Josh Gross, Sam Lightner

❏ 5. **EVISCERATE** 5.12a 35' ★★
Shares anchors with *Tender to the Touch*.
Gear: 5 draws
FA: Sam LIghtner, Josh Gross

❏ 6. **THE BUTTERFLY** 5.13a 70' ★★★
Climb *Tender to the Touch* and continue past the chains for seven more bolts.
Gear: 12 draws
FA: Josh Gross, Sam Lightner

❏ 7. **TENDER TO THE TOUCH** 5.11a 40' ★★★
Start on *Staph*, follow this past two bolts and break right for three more bolts.
Gear: 5 draws
FA: Sam Lightner, Josh Gross

❏ 8. **STAPH** 5.12c/d 45' ★
Hard boulder problem and weird anchor clip.
Gear: 9 bolts
FA: Josh Gross, Sam Lightner

❏ 9. **THE FLAPPER** 5.11c 35' ★★★
follows a flake feature
Gear: 6 draws
FA: Sam Lightner, Josh Gross

❏ 10. **PROJECT**

❏ 11. **THE ZIPPER** 5.12c 45' ★★★★
Slopers, crimp and stems; probably the best route at The Scar.
FA: Josh Gross, Sam Lightner

The Water Streak 🔆 SE

The Water Streak is just a stone's throw to the left of the Scar, but lower down, close to the road. There is just one climb. Look for the bolts ascending the black water streak.

❏ 1. **NERVE NET** 5.12b ★★★★
Two sport pitches lead to a trad third pitch. By avoiding the third pitch you will eliminate an epic downclimb.
P1: Follow the line of eight or nine bolts. No gear needed (5.12a, 80').
P2: A dozen bolts reaches a belay stance at 95'. Or, continue 20 more feet and past two more bolts to a spacious ledge (5.12b, 120').
P3: Clip one bolt then climb a left-facing corner that takes gear (5.8, 40').
Gear: about 14 draws, a few cams up to 1.5"
FA: Mark Howe

> The Jaycee Campground is located 3.9 miles from the 191/Potash intersection, between the Scar and Wall Street. It's a BLM-managed walk-in campground with six sites, a bathroom, dumpster and really good shade. There's no drinking water and no hook-ups, but there are firepits and picnic tables; cost is $12 per night.

A busy day on Wall Street

Josh Gross on *The Zipper* 5.12c   photo: Tom Perkins

Potash Road

WALL STREET E-SE

Wall Street is a workhorse for the Moab climbing scene, and for good reason. There are around 130 routes here, squeezed into one linear mile. There is no aproach and the routes are literally right off the road. Expect a gym-like ambiance, with a touch of the surreal. Wall Street can be a great source of entertainment. If you bring your hound, be very careful; trucks race up and down this road. Please pick up all of your trash, as this is a high volume area.
Approach: Drive 4.2 miles down Potash Road. Look for a "PARK IN DESIGNATED AREAS ONLY NEXT 1 MILE" sign. *Seibernetics* is found 100 yards beyond this sign.

☐ 1. SCRATCH AND SNIFF 5.11 ★★
An old, meandering bolt-protected slab climb, 20 feet right of *Seibernetics*. Bolts may be missing...
Gear: Draws, optional 0.75 for the bottom moves
FA: Kyle Copeland

☐ 2. SEIBERNETICS 5.8 70' ★★★
A slabby right-facing corner. Climb the slab, past two drilled angles, to a right-facing corner protected with fingers- and hand-size gear.
Gear: draws, 0.3–2.0
FA: Paul Seibert

☐ 3. UNEMPLOYMENT LINE 5.10+ 125'
Just left of *Seibernetics*. Two pitches.
P1: A shallow right-facing corner with a pin.
P2: Walk left on the ledge until under the first pin. Face climb, trending right, for 45 feet, past three drilled pins.
Gear: Tips to a 2.0, 3 draws
FA: Linus Platt, Kyle Copeland

☐ 4. SEAM AS IT EVER WAS 5.11b
Left of *Unemployment Line*, behind a tree, is a splitter seam in a groove. One bolt, just after a bulge.
Gear: 1 draw, tips cams, small nuts.
FA: Dan Mannix, Alison Sheets, 1987

☐ 5. RUDE OLD MEN 5.12 ★★
Great meandering slab. Some relic bolts and hangers.
Gear: 6 draws
FA: Charlie Fowler, Kyle Copeland

Wall Street

Coup d'Etat #11   **El Cracko Diablo** #10   **El Cracko Diablo Direct** #9   **Faith Flake** #8

Unnamed #13   **Warsteiner** #12

Midnight Frightening #15   **Smoke-Filled Rooms** #14

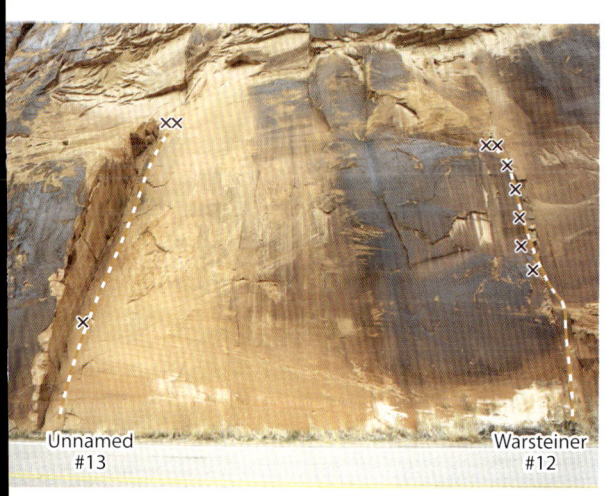

❑ 6. **RAIN CATCHER** 5.10+ 90'
Left-trending, slabby, tips corner to a varied crack system to hard-to-see chains on the left wall of an alcove.
Gear: Blue Alien to #3, (extra blue Alien)
FA: Mark Howe

❑ 7. **JUNK IN THE TRUNK** 5.12 85' ★★★
Left-trending face with nine bolts.
Gear: 9 draws, couple hand-size pieces for the lower part
FA: Mark Howe

❑ 8. **FAITH FLAKE** 5.11a 60'
Girth the flake with a double sling. Delicate climbing brings you past three fixed pieces.
Gear: Single rack to #2, 3 draws
FA: Jake Tradiak

❑ 9. **EL CRACKO DIABLO DIRECT** 5.11+
Aka *El Face o' Diablo*. Boulder to a high first bolt (stick clip advised). Climb edges up and left, past three bolts, to shared anchors with *El Cracko Diablo*. Harder than it appears. Usually toproped.
FA: (TR) Linus Platt, 1990

❑ 10. **EL CRACKO DIABLO** 5.10 50' ★★
Ascend a cool wedge feature, with fingers, to good hands over an overlap. Finish with more fingers. Fun!
Gear: Fingers and a single hands piece should do it
FA: Charlie Fowler, Sue Wint, Nancy Pritchard, 1989

❑ 11. **COUP D'ETAT** 5.11+ 50'
Shallow right-facing corner. Climb past a drilled pin and a bolt. Hard start!
Gear: 2 draws, tips-size cams, a set of nuts
FA: Linus Platt

❑ 12. **WARSTEINER** 5.11 50' ★★
Forty feet left of *Coup d'Etat*. Climb a body-length onto the ledge. Step off the ledge and follow a line of broken rock (reminiscent of a dike) passing five bolts.
Gear: 5 draws
FA: Mark Howe

There is a small parking area just left of *Warsteiner*.

❑ 13. **UNNAMED** 5.11b 70' ★★★
Thirty feet left of *Warsteiner*. Start in a shallow stembox, with a bolt at 15 feet, in a right facing corner. Continue up the corner, with gear, to another bolt high on the route.

❑ 14. **SMOKE-FILLED ROOMS** 5.11 60' ★
Thirty feet left of the previous route. Make a few moves onto a ramp. Continue up a shallow left-facing corner with one fixed piece just below the crux. Sequential!
Gear: 1 draw, gear from yellow TCU–#2
FA: Billy Smallen

❑ 15. **MIDNIGHT FRIGHTENING** 5.12b 70' ★★★
Just left of *Smoke-Filled Rooms*. Hard crimps lead to a bolt just under a flake/overlap. Follow the overlap, trending right, then climb over the overlap, passing another bolt on the right. Straight up to the anchors.
Gear: 2 bolts, 0.3-2.0
FA: Herb Crimp

Why not bring your own couch?

WE KNOW SHOES | WE KNOW GEAR
NOW WE'VE GOT BOTH

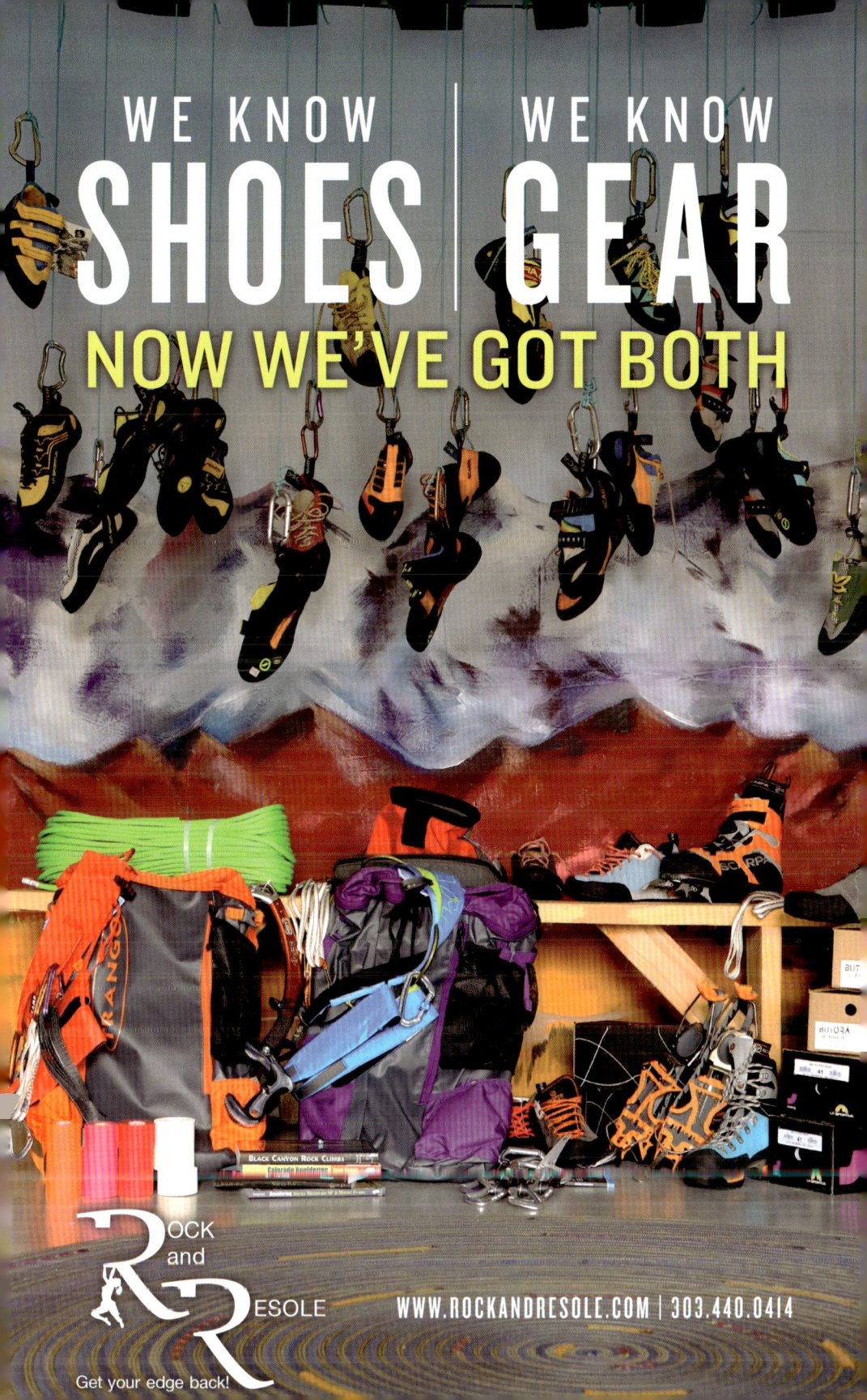

Rock and Resole
Get your edge back!

WWW.ROCKANDRESOLE.COM | 303.440.0414

Potash Road

☐ 16. **STEGO SLAB** 5.9 40' ★★
The last route before the School Room slabs. Face climb past five bolts, on swirly rock, to a three-bolt anchor.
Gear: 5 bolts
FA: Lynn Sanson, Josh Gross

☐ 17. **SCHOOL ROOM 1** 5.4–5.8 60'
This is a swath of easy-angle slabs, 60 feet high, 80 feet wide. Lots of fun, moderate topropes can be be established from anchors on the bench above these slabs. To reach the bench, scramble up a 4th-class route behind the large tree on the left. Individual lines are not described.

The next routes are found 100 feet to the left of School Room slabs on a 40-foot-tall buttress.

☐ 18. **UNNAMED** 5.11 40' ★★★
The bolted, right edge of the *Fistful of Potash* formation. Between this route and *Fistful of Potash* are bolt studs from an old (and unfinished?) Kyle Copeland line, *Dr. Strange Flake*.
Gear: 5 draws
FA: Canyon Cain, Keith Reynolds

☐ 19. **A FISTFUL OF POTASH** 5.10 40' ★★★★
Face climb past three bolt to a finger crack. Continue up the finger crack to the anchor.
Gear: 3 draws and some finger-size gear
FA: Charlie Fowler, Geoff Tabin, Tom Dickey, 1987

☐ 20. **RALPH THE RAT** 5.11 40' ★★★
Start left of the previous route. Trend left toward the arête then back right to share anchors with *A Fistful....*
Gear: 5 draws
FA: Dave Medara

☐ 21. **ABOVE A FISTFUL** 5.11
P1: Climb *Ralph the Rat*.
P2: Climb the chimney above.

☐ 22. **MINI ME** 5.9 40' ★★
Just left of *Ralph the Rat*. Face climb past two bolts to a shallow left-facing corner. Climb the varied size corner to the anchor.
Gear: 2 bolts, single rack to #3
FA: Josh Gross

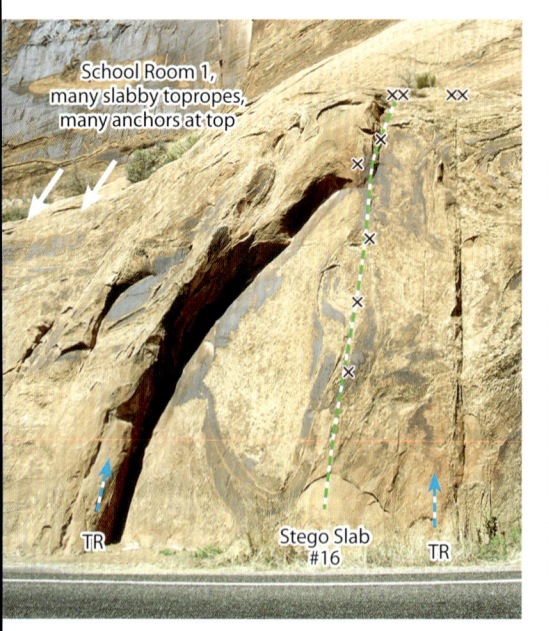

☐ 23. **LAST TANGO IN POTASH** 5.11b 60' ★★★★
Thirty feet left of *Fistful of Potash*, 40 feet right of *Potash Sanction*. Follow sequential edges up seams and past a few bolts. Great rock.
Gear: 5 draws, set of nuts, set of TCUs
FA: Kyle Copeland, Alison Sheets, 1987

☐ 24. **THE TWO SIDES OF PURPLE** 5.10 ★★
Start on *Pinhead* then head right to a right-facing corner with tips and wide. Anchor on the left wall. The route continues to the rim in two more pitches but this is not recommended by the first ascentionist.
Gear: 0.0–5.0
FA: Josh Gross, Lynn Sanson

☐ 25. **PINHEAD** 5.10b 40' ★★★
Fun climbing with plenty of features from which to choose. Start up a cluster of cracks and continue upward, protecting with a bit of everything.
Gear: Single rack to 3.0, set of nuts helpful

☐ 26. **UNNAMED** 5.12 50'
Bolted face in a left-facing corner.
Gear: 4 draws, a few off-fingers or tight-hand pieces
FA: Chris Baird

☐ 27. **POTASH SANCTION** 5.11 60' ★★★★
Start in a left-facing corner. Climb a variety of sizes to a bolt just under the roof. Lieback the offwidth roof. Continue up the broken corner to the anchor. Two more pitches have been added, at 5.12.
Gear (for P1): 0.5–5.0 (a new 5.0 will work but an old 5.0 is better)
FA: Charlie Fowler. FA, P2, P3: Mark Howe, Josh Gross

☐ 28. **NO FLY ZONE** 5.12c 65' ★★
Start on *Potash Sanction* and break left, passing five bolts under and around the roof.
Gear: 5 draws
FA: Josh Gross

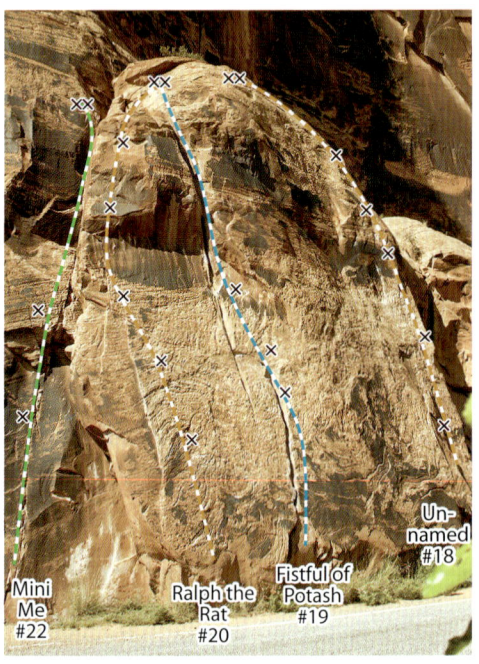

Wall Street

The next route, *Astrolad,* is located at mileage 4.4 from the Potash Rd/Hwy 191 intersection. There are a few aid routes between *Potash Sanction* and *Astrolad* but these are neither described nor recommended.

☐ 29. **ASTROLAD** 5.11 50' ★★★★★
Sixty feet left of *Potash Sanction*, identify a prominent right-facing corner (only the first pitch is described here; the route continues via aid for two more pitches). Begin with fingers and a hand jam or two. The seams arc out over the arête (two bolts). From here, a crack on the left and stems on the right will be useful. Finish at chains.
VAR. Don't go to the arête, continue straight up the corner at 5.11+.
Gear: Mostly tips, a few hand sizes, couple of draws.
FA: Jim Beyer; Var: Steve "Roadie" Seats

☐ 30. **ANOTHER ROADSIDE DISTRACTION** 5.10b 40' ★★★★
Start by climbing a broken blocky right-facing corner, continue up a nice section of fingers to the chains.
Gear: 0.3–0.5 (& optional big piece for just off the ground)
FA: Jim Beyer

☐ 31. **CHEMISTRY** 5.12 70' ★★★
Start on *Roadside Distraction*, break left through the bulge and finish up the obvious crack line.
Gear: 3.0, some fingers gear, 4 draws
FA: Josh Gross, Sam Lightner

☐ 32. **PROJECT** 5.?
Thin face climbing past three bolts. Trend right and meet up with *Chemistry*. Abandoned project?

The next routes are found 80 feet left of *Astrolad* and *Another Roadside Distraction*. A good landmark is the left-facing, left-arcing dihedral of *Mother Trucker.*

☐ 33. **UNKNOWN** 5.? 40'
Twenty feet right of *Mother Trucker* is a left-facing corner seam, with four drilled pins, to chimney.

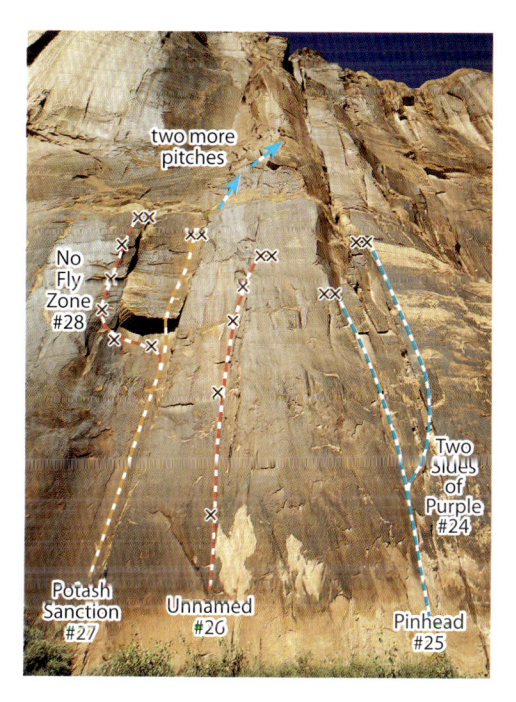

Kief Dogs enjoys a Potash Bong Hit 5.10

Potash Road

☐ 34. **TAKE A CHANCE ON ME** 5.12b 35' ★★
Facey arête just right of *Mother Trucker*.
Gear: 5 draws
FA: Sam Lightner

☐ 35. **MOTHER TRUCKER** 5.11c 50' ★★★★
Left-facing corner, arching left. Climb with laybacks and stems, placing pro when available.
Gear: blue TCU–1.0
FA: Jim Beyer

☐ 36. **KNAPPING WITH THE ALIEN** 5.11c/d 55' ★★★★★
The steep, chalked-up face 20 feet left of *Mother Trucker*. Nice edges. Popular!
Gear: 5 draws
FA: Kyle Copeland

☐ 37. **ROOM WITH A VIEW** 5.11+ 60' ★★
Splitter seam, with four bolts. Crux at second bolt.
Gear: 4 draws, stoppers, a few small to hand-size cams
FA: Equipped by Luke Malatesta; FFA: Jason Lantz

☐ 38. **SMOKE ON THE WATER** 5.12+ 85' ★★★★
Shallow right-facing corner to thin face to a final bulge to chains.
Gear: 10 draws
FA: Keith Reynolds

☐ 39. **HALF PIPE** 5.10+ 50'
Shallow left-facing corner with some stems and just enough gear placements. Pass a bolt up high on the face then a drilled angle on the right wall just before the chains.
Gear: 2 draws, set of nuts, heavy on small cams
FA: Jim Beyer

☐ 40. **WELCOME TO ANEXIA** 5.12 40'
Start on *Half Pipe*. Continue up the left-trending face.
Gear: 5 bolts
FA: Jake Tradiak

☐ 41. **UNNAMED** 5.6
Start just right of the *Bad Moki Roof* overhang. Meander up to a slab with two bolts, to the anchor.
Gear: 2 draws

☐ 42. **HORIZONTAL MAMBO** 5.12d ★★★★
Start up *Bad Moki Roof*. Instead of busting over the roof, traverse right on a flake on the underside of the roof.
Gear: 4 draws
FFA: Mason Earle

☐ 43. **BAD MOKI ROOF** 5.9 45' ★★★
The obvious, gigantic roof. Start in a right-facing corner with fingers, off-fingers, hands, then through the wedge at the lip of the roof (this is often sandy to add spice)
Gear: 0.4–3.0
FA: Kyle Copeland

☐ 44. **EYES OF FALINA** 5.9 90'
Just right of *Flakes of Wrath*. Not recommended.
FA: Kyle Copeland

☐ 45. **EAST OF WRATH** 5.9 80'
Start on *Flakes of Wrath*. Break right at the first horizontal, continue with face holds to the anchor.
Gear: Set of nuts and a single set of cams to a 3.0
FA: Josh Gross, John Brewer

☐ 46. **FLAKES OF WRATH** 5.9+ 60' ★★★★★
A striking line. Start up the flake with hands, then cruise finger pockets to the left-trending undercling, then to the anchors.
Gear: 0.5–2.0 (nuts provide great threads in the finger pockets)
FA: Alison Sheets, Paul Firestone, 1988

☐ 47. **FLAKES OF WRATH DIRECT** 5.11+ ★★★★
Start just left of *Flakes of Wrath*. Climb awesome hands to a crack switch, then things start to go thin.

☐ 48. **MISSISSIPPI HIGH STEP** 5.12- 40' ★★★
Start just left of an overlap, left of *Flakes of Wrath Direct*. Climb past two bolts. Climb a flake/overlap just right of the bolts, clip three more bolts to the chains.
Gear: 5 draws
FA: Linus Platt

Stella Noble, age 9 at the time, on *Horizontal Mambo* 5.12d

Potash Road

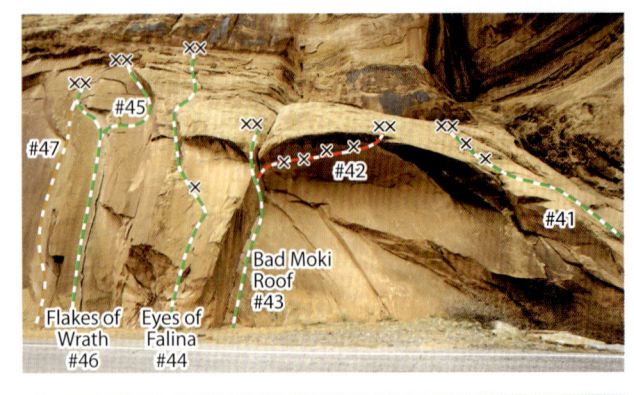

In the next 200 feet before reaching *Zigzag*, blank rock prevails and only two routes have been established.

❏ 49. UNNAMED 5.12 ★★★
Shallow switching corner, 25 feet left of *Mississippi*.... This might be Wall Street's toughest gear lead!
FA: Keith Reynolds

❏ 50. UNNAMED 5.10+
A chimney, just left of a smooth face.
Gear: 5 bolts & gear
FA: Keith Reynolds

❏ 51. ZIGZAG 5.10
This is about 200 feet left of *Mississippi High Step*. Climb some fun edges and trend left to a stance. Work back right to the arête, then leftward to the anchor.
Gear: 5 draws, a few off-finger pieces
FA: Jim Beyer

❏ 52. FROGS OF A FEATHER 5.10c 80' ★★★★
Start at a steep right-facing flake, 25 feet left of *Zigzag*. Climb fingers up the flake to a bolt up high. Work past a flake/column (heavily rope scarred) and work left and follow the weakness to anchors.
Gear: Couple sets of TCUs–2.0, a long sling
FA: Kyle Copeland, Paul Seibert, 1989

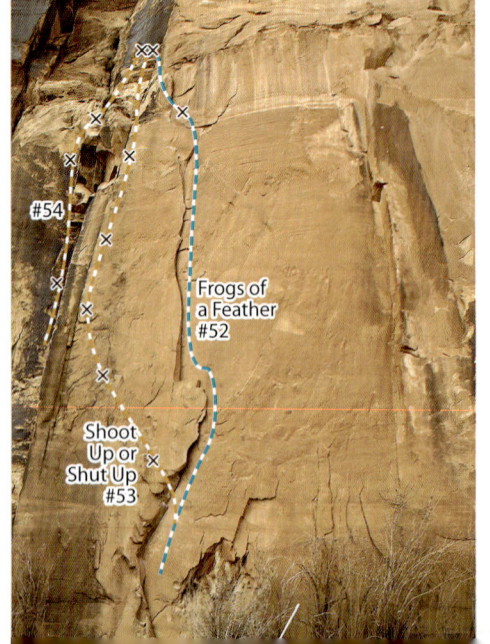

Kiefer Kelley on *Nervous in Suburbia* 5.9+

Wall Street

❐ **53. SHOOT UP OR SHUT UP** 5.11 80' ★★★
Start as for *Frogs of a Feather*; trend left to climb on the arête passing six fixed anchors.
Gear: 6 draws, set of nuts, small cams
FA: Kyle Copeland, Charlie Fowler, Marc Hirt, Tim Hudgel, 1989

❐ **54. SHOOT UP OR SHUT UP CORNER** 5.11a 80' ★★
An old toprope, recently equipped as a lead. Start up the corner and pass some bulges via four bolts (hard to see). Shares anchors with *Shoot Up or Shut Up*.
FA: Kyle Copeland

❐ **55. WAKE OF THE FLOOD** 5.10c 65' ★
Climb the crack/seam, passing a fixed anchor on the right, then another on the left. Work through the pod/bulge up to the belay.
Gear: 2 draws, single set of cams, a set of nuts
FA: Kyle Copeland

❐ **56. FLASH FLOOD** 5.11 65'
Face and seam. Trend left up to an arching right-facing undercling. Shares anchors with *Wake of the Flood*.
Gear: 0.75–2.0, set of nuts
FA: David Dawson, Kyle Copeland, 1989

❐ **57. HIGH OVER DATURA** 5.11+ 65' ★★★
Hard face climbing! Pass a pin, bolt, pin, bolt, bolt.
Gear: 5 draws
FA: Charlie Fowler

❐ **58. VISIBLE PANTY LINE** 5.10 65' ★★★★
Triple cracks/seams. Fun route, with gear just when you need it. A fixed piece marks the crux.
Gear: Set of nuts and TCUs should do it
FA: Kyle Copeland, Layton Kor, 1988

❐ **59. POUNDING THE FROG DIRECT** 5.11 65'
Face just left of *Visible Panty Line*. Climb past three fixed pieces then trend right to rejoin *VPL*. A bit "heady."
FA: Kyle Copeland, Marabel Loveridge, 1990

❐ **60. POUNDING THE FROG** 5.10b 40'
Yikes! Have your head on tight for this one. Face climb past a couple of fixed anchors, trend left to the *Smell of Dead Euro-peons* anchor.
Gear 2 draws
FA: Kyle Copeland, Paul Seibert, 1989

❐ **61. SMELL OF DEAD EURO-PEONS** 5.11
Toprope problem.

❐ **62. BOLTS TO BUMPY LAND** 5.11 135' ★★★★★
Face climb and friction up a long, rounded arête.
Gear: 14 draws, 70m rope, set of calves that don't burn!
FA: Jake Tradiak

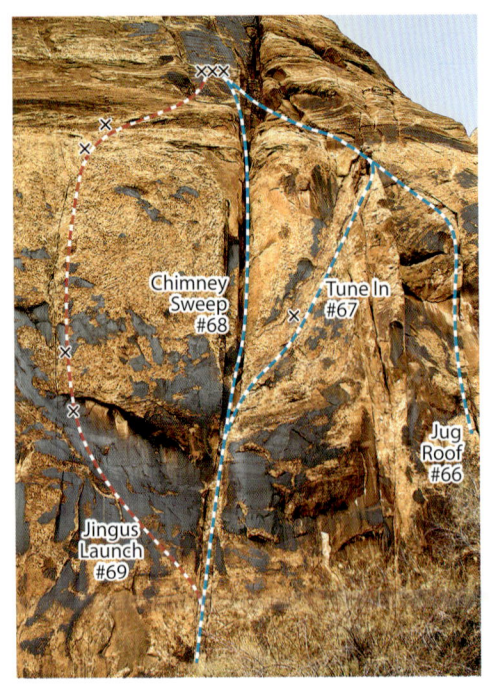

Potash Road

❐ 63. **WILLOW WHIP** 5.6 ★
This sits at the left edge of the parking; look for a left-facing ramp/corner with painted chain anchors.
FA: Josh Gross

❐ 64. **HIGH DESERT DRIFTER** 5.8 30' ★★★
Just left of *Willow Whip*. Climb a rightward curving flake (crux). Above, a ramping splitter leads to some horizontal cracks then the anchor.
Gear: tips to tight hands
FA: Josh Gross, Madoline Wallace

❐ 65. **RING PIN BOULDER** 5.9
Not recommended.

The next climbs are 100 feet farther left. Four routes, close together, share anchors.

❐ 66. **JUG ROOF** 5.10 ★★★★
Start behind some bushes. Climb to a large chockstone (the jug roof), pass it on its right. Follow the obvious left-trending splitter and at its end work left, cross *Tune In*, and clip the anchors atop *Chimney Sweep*.
FA: Jim Beyer

❐ 67. **TUNE IN** 5.10b
Start on *Chimney Sweep* then follow two bolts up and right to a ledge. Head back left to *Chimney Sweep*.
FA: Jim Beyer

❐ 68. **CHIMNEY SWEEP** 5.10
Yuk!
FA: Jim Beyer

At 4.6 miles from the Potash/Hwy191 intersection is a break in the cliff with a scrub-filled drainage. At the base of the drainage is some parking. *Bolts to Bumpy Land* is located on the right, *Willow Whip* on the left.

Wall Street

❑ 69. **JINGUS LAUNCH** 5.12 R/X
Not recommended.
FA: Jim Beyer

There is a small pullout just before the next two routes.

❑ 70. **UNNAMED ROUTE** 5.11d
A chossy, right-facing corner of various sizes brings you to a shelf with a large boulder and the anchors.
Gear: fingers to fist, set of nuts

❑ 71. **SUMMIT CHIMNEY** 5.9
Four pitches of chimney and offwidth. Further information is sparse to non-existent. Let the epic begin!!
FA: Jim Beyer

❑ 72. **WILD-EYED DEAR** 5.12 65' ★★★★★
(Aka Dark Horse) Just left of Summit Chimney. Face climb on really good Wall Street rock.
Gear: 7 draws
FA: Jim Beyer

❑ 73. **TWITIN' SHINKIES** 5.11b 50' ★★★★
Shallow left-facing corner, angling left to right past three fixed pins.
Gear: 0.4–#3, 3 draws
FA: Kyle Copeland

❑ 74. **BLOWIN' CHUNKS** 5.11b 60' ★★★
Ascend an obvious, shallow, left-facing corner to where it turns to a right-facing corner and clip the anchor.
Gear: 0.0–0.75, 4 draws
FA: Kyle Copeland

❑ 75. **FULL SPECTRUM** 5.11+ ★★★
(Aka Rainbow Route) Follow bolts up and left. Nice line.
Gear: 7 bolts
FA: Luke Malatesta, Jason McDannald

❑ 76. **SAND AND STEEL** 5.11b 60'
The right-facing corner just left of Full Spectrum. Climb with fingers and tips, pass the fixed pin and solve the overhang at the top.
Gear: 0.0–3.0, set of nuts, quickdraw
FA: Tony Calderone

❑ 77. **NO NAME** 5.11
Thirty feet left of Sand and Steel. Negotiate a thin seam protected with five fixed pins. Stem past some wide up to a final pin before the anchor.
Gear: 6 draws, gear

❑ 78. **RIGHT SIDE IN** 5.9
No anchor and not recommended.

❑ 79. **UNNAMED** 5.12b
The arête right of 30 Seconds.
Gear: 7 bolts

❑ 80. **30 SECONDS OVER POTASH** 5.8 50' ★★★★★
A left-facing corner, 100 feet left of Full Spectrum. A bit of liebacking at the start, to some jamming. POPULAR!
Gear: 1 set TCUs–3.0, nuts, a few extra hand size
FA: Kyle Copeland

There is a parking area at 4.7 miles

❑ 81. **LUCY IN THE SKY WITH POTASH** 5.10 60' ★★★★
A shallow left-facing corner with a tricky sequence at mid-height!
Gear: TCUs, a rack of cams to a 2.0
FA: Linus Platt

❑ 82. **NERVOUS IN SUBURBIA** 5.10 60' ★★★★★
Very popular face. Climb edges past four bolts. Sporty!
Gear: 4 bolts
FA: Kyle Copeland, Joy Kor, 1988

❑ 83. **PROJECT**
Bolted project just left of Nervous in Suburbia. At time of writing, 14 bolts in place.
FA: bolted by Keith Reynolds

❑ 84. **UNNAMED** 5.9
Ramp in gully with a single bolt.

❑ 85. **UNDER THE BOARDWALK** 5.12b/c 60' ★★★★★
Start just right of the arête. Work left and climb the arête.
Gear: 9 draws
FA: Charlie Fowler

Under the Boardwalk #85

Nervous In Suburbia #82

Lucy in the Sky with Potash #81

30 Seconds Over Potash #80

Dave Medara on *Under the Boardwalk* 5.12b/c Photo: Todd Bogan

Wall Street

❑ 86. **SOMETHING NASTY** 5.12 60' ★★★★
There is a gully/drainage between *Under the Boardwalk* and *I Love Loosey*. Inside, an arching finger crack splits the left wall. Climb it.
Gear: 2 sets of TCUs, add a couple of 0.5s
FA: Kyle Copeland, 1988

❑ 87. **I LOVE LOOSEY** 5.11+ 45'
Shuffle up a slabby, rounded arête with five bolts.
Gear: 5 draws
FA: Charlie Fowler, Kyle Copeland, 1988

❑ 88. **FERNANDO** 5.11 45' ★★★★
Climb a well-bolted face on dark varnish to a reachy finish. Hard for the grade.
Gear: 6 draws
FA: Sam Lightner, Josh Gross

❑ 89. **BABY BLUE** 5.11 45' ★★★★★
In a left-facing corner, climb fingers and face features to a tips finish.
Gear: 0.0–0.5 TCUs (heavy on blue TCU)
FA: Charlie Fowler, Kyle Copeland, 1989

❑ 90. **MAN AFTER MIDNIGHT** 5.12- 65' ★★
Start in a broken left-facing corner, eventually moving onto the arête passing seven bolts.
Gear: 7 draws
FA: Josh Gross, Sam Lightner

❑ 91. **DESP-ARÊTE** 5.12b ★★★★
This climbs an arête 50 feet left of *Baby Blue*. Start on the left side, passing a pin. Then, climb on the arête passing four bolts.
Gear: 5 draws
FA: Kyle Copeland

Potash Road

❏ 92. BEYER OFFWIDTH 5.9+
Not recommended; but if you do like it chossy and wide, this is for you!
FA: guess who?

Just past mile 4.7 there is a large parking area. This extends from near *Beyer Offwidth* to *She-la the Peeler*.

❏ 93. SLAB 5.8 50' ★★★
Fifty feet left of *Desp-arête*. Friction your way up the tongue-like feature, passing five bolts.
Gear: 5 draws
FA: Jake Tradiak

❏ 94. GUMBY GULLY 5.4 40'
A chossy stembox located just left of *Slab*.
FA: Amy Barnes

❏ 95. EAT THE RICH 5.10c 40' ★★★
Shallow right-facing corner in black varnish. Mostly tips. Short and fun.
Gear: 0.0 TCU–0.4, 1 hand piece
FA: Kyle Copeland, Ron Olevsky, 1989

❏ 96. KNIGHT MOVES 5.11 40'
The left-facing corner system left of *Eat the Rich*. Start with hands, cruise past a couple of pins to a broken splitter. There's one more pin before the anchors.
Gear: 0.3–2.0, 3.0 draws
FA: Kyle Copeland, Ron Olevsky, 1989

❏ 97. THREE SHEEPS TO THE WIND 5.11
This climb is very near to some petroglyphs. DO NOT CLIMB! This route is included for historical purposes only.
FA: Dave Dawson, Kyle Copeland

❏ 98. TIRED OF TALUS 5.11 ★★
Three pitches but only the first is described. Pitch 2 works left to access the 5.12 right-facing corner of the third pitch, but has poor rock and is not recommended.
P1: Start in a left-facing corner. A few wide moves access a mostly fingers crack that reaches the anchors.
Gear: (P1) old 4.0 (or new 5.0), fingers size cams, nuts
FA: (P1) Bret Ruckman, Gary Olsen; (P2,3) Jim Beyer, Pat McInerney

❏ 99. PERVERSE TRAVERSE 5.11 ★★★
Two new, high quality pitches have been added above the end of pitch 1.
P1: Follow *Tired of Talus* (5.11).
P2: Downclimb a bit to the right then follow a line of bolts across a frictiony face to a bolted anchor (5.10b).
P3: Climb a beautiful crack in a steep, shallow, left-facing corner. Tips to tight hands. Great pitch!
Descent: Single 70m rappel, just, from atop pitch 3.
Gear: tips–4.0, 6 draws
FA: James Webster

❏ 100. STATIC CLING 5.11a 70' ★★★★★
Climb a left-facing corner to a roof at half height, work left, pass the roof and continue up the left-facing corner. Popular, and for good reason.
Gear: set of TCUs, single rack to 3.0
FA: Jim Beyer

❏ 101. POTASH BONG HIT 5.10 70' ★★
Start up a hand crack to a flake that trends right to the *Static Cling* anchors. The flake has a hollow sound to it when you plug cams.
Gear: 0.75–3.0, a few shoulder slings, optional big piece
FA: Jim Beyer

❏ 102. THE GOOD, THE BAD, THE POTASH 5.11b/c 45' ★★★
Start up *Potash Bong Hit*, then break left for three bolts.
Gear: 3 draws
FA: Sam Lightner

❏ 103. SKELETONIC 5.11+ 55' ★★★★★
Stem up a right-facing, well-chalked corner.
Gear: 4 bolts and trad gear
FA: Eric Decaria

❏ 104. TOP 40 5.8 50' ★★★
A left-facing corner with some fingers and edges, passing two bolts to the final anchor. Note: if you bring a few hand-size pieces and continue past the anchor, you can access the anchors atop *Skeletonic* for toproping.
Gear: TCUs and a set of nuts.
FA: Jeff Slider

❏ 105. UNNAMED 5.12+
Splitter seam.
Gear: 6 bolts
FA: Keith Reynolds

PHOTO: ©ARJAN DE KOCK

LA SPORTIVA
innovation with passion
WWW.LASPORTIVA.COM

Potash Road

☐ 106. **BROKEN ENGAGEMENTS** 5.10 A3
This is above, and is accessed from, the School Room.
P1: Bolts to beaks (A3).
P2: Thin pins to easier clean aid (C1 A2+).
P3: Left-facing corner to loose rock (5.10 C1).
FA: Luke Malatesta

☐ 107. **LACTO MANGULATION**
5.10b 50' ★★★
Right-facing corner. Start up some shelfy features to a thinning corner protected with fixed gear.
Gear: 3 draws, set of nuts
FA: Jorma Hayes

☐ 108. **LITTLE TUFAS** 5.10b 50'
Just left of *Lacto Mangulation*, directly behind the tree. Start at a shallow corner with a bolt in white calcite on the left. Clip two more bolts that lead to a short slot and chockstone, up this to a two-bolt anchor.
Gear: 0.75, 3.0, 4.0, one tips piece, 3 draws
FA: Josh Gross, Lynn Sanson

☐ 109. **BANANA PEEL** 5.10b 55' ★★
Left of *Little Tufas*, on the black and white, calcite-blotched face. Edge and friction over the rounded slab.
Gear: 6 draws

☐ 110. **BROWN BANANA** 5.9 60' ★
Slide up calcite edges just left of *Banana Peel*.
Gear: 5 bolts

School Room 2: For 200 feet left of *Brown Banana* the cliff forms a low-angle slab with convenient parking (look for the sign on left) and a convenient ledge sytem above. Traditionally this has been a popular toprope area. Multiple bolted toprope anchors are installed on the ledge, which is accessed via a 4th-class gully across from the mileage post.

Recently a few protection and lower-off/rappel bolts have been appearing, providing a number of easy bolted leads, great for beginners. Please rappel from the top anchors of these routes; lowering on these low angle, rounded slabs creates nasty rope grooves.

☐ 111. **GRAMA & THE GREEN SUEDE SHOES** 5.7
Climb a chossy gash immediately left of *Brown Banana*. No anchors: either traverse left or right to clip nearby top-anchors or belay from a large block at the back of the ledge and walk off.
Gear: hand/fist and larger cams

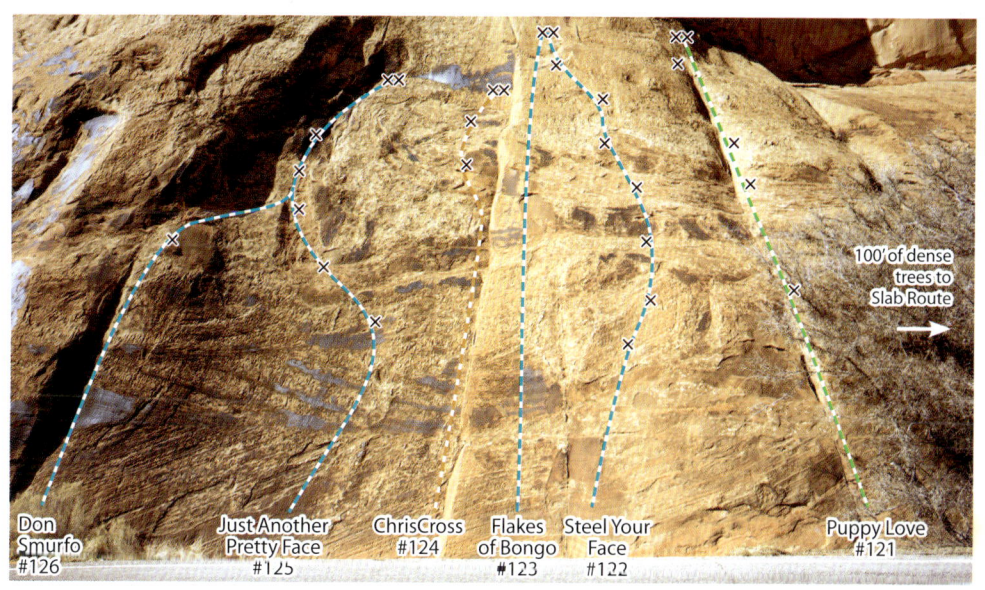

Wall Street

Photo labels (top): Don Smurfo #126 · Just Another Pretty Face #125 · ChrisCross #124 · Flakes of Bongo #123 · Steel Your Face #122 · Puppy Love #121 · 100' of dense trees to Slab Route →

❒ **112. HOLY MOLEY** 5.5
Four bolts.
Gear: 4 draws

❒ **113. PRACTICAL RELIGION** 5.5
Four bolts.
Gear: 4 draws

❒ **114. YOGINI** 5.7
Five bolts.
Gear: 5 draws

❒ **115. CHOCOLATE CHUNK** 5.3
Three bolts in black varnish. Short.
Gear: 3 draws

❒ **116. NEOPOLITAN** 5.7
Takes a small overhang halfway. Eight bolts.
Gear: 8 draws

❒ **117. HIDDEN MESSAGE** 5.5
Only two bolts and a pin!
Gear: 3 draws

❒ **118. ARC ANGEL** 5.10
Previously a toprope, now equipped with nine bolts.
Gear: 9 draws
FA: Tony Calderone, Dave Carrol

❒ **119. SHE-LA THE PEELER** 5.9 90'
Face with six bolts. Anchors are hard to see.
Gear: 6 draws

❒ **120. SLAB ROUTE** 5.7 95' ★★
Close bolts make this a terrific first lead. Crux is getting off the ground; difficulty eases and angle lessens. Rappelling from the top anchors recommended.
Gear: 9 draws
FA: Sam Lightner

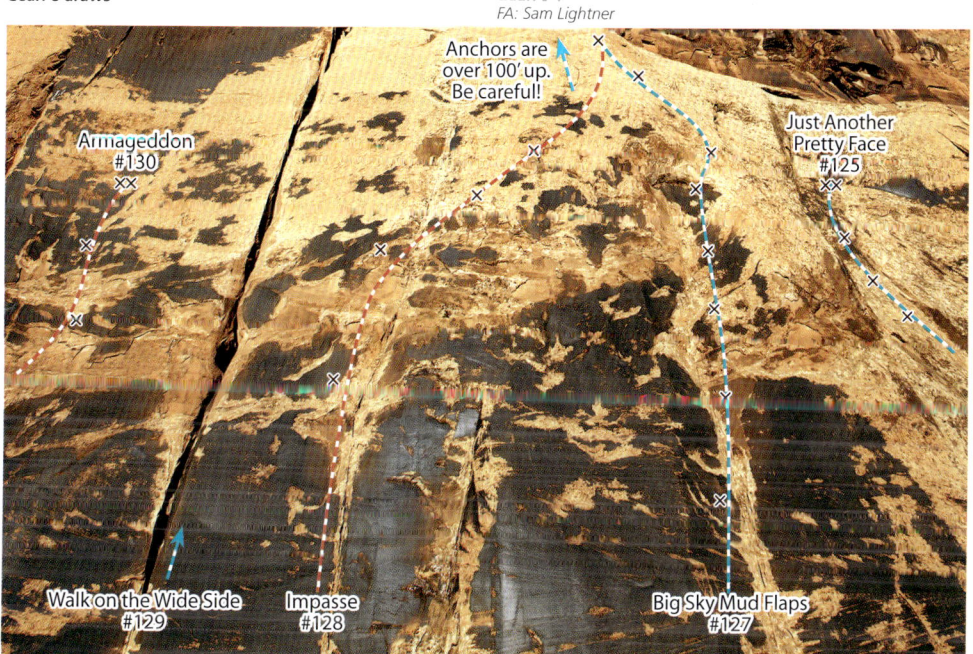

Photo labels (bottom): Armageddon #130 · Anchors are over 100' up. Be careful! · Just Another Pretty Face #125 · Walk on the Wide Side #129 · Impasse #128 · Big Sky Mud Flaps #127

Potash Road

Left of *Slab*, thick trees obscure the cliff. The next route is 100 feet left, at the left margin of these trees.

❒ 121. **PUPPY LOVE** 5.9 X 60' ★★
Climb the obvious seam, past four fixed pieces. Warning: ground-fall potential. Be on it!
Gear 4 draws
FA: Mike Baker

There is roadside parking from near *Puppy Love* all the way to the the left end of Wall Street.

❒ 122. **STEEL YOUR FACE** 5.10 80' ★★★★★
Just left of *Puppy Love*. Edge and friction up the face. A coveted tick for the slabsters amongst you.
Gear: 7 draws
FA: Kyle Copeland, Charlie Fowler, 1988

❒ 123. **FLAKES OF BONGO** 5.10
Toprope from the *Steel Your Face* anchors. It has been bolted and chopped more than once. At time of writing bolts are out, with two in but flattened.

❒ 124. **CHRISCROSS** 5.11a
A shallow left-facing corner with a few face moves past a couple bolts on the left just before the anchors.
FA: Chris Pendelton, Gary Olsen, 1984

❒ 125. **JUST ANOTHER PRETTY FACE** 5.10 70' ★★★
The face just left of *ChrisCross*. Follow crimps and slopers up the pretty (pretty runout!) face. Long way to first bolt, though the crux is higher, above the third bolt.
FA: Kyle Copeland

❒ 126. **DON SMURFO** 5.10
Face climb up a faint right-facing dihedral system. Work right to the *Just Another Pretty Face* anchors.
Gear: nuts and draws
FA: Kyle Copeland

Wall Street

Petroglyphs! No Climbing Left of Here!

White Way #135

❏ **127. BIG SKY MUD FLAPS** 5.10+ 110' ★★★★
Follow a seam then work right on face holds. Eventually work back left above the seam to the anchors. Be careful lowering, a 70m rope is required.
Gear: 9 draws
FA: Kyle Copeland, Charlie Fowler, Marc Hirt, 1988

❏ **128. IMPASSE** 5.12+ 110'
A crack/seam system. Climb past a couple of pins then work right, past two more pins, and join *Mud Flaps*.
FA: Kyle Copeland

❏ **129. WALK ON THE WIDE SIDE** 5.10 90'
Striking splitter offwidth.
Gear: 3.0–6.0 (and a pair of Carhartts)
FA: Peter Gallagher

❏ **130. ARMAGEDDON** 5.12a/b 50'
Just left of the *Walk on the Wide Side*. A face route that meanders right.
Gear: 5 draws
FA: Linus Platt

❏ **131. UNKNOWN** 5.? 90'
A seam between *Armageddon* and *Jacob's Ladder*.
Gear: 8 draws

❏ **132. JACOB'S LADDER** 5.10+ 40'
Gear: 4 draws
FA: Jake Tradiak

❏ **133. SHADOWFAX** 5.11- 50'
Gear: 5 draws
FA: Kyle Copeland, Bego Gerhart

❏ **134. POTSTASH** 5.9+ 60' ★★★
(Aka *Little Thailand*) A roadcut at the extreme left end of Wall Street. Climb bulges up blasted stone. Popular.
Gear: 5 draws
FA: Keith Reynolds

❏ **135. WHITE WAY** 5.11 100' ★★
Twenty feet left of *Potstash*. Friction up a rounded fin with distinctive white calcite.
Gear: 4 draws
FA: Peter Gallagher, Kyle Copeland, Layton Kor

Left of *White Way*, there are a few more routes that have been climbed. They are not listed here because they climb over or very close to petroglyphs. People, there are over 130 routes in one linear mile, please be respectful and don't climb over the petroglyphs!!!

The William's Bottom Campground is 5.3 miles from the 191/Potash intersection, just after Wall Street. There are 17 drive-in sites, each with fire pits, picnic tables and space for two cars, two tents, six people max. Animals must be tied up. Two bathrooms, one dumpster. There's no drinking water and no hook-ups. Quiet hours are 10 pm to 6 am; cost is $8 per night.

Potash Road

Beyond Wall Street, the roadside cliffs continue as the canyon meanders downstream, but without anything like the same concentration of quality climbs that Wall Street offers. There are, however, a few climbs, and one gem.

8.5 Miles

Approach: Drive 8.5 miles from the Potash Rd/191 intersection. Park on the left side of the road. Look for a right-facing dihedral starting from a bench. Scramble from the left or the right to access the route.

❏.1 **WHERE EGOS DARE** 5.10+ 70' ★★★★
This is my wife's favorite route along the road. It is mostly hands to off-fingers in an arcing, right-facing corner.
Gear: 0.75–2.0, optional extra fingers-size piece just before the anchors
FA Kyle Copeland

Michelle Kelley on *Where Egos Dare*

Gold Bar Camping is at 9.8 miles from the 191/Potash intersection, on the left side of the road, next to the river. There are four group sites, each with a bathroom. There is a $12 minimum per site. Reservations: phone 435.259.2100. Sites, if not reserved, are available for use. There are three big awnings, one dumpster and a boat ramp.

Spur of the Moment Tower

This tower is easily seen, directly across the river from the Gold Bar Camping area. The only existing route to the summit is named for Maribel Loveridge, who died in an avalanche in the La Sal Mountains in February 1992.

❏ 2. **THE LOVERIDGE** 5.12 C2 ★★★ ✨W
Linus Platt believes this has not seen a second ascent but feels it's very worthy and may possibly go free. Enjoy your adventure.
FA: Kyle Copeland, Linus Platt, Marc Hirt

Kyle Copeland on the FA, Linus Platt photo

SPUR OF THE MOMENT

CULVERT CANYON

Culvert Canyon is a side canyon located at 10.1 miles, just beyond Corona Arch. It has a few cragging routes, a few towers and some pretty good bouldering in a cool cave. Park in a small pull-out in front of the culvert.

If you are heading to the Ninja Training Center, walk through the culvert and follow a wash to the cave (five minutes). For the Layton's Tower area and adjacent routes, instead of walking through the culvert, head up and right to the railroad tracks, then walk down the tracks to some big boulders pockmarked with bullet holes. Locate a gate on the left to get through the cattle fence if you are heading toward the Layton's Tower area.

Block Tower Area

Beyond the cattle fence, look for a path that accesses the bottom of Layton's Tower. The *Southeast Face* is on the right side of the tower. For the cragging routes, walk up the talus on the left side of the tower. Routes are listed from right to left.

1. SOUTHEAST FACE 5.11 ★★★ SE
Excellent rock, aside from a couple of very loose sections. The 20-foot roof on the first pitch is exceptional.
P1: Start up loose rock, past a bolt 10 feet up. Climb a thin-hands slot through the first overhang to jugs. Jam a fist-crack through the second roof to a vertical 5.10 offwidth above to a bolted belay (5.11).
P2: Climb 5.10 offwidth/squeeze through a weird flake. Where the crack splits, go left to a small ledge. Go up and left (some loose rock) to an unprotected 5.8 corner which gains a big ledge and two-bolt belay (5.10).
P3: Scramble to the summit, downclimb to the ledge.
Descent: Rappel the route in one 60-meter rappel or two shorter ones.
Gear: 2 sets of cams from 0.5 to 4.0
FA: Paul Irby, Ben Folsom

The next five routes are just left of Block Tower in a west-facing alcove. Routes are described right to left.

2. ROUNDHEAD RUCKUS 5.10 W
Two pitches to the top. Not recommended, as the climb wanders past some very dangerous blocks.
FA: Bob Novellino, Tom Gilje, 1994

3. UNNAMED CORNER 5 11 45' ★★★ W
Start off stacked blocks in a right-facing corner. A knee jam gains steep fingers (look for face features). Rest at a small ledge at the switching corners. Punch it up the left-facing corner. Clipping the chains can feel rough.
Gear: 0.0 TCU–0.75
FA: Eric Decaria

4. EL NACHO 5.9 95' ★★ W
A left-facing corner that starts with some tighter hands. Climb past some blocks on lower-angle terrain and back into a steeper hands corner. Finish things off with a mantel in a notch looking down the opposite side of the tower. Fun climbing. On the upper part of the climb you can see through the crack to the other side. Gets morning shade.
Gear: 1.0–3.0
FA: Todd Marder, Millie Birdwell, 1994

5. FINGER FOOD 5.9 70' ★★★ SW
Start off the block. Climb the left-facing corner with hands. Some cool stemming brings you to the obvious flake. Fun, wider moves bring you around the flake to the anchor.
Gear: 0.5-4.0
FA: Todd Marder, Millie Birdwell, 1994

6. LK & KC 5.9 (SW
Three pitches to the summit of the formation behind the Block Tower.
P1: Start with a tricky offwidth move. Continue up the arching splitter (5.9) with varied climbing to the belay.
P2: Lots of big hands and offwidth.
P3: Third class to a groove, loose 5.5 to the summit.
Descent: Rappel 180 feet back down pitch 3. Walk down the bench.
Gear: 1.0-6.0 (heavy on big cams for P2)
FA: Thought to be Layton Kor, Kyle Copeland

Potash Road

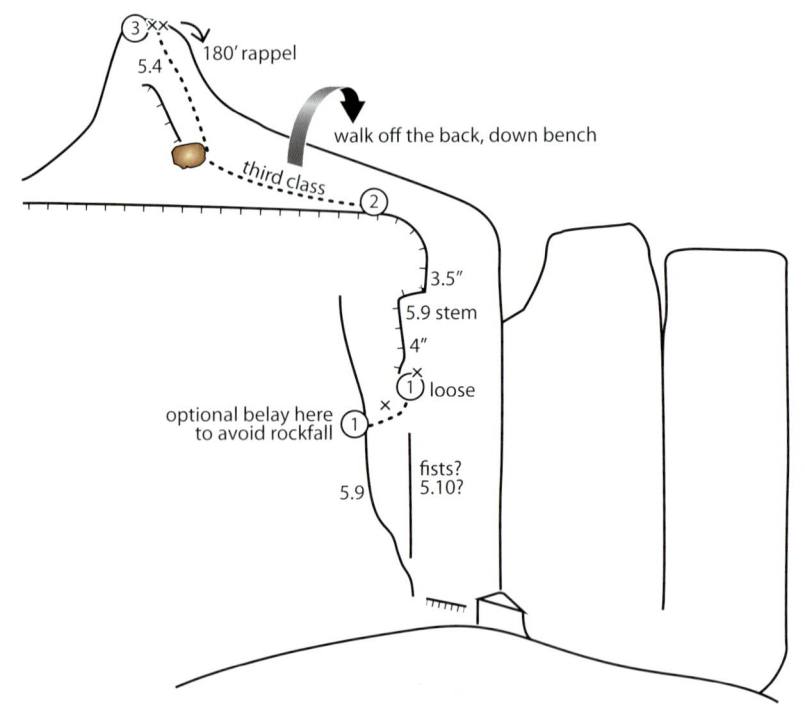

BLOCK TOWER

180' rappel
5.4
walk off the back, down bench
third class
3.5"
5.9 stem
4"
loose
optional belay here to avoid rockfall
fists? 5.10?
5.9

Mirek Hladik loving the *Finger Food* 5.9

GOLD BAR TOWER AREA

To access Gold Bar Tower, hike up to the railroad tracks and head left until you see a wire fence with a gap in it (left above the wash). Walk along the rim of the wash. After about 15 minutes you should be able to see Gold Bar Tower, and an intereresting-looking "hang nail" nearby. Keep walking a bit farther past the hang nail for Gold Bar Tower.

❏ 1. **HANG NAIL** 5.8 45'
The rock is not exactly killer Wingate but climbing is fun and there are some sweet photo opportunities. Climb the far side, between the formation and the main wall.
Gear: single set

Gold Bar Tower S

❏ 2. **DRAGON'S BREATH** 5.12 120' ★★
This is the only crack on the south face. Climb fingers then hard face moves before an unprotected 5.8 traverse right on small (and crumbling!) holds. Finish with a nice hand- and big-hands crack. Tricky gear anchor on top.
Descent: Downclimb to the east, rap from fixed anchors above the Fort Knox route (single 70m rope).
Gear: double set from small tips to big hands, 2 draws, extra thin-hands pieces for the summit anchor

Michelle Kelley rapping

NINJA TRAINING CENTER

This beautiful bouldering area is a five-minute walk beyond the culvert near the wash's end. Thanks to Zack Smith for the beta.

❏ 1. **ZEN GARDEN** V10 ★★★
The classic line following the crack.
FA: Dean Potter

❏ 2. **THE FLYING GUILLOTINE** V8 ★★★
Starts on flat edges and goes out a series of rails and ends at a big jug crack. An extension goes to the top but was never finished. It's probably V9.
FA: Zack Smith

❏ 3. **THE SHAOLIN FINGER JAB** V7 ★★★
Sit start to an obvious pocket then to a jug and a committing topout.
FA: Zack Smith

❏ 4. **THE VIETCONG DOUBLE CLUTCH** V7 ★★★★
A mega dyno to a committing topout over pungi-stick-like tree branches.
FA: Zack Smith

To the right lies the Black Belt area with a bunch of crispy warm-ups.

Noah Bigwood on *Zen Garden*. Photo: Eric Odenthal

Potash Road

Day Canyon

Pete Rensing on *Pocket Rocket* 5.10

DAY CANYON

Day Canyon is super awesome! Most of the routes here are long, fun, and really good quality. The climbs are a bit spread out but it's well worth the effort finding them.
Approach: At 11.4 miles from the Potash Rd/Hwy 191 intersection, park on the roadside. Head into the canyon through a tunnel of willows and tamarisk until you hit a wash, then follow this wash into the canyon. *Pocket Rocket* will be seen on the right. Farther up the wash you will hit an old mining road. For routes far up the canyon, like Mission Tower, there is an alternative approach from the top, described on page 140.
Routes are described from the bottom to top of the canyon.

1. POCKET ROCKET 5.10c 70' ★★★ S
Huecos? Solid? In the desert? Hell, yeah! After a bouldery start, climb overhanging buckets for the first two bolts. Getting above the second is a reachy crux. The rest of the way is a cruise on swiss cheese, except the clipping-the-chains move where your feet disappear. Really fun route.
Gear: 8 quickdraws excluding the anchors.
FA: Tom Perkins

The next three routes are on the left side of the canyon just before some slickrock in the drainage.

2. KISS OF THE SPIDER WOMEN 5.12 80' ★★★★ NW
Start in a right-facing corner. Go through some broken rock into a fingers corner. Take a deep breath, undercling and lieback a flake to the anchor … exhale!
Gear: blue TCU–3.0 with extra 0.5
FA: Jimmy Dunn, Craig Luebben, Lisa Hathaway

3. WORKING CLASS HERO 5.9 65' ★★★ N
A slabby, left-arcing, fingers splitter.
Gear: #1 TCU–0.75
FA: Kyle Copeland

4. UNNAMED 5.9 60' ★ N
The next climb right of *Working Class Hero*. Thin hands to off-fingers splitter. Good climbing on mostly good rock (a bit loose at the top, should clean up).
Gear: 0.4–3.0

The next three routes are across the canyon on the right, just up from the previous routes. SW

5. CHICKEN TEJERO 5.11 ★★
Left-facing corner. Starts wide and steep, passing a bolt. Then the angle eases off; cruise with tight hands and off-fingers to a final fingers bulge.
Gear: 0.3–2.0
FA: Dave Medara

6. KENTUCKY BROWN WATER A2
A three-pitch aid route up a prominent flake feature, not described here in detail but useful as a landmark.

7. BEE LINE 5.10+ 90' ★★
A bouldery start on suspect rock leads to splitter going through the sizes. Steep.
Gear: 0.0–4.0
FA: Katy Cassidy, Earl Wiggins, 1988

8. JUNE'S BOX 5.10 70' ★★ SW
Left-facing, loose corner for a body-length to a stem-box with tips.
Gear: Blue TCU–1.0 (heavy on tips)
FA: K3

9. CONCEPCIÓN 5.13- 220' ★★★★★ W-SW
This was an obscure two-pitch aid route called *Acromaniac* until Dean Potter gave it a free ascent (in one pitch) and a new name. Since then there have been a few more free ascents. Without a doubt a very eye-pleasing line—if you can imagine it without a gazillion tick marks!
Gear: Double set Metolius 0.0–3.0 (heavy on 0.75s)
FA: Kyle Copeland. FFA: Dean Potter

On the wall just behind the towers there are four sweet routes across the canyon from *Concepcion*. These are listed right to left. NE

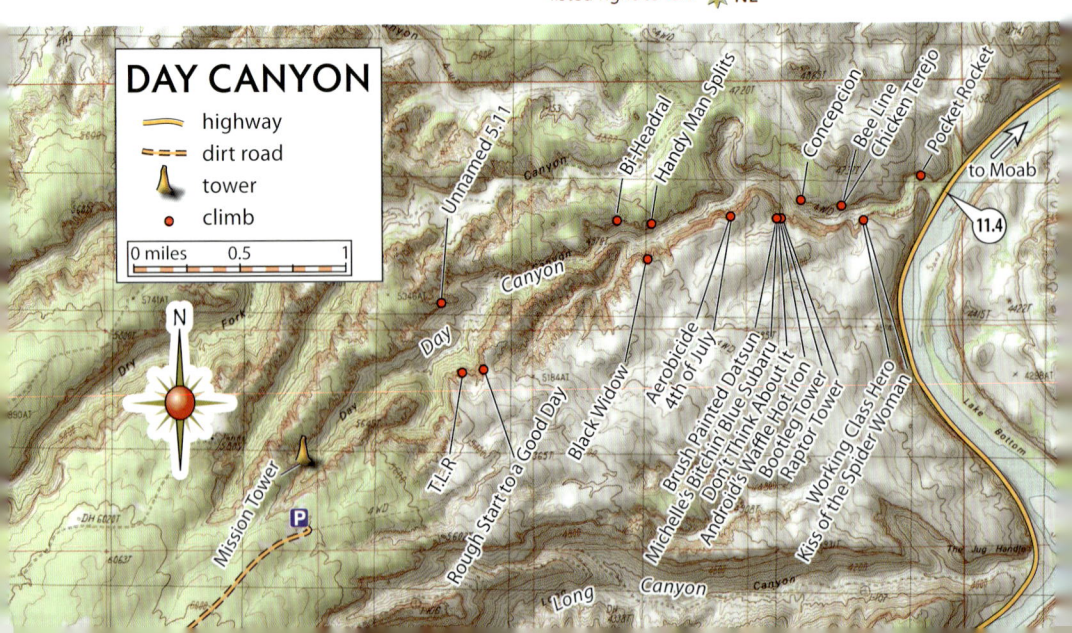

Day Canyon

❏ 10. **BRUSH-PAINTED DATSUN** 5.10 95' ★★★★★
Climb up and onto a bench and climb a killer hands flake that pinches down to off-fingers just before the anchors. Money!!
Gear: 0.75–3.0
FA: Kyle Copeland

❏ 11. **CHRISTINE'S WAY-BUFF SAAB** 5.9 60' ★
Same start as *Brush-Painted Datsun*, but veer left through a set of mantels then onto a right-facing corner with hands.
Gear: 0.5–2.0
FA: Kyle Copeland

❏ 12. **MICHELLE'S BITCHIN' BLUE SUBARU** 5.10+ 135' ★★★★
Start by climbing *Christine's Way Buff Saab*, pass the anchor and keep cruising. Pass a short section of fist, continue with steep off-fingers to a rest. Go through the pod with fingers and continue up using face holds protected by tips-size gear in a splitter to the anchor. Descent: rappel with two ropes or make two rappels via the anchors of *Christine's Way Buff Saab*.
Gear: #1 TCU–4.0
FA: K3

❏ 13. **FINGER BANDIT** 5.12 55' ★★★★
Splitter fingers to off-finger and tips in a white shield.
Gear: purple TCU–0.75
FA: Ben Riley; FFA: Zack Alberts

❏ 14. **ANDROIDS WAFFLE HOT LINE** 5.10+ ★★★★
P1: Mostly splitter big-hands and fist with some stems in a right-facing corner.
P2: A big-hands double crack leads to a crack switch with fingers. Then clip the chains.
FA: Kyle Copeland, Eric Johnson

Across the way from *Concepción* there are two obvious towers, Bootleg and Raptor.

Bootleg Tower

Approach as for *Brush-Painted Datsun* and keep walking up the hill. Bootleg is the smaller and closer of the towers. *Moonshine* is closer, *Buzz Lust* farther.

❏ 15. **MOONSHINE** 5.10+ ★★
Start between the tower and the wall behind. Stem past four bolts, then ascend a crack up and right of the bolt line. At the horizontal, go left to the obvious crack and summit.
Descent: Single-rope rappel
Gear: 4 draws, 1.0–3.5
FA: Eric Bjørnstad, Ron Wiggle, Terry McKenna, 1974

❏ 16. **BUZZ LUST** 5.12 100' ★★★
Hard face climbing. The route starts on the south-facing side (facing Raptor Tower) for the first bolt, then moves left and climbs the west face the rest of the way.
Gear: A dozen draws
FA: Kevin Chase

Raptor Tower

❏ 17. **PROHIBITION CRACK** 5.11+
Start on the north side of the tower.
P1: Climb the wide, splitter crack. A few chockstones provide the occasional reprieve from the grunting. Climb past the final chockstone to the bolted belay ledge (5.10+, 120').
P2: Hard offwidth and chimney, past a few fixed pieces. At the top of the chimney, face climb left over to a finger-to-fist crack and gear belay (5.11+, 100').
P3: Face climb up and left past a couple bolts (and some lichen, to spice things up for ya!) to the summit belay bolt (5.11+, 30').
Gear: 4.0s and up... up to a blue Big Bro. Bring a few smaller pieces for the belay atop P2. Also bring a couple quickdraws, shoulder-length slings, and a healthy appetite for the wide.
FA: Keith Reynolds, Alan Stevenson

❏ 18. **BOOGNISH TOWER** 5.10 100' ★★
Bolted chimney requiring various chimney techniques.
Gear: 15 draws
FA: Paul Bucher, Taylor Bond, Drake Buckingham

Potash Road

The next three routes are accessed by hiking up-canyon for a few minutes. They are on the left. You can see *Another Fine Day*'s anchor from the main trail. *Fourth of July* is 20 feet right of this and facing up the canyon. *Aerobicide* is just up-canyon, facing toward the highway.

19. ANOTHER FINE DAY 5.10 ★ N
This right-facing corner is easily seen from the trail. A hard start on less-than-perfect rock turns to hands.
FA: Joel Hickok

20. FOURTH OF JULY 5.10 ★★ NW
Start in a right-facing corner. Climb big hands to a body-length of offwidth. Continue with big hands and hands to a rest on a ledge. Work your way to the left splitter (hands to off-fingers) to the chains.
Gear: 0.75–4.0
FA: K3

21. AEROBICIDE 5.11+ ★★★★★ NE
P1: Start with a big-hands splitter which quickly pinches down to tight hands. When it pinches even more, switch cracks, and climb off-fingers and back to tight hands to the belay
P2: Mostly offwidth.
Descent: Two raps with a single 70m rope.
Gear: (P1) 0.75–3.0 (P2) 2.0–5.0 (heavy on 4.0s)
FA: Kyle Copeland, Carl Diedrich

The next four routes are on the right side of the canyon a little way beyond *Aerobicide*. *Handy Man Splits* is easy to spot; it faces up-canyon, so as you walk by it will be visible behind you. A few minutes more walking gets you to *Bihedral*, which follows a beautiful and very obvious stembox. The unnamed 5.11 is very close to *Bihedral*.

22. HANDY MAN SPLITS 5.10 65' ★★★ W
Stem the right-facing corner eventually climbing a hands splitter in the right wall (this wall faces up-canyon). This crack thins down to off-fingers just before the chains.
Gear: #2 Friend–3.0
FA: Carl Diedrich

23. BIHEDRAL 5.10 130' ★★★★ SW
Really cool climbing! Start up a right-facing corner with big hands, traverse left to the bottom of the obvious stembox. If you are not comfortable back cleaning your gear then set a belay here. Otherwise continue climbing. Awesome stems almost all the way, using everything from fingers to knees. Super fun!!
Descent: two 60m ropes.
Gear: 0.5–6.0
FA: Kyle Copeland

24. UNNAMED 5.11 100' ★★★ SW
This is located behind a pillar, not far left from *Bihedral*, in a left-facing corner. Bouldery moves access a flare with tight hands in a slot. After the slot, continue with a short splitter section past a scary block (more secure than it appears) then into a left-facing flake with tight hands and off-fingers. Great climb!
Gear: 0.5–3.0

25. BLACK WIDOW 5.12- 165' ★ N
Left-facing corner in whitish rock. A bit silty. Start with tips and fingers. When this cracks seams out, face climb past a bolt to a hand section and some funky rock with a bolt. Continue through 10 feet of offwidth to 30 feet of clean off-fingers.
Gear: Tips-size cams up to 3.0, one big piece (old 5.0)
FA: Paul Irby

Steven Lucarelli on *Aerobicide* 5.11+

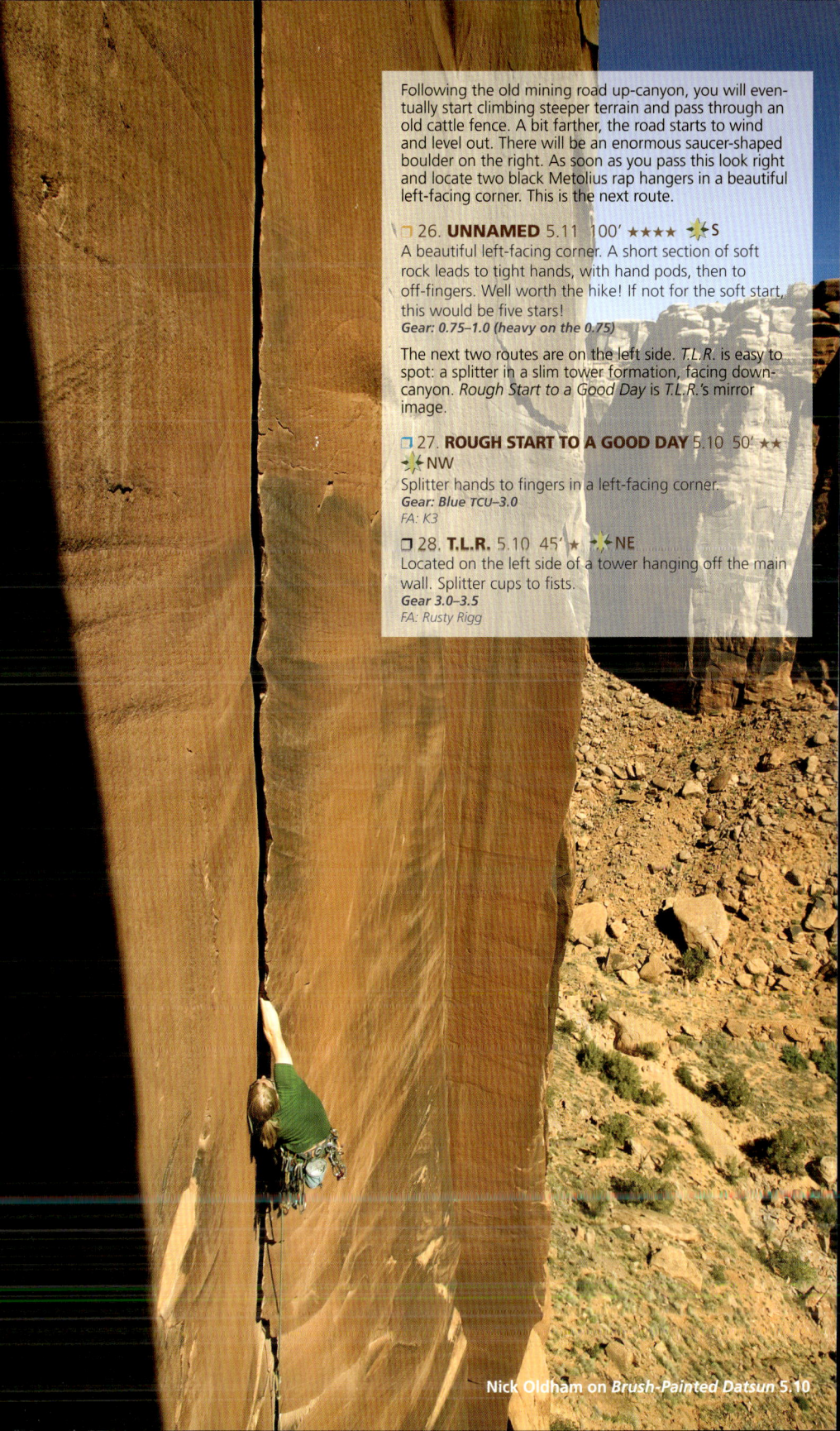

Following the old mining road up-canyon, you will eventually start climbing steeper terrain and pass through an old cattle fence. A bit farther, the road starts to wind and level out. There will be an enormous saucer-shaped boulder on the right. As soon as you pass this look right and locate two black Metolius rap hangers in a beautiful left-facing corner. This is the next route.

☐ 26. **UNNAMED** 5.11 100' ★★★★ ☀ S
A beautiful left-facing corner. A short section of soft rock leads to tight hands, with hand pods, then to off-fingers. Well worth the hike! If not for the soft start, this would be five stars!
Gear: 0.75–1.0 (heavy on the 0.75)

The next two routes are on the left side. *T.L.R.* is easy to spot: a splitter in a slim tower formation, facing down-canyon. *Rough Start to a Good Day* is *T.L.R.*'s mirror image.

☐ 27. **ROUGH START TO A GOOD DAY** 5.10 50' ★★ ☀ NW
Splitter hands to fingers in a left-facing corner.
Gear: Blue TCU–3.0
FA: K3

☐ 28. **T.L.R.** 5.10 45' ★ ☀ NE
Located on the left side of a tower hanging off the main wall. Splitter cups to fists.
Gear 3.0–3.5
FA: Rusty Rigg

Nick Oldham on *Brush-Painted Datsun* 5.10

Mission Tower

Approach: This is a long walk from Potash Road—not recommended. The first ascent team drove in on dirt roads above Day Canyon, rapped in, and jugged out. An old cowboy path bypasses the rappel, and is described here. There are two driving approaches:

1. From Maverick Buttress in Long Canyon, drive 1.8 miles up-canyon, turn right. Drive through a big graded clearing, continue straight over some rougher road. One mile from the main Long Canyon road there is a fork; don't go right, stay straight, a short distance later the road ends. Park here. In front you should see the head of Day Canyon.

2. From Hwy 313, drive 13.7 miles to the left turn heading toward Deadhorse Point. Reset your odometer here. Drive 1.3 miles, turn left onto a dirt road (this is the top of the Long Canyon road). Head down this road. At 4.9 miles, take another left and follow this road through the clearing, continuing straight. At a fork, keep going straight to the end of the road and the head of Day Canyon.

The Cowboy Trail: From the parking, a short walk around to the other side leads to a trail down the slickrock into the canyon. It's a 10–15 minute hike.

29. STICK TO THE MISSION 5.11 ★★★ SW

Named for the Todd Skinner mantra, "Stick to the mission!" Start on the southwest face.
P1: Climb mostly hands in a shallow right-facing corner on softish rock to a bolted belay.
P2: Some challenging and fun face moves lead right, past a bolt, to the obvious splitter. This starts with hands and goes through the sizes until you are into offwidth. Continue into a wide pod. Exit this via a steep bombay move, then more offwidth leads to a spacious belay ledge. Gear belay with 0.75–2.0.
P3: Follow the obvious, easy chimney with some soft rock to the summit.
Gear 0.75–6.0 (heavy on the big stuff), long slings, draws
FA: Sam Lightner, Josh Gross

Nice timing, boyz. I scoped this from the rim, saw no anchors, and came back three days later with the drill and gear ... BAM, IT WAS ALREADY DONE!

Roadside Select—Day Canyon to Long Canyon SSE

Between Day Canyon and Long Canyon are some selected pitches along the main road.

12.0 Miles

❏ 1. **UNO MO-MO** 5.10 45' ★★
Tight fingers in a right-facing corner that turns into shallow offwidth with fingers in the back. Finish by traversing right to the anchor.
Gear: 0.3–4.5
FA: Ron Olevsky

❏ 2. **DOS MO-MOS** 5.10 90'
Steep right-facing corner. Fingers to stacks, finishing on a ledge with anchors.
Gear: 0.4–3.0 (5.0 helpful)
FA: Kyle Copeland

❏ 3. **SKINWALKER** 5.11+ 110' ★★★★★
A locals' favorite, for sure!! A quick approach across the railroad tracks brings you to the base. Climb huecos and edges past two bolts. At the second bolt, traverse right to the base of the splitter. It begins with fingers and goes through the sizes; up a barndoor offset to steep hands out a large pod to the anchor.
Gear: 0.4–2.0 (bring a few extra #2 Friends)
FA: Jay Smith

❏ 4. **SAY YOUR PRAYERS** 5.13? ★★★
Still not freed yet. This is the line just left of *Skinwalker*. GOOD LUCK!

12.4 Miles

❏ 5. **OFFWIDTHS ARE BEAUTIFUL** 5.10 175'
★★★★
Two pitches. Aka *Frenchy's Nightmare*. A classic Craig Luebben creation.
P1: Wide the whole way. Right-facing 5.9 and 5.10 offwidth, easy to layback with a toprope, hard to lead. Belay from bolts inside of the pillar. There are probably some big cam placements if you have any left.
P2: Chimney to the top between the pillar and the main wall. No worthwhile pro, 5.8.
Gear: P1: mostly 4.0–6.0. P2: some poor purple and blue TCUs
FA: Craig Luebben, Sari Schmetterer, Earl Wiggins, Katy Cassidy, George Hurley, 1988

Inset: Adeline Guay on *Skinwalker* 5.11+

Jay Anderson on *Offwidths are Beautiful* 5.10
Photo: Andrew Burr

DESERT BISTRO

Casual fine dining in the heart of downtown Moab

Reservations recommended: www.desertbistro.com/reservations
Open seasonally Tuesday – Sunday at 5:30pm, closed Mondays

36 South 100 West, Moab, UT | (435) 259-0756

Long Canyon

Pamela Shanti Pack on *Sidewinder* 5.11+   Photo: Andrew Burr

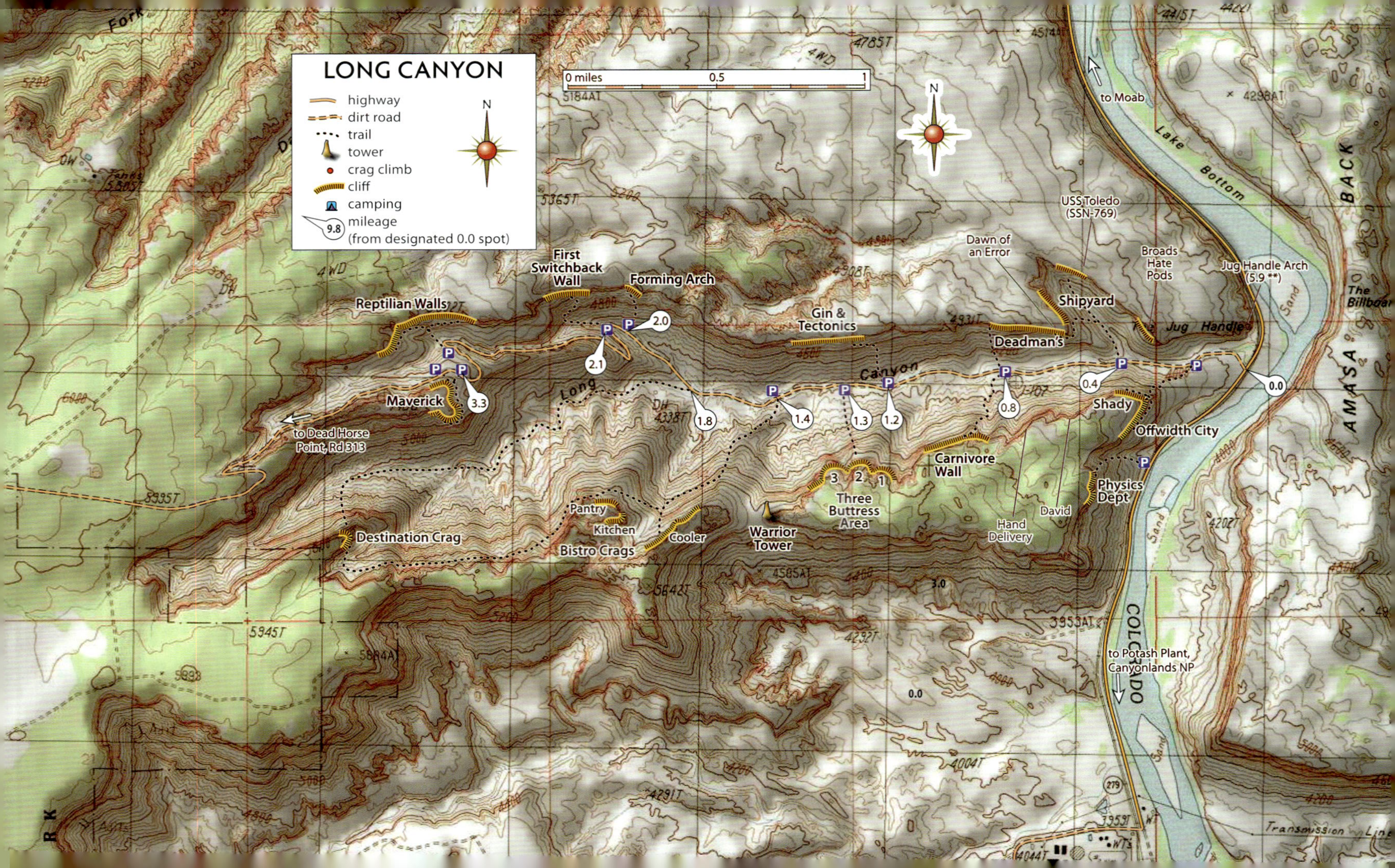

LONG CANYON
highway
dirt road
trail
tower
crag climb
cliff
camping
mileage
(from designated 0.0 spot)
9.8
N
0 miles
0.5
1
to Moab
Lake Bottom
BACK
AMASA
The Billbgar
USS Toledo (SSN-769)
Broads Hate Pods
Jug Handle Arch (5.9 **)
Jug Handle
Dawn of an Error
Shipyard
Deadman's
Gin & Tectonics
Long Canyon
First Switchback Wall
Forming Arch
Reptilian Walls
Maverick
to Dead Horse Point, Rd 313
Destination Crag
Pantry
Kitchen
Bistro Crags
Cooler
Warrior Tower
Three Buttress Area
3
2
1
Carnivore Wall
Hand Delivery
David
Physics Dept
Shady
Offwidth City
0.0
0.4
0.8
1.2
1.3
1.4
1.8
2.0
2.1
3.3
COLORADO
to Potash Plant, Canyonlands NP
Transmission Line
4WD
Sand

LONG CANYON

Long Canyon. Without a doubt my favorite place to crag in Moab! The rock is generally excellent Wingate and the views are outstanding even by Utah standards. This canyon fills all my needs: there is plenty of shade on the left side to keep me busy in the summer months and plenty of sun on the right for the cooler days. There are some amazingly long pitches here, on both sides of the canyon, as well as some rim shots.
Crags and routes are listed starting with the right side of the canyon from bottom to top, then the left side of the canyon from bottom to top.
Approach: Jug Handle Arch looms over the road, 13.5 miles from the intersection of Potash Road and Hwy 191. Take a right here into Long Canyon. RESET YOUR ODOMETER.

LONG CANYON RIGHT SIDE

When you first pull in and cross the tracks there is a parking spot on the left side. Park here if you want to climb the routes on the right before reaching the Shipyard, Jug Handle Arch, Porcupine Flake, an unknown 5.8 chimney, and the 5.10 splitter. Detailed descriptoins for these routes are not included. Just beyond this parking is the much higher quality Shipyard.

Shipyard

The Shipyard is a horseshoe-shaped alcove of prime Wingate. Parking for the Shipyard is at 0.4 miles on the left side of the road, just past the entrance to the Shipyard. Routes are listed first on the right side from front to back, then left side front to back.

SHIPYARD RIGHT SIDE SW
The first two routes are located at the front right of the Shipyard and just a few feet from each other. Then there is a large gap between the next climbs which are located at the back of the Shipyard. If you are going to climb the cluster of climbs in the back, it is easiest to walk along the bottom of the drainage until an obvious cairned trail brings you through the talus to the bottom of the climbs.

❐ 1. **BUTT PYGMIES** 5.11 60' ★★
A cool line, with a neat pod/chimney feature. Climb the pod to a small off-fingers roof, pull into a right-facing corner with off-fingers to tight hands.
Gear: 0.3–2.0, heavy on the off-fingers, big piece optional

❐ 2. **BROADS HATE PODS** 5.10+ 80'
A fun but awkward climb. Begin on face moves with sidepulls and good feet. Step left into the main crack, continue up a flaring crack which takes off-fingers pro. Work up and through the pods. Chockstones in the first pod are solid. It seems like no matter which way you are facing, you wish you were facing the other way.
Gear: Blue TCU–5.0 (heavier on the off-fingers)
FA: Topher Donahue

❐ 3. **NIGHT VISION** 5.11+ 120'
Near the center of Shipyard Right this route features a flake and some face climbing.
Gear: 0.0–4.0
FA: Josh Gross, Ralph Ferrara

❐ 4. **SHIPWRECKED** 5.10 80' ★★
Climb the left side of a pillar leaning against the wall.
Gear: Blue TCU–3.0
FA: Kevin Chase

❐ 5. **USS TOLEDO (SSN-769)** 5.11+ 120' ★★★
One crack system left of *Shipwrecked*. Locate two bolts protecting face moves to a small left-facing corner. Climb the face then move right into an offwidth flake. Make an offwidth move around the flake and pull into hands narrowing to less-than-tips then back to hands.
Descent: Rap the route. A single 70m rope just barely makes it.
Gear: double set from gray TCU through 2.0 with extra less-than-tips, (1)4.0, offset nuts useful, draws
FA: Herb Crimp

THE SHIPYARD

LEFT   RIGHT

Tom Gwinn on *Dawn of an Error* 5.11

Long Canyon

❏ **6. TORPEDO BAY** 5.12 60' ★★★★★
Splitter fingers to off-fingers.
Gear: 0.4–0.75
FA: Eric Decaria

❏ **7. NINA** 5.10+ 60' ★★
Start in a left-facing corner. Steep cups/fists turns to hands, then to a fingers splitter.
Gear: 0.5–3.5
FA: Eric Decaria

❏ **8. ELECTRONIC BATTLESHIP** 5.10 60' ★★
Good rock! Splitter fingers to fist. Actually, for most people, just a bit bigger than fist.
Gear: 0.5–4.0
FA: Kevin Chase

❏ **9. ALBERTS-WEBSTER** 5.12+ 150' ★★★★
Slopey face climbing on white rock, featuring a mandatory, all-points-off sideways dyno.
Gear: 18 bolts
FA: Zach Alberts, James Webster

SHIPYARD LEFT SIDE E

Approach: Start hiking into the drainage, as for Shipyard Right. Just inside the Shipyard is a large boulder. From the boulder, locate a trail leading toward Deadman's Buttress (the cliff just left of and outside the Shipyard). Start hiking this trail but veer off rightward just before reaching the cliff. Walk along the base to your route.
Routes are listed left to right.

❏ **1. STEWING OVER ART** 5.12- 100' ★★★★
A steep, shallow right-facing corner, mostly off-fingers.
Gear: 0.3–0.5
FA: Stuart Ruckman, Bret Ruckman, 1988

❏ **2. UNNAMED** 5.12d A0 ★★
Splitter with a funky traverse to another splitter. Mostly tight hands and fingers. Not yet freed?
FA: Marco Cornacchione

❏ **3. THE PROUDEST MONKEY** 5.12 ★★★★
Three pitches, sweet line.
P1: A fingers splitter leads to a pod. Here, switch to another splitter on the right. Follow this, fingers/off-fingers, to a small belay ledge with bolts (5.12, 65').
P2: Climb a roof, then hands/big hands up a crack. Belay in an obvious pod on the right wall (5.10, 65').
P3: Exit the pod with good, steep hands into a flare with more hands and big hands. Pass the roof on its left side (5.11, 75').
Descent: Rap the route with double 60m.
Gear: P1: 0.3–0.75, P2 & 3: 1.0–4.0
FA: Steve "Roadie" Seats

❏ **4. APE INDEX** 5.10+ 65' ★★★
Really fun. Start under a right-facing corner. Fingers and off-fingers gain a square slot with more off-fingers. Exit the slot with some funky, cool, reachy moves up to a flake. Climb the flake past a bolt then clip the anchor.
Gear: blue TCU–1 (heavy on 0.75), quickdraw
FA: K3

❏ **5. UNKNOWN** 5.13 ★★★
A shallow right-facing corner with a sweet finger crack. This line is super pleasing to the eye... but looks very hard. A bolt at the start suggests this was a rope solo first ascent.
Gear: A ton of fingers/off-fingers
FA: Mason Earle

❏ **6. THE 100TH MONKEY** 5.11 65' ★★★
This, the last climb in Shipyard Left, takes a shallow left-facing corner that starts behind a pillar. To get to the start, walk past the climb, scramble up to a "sidewalk" and traverse back to the base. Start in a cool slot, hands, continue with off-fingers and tight hands to a final slot with hands in the back.
Gear: 0.75–3.0

Proudest Monkey 5.12

Herb Crimp on Torpedo Bay 5.12

Deadman's Buttress ☀S

Deadman's Buttress is the section of cliff just left and up-canyon of the Shipyard entrance. It extends for nearly half a mile along the right side of the canyon (from about 0.4–0.8 miles). Pamela Pack has recently added two new routes between routes 4 and 5: *The Dark Passenger (5.12)* and *Tooth Fairy (5.10+)*. Routes are listed right to left. Two access methods exist:
1. For the routes at the right (Shipyard) end of the cliff, park as for the Shipyard and start hiking on the same trail. Just inside the entrance to the Shipyard there is a large boulder. Here, a trail splits off to the left and scrambles through and over some lower cliffy sections. Follow this faint path to the base of the cliff.
2. For the left end of the cliff (*Program Director* area) park at 0.8 miles. Ascend the obvious talus drainage (with a tree near its top) to the base of the cliff.

☐ 1. **SNAKES AND SNAILS** 5.11 90' ★
This easy-to-see line ascends the prow where Shipyard Left meets Deadman's Buttress. Mostly wide. Start with splitter hands to an offwidth. Then through a chimney with a rough exit, finally back to hands.
Gear: 2.0–6.0, Big Bros, heavy on big stuff
FA: Michael Dorsey, Keith Gotschall

☐ 2. **PUPPIES AND TAILS** 5.11- 90' ★
The wide counterpart to *Snakes and Snails*. Shares anchor.
FA: Michael Dorsey, Keith Gotschall

☐ 3. **FUNNEL CAKE** 5.8 70'
Hands lead to a squeeze/dihedral with fingers.
Gear: 0.4–2.0
FA: Tom Perkins

☐ 4. **FIST TO CUFFS** 5.11b 70' ★★
A splitter hand-crack to a bulge with big hands. Tunnel through a hole to a splitter that gains the anchor.
Gear: 1.0–4.0 (heavy on 3.0 & 3.5)
FA: Tom Perkins

☐ 5. **DRAGON'S LAIR** 5.11 140'
Another wide one! Grunt and bleed through bulges.
Gear: Mostly offwidth pieces
FA: Craig Luebben, Greg Murphy, 1994

☐ 6. **NECRO DANCER** 5.10+ 150' ★
Kinda dirty left-facing corner. All varieties of hands with some wide spots thrown in.
Gear: 1.0–4.5 (heavy on hands)
FA: Kyle Copeland, Sue Kemp, 1987

☐ 7. **ANGLE RUNNER** A2
Splitter, then, partway, switch to another splitter.

☐ 8. **DAWN OF AN ERROR** 5.11 85' ★★★★★
Sweet pitch! Start in a slot with big hands. Turn an overlap with hands then cruise through the sizes in a beautiful splitter in the middle of the shield. End with fingers at the first anchor (5.11) or keep going for 25 feet of fingers and tips (the rock deteriorates a bit) to the second anchor (5.11+).
Gear: 0.4–3.0 (heavy on your hard sizes)
FA: Kyle Copeland, Sue Kemp, 1987

☐ 9. **UNNAMED** 5.11 120' ★★
Start with fingers to a stembox. Stem to an overhang, pass this with fists and continue up an arcing offwidth.
Gear: 0.3-6.0 (heavy on the wide)

There is a gap of about 200 feet until the next route.

☐ 10. **UNNAMED** 5.10 50'
Climb some choss to a left-pointing, jutting flake. Pass the flake protecting with a wide piece.
Gear: 1.0–4.0

☐ 11. **UNNAMED** 5.10 190' ★★★
Two pitches, featuring a left-facing corner.
P1: Broken rock past a bolt to a hard-to-see anchor (60').
P2: Step left into a beautiful left-facing corner. Cruise with hands to a somewhat hidden double Metolious anchor on the left wall (130').
Gear: Blue TCU–3.0 (heavy on tight hands)

☐ 12. **TANK BRAIN** 5.12 ★★★
A tribute to Dave and Emma's late canine companion, Mr. Hobbs. Start by clipping two bolts, then head up a left-facing corner, finish with a fingers roof. Burly!
Gear: Yellow TCU–1.0 (heavy on yellow TCU size)
FA: Dave Medara

Long Canyon

☐ 13. CHALK IS CHEAP 5.12 ★★★★
Two pitches. Stars are for pitch 2, which takes a beautiful, bulging, dark, left-facing corner. Simply stellar!
P1: Meander up a face, past bolts to a stance with anchors (5.12).
P2: Pull a sweet bulge, hands, and continue up the left-facing corner with thinning hands (5.10+).
Gear: 7 draws, 0.3–3.5 (heavy on big hands)
FA: Kyle Copeland

☐ 14. MOCHA CHOCOLATE YAYA 5.9 60' ★
Climb broken rock to a slabby finish with fingers.
Gear: 0.4–2.0, couple shoulder-length slings
FA: Tom Perkins

☐ 15. DEAD RINGER 5.11+ 50'
This route is just right of the start to *Chopper*. Unfortunately, the start fell off. There are some large, light-colored blocks, once part of the route, at its bottom. Splitter fingers to a flake with tight hands.
Gear: #1 TCU–2.0
FA: Tom Perkins

☐ 16. CHOPPER 5.10+ 150' ★★★★★
Awesome! Start on a bench. Begin with big hands in a slot, then hands. Pass the belay and keep truckin. Long, left-facing, tight hands to off-fingers, to the anchor.
Gear: 0.75–3.5 (heavy on 2.0)
FA: Katy Cassidy, Carol Petrelli, Earl Wiggins, 1988

Looking up at the roof of *Get Over It* (#17)

☐ 17. GET OVER IT 5.12 C1 ★★★★
This is an excellent three-pitch extension to *Chopper*. Pitch 3 will likely go free in the near future.
P1: Climb *Chopper* (5.10+, 165').
P2: From the belay, walk right and clip a bolt. Down-climb from the ledge (an off-fingers piece for the follower?) then traverse right with pretty good holds. Reach around the arête and clip a second bolt. Move around the arête to a small, bolted stance (5.10+, 30').
P3: Traverse right on a hand-rail to a splitter. Start with some aid (blue TCUs, 0.3, C1). The crack widens to a section of bulging 0.4. After this bulge there is a small roof with better feet. Pass this roof with off-fingers (0.5). Another small roof requires more off-fingers (0.75s). More off-fingers gains a "thank god" hand jam and a bolted belay in a wedge (5.12,C1,65').
P4: The roof pitch. Climb tight hands in a right-facing corner, past a bolt, to the roof. Take a deep breath, start with tight hands and continue with hands and occasional feet. Pass a bolt and continue (exposed!) to the lip. Turn the lip (3.0 Camalot-size) and reach a bolted anchor (5.11, 70').
Descent: Rappel the route. Make sure to tie a tag line to the belay before the roof, so you can get back to the top of the splitter pitch. From atop the splitter pitch, a double rope (70m) rappel reaches the ground.
Gear: P1: 0.75–3.0 (heavy on 2.0). P2: 2 quickdraws, 0.75. P3: #1TCU–0.75 (heavy on fingers). P4: 2 quickdraws, 1.0–3.0 (4 each, minimum, recommended), tag line (70m)
FA: P1: K3, Joe Smith. P2: K3, Adeline Gauy. P3: K3, Paul Irby

DEADMAN'S BUTTRESS

| 23 Chasin' Skirt 5.10+ | 21 | 19 Program Director 5:10 | 18 | 16 Chopper 5.10+ | 15 Dead Ringer 5.11+ | 14 Mocha Chocolate Yaya 5.9 | 13 Chalk is Cheap 5.12 | 12 Tank Brain 5.12 | 11 Unnamed 5.10 |

Potash Road

18. UNNAMED SPLITTER 5.looks hard... 60'
Face climb past three bolts into a shallow left-facing corner with fingers. Then reach around the arête to a splitter that starts with tips and continues to hands.
Gear: 3 draws, tips–2.0

19. PROGRAM DIRECTOR 5.10 170' ★★★★★
A boulder problem on dubious rock gains a beautiful splitter. This starts out a bit tight (pass an abandoned belay station) but soon shifts gears into an epic big-hands journey to the anchor. Clip at your waist and save yourself from a heavy rope!
Gear: 0.75–3.0 (heavy on the 3.0s), optional tips piece at the boulder problem which won't keep you from hitting the deck but it will keep you from yard-sale-ing off the ledge from which you start)
FA: Katy Cassidy, Peter Gallagher, Earl Wiggins, 1988

20. UNNAMED 5.11 ★★
Start in a left-facing corner. Climb to double cracks on the left wall with off-fingers and tight hands. Move up and left past an overlap (drilled angle) to a short, ramping, left-facing corner to the anchor.
Gear: 0.3–3.0, 1 draw
FA: Jeff Ofsanko, the Betty sisters

21. CHASIN' SKIRT 5.10+ ★★★★
P1: Start in a shallow left-facing corner with hands. It soon turns into splitter with tight hands and some off-fingers. The rock quality does deteriorate a bit just before the anchor but this should not deter you from climbing this otherwise sweet splitter (65').
P2: Step left and climb left splitter with mostly fists to an anchor hidden in the obvious pod.
Gear: 0.75–4.0
FA: Jeff Ofsanko & the Betty sisters

22. SHIT EATIN' GRIN 5.12 ★★
A double crack system for two pitches. Face holds save the day at the really thin parts.
P1: Begin in a shallow right-facing corner/wedge which disappears, move right (fingers) and climb to the horizontal break with anchors (5.11+, 50').
P2: Climb the splitter above, with hands down to tips as the crack disappears. Move right to the other splitter and climb tips all the way up to some offwidth before clipping the anchor (5.12). Rap the route.
Gear: Tips to offwidth

23. TWO HEATHENS & THE PROPHET 5.12 90' ★★★
Not yet all free. With some traffic should be a fine route. Start by turning a low roof. Climb the left of a wide stembox with tight hands that go through the sizes down to fingernails. Clip a bolt and move to the right of the stembox before moving onto the arête and following it past seven bolts.
Gear: 0.0–1.0, 8 draws
FA: K3, Joe Smith, Jay Ackerman

Michelle Kelley on *Chasin' Skirt* 5.10+

Gin and Tectonics Area S

Drive 1.2 miles from Potash Road and park. Hike the obvious talus slope that allows access through a lower rockband. Above this band, trend left past a large, chossy pyramid formation. To identify *Gin and Tectonics* examine the rim top and locate a distinctive diving-board boulder hanging over the edge. There is a right-facing corner under this; this is *Gin and Tectonics*. Follow the corner all the way down and you will see where the route starts on a sloping bench. The routes in this area are long and generally very good! Routes are listed right to left.

☐ 1. **SPRING FLING** 5.11d ★★★
Four pitches, up a right-facing corner, to the rim. Start on the same sloping bench as *Gin and Tectonics*.
P1: Right-facing, offwidth corner—consider taping your ankles (5.11).
P2: Varied sizes to a bolted boulder problem (5.11d or 5.10, A0).
P3: Hands and off-fingers to a mantel with a bolt (5.10).
P4: Sweet hands to the rim (5.10). Note: Pitches 3 and 4 could be combined easily with some long runners.
Descent: Rap the route with a single 70m rope.
Gear: Blue TCU–5.0
FA: K3 and Joe Slansky; FFA: Herb Crimp

☐ 2. **GIN AND TECTONICS** 5.11+ ★★★★★
Three pitches. Legend has it that the Ruckman brothers felt this was one of the best desert lines they put up.
P1: Widening right-facing corner, fingers to hands, with a *ton* of the latter (5.11, 140′).
P2: Traverse right to a drilled pin and the face-climbing crux. Next, negotiate a long, pumpy right-facing corner of mostly small sizes and belay below a squeeze (5.11+, 140′).
P3: Squeeze through the chimney and up the steep, big-hands finish (5.10, 120′).
Descent: Rap Spring Fling
Gear: Triples from tips to wide hands, singles of bigger stuff to #6 Friend. The first pitch can swallow lots of #2 Camalots.
FA: Stuart Ruckman, Bret Ruckman, 1988

☐ 3. **THE HEADSTACK** 5.12 75′ ★★★
Climb past some blocks to a splitter offwidth. "Industrial" offwidth. Donahue explains, "At one point I was doing hand jams against my head to keep from falling out of the crack—thus the name."
Gear: Many 3.0–4.0, Bigbros
FA: Topher Donahue

☐ 4. **UNNAMED** 5.? 80′ ★★★
Start in a left-facing corner with fingers. Then switch cracks to a splitter on the right wall that begins with fingers. Work through a pod finishing with a tight hands splitter.
Gear: Blue TCU–2.0 (heavy on tight hands)

☐ 5. **PECCADILLO** 5.11- 180′ ★★★★★
Splitter and steep; gotta love it! Mostly big and cupped hands. Start up some broken ground to a fixed piece. This could be used as an alternate belay, or else just clip it and keep cruising. Partway, there are some flakes that overlap the crack (fun) then it steepens to a surprise just before the anchor. MONEY!!!
Gear: 1.0–4.0 (heavy on the 3.0s)
FA: Bret Ruckman, Stuart Ruckman, 1988

☐ 6. **HOT LIPS** 5.11+ 80′ ★★★
Start with a curving splitter, up through a flare. Once past the flare, pull through the bulge then up the splitter with mostly pumper big hands on overhanging rock to an off-fingers crux.
Gear: 2 Friends – 5.0, heavy on big hands
FA: Topher Donahue, Jimmy Dunn, the Betty sisters

☐ 7. **THE MONSTER** 5.11 200+′ ★★★
WOW! somebody is serious about their o-dubs! Most of us merely used this feature as a landmark. When you are coming down from Maverick Buttress, you can see the entire cliff down to the head of the canyon. This feature is the prominent splitter.
Gear: besides lots of endurance and a huge set of cahones, the first ascent went with 16 Bigbros and 3 #6s
FA: Tom Eichenburger

☐ 8. **SPICY MEATBALL** 5.11 200′ ★★
This long splitter finishes with a short left facing corner.
Gear: Fingers–4.0

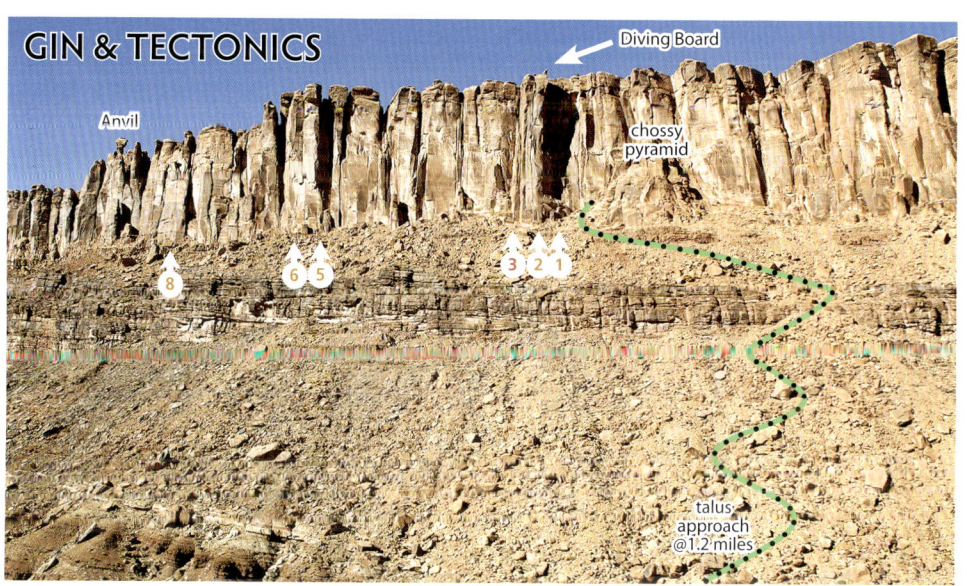

Potash Road

Jim Madore on *Gin and Tectonics*, 5.11+ (3rd pitch – 5.10)

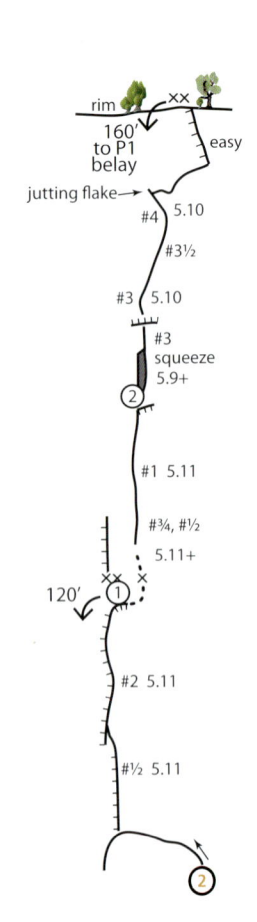

Charley Graham and Jim Madore on the second pitch (5.11+)

rim
160' to P1 belay
easy
jutting flake
#4 5.10
#3½
#3 5.10
#3 squeeze 5.9+
②
#1 5.11
#¾, #½
5.11+
120' ①
#2 5.11
#½ 5.11
②

Long Canyon

Forming Arch Area ☼SW

Drive until the odometer reads 2.0 miles. Park at a small pullout on the right. Hike up the drainage to the base of a huge forming arch. At the arch start walking right. There are a few warm-ups along the way to *Two Plumb*.

Routes are listed from left to right.

❏ 1. **THE BEGINNING** 5.10b 50' ★★★
This route is on the lower, Chinle band of rock, below and slightly right of *Two Plumb*. It is best seen and approached from beside the roadside hoodoo (just before a big dip in the road). This left-facing corner goes from off-fingers to tight hands, and is steeper than it looks.
Gear: 0.75–2.0
FA: Kiefer Kelley

❏ 2. **STINGRAY** 5.11+ 90' ★★★★
The right side of the gigantic forming arch. Start under the left-facing corner. Work up broken rock to the corner, then continue, with steep off-fingers, to a bulge that tightens slightly; the angle eases just before the anchor.
Gear: 0.3–0.75, set of nuts may be useful
FA: Jay Smith

❏ 3. **PROJECT** 5.hard 135' ★★★★★
Not yet free. But when it is, it'll be an amazing route! Finger heaven...or is it hell? Climb face to an aid move past a bolt and then to an incredible fingers splitter.
Gear: Lots of finger pieces (heaviest on 0.4)
FA: Jay Smith

❏ 4. **BEAR BONES** 5.11 ★
Steep off-fingers to a left-leaning corner with big hands.
FA: Charley Graham

❏ 5. **KID'S DAY OFF** 5.10+ 110' ★
A right-facing corner with lots of tight hands and a fingers crux.
Gear: 0.4–2.0
FA: Dylan Warren

❏ 6. **LOOMING** 5.9 70' ★★★
Hands in a left-facing corner brings you to fist and a little bigger ... but don't worry, there are some face features just where you want 'em.
Gear: 1.0–4.0 (heaviest on hands)
FA: K3

❏ 7. **NEANDERTHAL** 5.11 40' ★★
Harder and steeper than it looks. And, a horrible size! An awkward start puts you into a steep off-fingers splitter that turns into an off-fingers offset. After this, climb welcome jugs on thinner gear to a perfect belay ledge.
Gear: 0.3–0.75 (heaviest on 0.5 & 0.75)
FA: K3

❏ 8. **PRICKLY PEAR** 5.9 50' ★
Left-facing, ramping corner. Mostly sharp, tight hands. See if you can figure out the secret "behind it."
Gear: 1.0–3.0
FA: K3

❏ 9. **WICKED** 5.13 45' ★★★★★
Off-fingers to tips splitter. Push through the tips section to a needed hand jam, up to a stance. Clip the anchor just past the horizontal break.
Gear: 0.5–blue TCU
FA: Zach Alberts

The next two routes are located just right of *Wicked* and start 15 feet up on a large ledge known as "the Hang." Both routes share a common anchor.

❏ 10. **HANG ON** 5.11 45' ★★★
A left-facing, shallow corner that starts steep, with tips and face, up to a beautiful fingers layback.
Gear: 0 TCU–0.5 (heavy on yellow TCU), optional hands piece
FA: K3

❏ 11. **HANG OVER** 5.11 45' ★★
A left-diagonaling offset splitter. Climb fingers through hands to a sloping stance and belay just below some stacked blocks.
Gear: 0.3–2.0
FA: K3; FFA: Anne Merchandise

❏ 12. **TWO PLUMB** 5.11+ 200' ★★★★
Wow! A very beautiful line. However, it does has a problem with run-off and can sometimes have a powdery feel. Just over vertical, just under hands.
P1: Offset splitter that changes aspect several times in the first 20 feet. Continue with tight hands (5.11+, 100').
P2: Step right, fingers through big hands (5.11, 100').
Gear: P1: 0.75 Camalots–#2 Friends, heavy on #2. P2: Yellow TCUs–3 Friends
FA: K3, Joe Slansky. FFA: Anne Merchandise

Jay Smith on the FA of *Stingray* 5.11+

13. SCHOOL MASTER
5.11+ ★★★★

School Master is just right of *Two Plumb* and faces up-canyon (toward Maverick Buttress). There are two curving cracks next to each other that form the shape of a key or violin. The route climbs the right one of these cracks.

P1: Climb a crack that jogs right and passes a large boulder (that seems solid) to a ledge. Climb the left-facing corner, first with fingers and feet features then with perfect hands to a two-bolt belay (5.10, 100' ★★).

P2: Move right to a right-facing offset, fingers to rattly fingers. The offset diagonals left and goes through a short section of cups and fist. Finish with tight hands to a two-bolt belay (5.11+ ★★★★).

Gear: 1.0 TCU–3.5 (heaviest on 0.4s and 0.5s)
FA: Jay Smith, K3

Zach Alberts on FA of *Wicked* 5.13

Potash Road

First Switchback ☀ SW

At 2.1 miles, park at a small pullout on the left. Walk just a little bit up the road. Look for a faint trail on the right side of the road (sometimes cairned); follow this trail as it trends left. The hike dumps you out around *Two Buck Chuck*. Routes are listed from right to left.

1. CAPTAIN HOOK 5.11 60' ★★★
Begin from the same ledge as *Why Does It Hurt*. Start out with hard fingers and tricky feet around an overlap. Above the overlap, crank the zigzagging splitter.
Gear: 0.5–4.0 (heavy on hand sizes)
FA: Tom Perkins

2. WHY DOES IT HURT WHEN I PEE 5.11 130' ★
This thing feels hard! The entire climb is in a left-facing corner that feels reminiscent of a tidal wave crashing over your back. It is also dirty and an insecure size. But from the ground it appears long and sweet. For most folks it will be too big for a fist, and too small for a knee. Oh yeah, it's steep too!
Gear: 3.0–4.5
FA: Dave Jones, Kyle Copeland, Sonja Paspal

3. VAN GO 5.6 30'
A short, fun something to do. A good first lead.
Gear: 1.0–30
FA: Tom Perkins

4. THE MOTHER SHIP 5.11 65' ★★
Right-facing corner. Climb past two bolts, continue up the corner going through the sizes. Finish with some offwidth.
Gear: 0.0–5.0
FA: Tom Perkins

5. TWO BUCK CHUCK 5.9 50' ★★★
Start in a left-facing corner with off-fingers, up to a dihedral with hands, finish with hand stacks.
Gear: 0.75–4.0
FA: Tom Perkins

6. FOUR GUITARS AND A PIANO 5.10 50' ★
Left-facing tips to flakes. After the flakes, it turns to a right-facing corner with hands.
Gear: 0.5–4.0 (heavy on 0.5s and 0.75s)
FA: Tom Perkins

7. DR. YU 5.11 50'
Face moves past a bolt mark the start. Continue up a finger crack that eventually turns to hands.
Gear: 1 draw, 0.5–3.0
FA: Tom Perkins

8. CROCK POT 5.10+ 50'
Start in a right-facing corner with tips. Pass a hole to left-facing corner with off-fingers/tight hands.
Gear: 0.3–2.0
FA: Tom Perkins

9. THREE DOORS DOWN 5.10b 100'
Long left-facing corner. A chossy start leads to wide hands, to fingers, and finally offwidth.
Gear: 0.4–4.5
FA: Tom Perkins

10. GOOD GRIEF 5.12 70' ★★
Start with a short, double fingers splitter to a left-facing corner with all sizes.
Gear: 0.0 TCU–4 (heavy on #3s and #4s)
FA: Tom Perkins

11. NO MORE TEARS 5.11 120' ★★★★
Left-facing corner with a couple of pods. Start with bulging off-fingers, which becomes tight hands and hands. Anchors are under a huge roof.
Gear: 0.75–3.5
FA: Judy Ruckman, Bret Ruckman

Tom Perkins on Captain Hook 5.11

FIRST SWITCHBACK

Reptilian Walls ☼S

Park at a small pullout at the second switchback (3.1 miles). The Reptilian Walls will be behind you. Also behind you is a drainage. Enter the drainage from the left (up-canyon) to avoid a step/roadcut while staying below a small cliffband, as in the photograph below. Once in the drainage, the directions differ depending on your destination.
Reptilian Left: Keep cutting left to the top of the rock rim/ledge band. It's best to stay low, locate the climb you desire and cut up the short, steeper talus.
Reptilian Right: Cross the drainage and trend right to a rock rim/ledge below the cliff. As for Reptilian Left, walk this rim/ledge till you locate the desired climb and hike up the short talus.
Note: Along the way you may see some petrified wood, perhaps even sections of tree. Please leave these for others to enjoy!

REPTILIAN WALL RIGHT
Routes are listed left to right.

❑ 1. **CHAMELEON** 5.11 50' ★★
Start up a big-hands splitter for 15 feet then bust left through a big hole. Climb out of the hole, hands, into a wedge. Exit this, past a roof with fingers and tips (bolt), then to the belay ledge with a two-bolt anchor (can't be seen from the ground).
Gear: 0.0–3.5, 1 quickdraw, shoulder-length slings
FA: Tom Gwinn, K3

The next route starts from a ledge 40 feet up. Access this ledge by 1) a third-class scramble behind a large boulder, by 2) reaching the start from the top of *Chameleon*, or 3) by a brief 15-foot pitch just right of *Chameleon*.

❑ 2. **FADED MIDGET** 5.11 115' ★★★★
Links up nicely with *Chameleon*. Begin with 10 feet of wedging to a small ledge. Climb this with hands and tight hands, pass a bolt and continue with off-fingers and fingers to a two-bolt belay (hard to see).
Gear: #1 TCU–4.0 (heavy on fingers and off-fingers)
FA: Charley Graham

The next three routes all ascend a pillar in a corner, the Triceratops Pillar. The anchors on top are shared by all three climbs, allowing for fun toproping possiblities.

❑ 3. **TRICERATOPS LEFT** 5.10 50' ★
The left side of the pillar. Start up blocky terrain to the main offwidth/chimney system. Stems and face holds make it less grueling than it appears. Almost fun.
Gear: 2.0–5.0 (heavier on the big sizes)
FA: K3, Jay Ackerman, Tom Gwinn

❑ 4. **TRICERATOPS MIDDLE** 5.12- 50' ★★★
The obvious finger splitter. Start as for *Triceratops Left* and traverse out on ledges to meet the bottom of the crack. Tips, supplemented by crimps, lead to a fun section of nice fingers, up to a flare. Some off-fingers gain an awkward finish. May clean up to be a 4-star route.
Gear: 0.0–0.75, some hands pieces for the corner start
FA: K3, Jay Ackerman, Tom Gwinn

❑ 5. **TRICERATOPS RIGHT** 5.10- 50' ★★★
The right side of the formation. A left-facing corner with great hands leads to a ledge. Climb past a small pod to a short offwidth/chimney. Continue with big hands, to fists, to a wide final move.
Gear: 2.0–4.5 (shoulder slings)
FA: K3, Jay Ackerman, Tom Gwinn

The next two routes are very close to each other.

❑ 6. **UNNAMED** 5.10 80'
A zigzagging, right-facing corner.
Gear: 0.75–3.0

❑ 7. **VERTICAL FLU** 5.10+ 60'
A mostly tight-hands splitter. Quality lessens near the top.
Gear: 0.5–3.0

❑ 8. **UNNAMED SPLITTER** 5.10+ 160' ★★★
Start in a shallow left-facing corner with fingers. Continue past a short wide section and rest in the slot just under a block (seems quite solid). Work out over the block (fun) then enjoy the long, beautiful hands splitter.
Gear: 0.3–4.0 (heavy on hands)

Potash Road

9. STEALTH BELLY 5.10 75' ★★
Start on a pillar/pedestal (some soft stone) up to a left-facing dihedral. Climb this with mostly tight hands. Look for some rest ledges on each wall. Great warm-up.
Gear: 0.75–3.0

10. LIZARD LUST 5.11 65' ★★
Start on the same pillar as *Stealth Belly*, but traverse right and lean over to the shallow left-facing corner/offset. Continue, fingers, to a small overhang. Above this, an off-fingers crack continues up a left-arching offset to a belay ledge. Pumpy.
Gear: 0.4–2.0, heavy on 0.5
FA: Dave Dawson

11. ANACONDA 5.11 ★★★★
Two pitches up a left-facing dihedral. Another great contribution from Mr. Platt.
P1: Tight hands leads to a chimney protected by a bolt.
P2: Sustained, with tight hands and off-fingers.
Gear: 0.4–3.0 (heavy on #2 Friends)
FA: Linus Platt

12. DON IGUANA 5.10+ 85' ★★★
Right-facing corner. Mostly hands, with some really fun hueco climbing just befor the anchor. Good warm up!
Gear: 1.0–3.5
FA: Linus Platt, Dave Dawson

13. SHED YOUR SKIN 5.10+ 65' ★★★
Start with a body-length of face climbing over soft stone, up to a right-facing offset with fingers. Continue with all sizes of fingers, switching aspects several times. Finish with tips (and some tricky feet) to a belay ledge with two Metolious rap hangers.
Gear: #1 TCU–0.75
FA: K3

14. THE COBRA 5.12 140' ★★★★
(Aka *Snake Charmer*) Start out on some softer rock passing a low bolt. Then climb the long, left-facing corner passing a huge bulge before the anchor. The *Quarter of a Man* of Longs.
Gear: 1 quickdraw, 0.3–1.0 (heavy on off-fingers)
FA: Topher Donahue

Kiefer Kelley on *Wiggle* 5.10

15. WIGGLE 5.10 70' ★★
Strange route. Strange as in awkward. The route features a narrow dihedral that will make you wiggle your way up while jamming fingers and tips. Even more strange, this route calls out to be climbed!
Gear: Purple TCU–0.75
FA: Topher Donahue, Patience Gribble, 1996

REPTILIAN RIGHT

Long Canyon

❏ 16. **HIDDEN DOOR** 5.11- ★★★★
Unique and super cool. Stars are for pitch 2. You have to deal with some choss on the first pitch to get to the goods on pitch 2, but it's well worth it.
P1: Start out soft and wide. As you get higher the rock gets better—but the crack becomes wider. Pass some chockstones until you can get your body in, eventually getting to the "door." Set a belay with hands-size gear.
P2: Climb through the door and exit with great hands and frictiony feet. Continue up the thinning, arcing splitter to a belay ledge with an anchor.
Descent: Double-rope rappel.
Gear: 0.5–6.0 Camalots
FA: Topher Donahue

❏ 17. **THE LIZARD'S HEX** 5.10b 75' ★★★
Just right of *Hidden Door* is a 40' pillar leaning against a left-facing dihedral. Climb the right side with hands and off-fingers, mantel onto the top. Continue up the corner using the corner crack and a finger crack on the right. Anchor on the right wall. Named for an old Hexcentric anchor found atop the pillar.
Gear: #1 TCU–4.0 (more #1 TCUs if you pro the finger crack)

❏ 18. **UNNAMED** 5.?
Just right of *Lizard's Hex* is an obvious splitter with an escape biner anchor. Unfinished project?

REPTILIAN WALL LEFT
Routes are listed from right to left.

❏ 1. **FOREPLAY FOR A SERPENT** 5.10 50'
A short, left-facing, big-hand to fist corner. Needs a second pitch (this will be wide).
Gear: 3.0–4.0
FA: K3

❏ 2. **SEVENTH SERPENT** 5.11 120' ★★★★★
Stellar! An obvious squiggly splitter in a shield of caramel colored Wingate, easily seen from the Maverick Buttress parking. Low down, there is an awkward slot that takes a big piece. Above, work up a right-angling tight-hands offset, followed by a left-trending rampish section. Then comes a squiggly splitter, off-fingers, which leads to a plumb tight-hand splitter.
Gear: 0.5–4.0
FA: Dave Dawson, Kyle Copeland, 1989

❏ 3. **SEVENTH SERPENT EXTENSION** 5.12- ★★★★★
Climb *Seventh Serpent*, clip the anchor and continue through the bulge and on up the splitter, with tight hands and off-fingers. Pass another roof, finish with less-than-vertical fingers.
Descent: Rap to the ground with two 60m ropes.
Gear: as for *Seventh Serpent*, plus 0 TCU–#2 Friend
FA: Charley Graham

❏ 4. **GECKO** 5.10 45' ★
Right-facing corner with an offwidth on the left wall.
Gear: Single rack with extra blue TCU
FA: K3

❏ 5. **HALF SNAKE, HALF CHICKEN** 5.10+ 65' ★★
Start with hands up a right-facing corner then scramble over some soft rock to a stembox. Climb this, with off-fingers. The crack works left to a big ledge with anchors.
Gear: 0.5–3.0 (heavy on off-fingers and tight hands)
FA: K3

The next two routes climb a small pillar leaning against the wall, just right of *Two Scorpion Telsons*.

❏ 6. **MANUS RIGHT** 5.9 35'
Climb the right side of the pillar, mostly hands.
FA: Jay Ackerman

❏ 7. **MANUS LEFT** 5.8 35'
The left side of the pillar. The crack starts with fingers (and footholds) then widens to hands. When it gets still wider there is a hidden trick....
FA: K3

❏ 8. **TWO SCORPION TELSONS** 5.12- 85' ★★★★
An arcing crack that starts thin, widens up then narrows back down. Bouldery moves, protected by microcams, start things off. Continue with fingers and up through the sizes to fists at the midpoint. Two bolts protect moves past a large chockstone, then the upper part of the crack starts with hands, eventually going back down to fingers.
Gear: 0.0–3.5, 2 draws, a solid spotter at the bottom.
FA: K3

❏ 9. **METASOMA** 5.10 125' ★★
A bit of everything. Start in a left-facing corner with fingers and climb a pillar. Next, take the left-facing corner (off fingers) to a ledge. An offwidth, on the right wall, gains a massive block. From the block use double cracks (big hands, and offwidth) up to and past a bolt. Thin hands gains the upper splitter, where sharp hands lead to off-fingers then another double crack.
Descent: A single 70m can work, but you must rappel rightwards to have enough rope to reach the ground.
Gear: single set of fingers, double set from 0.75–3.0, a couple of big cams (4.0, 4.5)
FA: K3

❏ 10. **FIST A LIZARD** 5.10b/c 65' ★★
Start with fun moves (hands) up a steep, hollow-sounding flake in a left-facing dihedral. Pull around the arête with big hands then continue with fists in a right-facing corner, passing a small pod. Finish with more steep fists.
Gear: 2.0–4.0
FA: K3

❏ 11. **POWDER MY LIZARD** 5.10+ 60'
Start in a short section of left-facing wide choss which turns to tight hands and off-fingers. Then reach right and switch cracks. Hands turns to big hands and steep fists.
Gear: 0.75–4.0 (6.0 optional at start)
FA: K3

❏ 12. **LEAN LIZARD** 5.11 65' ★★
Starts up a splitter with finger stacks utilizing a stem on the right. After the stems run out the splitter turns into a right-facing flare.
Gear: 0.3–0.5
FA: K3

MISCELLANEOUS RIGHT-SIDE ROUTES

❏ 1. **SIDEWINDER** 5.11 ★★★★
This offwidth test-piece sits far up-canyon. Drive past Maverick Buttress. Just beyind the fallen slab of rock that forms a brief road-tunnel, look right and locate this beautiful, left-facing offwidth/squeeze.
Gear: 2.0–Big Bros (12 placed on the FA)
FA: Craig Luebben, Thor Keiser, 1990

Charley Graham on the FA of *Seventh Serpent Extension* 5.12-

Long Canyon

Maverick Buttress

Driving up Long Canyon, Maverick Buttress dominates the view and draws the eye. These cliffs are, by far, the most popular area in Long Canyon, and for good reason. The cracks are superb, the approach from the road very short. This is a close second to Wall Street for convenience.

The buttress has three distinct facets, Maverick Left, Center, and Right, separated by two 90-degree outside corners. As you drive up the canyon, the east-facing Maverick Center stands out prominently. As you drive past the cliff, the north-facing routes of Maverick Right becomes visible, right above the road. The south-facing Maverick Left is the continuation, out of sight, of the cliffs beyond Maverick Center.
Approach: Hard to miss, but your odometer should read 3.3 miles. There is parking below Maverick Center and a bit farther up the road under Maverick Right.
Note: This is a bighorn sheep feeding area. If sheep are present, please go elsewhere to climb, give the sheep some room and time to feed!

MAVERICK CENTER ☀ E
Routes are listed from right to left, starting with the three splitter cracks on the majestic, vertical face of varnished Wingate that looms over the road at its closest approach.

☐ 1. **RAWHIDE** 5.11+ 110' ★★
Start with fists to big hands. Pass a flake and a bit of wide to a seam. Continue with off-fingers.
Gear: 1 set of TCUs–3.5 (heavy on off-fingers)
FA: Charlie Fowler, Jack Roberts, 1987

☐ 2. **MISS KITTY LIKES IT THAT WAY** 5.11+ ★★★★★
Splitter hands, to a pod with tight hands, then the business: off-fingers to the chains.
Gear: 0.5–2.0
FA: Charlie Fowler, Jack Roberts, 1987

☐ 2a. **MISS KITTY LIKES IT RAW** 5.11+ ★★★
Combination/variation of the previous two routes. Climb Miss Kitty. At the anchor, face climb over to Rawhide and finish at Rawhide's anchors.
Gear: Same as Miss Kitty, plus extra red Camalots

☐ 3. **GUNSMOKE** 5.11 110' ★★★★★
Great! Long splitter that starts with all sizes of hands to a rest. Above, punch it with off-fingers and fingers in a short section of right-facing dihedral.
Var: bump the grade by a half with a direct start just left.
Gear: Yellow TCU–3.0
FA: Charlie Fowler, Jack Roberts, 1987

☐ 4. **BOOT HILL** 5.12 120' ★★★★
After a sandy start, a steep #2 Friend-size crack leads to a weird move into a chimney. Relaxing wriggling past a fixed piton sets you up for the upper face, with its ring-lock and thin-hand madness. Don't stop....
Gear: Quickdraw, 0.5–3.0 (heavy on off-fingers)
FA: Linus Platt, Jimmy Dunn

☐ 5. **CLANTONS IN THE DUST** 5.10+
A right-facing offwidth. Can be dirty.
Gear: 0.75–5.0
FA: Jimmy Dunn

☐ 6. **HIGH NOON** 5.11 35' ★★
Short, stout, right-facing corner with layback tips, face climbing, and off-fingers.
Gear: Purple TCU–0.75

☐ 7. **TEQUILA SUNRISE** 5.10+ 80' ★★★★★
Start with off-fingers with some slabby pods for the feet. Then tight hands and hands, with a leftward traverse to meet up with Hot Toddy. Sweet warm-up.
Gear: 0.75–3.0
FA: Charlie Fowler, Jack Roberts, 1987

☐ 8. **HOT TODDY** 5.10 80' ★★★
A right-facing corner that offers another sweet warm-up. Shares anchors with Tequila Sunrise. Start things off with a wide move then climb mostly big hands.
Gear: #3 Friends–3.0
FA: Charlie Fowler, Jack Roberts, 1987

☐ 9. **HOE DOWN** 5.12
This crack is found just before the cliff turns into a large alcove/gully. Mostly splitter, with some soft rock.
Gear: Mostly tight-hands and off-fingers size cams

Brittany Griffith on *Boothill* 5.12, photo: Andrew Burr

The next five routes sit in the alcove just left of *Hoe Down*. To access this alcove, scramble up and over some boulders. Routes are listed in a counter clockwise direction (right to left).

❒ **10. FESTUS** 5.12 40' ★★
Steep tips with finger pods up a left-facing corner.
Gear: Purple TCU–0.4, heavy on blue
FA: K3

❒ **11. TEXAS TWO STEP** 5.10 60' ★★★
Start on top of the boulder and step across to a right-facing corner with tight hands. Switch into a left-facing corner, with hands rapidly widening to fist.
Gear: #2 Friend–3.5
FA: Chris Begue, Tim Begue, 1988

❒ **12. ROUND UP** 5.11 70' ★★★
Begin with delicate moves and thin gear, to an ever-widening splitter. Good fun!
Gear: Blue TCU–3.0
FA: Mia Axon, Dougald MacDonald

❒ **13. SADDLE SORES** 5.10 ★
A left-facing dihedral adjacent to *Round Up*. Start with hands, finish with wide, just before the anchors.
Gear: 2.0–4.5 (mostly hands and big hands)
FA: Dougald MacDonald, Mia Axon

❒ **14. UNNAMED** 5.10 45'
Close to *Texas Two Step* and *Saddle Sores*. Start up soft rock to a bigger-than-fist splitter, using stems on the right wall. Anchors are visible on the right wall.

❒ **15. UNNAMED AID ROUTE** 65'
Pin scars to a tips splitter.

❒ **16. MUSTANG MAN** 5.11+ 65' ★★
Mostly a fingers splitter.
Gear: Yellow TCU–1.0
FA: Galen Rowell, John Laurtig, 1994

❒ **17. UNNAMED** 5.11 70' ★
Fingers to off-fingers splitter.
Gear: Yellow TCU–#2 Friend

MAVERICK LEFT ☀ S
This is, effectively, the continuation of Maverick Center, as it bends round beyond *Mustang Man* to face south, the side that is not visible from the road. Routes are listed right to left.

❒ **1. MAV 1** 5.10 35' ★
A bouldery twin-crack start gives way to an ever widening crack. An apparently solid chockstone provides an awkward mantel just before the chains. Short and fun!
Gear: 1.0–4.0
FA: Dylan Warren

❒ **2. UNNAMED** 5.10 90' ★
Just left of *Mav 1*. Stand back from the cliff a bit to see the anchor, above a shelf. Climb blocky terrain to reach a right-facing fists corner.

❒ **3. UNNAMED** 5.10+ 115' ★★★★
Up a stembox to a shallow, right-facing corner. Sweet! If this were on the front of Maverick and better documented, it would be as popular as *Gunsmoke*.
Gear: 0.4–4.5

4. UNNAMED 5.11 100' ★★
Right-facing corner. Start with hands, gain an offset splitter with off-fingers and tight hands.

5. UNNAMED 5.10 80' ★★
A right-facing dihedral. A spotter is nice for the start. Being tall may be helpful. A thin start then goes up through the sizes. Physical!
Gear: #1 TCU–6.0 (long pants)

6. QUICKDRAW 5.11 60' ★★
Reachy, sequential edges. Fun!
Gear: 6 quickdraws
FA: K3, Michelle Kelley, Tom Gwinn

7. UNNAMED 5.11 100'
A left-facing corner. Start with fingers and tips, and continue to hands and off-fingers.

8. 2012 5.11 70' ★★★
A zigzagging fingers splitter up to a left-arcing corner. A boulder problem gains the splitter. The corner starts off-fingers and gets steeper and wider the higher you go, ending with offwidth.
Gear: 0.0–4.5 (old 4.0 Camalots are best for the ow; new 4.0 are umbrella-ed, new 5.0s crammed)
FA: K3

MAVERICK RIGHT ☀ N
This is the rightmost sector, north-facing, close to the road and parallel to it. Routes are listed left to right, starting from the big prow just right of *Rawhide*.

1. SHOOT OUT 5.11b 65' ★★★
This is located just around the corner and right from *Rawhide*. Start with hands, pass a block and continue with tight hands and awkward off-fingers. Finish with some fingers and a desperate anchor clip.
Gear: 0.3–3.0
FA: Jay Smith

2. SHOWDOWN 5.11 85' ★★★
This is 100 feet right of *Shoot Out*. A broken start leads around a block and through a small roof. Climb a sustained thin-hands corner that pinches down to fingers in a flare.
Gear: 0.3–4.0
FA: Jay Smith

3. UNNAMED 5.?
Offwidth.

4. SHORT CRACK 5.11+ 50' ★★★
Start up a short splitter, with tight hands to off-fingers, mantel onto the ledge. Move a tad right and continue up the crack with hands through a bulge, then with fingers through another bulge. More fingers gain the anchor.
Gear: 1.0 TCU–#3 Friend.

Heather Hillier on *Texas Two Step* 5.10

LONG CANYON LEFT SIDE

The left side of Long Canyon hosts some spectacular climbing, yet the routes see little traffic. The cliffs generally face north and get lots of shade, making these crags great for the warmer months. The established routes are mostly clustered at several crags, with the occasional gem in between.

Shady Crag N

Some good climbs and a short approach. Park almost immediately after pulling into Long Canyon, just after the railroad tracks. Step over the half-buried cattle fence and find an old road (now closed to vehicles). Follow this road toward Offwidth City. Watch for a faint trail (sometimes cairned) leading to the right. All the routes are within a five-minute walk of each other.

1. DONE LUBIN' 5.11 ★★★★
Offwidth climbing. This goes to the rim in four pitches.
Gear: A bunch of shoulder slings, one set of cams with lots of large cams, couple of #4 Big Bros
FA: Jimmy Dunn, Craig Luebben, 1994

2. FINGER BANG 5.11 70' ★★★★
A bouldery start leads to fists in a flare, to a ledge. Reach over right and continue up a beautiful, left-facing finger crack. Great rock.
Gear: Yellow TCU–3.5 (0.4 Camalots work well for the meat of the fingers section)
FA: K3

3. SEPTEMBER SWEAT 5.10+ 65' ★★
Fist to offwidth in a slot.
FA: K3 and Michelle Kelley, 2017

4. DOUBLE CRACKS 5.11 100' ★★★
Start up a chossy looking left-facing corner that climbs better than it looks. Continue up the right splitter crack (hands) and eventually switch to the left crack. Up and into some wider climbing. After some offwidth continue with hands to some face moves that gain the obvious ledge (and hidden anchor). Physical!
Gear: 0.75–6.0
FA: Jimmy Dunn

5. MCL 5.10+ 2 pitches ★★
P1: Climb the left side of a block via ow, passing two drilled angles and a bolt. Bolted belay. 65'
P2: Climb a steep left-facing corner of mostly big hands/fist, passing a tricky pod marking the crux. 95'
FA: K3, Jay Ackerman 2017

6. UNNAMED 5.11 30' ★
Is this a tower or a bolted boulder? You decide! Follow the bolt line, using both sides of the arête, to a mantel and traverse left to the oddly placed anchor.
Gear: Quickdraws

7. UNNAMED 5.10 75' ★★★
Start behind a leaning pillar. Climb the left-facing corner with all sizes of hands and a few off-finger moves.
Gear: #2 Friend–4.0
FA: Jimmy Dunn?

7a. MINI SKIRTS & HALTER TOPS 5.11 ★★★★★
P1: Clip the chains of #7, keep going up a face past two bolts to a shallow stembox with fingers, passing two more bolts, to the belay (5.11, 115').
P2: Continue up the right side of the stembox to a horizontal roof crack with perfect hands (5.11, 50').
Gear: #1 TCU–4.0
FA: K3

7b. JOCK STRAPS AND BANANA HAMMOCKS 5.11+ 115' ★★★★
From the belay of *Mini Skirts*, climb the left side of the stembox with fingers. (5.11+, 50').
Gear: (1)0.3, many 0.4s
FA: K3

8. UNKNOWN 5.10 40'
Fist to offwidth in a slot.

9. FOR JOEY 5.10
A bit chossy but not deadly. Good tower training! Start in a right-facing corner, pass a hollow flake in the crack. Make a couple of slab moves right and continue up a right-facing, silty corner to a two-bolt anchor.
Gear: 1.0–3.5
FA: K3

Long Canyon 165

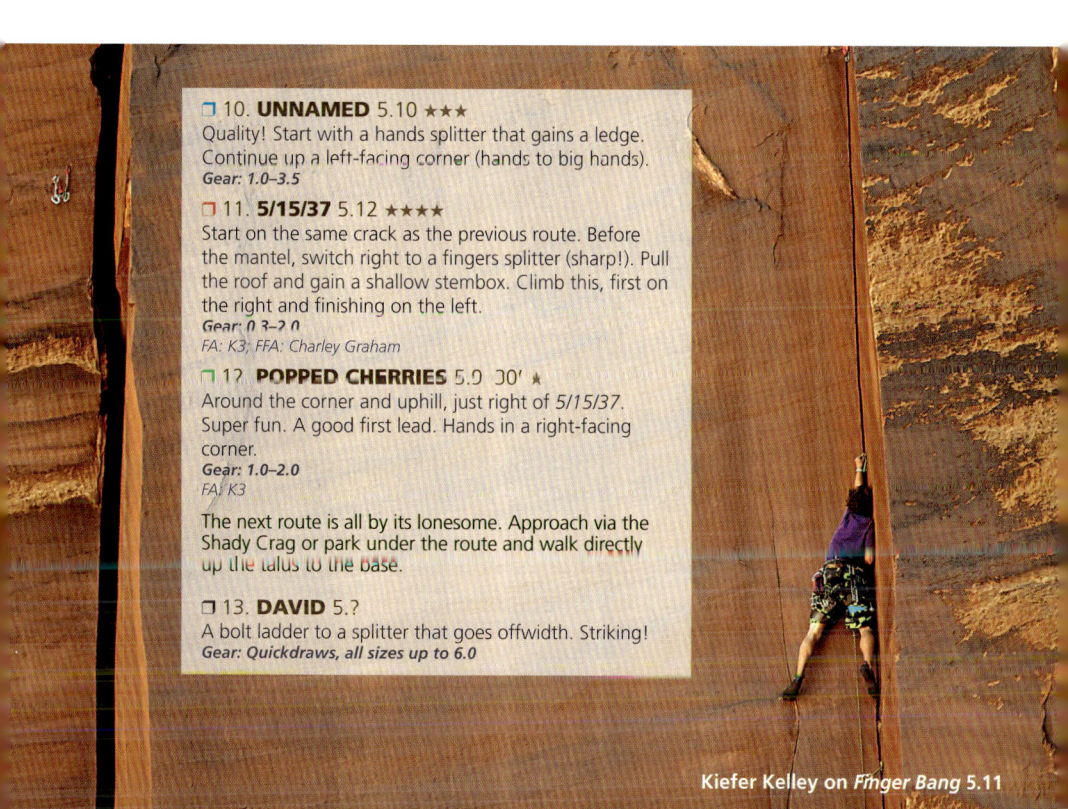

Ben Riley on *5/15/37* 5.12

☐ 10. **UNNAMED** 5.10 ★★★
Quality! Start with a hands splitter that gains a ledge. Continue up a left-facing corner (hands to big hands).
Gear: 1.0–3.5

☐ 11. **5/15/37** 5.12 ★★★★
Start on the same crack as the previous route. Before the mantel, switch right to a fingers splitter (sharp!). Pull the roof and gain a shallow stembox. Climb this, first on the right and finishing on the left.
Gear: 0.3–2.0
FA: K3; FFA: Charley Graham

☐ 12. **POPPED CHERRIES** 5.9 30' ★
Around the corner and uphill, just right of *5/15/37*. Super fun. A good first lead. Hands in a right-facing corner.
Gear: 1.0–2.0
FA: K3

The next route is all by its lonesome. Approach via the Shady Crag or park under the route and walk directly up the talus to the base.

☐ 13. **DAVID** 5.?
A bolt ladder to a splitter that goes offwidth. Striking!
Gear: Quickdraws, all sizes up to 6.0

Kiefer Kelley on *Finger Bang* 5.11

Hand Delivery Area ☀ N

At about 0.7 mile you will see a drainage that allows access between the lower cliffs. Ascend this drainage looking left at the top for the obvious lines—listed right to left.

1. HAND DELIVERY 5.11+ 150' ★★★★
A 5-star route spoiled only by a funky beginning. Start with some shallow stemming with thin gear, continue up a crazy-looking roundish block with a hand jam. This is where things get sweet. Pass the block and continue past a zigzagging splitter with off-fingers to a roof. Over the roof, climb tight hands to a pod. Beyond, an absolutely stellar hand crack awaits.
Gear: Small to medium nuts, 0.75–3.0, heavy on hands.
FA: Stuart and Bret Ruckman

2. PEANUT DELIVERY 5.11- 80' ★★
Start with face moves protected with a fixed DMM Peanut. Continue through a short offwidth to an off-fingers and fingers flake to a belay ledge.
Gear: 0.4–4.0, heavy on off-fingers
FA: K3

3. DELIVERANCE 5.11 80' ★★★
Begins off-fingers splitter into a massive off-fingers slot, then continue out the roof of the wedge, stemming and protecting the tips crack.
Gear: Blue TCU to 0.75
FA: K3

165'
#3½
5.11-
arete
#3
#2½
5.10+ #2½
#2
5.11+
cut left into splitter #2
at last opportunity
#3
protect in #1½
bottom of splitter
to reduce drag
block
#3
small/med nuts
5.10- stems

Herb Crimp on *Hand Delivery* 5.11+   Photo: Andrew Burr

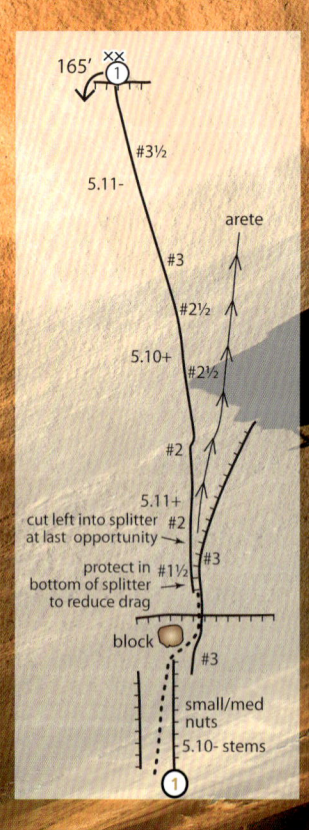

Long Canyon

Carnivore Area N

Park at 0.9 miles, just before the road goes over a wash. Look left and you will see an obvious talus cone. Hike the cone and you end up just beneath the bolted flake, *Shaken, Not Stirred*.
Routes are listed left to right and are in close proximity to each other.

1. UNNAMED 5.10+ 120' ★
A splitter crack begins with fingers then turns to hands. Continue to a right-facing corner with all sizes.

2. SHAKEN, NOT STIRRED 5.10 100' ★
A left-facing corner (fists) leads to a shelf then continues via a bolted, hollow-sounding flake. Pumpy.
Gear: 4 draws, #2 Friend–4.0
FA: K3

3. CARNIVORE 5.12 60' ★★★★
Start with fingers in a right-facing offset with some feet on the right side. This switches to fingers in a left-facing offset. Continue up more fingers in a shallow, right-facing, right-leaning corner. Great rock!
Gear: #1 TCU–0.5
FA: Jay Smith, 1991

4. HERBIVORE 5.11 ★★★
Splitter offwidth. There's something about a woman who throws on the Carhartts and goes big! Nice one, Sam! All sorts of stacking here. Starts wide and gets wider. Near the top it dog-legs left. Great rock!
Gear: 4.0–6.0
FA: Sammy Burrell

5. MADE IN THE SHADE 5.12 ★★★★★
Right of *Carnivore*. Two or three pitches, mostly straight-in fist/offwidth. May not be all free.
FA: Mike Klien, Bob Novellino, John Rosholt

6. FELIX DREAM 5.12+? 80'
Shallow right-facing corner.
Gear: Heavy on 0.75
FA: Herb Crimp

TRIPLE BUTTRESS AREA

This area features three prominent buttresses. From left to right these are Buttress 1, Buttress 2 (aka Bond Buttress) and Buttress 3. All three offer up great routes on generally really good rock. Buttress 2 offers (to date) the most climbing, yet each has some 4- and 5-star gems.

All the climbs are accessed via the same approach. Drive 1.3 miles from the Potash/Long Canyon intersection. Park on the left side in a faint parking spot just before the road dips. Hike up the steep middle rib on a faint trail for around 650 vertical feet to the base of Buttress 2.
Note: this area seems very popular with rattlesnakes. They are usually found in the shade. Beware!

BUTTRESS 1 N

1. ONATOPP 5.10 180' ★★★★
Referred to as *Onatopp*, this may not be the correct name. Locate a left-facing corner with the left wall covered by lichen. The climb can be broken up into three pitches or stretched into one long pitch. Start with beautiful hands, pass the first anchors and lieback an ear (off-fingers gear). Pass the next set of anchors and climb offwidth, past fixed gear, to the final set of anchors. Super fun climbing on mostly good rock.
Gear: 0.5–4.0

2. UNNAMED 5.11 80' ★★★
A switching splitter. A straight-in hand crack quickly pinches down to fingers before its end. Switch cracks (more fingers), gradually working back up to a section of off-fingers in a left-facing, offset splitter. More fingers leads over the lip and to the belay ledge.
Gear: 0.3–2.0

BUTTRESS 2 (BOND BUTTRESS) NE

Recently developed, this area may hold the best concentration of hard, 5-star routes in Long Canyon.

1. TRIPLE SHAFT DRIVEN 5.11 ★★
Two pitches. Always a pleasure to climb with THE Leonard Coyne! A lunatic in an awesome way!!
P1: A left-facing corner begins with offwidth, continuing with hands to off-fingers, to a bolted belay ledge.
P2: Hands lead to a tips layback, then to some friendlier sizes.
Gear: 0.0–5.0 (a few extras in ow and off-fingers sizes)
FA: K3, Leonard Coyne, Jay Ackerman

Potash Road

☐ 2. UNNAMED 5? 80' ★★
Mostly chimney and offwidth. Look for some tiered pillars that lean into a large dihedral system that goes halfway up the cliff. The climb takes the left side of this formation. Start in a wide, right-facing corner and climb to a drilled-piton anchor at half-height on the pillar.
Gear: 4.0–6.0

☐ 3. JUST WHISTLING DIXIE 5.11 135' ★★★
This long, physical pitch ascends the right side of the same pillars described in the previous climb. After a couple moves on loose-looking but solid rock (place and back-clean an old 4.5?), move right onto a sloping ledge and the base of the left-facing dihedral. Climb fingers to a sweet section of off-fingers and steep tight hands. Next, cruise a hands flake to steep big hands to a pod (and a rest!). Negotiate the pod, and the crack above, with cups and fists (and a stack, optional 4.5) to a final, sharp, fists flake.
Gear: 0.3–3.5 (optional 4.5)

☐ 4. DR. NO 5.9 A0 45' ★★★
This takes the stunning offset hand crack just above *Just Whistling Dixie*. If it were longer, it would be a 5-star pitch. From the anchor atop *Just Whistling Dixie*, tension to a bolt and pendulum right to the offset splitter. Hands and big hands gain the belay ledge.
Descent: Two 60m ropes just reach the ground
Gear: 2.0–3.0
FA: K3

☐ 5. UNNAMED SPLITTER (2 PITCHES) ☀ N
Most likely an aid line. Look for a drilled pin at the bottom.

The next five pitches are around the corner to the right and offer shade all morning. ☀ NW

☐ 6. SOLAR FLARE 5.10 50' ★
A wedge, climbed with fingers to off-fingers.
Gear: 0.4–1.0
FA: Charley Graham

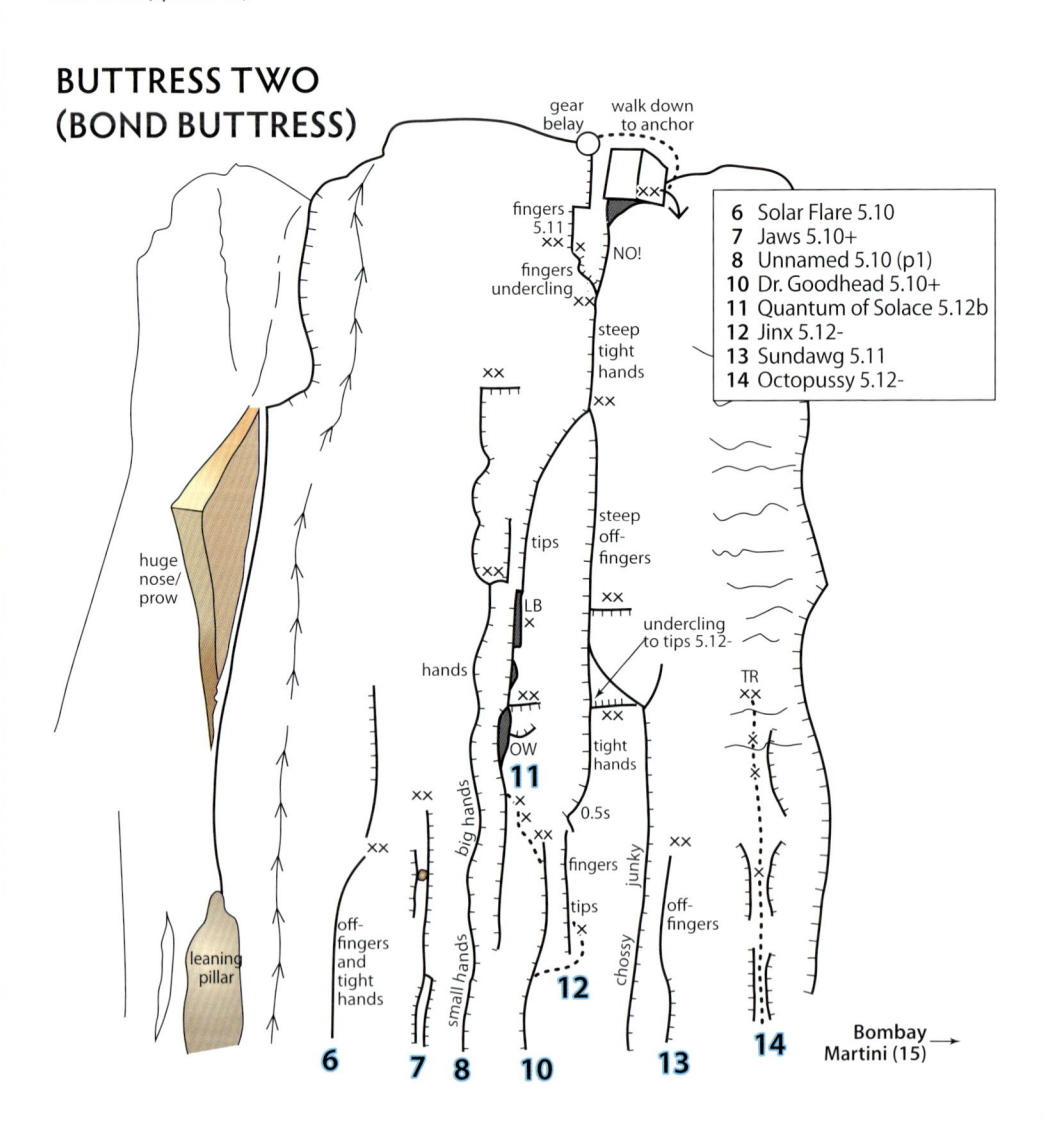

BUTTRESS TWO (BOND BUTTRESS)

6 Solar Flare 5.10
7 Jaws 5.10+
8 Unnamed 5.10 (p1)
10 Dr. Goodhead 5.10+
11 Quantum of Solace 5.12b
12 Jinx 5.12-
13 Sundawg 5.11
14 Octopussy 5.12-

Bombay Martini (15) →

Long Canyon

☐ **7. JAWS** 5.11 70' ★★★
A cool route. Jam and stem double cracks to a bulge. Climb to a horizontal, continue up the square slot (off-fingers) to a chockstone. Clamber over this, then tackle fingers and face to the anchor.
Gear: 0.3–3.0 (heavy on off-fingers)
FA: K3

☐ **8. UNNAMED CORNER** 5.10 ★★★★★
Aka *the Ruckman Route* (though Bret does not recall doing this). A stellar, long pitch of hands up a wavy, shallow left-facing corner. The crack varies from tight hands to baggy fists but mostly it's great hands.
Gear: 1.0–4.0 (plenty of gold Camalots)
FA: Bret Ruckman?

☐ **9. UNNAMED CORNER 2** 5.11- C1 ★★★★
Recently, 80 feet of hard climbing, broken into two pitches, has been added to the previous route.
P1: Follow the *Unnamed Corner* (5.10).
P2: Awesome jamming, reminiscent of the crux of Indian Creek's *Battle of the Bulge*. Gear belay at a no-hands rest (5.11a, 40').
P3: The corner goes to doubly overhanging, the crack shrinks to less-than-tips, and the rock is a bit sandy; the exposure bites while the cams, not so much. Free, this will probably be 5.12+ or harder (5.11, C1, 40')
Gear: 0.75–1.0, P3: tips and fingers gear
FA: Charley Graham and Herb Crimp

☐ **10. DR. GOODHEAD** 5.10+ 55' ★★
Pull a bouldery move to stand on a small pedestal. Continue up a shallow right-facing corner with fingers. Pass a ledgy section to sustained steep fingers to a Thank-God hand-pod to clip the anchor.
Gear: 0.3–1.0
FA: K3

☐ **11. QUANTUM OF SOLACE** 5.12- ★★★★★
P1: Climb *Dr. Goodhead* until just below its anchors. Go left, around a balancy arête to a right-facing corner. Climb tips and face past two bolts up to a great finger crack. Next, take a deep breath … man up! Lieback a steep, wide bulge and clip the anchor (5.12).
P2: Climb easy wide up to a chimney, clipping a bolt out right. Continue up double corners, off-finger on the left and finger pods on the right. Eventually, move to the right one and, shortly after, the angle eases. Continue more easily to a bolted belay stance. Here the route merges with the top of *Jinx*'s second pitch (5.11). Follow the last two pitches of *Jinx* to the rim.
Gear: 2 draws, many fingers-size cams, 4.5, 6.0
FA: Charley Graham, K3, Tom Gwinn

☐ **12. JINX** 5.12- 390' ★★★★★
Jinx is a great four-pitch route: steep, unlikely and surprising. The first pitch is an excellent 5.11. Above this, three highly recommended pitches forge their way to the rim.
P1: Start as for *Dr. Goodhead* and move right at a horizontal break. Rest, then make thin moves past a bolt and continue up the right-facing corner with some steep tips/fingers to a foot-ledge (rest) at the height of *Dr. Goodhead*'s anchor. Varied climbing leads to a bulge (off-fingers) to the final tight-hands section. The anchor is below a big chockstone roof (5.11, 90').
Var: To avoid a hanging belay bypass this belay and move left out under a bulge. Underclinging and layback the bulge (crux) and then climb easier terrain to a bolted belay ledge under a corner (5.12+).
P2: Climb steep off-fingers in the beautiful corner to some lesser-quality rock, traverse left (easy) to a sloping belay stance shared with the top of pitch 2 of *Quantum of Solace* (5,11-).
P3: Climb steep tight hands in the right-facing corner. When the corner starts to seam you will see an anchor out left under an underclig (placed during a lightning storm). Clip the anchor but keep cruising with more underclings. Continue across the horizontal break, pass the "chicken bolt" and make a blind move around the arête to a really cool bolted belay stance (5.12-).
P4: A shallow, right-facing corner with fingers quickly leads to a ledge. Keep going up the corner with less-than-vertical off-fingers and build a belay on the rim with a few off-fingers/tight hand pieces (5.11-).
Descent: Walk climber's right of the route and down-scramble to the right side of the huge square block that looms above you the entire route. Rap the route from here or swing right and catch the anchor on Octopussy and rap to the ground. **Two 70m ropes needed.**
Gear: 0.0–3.0 (heavy on fingers and off-fingers), draws, shoulder-length slings
FA: K3, Michelle Kelley, Charley Graham

☐ **13. SUNDAWG** 5.11 55' ★★★★
Sequential and balancy climbing. Begin up a face protected with tips gear. Then climb a shallow left-facing corner with off-fingers (can be slippery) to a no-hands rest. Finish up a wavy off-fingers splitter with help from some face features. Nice one, Herb!
Gear: 0.0–0.75
FA: Herb Crimp

☐ **14. OCTOPUSSY** 5.12- 100' ★★★★★
An awesome link up of cracks, edges, flakes, and stems. A trickier start than it appears. Begin by balancing your way up to the short squeeze for a rest. After the squeeze, climb some really fun fingers. When this crack peters out, stem your way up to the bulge passing a bolt. Small face holds bring you around the roof and up to a finger-jug flake. Some sequential moves past two more bolts bring you to a final stem and the anchors.
Gear: 3 draws, blue TCU–1 (heavy on tips through fingers)
FA: Charley Graham

☐ **15. BOMBAY MARTINI** 5.12- 40' ★★★
Start with a brutal bombay chimney. Exit to off-fingers in a shallow right-facing corner with steep, sharp, but bomber rock. Soon the angle eases and the fingers become secure; negotiate a horizontal band and clip the chains.
Gear: 2.0, 4.0 for the bombay, blue TCU–0.75 for the rest (meat is baggy purples or crammed 0.75s, red Metoliuses work best)
FFA: Charley Graham

BUTTRESS 3

☐ **1. PUSSY GALORE** 5.10 70' ★★ NE
Scramble onto a ledge with an obvious splitter. Hands transition to offwidth. The anchor is hidden in the offwidth.
Gear: 2.0–3.5
FA: K3

☐ **2. UNNAMED** 5.10+ 160' ★★★★ NW
This route is five minutes around the corner by itself. A really cool climb with a "rodeo rest." Start in a right-facing corner, take a seat on a loose-looking block (the rodeo rest). Soon, switch to the obvious arching splitter on the left wall which eventually arcs back to the corner.
Gear: 0.5–4.0 (heavy on hands and tight hands)

Charley Graham on FFA of *Octopussy* 5.12-

Long Canyon

Warrior Tower

From the Bond Buttress, hike right to Buttress 3. Traverse the buttress for about 15 minutes to the tower

1. HAPPY HUNTING GROUND 5.12- ★★★★
P1: Look for a plaque, climb the right-facing corner above, hands to fingers, to a ledge. Continue up and left though a wide corner and chimney that gains the belay ledge. Traverse right to a two-bolt belay (5.10).
P2: Start up a steep, thin crack with face moves and then easier jamming as the crack opens up and zigzags, before steepening up again. When it ends, traverse blindly right around the arête past a couple bolts and belay on a large ledge, red Camalots useful (5.12-).
P3: Move to the other side of the ledge and face climb past one bolt to the summit (5.8).
Variation to pitch 1: Begin to the right. Start with devious, thin crack climbing to a bolted and sustained stemming corner. Belay as for the regular pitch 1 (5.12).
Descent: Two 60m ropes reach the ground in one rap.
Gear: Doubles from tiny to #2 Camalots and one or two extra 0.5, 0.75 and #1 Camalots
FA: Alan Hunt, Jim Olsen. FFA: Steph Davis

Bistro Crags

This is a wonderful area with a bit of everything, except crowds! The approach takes a pretty solid 40 minutes, but there are nice views along the way. If you look carefully you will see Corona Arch. Sweet!
Approach: Park at 1.4 miles in a small, two-car-size pullout on the right. Cross the road to the obvious wash and scramble up its right side to a faint path. Walk up and slightly right until you hit an old mining road. Continue along this road as it follows a rib under a small cliffband and skirts rightwards. The road heads to the right side of the gap behind Warrior Tower. You will pass a boulder on the mining road, and after this, watch for a talus-filled drainage on your left. Scramble up this, finding the path of least resistance. At its top go left for the Cooler Wall, straight for the Kitchen Wall, and right for the Pantry.

BISTRO: COOLER WALL

COOLER WALL ☀ NW

☐ 1. **FOODBORNE ILLNESS** 5.10 50' ★★
There is something a bit unnerving about being on virgin sandstone, slightly gripped, and looking down to see your belayer puking his guts out.... A hand crack in a right-facing corner to a fist roof.
Gear: 0.75–3.5
FA: K3

☐ 2. **TWICE BAKED** 5.11 100' ★★★
Boulder past a bolt to gain a beautiful tight hands splitter.
Gear: yellow TCU–1.0 (heavy on the 1s, #2 Friends)
FA: Dylan Warren

☐ 3. **UNNAMED** 5.10+
Offwidth splitter crack with a bolt.
FA: Dave Sadoff

☐ 4. **SMASHED FRUIT** 5.10+ 110' ★★★
Fun and varied. Start by passing a bolt on slippery ground then move to a bolted chimney. Exit this to a stellar, left-facing hand crack. Long pitch, physical climbing.
Gear: 0.75–3.5, 3 draws
FA: K3

☐ 5. **EXTRA LEAN** 5.11 40' ★★★
Similar to *Baby Blue* on Wall Street. A right-facing corner with tips. Lean and mean!
Gear: #1 TCU–0.4
FA: K3

BISTRO: KITCHEN WALL

Long Canyon

☐ 6. **BEEF TIPS** 5.11 90' ★★★★
A left-facing corner. Start with off-fingers and finish with big hands. Steep and pumpy! Dylan pulled this off onsight, cleaning along the way, the normal amount of choss that comes with new desert routes. Good one D!
Gear: 0.5–3.0 (heavy on off-fingers)
FA: Dylan Warren

☐ 7. **REACH IN** 5.10 50'
Chossy, fun corner.
FA: K3

☐ 8. **MUTTON FOR PUNISHMENT** 5.10+ 75' ★★
A right-facing corner that starts with fingers and goes up to hands.
Gear: 0.4–2.0
FA: K3

☐ 9. **SPELUNKING SPANKY** 5.11 ★★★
Four pitches, to the rim. The name? It's a long story....
P1: Fingers all the way up to knees and stacks. Anchor visible on the left wall (5.11).
P2: Chimney upward past some fixed pro to easier ground and a belay on the right wall (5.10+).
P3: Super and unique horizontal pitch. Traverse left by walking inside the cliff. At about halfway through there is a gap. Clip a drilled angle and chimney sideways, back to solid ground. Continue to its end (5.9).
P4: Ascend the triangular chimney until it is possible to scramble to the top (5.9+).
Descent: Walk to a spot directly above the horizontal pitch and look for a perfect, square hole in the rim. Rap through to above the baby angle on pitch 3, then rap the route.
Gear: #1 TCU–4.5, optional headlamp for pitch 3
FA: K3, Dylan Warren

☐ 10. **CHEF'S SPECIAL** 5.10 50' ★★★★
The first route to be put up at the Bistro Crags. Splitter hands.
Gear: 1.0–3.0
FA: K3

☐ 11. **PORK CHOPS AND KETCHUP** 5.10 60' ★★
A right-facing corner with mostly hands.
FA: Dave Sadoff

KITCHEN WALL ✴ NE
From the top of the talus wash, hike straight back. A good landmark is *Tomato Basil Appetizer*, a short, lightning-bolt splitter crack on the right side of the crag. Routes described left to right.

☐ 1. **FRENCH COOKING** 5.11 65' ★★
A tips-to-fist arching splitter. Cruxy off the deck.
Gear: 0.0-3.5
FA: K3

☐ 2. **WITH A SOUTHWEST FLARE** 5.10 65' ★
Off-fingers to offwidth in a right-facing corner. Shares anchor with *French Cooking*.
Gear: 0.5–2.0
FA: K3

☐ 3. **PLUMB AND PIT** 5.10 60' ★
Left-facing corner with hands and huecoes.
Gear: 1.0-3.0
FA: K3

☐ 4. **RARE** 5.10+ 70' ★★
Climb a left-facing corner, chimney to fist.
Gear: 2.0–3.5
FA: Dylan Warren

☐ 5. **MEDIUM RARE** 5.10+ A0 ★
Start as for *Rare* then clip a bolt and pendulum over left to a splitter.
Gear: quickdraw, 0.75–2.0
FA: Dylan Warren

☐ 6. **TOMATO BASIL APPETIZER** 5.9 30' ★★
Splitter hands in a lightning-bolt crack—a striking line. A good first lead for the aspiring crack aficionado.
Gear: 1.0–3.0
FA: K3

PANTRY ✴ NE
Some nice moderate climbs here.

☐ 1. **PASTA WORLD** 5.10 80' ★★★
A left-facing corner with hands.
Gear: 2.0–3.0
FA: Dylan Warren

BISTRO: PANTRY

Tenderloin Tower

Potash Road

Jay Ackerman on Chef's Special 5.10

❒ 2. **TOASTED SEEDS** 5.11 100' ★★
A left-facing corner with mostly fingers.
Gear: 0.4–3.0 (heavy on 0.5)
FA: Dylan Warren

❒ 3. **THE KUNDA** 5.10+ 60' ★★
Fist to offwidth, in a slot.
Gear: 3.5–5.0, tape for your ankles
FA: K3

❒ 4. **ROSEMARY AND THYME** 5.10 50' ★
A left-facing corner with hands.
Gear: 1.0–#3 Friend
FA: Dylan Warren

❒ 5. **HABANERO** 10+ 50' ★
A splitter that doglegs left and ascends a left-facing corner
Gear: 0.5–3.0
FA: K3

❒ 6. **BITTERSWEET** 5.10 ★
Climb *Semi-Sweet* and switch over to the left crack and climb a few more body-lengths.
Gear: 0.5–3.0
FA: K3

❒ 7. **SEMI-SWEET** 5.10- 50' ★★
Splitter hands. Another great lead for a beginner.
Gear: 1.0–3.0
FA: K3

The Destination Crag ☀ SE

The Destination Crag is a hike to get to but the routes are really good. They have length, great rock, solitude: all-round great climbs.
Approach: From the southwest face of Maverick Buttress, look behind you: that's the crag. So far we have found two ways to get there; neither very easy.
1) From the Bistro Crag, keep traversing up-canyon, following the cliff line.
2) Park at around 1.8 miles (just below the parking for the *Two Plumb* area) and hike up the drainage. This becomes narrower and narrower (a cool hike on its own!). After about 20 minutes, look for an escape from the draw, and scramble up the steep talus, skirting lower cliffbands, to the cliff.

❒ 1. **DESTINATION 1** 5.11 120' ★★★★★
A left-facing corner with some bulges. Start with fingers and go through the sizes up to big hands.
Gear: Blue TCU–3.0
FA Joe Slansky

❒ 2. **DESTINATION 2** 5.12 ★★★★★
Not far right from *Destination 1*. Hard start on some softish stone, then fingers and off-fingers in an offset that switches aspects several times. The jams ease into all sizes of hands.
Gear: 0.3–3.0
FA: K3

ROCK CLIMBS OF SOUTHWEST UTAH & THE ARIZONA STRIP

By Todd Goss

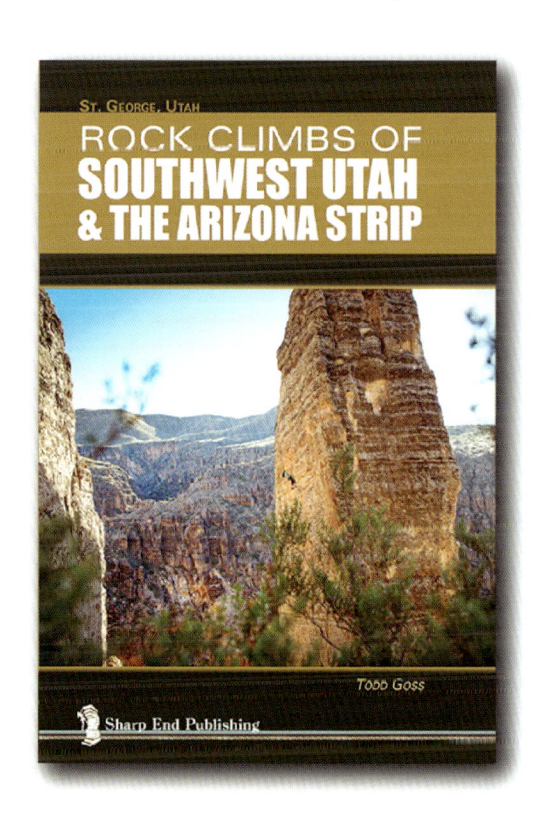

This full-color guide will make you want to pack up and buy real estate in St. George, Utah. With eight rock types, 50+ areas and many renowned crags, the St. George region has become the West's premier sport climbing venue. Routes run the gamut from novice to expert, and scenery from red rock to alpine. This diverse area, boasting nearly a thousand climbs, truly has something to satisfy any climber's taste.

Curious about our latest books? Follow us:

@sharpendpublishing

www.sharpendbooks.com

Potash Road

Long Canyon to the Potash Plant

Beyond Long Canyon, there are two more worthy areas: Offwidth City and the Physics Department. Offwidth City refers to the cliffs that loom over Potash Road just beyond Long Canyon. The Physics Department is located just a little ways beyond Offwidth City, but has separate parking and a separate approach.

Offwidth City SE

Offwidth City is located just a little left of the Shady Crag, but is outside Long Canyon, facing Potash Road. Park just inside Long Canyon immediately after the railroad tracks (as for the Shady Crag). Step over the half-buried cattle fence and find an old, closed road. Hike this road, which leads to Offwidth City. Routes are listed from right to left.

❏ **1. THE MAYOR** 5.11+ ★★★★
This is the obvious left-facing, offwidth corner just left of *Done Lubin'* on the Shady Crag. Four pitches.
Gear: 0.5–green Big Bro (heavy on the big stuff)
FA: Craig Luebben, Topher Donahue

❏ **2. RALPH** 5.12 ★★★
Craig Luebben intended calling this *Off*, because it involves lots of "off" sizes, but gastric difficulties provoked by the grueling first ascent inspired the moniker *Ralph*. Climb the switching splitter just left of *The Mayor*. Start with big hands and offwidth. Face climb right to switch cracks, finish with fingers-to-hands.
Gear: 0.3–6.0 (heavy on off-fingers)
FA: Craig Luebben, Kennan Harvey, Dave Anderson

❏ **3. BIRTH CANAL** 5.10 ★★
Holy Chimney, Batman! This awesome line is about 100 feet left of *Ralph*. Follow the cliffline, and when the cliffbase starts to ascend, look up and locate the anchors. Two pitches.
P1: Begin on the left, behind some stacked rocks that form a chimney. Climb weaknesses inside and at its top crawl through a hole on the right. Continue right into a wedge with a big chockstone. Ascend the right side of the chockstone, hands, to the anchor (90').
P2: Climb steep rock over the anchor into the chimney. Pass a bolt on the outside and keep going, past two more bolts, hidden inside. Eventually reach the top of the chimney; the anchor is on the left.
Gear: P1: 0.75–4, P2: 3 draws, Big Bros

❏ **4. FULL MOON APOLOGY** 5.11 ★★
Start up either side of a pedestal and climb the slot/wedge with fingers and off-fingers.
Gear: 0.4–1.0 (heavy on off-fingers)
FA: Jimmy Dunn

❏ **5. BLACK AND STACKS** 5.10+ ★★
Three pitches, just left of *Apology*. Pitch 1 is a fine fingers to hands outing. The latter pitches are for sickos who enjoy the wide.
Gear: 0.4–6.0
FA: Topher Donahue, Lisa Hathaway

❏ **6. PILLAR ROUTE** 5.10+ ★★★
Two pitches that ascend a pillar to a striking splitter.
P1: Start with some thin, heady moves off the ground up the broken corner. Climb the left side of the pillar with hands and a brief offwidth section to a rest. Continue with big hands and fists to the pillar's top.

P2: Move right off the belay and climb wider, softer rock to the obvious handcrack.
Gear: 0.75–4.0 (heavy on hands/big hands), nuts and a few tips pieces for the start
FA: Kyle Copeland, Craig Luebben, Kennan Harvey

The next three routes are a short walk left of *Pillar Route*. *Main Street* and *Side Street* are on each side of a small fin.

❏ **7. MAIN STREET** 5.11+ 80' ★★★
A shallow right-facing corner, mostly fingers.
Gear: 0.0 TCU–2.0 (heavy on fingers)
FA: Jay Smith

❏ **8. SIDE STREET** 5.10+ 80' ★★★
Climb a left-facing corner with off-fingers before pulling a bulge with tight hands. It's not over till you hit the chains.
Gear: 0.75–2.0
FA: Jay Smith

❏ **9. INCREDIBLE POOH** 5.11 ★★★
Start up some blocky terrain with thin gear then continue through the sizes to hands.
Gear: 0.0 TCU–2
FA: Eric Decaria

Tom Gwinn on *Black and Stacks* 5.10+

The Physics Department ❋E

At 13.8 miles from the Potash Rd/191 intersection (about one half-mile beyond Long Canyon) look for a pullout on the left. Park and walk back to the obvious drainage. Hike up this drainage and the cliff is at the top on the left.

1. RADIOACTIVE PORKSICKLE 5.13 ★★★★
Looks excellent.
P1: Climb over some blocks, past a bolt, to a wedging left-facing dihedral with off-finger and fingers (5.12).
P2: Splitter tips forever (5.13).
FA: Matt Lisenby

2. WEAK BOSONS 5.11+ 135' ★★★★★
A #2 Friend classic! Fingers to tight hands in a right-facing corner to a splitter. Traverse left on a two-foot ledge to clip the chains. A 70 meter cord gets you to the ground on rappel, but not if lowering off.
Gear: 0.3–1.0 heavy on 2 Friends and red Camalots
FA: Bret Ruckman, Gary Olsen

3. STRONG MUONS 5.12 ★★★
Previously a toprope, now a lead. A zigzagging splitter with a three-inch offset. Fingers to off-fingers.
Gear: 0.5–#2 Friend

4. ENERGY DECAY 5.10+ 75' ★★★
This left-facing dihedral is about 300 feet left of *Strong Muons*. Right-facing tight hands to big hands corner.
At the time of this writing, this worthy route has only a single pin anchor.
Gear: 3.0–3.5
FA: Bret Ruckman, Gary Olsen

5. BLOOD HUSH 5.12 50' ★★★
This is 300 feet left of *Energy Decay*. This fingers splitter begins on somewhat less-than-stellar rock that turns into bullet, black rock higher up. Feet disappear, but a saving hand jam allows for clipping the anchor.
Gear: Tips–0.5 (heavy on 0.4)
FA: Charley Graham

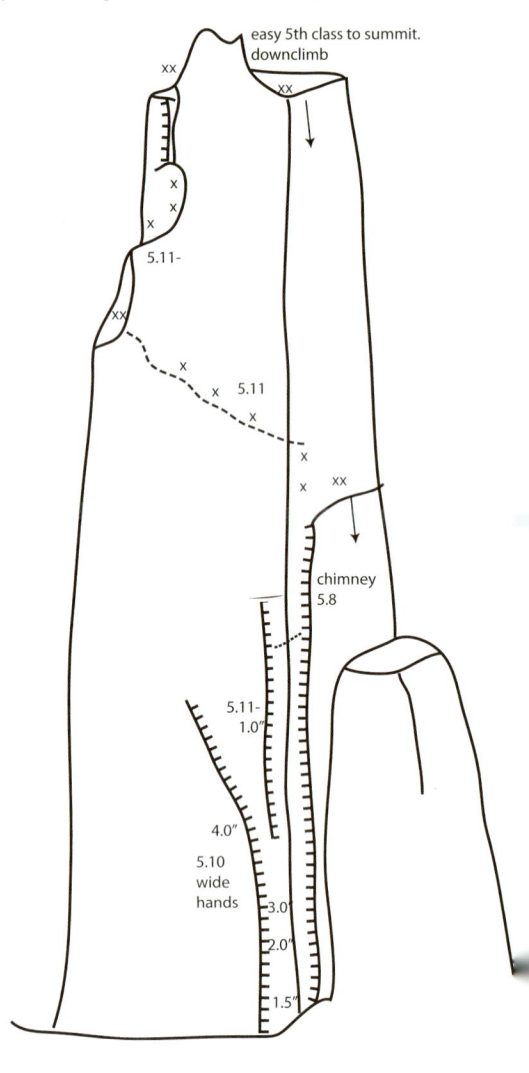

Nik Mirhashemi on Energy Decay 5.10+

Heisenberg Tower

4. THE UNCERTAINTY PRINCIPLE 5.11 ★★★
This 3-pitch route climbs Heisenberg via chimneying and face climbing.
Gear: 3.0–3.5
FA: Jake Warren, Kevin Kane

Chapter 6: River Road

Ben Riley on *Do'ofright* 5.11+

RIVER ROAD OVERVIEW MAP
N
paved road
unpaved road
tower
crag
parking
Arches NP boundary
camping (# of sites)
bathroom
trail
7.5
mileage (from 0.0 location)
HIDEOUT WALL DETAIL
(same scale)
Fisher Towers
The Titan
Onion Creek Rd (Fisher Valley Rd)
no!
12.1
Hideout Wall
Hideout CG
11.1
10.3
no!
0 miles
1
2
3
Hittle Bottom CG (12)
To I-70
128
21.0
Lower Onion Creek CG (4)
20.0
0.0 reset
Onion Creek Rd (Fisher Valley Rd)
Fisher Towers
The Titan
bridge @ 3.6 miles
Hindu
To Hideout Wall (see inset map)
Crooked Arrow Spire
16.1
15.4
hike or drive (4WD?) up creekbed
Voodoo Wall
0.0 reset
Sister Superior
Parriott Mesa
Priest and Nuns
Rectory
Castleton Tower
4.7
Castle Valley
Arches National Park
Theater
11.0
Big Bend Bouldering (7.9)
7.2
Big Bend Butte
Dolomite Lighthouse
The Big Bend
6.0
Podunk Mesa Tower
Big Bend: 5 campgrounds, 66 sites.
Listed from down- to upstream:
Drinks Canyon (17)
Hal Canyon (11)
Oak Grove (7)
Big Bend (23)
Upper Big Bend (8)
Trail of the Navajo
Fun Ramp (1.5)
Artist's Tears (2.9)
Barney Rumble
3.1
Goose Island CG (18)
Granstaff CG (16)
Sorcerer (1.0)
0.0
191
El Secondo
MOAB

RIVER ROAD

Hwy 128, which runs from Moab to Cisco, is one of the most scenic highways in the U.S. It parallels the Colorado River most of the way, offering easy access to the river at any number of launches and sites. It also offers access to some of the most well-known climbing areas in the Moab region, including the Fisher Towers, Onion Valley, Castle Valley, and the boulders at Big Bend. Hundreds of climbs along this spectacular road beckon the adventurous climber. Only a select amount are described here.

Sorcerer and Sorcerer's Apprentice

Driving down the road, the first objectives you will come to are the Sorcerer and Sorcerer's Apprentice—two toweresque formations that have routes on each side and are just a mile down the road. From Center and Main drive 2.5 miles north out of town, and turn right just before the bridge. Reset your odometer here and continue a mile. Park on the left at a pull out with a kiosk, walk across the road to an obvious trail to the base of the climbs.

Sorcerer NW

There are two routes on this formation. *Sorcerer's Crossing* is on the right side of the pillar. Thanks Pamela Pack for the beta!

1. SORCERER 5.11+
One of the best and most challenging offwidth towers in the desert (and first climbed in 1978).
P1: Slightly overhanging, left-facing offwidth dihedral on the left side of the pillar. Climb past 3 star-drive bolts to a 3-bolt anchor (old school 5.10 ow).
P2: Wild chimney/tunnel to a 3-bolt anchor on loose rock. Extremely unique. Don't fall on this pitch—but if there is any chance you will you shouldn't be on this route. Classic desert adventure climbing (5.9+).
P3: Strenuous and unique 5.11d off-width/squeeze chimney past two drilled angles and one lead bolt to 2-bolt anchor. Exposed and committing.
Gear: P1: (2)5.0, (1)6.0, green BigBro; P2: (1 each)1.0–3.0, (2)4.0, long runners; P3: TCUs, (1)1.0, (1)2.0, (1)5.0, (2)6.0, green Big Bro, blue Big Bro
FA: Jim Dunn, Leonard Coyne

2. SORCERER'S CROSSING 5.12
Sorcerer's Crossing starts on the right side of the formation and continues for two pitches before crossing through to the left side for the final pitch.
P1: Climb gnarly ow for an eternity up to three or so body-lengths of squeeze chimney (5.12, 130').
P2: More grueling ow until you can tunnel through to the other side (5.10+, 95').
P3: Follow the left side (original route) via hard chimneying and finish up with some ow (5.11+).
Gear: unknown
FA: Craig Luebben, Jeff Achey

Sorcerer's Apprentice

2. RIGHT SIDE 5.10+ ★★★★
The most popular route of either formation.
P1: Begin the climb on either of the two arching tight hand splitters found on the left or the right. Follow the flake with tips gear to a seam with a few face moves followed by a short wide section. From here, a bit more fingers to a slung chockstone and fixed Hex on a nice belay ledge.
P2: Climb the right-facing corner with some stacks up to a bulge with off-fingers and tight hands. Then continue with steep offwidth and stems to fingers and tips to finish up in the "eye." Set a belay here with gear from 0.4–2.0.
P3: Two options to summit. Left through the eye to meet up with the left-side route (5.11c), or the original right-side start. Face climb out from the belay on some softer rock until you come into some thin hands that tapers down to tips. A few offwidth moves on softer stone get you to the top.
Gear: 0.0 TCU-6.0, heavy on fingers (2 old #4 Camalots are nice).
FA: Chip Chace, Jeff Achey

3. LEFT SIDE 5.11+
P1: Start by climbing a couple body-lengths of wide crack up to a ledge. Continue up with good hands. Belay from the anchor out on the ledge to the left of the "eye" if you plan on finishing up the left side. Belay in the "eye" if you want to finish up the right side.
P2: Start off the belay just left of the "eye" with some fun and steep offwidth moves followed by off-fingers, passing two pitons. Continue with some rounded fingers in a flare. Pass the flare, clip a third pin and top out on softer rock.
FA: Jim Dunn, Bryan Becker, Ed Webster, Martha Morris, and Maureen Gallagher

Sorcerer's Apprentice (left), Sorcerer (right)

GOOSE ISLAND AREA

Some climbs worth mentioning reside on the north side of the river. They are covered in the Arches section of this book, as they are actually part of the Arches National Park, and as such fall under park rules and closures. As I write this, they are closed due to raptor nesting. YOU MUST check with the park before climbing to ensure its accessibility! As always, in the park, use no chalk or use sandstone-colored chalk! Follow existing paths or trails, and install no new fixed anchors without a permit.

River Road Dihedrals

N

From the junction of 191 and 128, drive 2.6 miles and park on the LEFT! This area has a couple of moderates and a couple of harder routes. Its north-facing aspect makes for some comfortable climbing on hot days. Routes are listed right to left.

1. **BLOODY KNEES** 5.9 125' ★★★
Left-facing corner that starts with a short section of tight hands. Continue up the widening crack, moving from hands to fists to stacks. Be on the lookout for face features and the occasional knee jam. Beyond the wide section, continue with hands to the top.
Gear: 0.75-4.5 (double rack up to 4.0, with 4.5 being optional)
FA: Steve Cheyney

2. **OXYGEN DEBT** 5.11+ 70' ★★
Just left of *Bloody Knees*, this route faces back down the River Road towards town. Start steep and thin, then into a wide section. Just past the first wide section, ride some fists to a lesser-angled offwidth. Grunt fest!
Gear: One fingers piece. Double rack from 2.0-4.0.
FA: Paul Gagner

3. **EAST DIHEDRAL AKA BLOODY ELBOWS** 5.9 80' ★★
Starts with a few face moves off the ground. The rock improves higher on the route. Continue up the crack going through the sizes.
Gear: 0.75-4.0 (a 4.5 may be nice for the fledgling leader)
FA: Jimmy Dunn

4. **KER-THUD** 5.9
Heads up to the new leader, this may feel a little runout! Starts just left of *Bloody Elbows*. Similar start as *Bloody Elbows*. Face climb past two bolts up to the left arching splitter with several pods.
Gear: 0.3 through 2.0, 2 draws, nuts helpful
FA: Billy Smallen

5. **ROOT CANAL** 5.8 ★★
On the Molar formation. Chimney climbing past five bolts. Step from the lower summit to the upper summit for an exciting finale. Really fun.
Gear: 5 draws

Serafina Gerard on *Root Canal* 5.8

Roadside

ADVENTURE

At 2.9 miles from the intersection of 191 & 128, on the right side of the road just before Negro Bill Canyon, residesa coveted aid line called *Artist Tears*. Park at the Negro Bill parking area and walk back down the road then up the short talus to the base of the route.

❏ ARTIST TEARS 5.8 C3 ★★★ ✺ N

This awesome, steep, and sheer route now goes clean. The anchors have been replaced and are now bomber. The route can be done several ways, and over the years another set of anchors has appeared, breaking the old-school pitch one into two short pitches. It is possible to link pitches 1 and 2 as well as pitches 4 and 5. The route (if you go from anchor to anchor) is 5 pitches long.

P1: Warm-up pitch. Climb 5.5 slab to a pin, hook to a bolt, hand place a #4 BD Angle (sawed off or tied off. Do not hammer. The hole is in poor shape and the move is above a bomber new bolt). Follow the bolt/rivet ladder, then do one reachy offset nut placement to belay anchors (C1+).

P2: Crux pitch. Make a couple of hook moves to a pin, hook to another pin, then start a string of tenuous placements (Tri-cams, hooks, and small offset wires) past two more pins to the belay (C3).

P3: This awesome pitch has just enough scarring to go clean. Make one or two small offset wire placements to a bolt, then start a string of small wires in an overhanging shallow seam with the occasional Tricam and cam placement. This nonsense ends at a bolt/rivet ladder (many of which have been replaced) which takes you to the next belay (C3).

P4: Casual Pitch. This is the longest and steepest pitch of the route. Bring a ton of tie-offs and rivet hangers. There are a couple of very reachy moves. Be prepared to lasso or improvise something to reach some of the fixed gear (getting into your top-steps is hard in some spots). Follow fixed gear and place decent gear along the way until you reach the final belay (C2).

P5: Aid/free climb past some fixed gear (nuts and pins) in a groove to the summit. There are new anchors off to the left on a small patch of varnish (5.9 or C1).

Rap: A short distance over the lip to the last set of anchors (25 ft) then make a double rope 60 m rap to the start of P3, then one more double to the ground. Fix a rope from the start of P3 to the top of P4, otherwise it is difficult to get back into the wall.

Gear: NO HAMMER, sawed off #4 Angle (normal one will work, just have to tie it off), 1-2 sets DMM Peanuts, 1 set HB offset brass nuts, doubles in 3 largest sizes (yellow, green, blue) 1 set Tricams pink–blue, double in red, 1 set offset Aliens, 1 set Aliens (full set including largest sizes), 1 set Camalots 0.5–2.0, 1 set stoppers, 25+ free biners, BD grappling and cliffhanger hooks, 12 rivet hangers, 20 tie-offs, screamers useful. Belay seat/ledge highly recommended, extra rope to fix pitches
FA: P1 & 2 Eric Bjørnstad, Jimmy Dunn; Entire route: Molly Higgins, Larry Brunce

Thanks to Luke Malatesta for the topo and description.

Serafina Gerard on *Bloody Knees* 5.9

Luke Malatesta, *Artist Tears*, photo: Chuck Burr

River Road

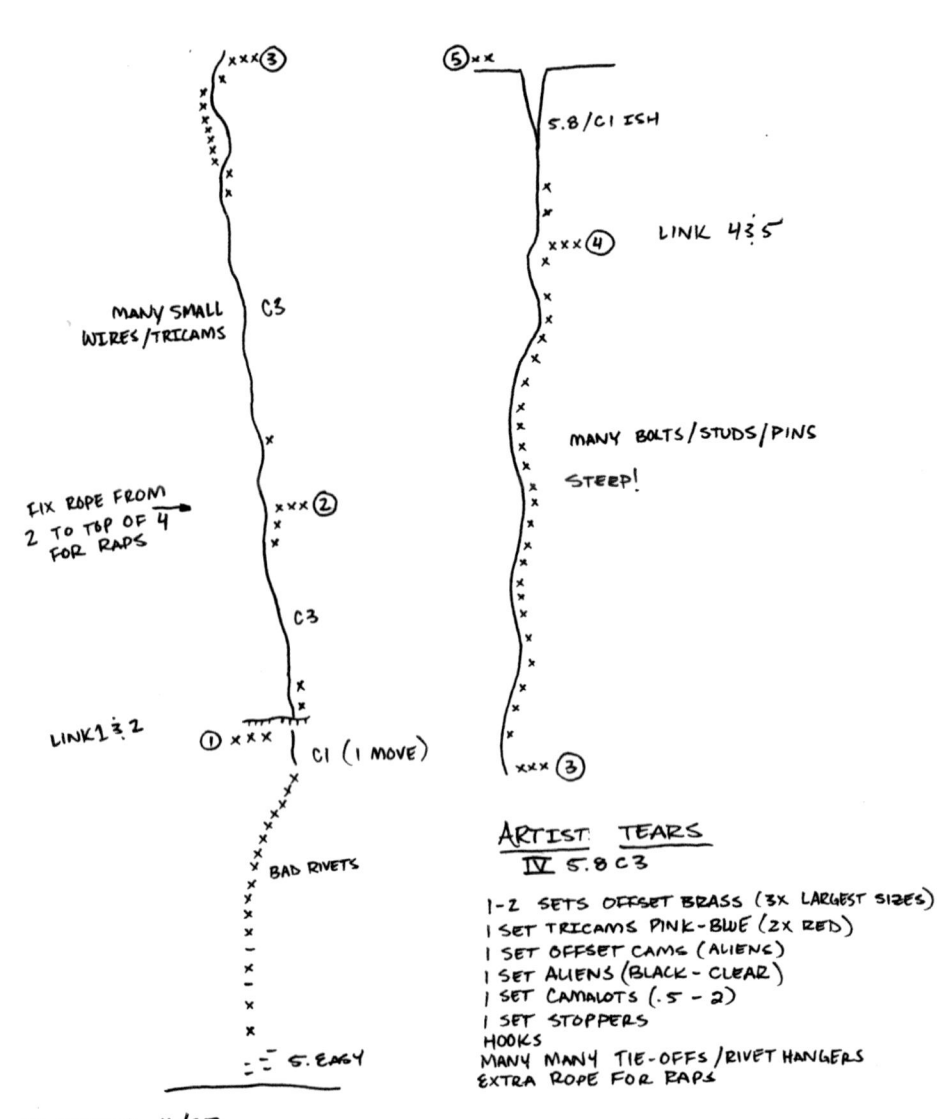

Many small wires/tricams — C3

Fix rope from 2 to top of 4 for raps

LINK 1 & 2

C3

C1 (1 move)

BAD RIVETS

5. EASY

L. MALATESTA 11/07

5.8/C1 ISH

LINK 4 & 5

Many bolts/studs/pins

STEEP!

ARTIST TEARS
IV 5.8 C3

1-2 SETS OFFSET BRASS (3X LARGEST SIZES)
1 SET TRICAMS PINK-BLUE (2X RED)
1 SET OFFSET CAMS (ALIENS)
1 SET ALIENS (BLACK - CLEAR)
1 SET CAMALOTS (.5 - 2)
1 SET STOPPERS
HOOKS
MANY MANY TIE-OFFS / RIVET HANGERS
EXTRA ROPE FOR RAPS

Protecting wildlife, appropriate use of fire, clean water, healthy parks and trails—all a reality when people learn about and practice Leave No Trace.

It all starts with your commitment.

Leave No Trace™
Center for Outdoor Ethics | LNT.org

LNT.org/join

River Road

Podunk Mesa Tower ⭐N

An odd little tower resides just before Lighthouse Tower and Big Bend, and it holds a terrific climb—visible from the road to a keen observer. From the junction of Hwy 191 and 128, drive 6.0 miles. Park in a campground with an information kiosk on the river side of the road, hike up the gully across the road (Spring Canyon) to a small cliff band with a spring at the base. Head up the steep talus slope to the base of the tower.

☐ 1. ADRENALINE CIRCUS 5.10+ ★★★

Adrenaline Circus starts on the west (facing the river) side of the tower. The first set of anchors is visible on a ledge, just below a dark face with cracks.

P1: The first ascentionist started on the south (facing the gully) side and ascended a pretty crumbly loose crack to get to the first belay ledge. It is 5.10 and not worthwhile. Nowadays, folks start up the easy (though sparsely protected) slabs directly beneath the first anchor on the west side. It is definitely the worst pitch of the route but luckily only about 5.5 and 50 feet.

P2: From the belay anchor, climb up and left past a bolt to gain a crack system that leads to a huge, comfy belay ledge after 80 feet. The crack eats up cams from 1.0 to 4.0 inches (5.10).

P3: From the anchor, go to the left edge of the ledge and climb a few body-lengths looking at a blank black slab with bolts. At 5.9, it climbs easier than it looks. Traverse right and then up a somewhat soft but slabby crack to the next belay ledge. This winding 60-foot pitch can generate some rope drag.

P4: This is where the route gets its name. Begin by stepping down and right from the belay until you can lean out to clip the first bolt. The exposure here is great, and some fairly exciting climbing follows. Climb the blunt arête up to a headwall and then move right a bit to the summit. This pitch is 80ft long, but the pucker factor might make it feel harder (5.10+).

Descent: Rappel 35 meters from the summit to the top of pitch 3, then two 60m ropes reach the ground. Otherwise rap the route.

Gear: 0.3-4.0, 10 long draws
FA: Josh Gross, Noah Bigwood

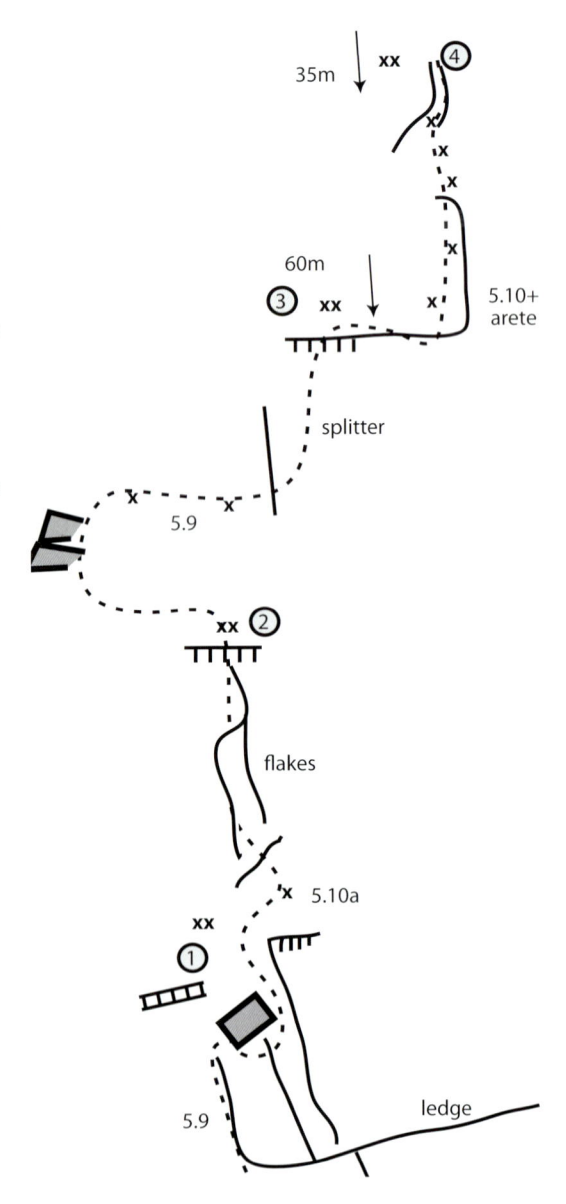

LIGHTHOUSE, DOLOMITE, AND BIG BEND BUTTE AREA

Across from Big Bend Rec Area are a host of fine towers and rim routes, clearly visible from the road. Park at 7.2 miles in a small pullout on the right side of the road. Look for a steep cairned trail going up an obvious talus cone/ridge towards the notch on the right of Lighthouse. The trail splits near the top of the talus—left will bring you to Dolomite Tower and the Big Bend Butte. Right brings you to the approach pitch for *Lonely Vigil* and *O'Grady*.

1. O'GRADY 5.12+ ★★★★
P1: Climb the obvious weakness from left to right to a belay ledge (5.8, 65').
P2: Make your way onto the block, then climb into the obvious slot. Steep, thin, nut-protected moves lead to a gorgeous off-fingers/tight hands splitter up the middle of the tower. Use the crack on the left to gain the summit (5.12+, 110').
Rap: Double ropes lead to the ground. A single 70m cord also works but requires swinging into the belay.
FA: Jay Smith; FFA: Kitty Calhoun

June Ray following pitch 2 of *Lonely Vigil* 5.10

Light House Tower

2. LONELY VIGIL 5.10 ★★★★ NE

This route is on the back side of the formation as viewed from the road. The best method of reaching the start is to climb a 40' 5.6 approach pitch in the notch between *O'Grady* and Lighthouse Tower. Once through the notch walk left for 50' or so and look for the stem box on the second pitch.

P1: Climb through some bulges and into the first squeeze (optional 6.0), then proceed (via stems, discontinuous cracks and face holds) up the left crack to a ledge. Set a belay with gear (2.0 Friends & 1.0 Camalots work well). Those savvy with shoulder length slings could combine this with the next pitch.

P2: Flip your trusty ol' two-headed coin for this pitch! Climb some tight hands in a right-facing corner until you can traverse right to the left-facing corner. Continue via ow to a chimney with a chockstone, until you can get a finger-sized piece of gear just under a roof. Make a steep traverse left—with stems and face holds—to a ledge. Get a solid piece of gear (small nuts helpful) and pull a few final thin moves to the next belay ledge.

P3: Walk left along a ledge to a bolt. Slab up towards a loose looking block (secure) with more easy slab moves bringing you to the anchors.

P4: A boulder problem to the summit block must be reversed!

Descent: You could rap the route, but I like to rap down the old Carter route between Dolomite Tower and Lighthouse in two raps. (From the third pitch anchors, you can look down and see your next rap station). From here a 70 meter rope will get you to the ground—30' right of where you began.

Gear: Double sets of cams to 3.0 and a set of nuts. Optional 6.0

3. IRON MAIDEN 5.12 ★★★★ W-SW

It's good and difficult. *Iron Maiden* is located at the top of the approach trail on the right side of the tower.

P1: Begin just left of a notch, up a short chimney to a ledge. Follow a right-facing corner that eventually thins down past a fixed piece. Avoid the optional belay stance and continue past a bolt, traversing right to the arête and a gear belay (0.5 and 0.75 work well). 5.12

P2: Follow the famed "harder than it looks" leftward horizontal crack to a crack system (big hands and fists). Pass through the blocky cave up to a corner with a gear belay (3.0s). 5.11

P3: Climb the flake (5.12) passing a pair of bolts, then traverse right past the *Lonely Vigil* belay and continue to the summit.

Descent: Rap as per Lonely Vigil

Gear: Triple sets of 0.0–3.5, nuts, shoulder length slings

FA: Ed Webster, Jeff Achey

Ben Riley on *Dolofright* 5.11+ R

River Road

Dolomite Tower ☀SW

☐ 4. **DOLOFRIGHT** 5.11+ R ★★★★
Heads up, boys and girls—Tom was perhaps feeling a bit spicy! The route has a reputation for great climbing but it's very bold! The story goes that after Tom put up the route, Dan Osman did it and wrote in the summit register "Great route but could use another bolt." Enough said!
P1: The crux pitch. Begins from the back side. Steep climbing leads past a piton to the arête. Some red Camalots will work in a horizontal as you continue on this sustained pitch.
P2: The climbing eases up but the bolt spacing gets wider and the rock is a little iffy. Take a good look at the final bolt—Tom left a message on it.
Gear: 8 quickdraws, (2)yellow Metolious TCU or equivalent, 1.0, large testicles helpful
Rap the route.
FA: Tom Gilje

Big Bend Butte ☀SW

☐ 5. **INFRARED** 5.12 ★★★★★
A modern classic! As seen from the road, looking up at the butte, this is the farthest right obvious route.
P1: Commence just right of where Dolomite Tower and the butte connect. Climb broken rock up and over some bulges, then follow a big hands crack to a bolted belay (5.10).
P2: Edge left past a bolt (5.10+) to a steep fist crack leading to a bolted belay.
P3: A stellar pitch of "man hands." This climbs the obvious splitter seen from the road. Pass a block with a bolt to good hand jams under and around the roof. Bolted belay.
P4: Exposed, steep face climbing follows the right-facing corner system. Trend left toward the summit. This is not a pure sport pitch—a single rack is recommended to supplement the bolts.
FA: Jay Smith, Conrad Anker
Descent: Rappel the route with two 60 meter ropes. There has been lots of confusion concerning the descent of this stellar route. There are absolutely rap anchors from the summit. You must have patience and a keen eye and you will find them. ALSO, The last pitch is very steep and to ensure you're not rapping back off into space you need to fix a line before climbing the last pitch to ensure you're able to get back to the cliff!
Gear: 1 set wires, 1–2 sliders, 0.3, (2)0.4, (2)0.5, (3)0.75, (2)#1 Friends, (2)1.5, (3)2.0,(3)2.5, (3)3.0, (4)3.5, (3)4.0, many long draws and runners for last pitch

☐ 6. **CLEARLIGHT** 5.11 ★★★
Another amazing route completes the Big Bend-Jay Smith hattrick. This is a bit of a meandering line. As seen from the road, it's the third splitter from the right.
P1: Climb fingers and hands (sometimes dirty) for 100+ feet to a bolted belay (5.10).
P2: The "Try Not to Fall" pitch. Travel left, passing a few bolts and utilizing any gear placements you find (your follower will thank you, as prussiks or an ascender would be necessary if they blew it on the traverse). An off-fingers/fingers splitter leads to the belay (5.11+).
P3: A sweet big hands splitter goes wide for a short bit. Good rock! (5.11)
P4: A runout 5.8 chimney leads to the summit.
Gear: 0.3, 0.4, (2)0.5, (4)0.75, (5)#1 Friends, (3)2.0, (4)3.0, (4)3.5, (2)4.0, (1)6.0, draws and runners
FA: Jay Smith, Kitty Calhoun

The route shown as "A" on the topo on the next page is the Big Bend Wall 5.10 A3

Roadside

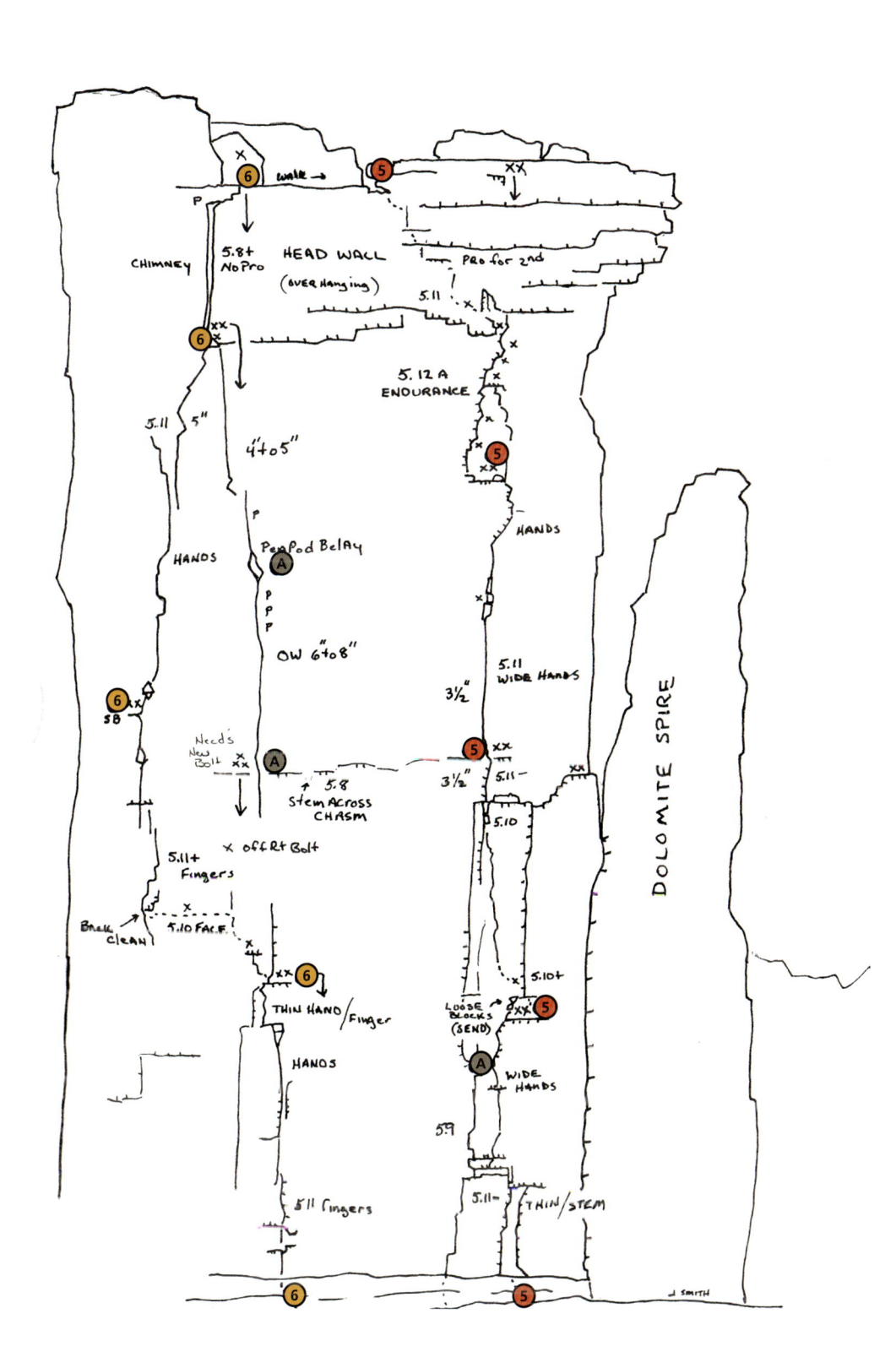

Ben Kiessel following pitch 3 (5.11) of *Infrared*

Ben Kiessel stemming to another good rest on the final pitch.   Both photos: Matt Pickren

BIG BEND BOULDERS

The Big Bend Boulders, located on the River Road near Big Bend Campground, have become quite popular with the cordless crowds. Ideal for a post-ride pump, a full day session, or a quick fix after a long drive, this boulderfield is stacked with quality sandstone problems. Park in the pullout about 7.9 miles up the River Road from Moab. The chalked boulders are obvious on the side of the road opposite the river. Thanks to Lisa Hathaway and Noah Bigwood for the descriptions.

Laurel Wright on *Circus Trick* V4
Photo: Andrew Burr

BIG BEND BOULDERING

For decades, Big Bend has been a roadside stop-over for the itinerant and peripatetic desert rat. Easily accessible, it offered great rest or rain day options for the likes of the Moab area's earliest route developers. It is often hard to say who "discovered" or FAd a lot of the problems, but without a doubt Eric Decaria and Tom Gilje spearheaded the development of most of the classic and harder lines with contributions in the double-digits from Noah Bigwood. Courtesy of the aforementioned efforts, in the past 10–15 years, Big Bend has evolved from being a handy, roadside novelty, to an area renowned for its compression test-pieces. Though lacking in sheer numbers of problems, there is at least one classic at each grade that can hold its own with the world's best. Not to be missed, in general order of difficulty are: *Washing Machine, The Black Box Arêtes, Washed Up, Silly Wabbit, The Circus Trick(s), Block Party, Army of Darkness, Black Angus, The Chaos, The Grim Reacher(s), Bluelight Special, Five Finger Discount,* and *The Hell Belly* (standing and sit variations).
-Lisa Hathaway

Block Top Boulder (#1)

This square boulder sits apart from the main areas and is the first boulder visible as you approach from Moab. Turn right onto a dirt campground access road across from the main Big Bend campground, and park in the overflow parking area on the right. The boulder sits about a hundred yards directly in front of the parking.

❐ 1. **BROWN POWER** V4
On the south (road) side of the boulder. Start on a good horizontal slot and go straight out the small roof using a lefthand sidepull and cool brown pockets.

❐ 2. **FIVE FINGER DISCOUNT** V9
Start right of #1 on the right side of the same horizontal slot. Go up and right, topping out near the arête.

❐ 3. **BLOCK PARTY** V5
Ten feet right of *Five Finger Discount* on the other side of the arête. Start under the roof on good pocket slots and go straight out the roof and up a series of thin crimps.

❐ 4. **WHODUNNIT** V8
Ten feet right of #3 and around the arête. Start low at the bottom of a shallow dihedral. One huge move left and then straight up on small holds.

❐ 5. **DESCENT** V0
Start in the same shallow dihedral as #4. Go straight up on good holds. Beware this is also the descent!

❐ 6. **SLAPPING THE BLOCK** V6
Five feet right of #5. Start sitting and go up through bizarre moves, finally slapping your left hand up a blunt arête and leap for the top.

❐ 7. **SLAPPING THE BLOCK SIT-START** V10
This problem can be made harder with a sit start to the left.

❐ 8. **BLOCK SHOCK** V2
Just right of #6 on a blunt arête on the left side of a brown face (facing the parking area). Start on good holds and go up through slopers to the top.

❐ 9. **BLOCK POCK** V1
Ten feet right of #6. Start on decent holds and move left to the biggest pocket on the face then straight up.

Lisa Hathaway on *Circus Trick*
Photo: Eric Odenthal

Jim "Wayne Bob" Maierhofer" on *Grim Reacher*
Photo: Eric Odenthal

Roadside

The Shackleton Boulder (#2)
The large boulder to the viewer's right of the Block Top. Not super popular, but there are three fun problems. The boulder is littered with numerous quality moderates. Approach carefully from pullout on 128 (preferred) straight up faint wash (or from Block Top, being careful to avoid the cryptos).

1. THE SHACKLETON TRAVERSE V7
Traverse the bloc on the best available holds.

2. V3
In the middle of the face that faces toward the Block Top there are two great problems adjacent to one another. The V3 uses edges and a good foot to attain the top.

3. V7
A great problem, though a bit of a contrivance as it is easy to access the good holds for # 3. As with any Big Bend problem, if it feels too easy, it likely is not the variation described. Start left of #3 and pull up and slightly left on small edges.

Army of Darkness (#3)
To get to this boulder, hike east (toward Lighthouse and Dolomite towers) for 300 yards from the main Big Bend parking area. The boulder is back in the second drainage on the left and is visible from the road.

1. BASKETBALL DIARIES V5
Start on matched crimps near the left arête of the east (uphill) side of the boulder. Traverse right on slopers and across a long flat rail to an obvious dyno move to a good flat edge above.

2. QUEEN AMADALA V7
A new hold appeared in 2013. The original problem, Jedi, can still be climbed at V9/10 as an eliminate, but now the obvious sequence uses the new crimp. Do the first ten feet of #1, then stay low.

2a. RETURN OF THE JEDI V10
For Jedi, the left-hand crams into a small finger-tip stack. Throw a big right-hand dyno to catch the edge of a crack between two boulders, and go straight up. This problem was originally done using the crack for feet to finish (V9), but was later done without (V10).

3. LEFT HAND OF DARKNESS V7
The left arête on the west (downhill) side of the boulder. Start on any of the good low jugs and continue straight up. Can also be started from a small flat rock just left of the arête with significantly reduced difficulty.

4. PROJECT V?
Between #3 & #5 several tiny and enticing crimps have shut down all attempts.

5. ARMY OF DARKNESS V5
Start with a good high right-hand crimp. Step up and move left topping out on slopers.

6. RIGHT HAND OF DARKNESS V8
Start as for #5 but go right to a sloping undercling, continue up and right to the top.

7. BASIC TRAINING V0
Ten feet right of #5 and # 6, go up an obvious black scooped slab.

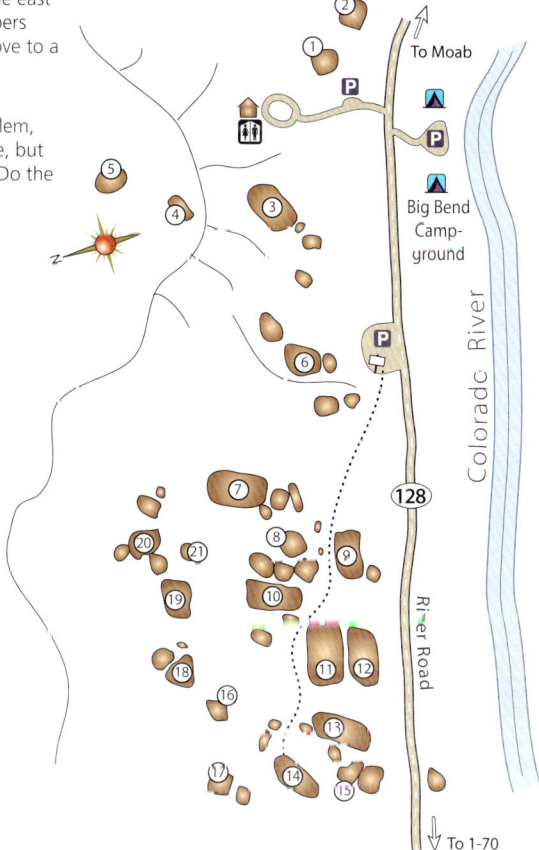

1. Block Top Boulder
2. Shackleton Boulder
3. Army of Darkness
4. Monster Block Boulder
5. Chevy Van Boulder
6. Wash Boulder
7. Highballs Boulder
8. Scoopula Boulder
9. Trail Boulder
10. Black Box Boulder
11. Chaos Boulder
12. Flat Top Boulder
13. Hueco Traverse Boulder
14. Sand Traverse Boulder
15. Punisher Boulder
16. The Orange Peel Boulder
17. The Split Boulder
18. Big Horn Beaver
19. The Belcer Traverse
20. Black Boulder
21. The Sloper Cave

Monster Block Boulder (#4)

Hike directly uphill behind the Army of Darkness Boulder to the first plateau. The boulder is vaguely triangular and all the problems are on the east side.

☐ 1. **DRUNKULA** V4
Sit-start with slopers and head right up the angling left-facing left arête.

☐ 2. **FRANKENSPANK** V7
Begin with a sit-start just right of *Drunkula*. Move up and left on interesting pockets and edges.

☐ 3. **QUASI-MONO** V4
Commence 10 feet right of *Frankenspank* with a tiny mono and an even smaller crimp. Dyno for the top.

Chevy Van Boulder (#5)

Like Monster Block, this stone is sadly overlooked due to the long (by Big Bend standards) approach and difficulty of the problems. In the past decade or so, quiet development of many hard problems has been going on up here. From the Monster Block, continue up the hill and left a bit (passing a few boulders with existing problems), to a split boulder with a cool scoopy-arête problem (V5/6) located on the right side of the split. (On the left side of the split is a hard sit-start problem.) The Chevy Van is directly above this boulder and is on an overhanging face, facing the cliff.

☐ 1. **CHEVY VAN** V11
A built-up landing helps identify this problem. Start as low as possible on a steep arête on crimps, climb right on the steep face and up to the slab crux.

Wash Boulder (#6)

From the main Big Bend parking lot, walk 100 feet north (away from the road) up a small wash; the boulder is on the right side of the wash.

☐ 1. **SLAB** V3
On the north (facing away from the road) side is a black slab. Start on two crimps and smear your feet. Deadpoint to an obvious right-hand crimp jug.

☐ 2. **WASHING MACHINE** V2
The arête that faces into the wash. Start on the good jugs at head height and dyno left to a jug around the arête then up.

☐ 3. **WASHED UP** V4
Just right of #2 is an obvious right-angling ramp. Start as low as possible and ascend, finishing with an interesting mantel.

☐ 4. **WASHED UP RIGHT** V5
Begin as for #3 but head right from the rail on sloping edges and finish at the triangle point.

☐ 5. **QUEEN OF CLEAN** V6
Start from a bad rail and move up and left.

Highballs Boulder (#7)

This huge boulder dominates the view from the parking lot. It sits on a hillside about 100 feet from the parking area and presents an impressive-looking slab above an equally impressive overhang.

☐ 1 **HIGHBALLS** V7
On the left side of the big overhang (facing the parking lot). Start on a good right-hand sidepull, go to a right-hand pinch in a small roof. Reach up to the notched jug and carefully negotiate the giant slab above.

☐ 2. **HIGHBALLS LEFT** V8
Start at the left side and go straight up to a high crux.

☐ 3. **PROJECT** V?
In the center of the big roof just right of #1. Start under the roof on tiny sidepulls and go to the lip then up the slab above.

☐ 4. **HIGH DESERT DRIFTER** V1
Fifteen feet right of #1 on the right side of the big overhang. Start with good holds above the lip and continue up on good holds through a high finish.

☐ 5. **LOW BALL** V3
On the backside (facing away from the parking) in a small flat-floored grotto. Start sitting with two decent holds and go straight up to mantel into a scoop.

☐ 6. **SATELLITE 1** V3
About 20 feet right of #4 on a separate boulder leaning against the Highballs Boulder. Start on crimps at the lip of a gentle roof, then continue on crimps and pockets.

☐ 6. **SATELLITE 2 (HIDDEN CRACK BOULDER)** V3
Ten feet right of #6 a thin, flat boulder leans against the #6 boulder. Climb the crack between these two, start as low as possible and move up and left.

Scoopula Boulder (#8)

One hundred yards from the parking area, the trail goes between two boulders. Scoopula is the one on the right and presents its namesake scoop directly toward the trail.

☐ 1. **SCOOPULA** V10
On the south side of the boulder (facing the road). This stellar problem starts matched on a low sloper with a hidden toe hook below the roof. Go up and left to the arête finishing with a thrilling dyno to the lip.

☐ 2. **STANDULA** V8
Start on the good right-hand crimp above the starting sloper and finish the rest of the problem.

☐ 3. **WUSSULA** V5
Start on the left arête and step off the boulder to do the last few moves and the dyno.

☐ 4. **SITULA** V11
Take it one move lower than #1 with a scooch start.

☐ 5. **LEFT** V3
Ten feet right of #1 around the corner. Start on an obvious vertical jug and go up and left (avoiding the boulder to the left).

☐ 6. **CENTER** V4
Five feet right of #2, start low on a good left-hand pocket and a not-so-good right. Go straight up.

☐ 7. **RIGHT** V1
Start in the huge pocket five feet right of #3, near the right end of the boulder, and go up.

Trail Boulder (#9)

Located on the left side of the trail (across from Scoopula) about 100 yards from the parking lot.

☐ 1. **BIG HUCK** V7
On the blunt lefthand arête nearest the trail (facing away from the road). Start with the left hand on the arête and the right hand on a distant sidepull. Step up

and jump for the top. As with most off-the-ground crux problems, stacking pads vastly reduces the difficulty of this problem.

❏ 2. **MIDDLE MAN** V2
Five feet right of #1. Start sitting with a good left-hand undercling pocket and the right hand on a vertical hueco. Big moves lead to big holds and the top.

❏ 3. **TRAIL TRAVERSE** V3
Fifteen feet right of #2 near the left end of the face. Start sitting with small crimps and traverse left along a horizontal crack using all available holds. Avoiding the top of the boulder adds a V grade. Top out at #2. Variation: Start on #2 and traverse right. Top out with a sloping mantel above the start of #3.

❏ 4. **HIGH STEP** AKA **STEP IT UP** V2
On the side facing the road, the left arête. Start with the left hand on the arête and step up on a very high foot to a hidden crimp over the lip.

Black Box Boulder (#10)
A great area to warm up, but watch out on really hot days as the black rock can actually be blisteringly hot. From the parking area, walk the trail 125 yards, past the Scoopula and Trail boulders, then go right for 50 feet.

❏ 1. **SLIMPER** V3
On the far left end, right of the arête, of the longest black face (facing away from the parking). Start with two high sloping crimps and go straight up.

❏ 2. **SHORTER TRAVERSE** V5
Ten feet right of #1. Start on a good sidepull jug and traverse low right for 20 feet to #5.

❏ 3. **SLOTS OF FUN** V2
Five feet right of #2. Start with two chalked up slots and go to a good right-hand sidepull then up.

❏ 4. **CENTER START** V1
Five feet right of #3. Start on good small crimps and go up and a bit right to the top.

❏ 5. **CENTER DIRECT** V3
Five feet right of #4 and 10 feet left of the arête. Start on two tiny sharp crimp/pockets with a huge sandy foot and go straight up.

❏ 6. **ARÊTE LEFT SIDE** V3
The left side of the arête. Either use a right hand on the arête and deadpoint to a good horizontal crimp, or traverse from #4 to the same crimp. Go up the arête. Variation: Dyno from the crimp to the top.

❏ 7. **ARÊTE RIGHT SIDE** V3
The right side of the arête. Start with a good right hand edge and the left on the arête (or edges near it). Go straight up.

❏ 8. **BLUE LIGHT SPECIAL** V9
Ten feet right of #7 lies a sharp right arête with a chest high roof below it. Start with a right hand on the arête and jump like Michael Jordan to catch a finger notch in the arête with the left hand. Get your feet up and continue using the arête to the top.

❏ 9. **BARRACUDA** V10
Start as for #8 and then traverse left to finish on #7.

❏ 10. **ABUCARRAB/FADE INTO BLUE** V6
Start as for #7 and finish on #8. Though a link-up, this is actually one of the sweetest problem in the cluster.

❏ 11. **BLACK ALLEY** V0
On the backside of the boulder in a corridor, about 15 feet right of #8. Start on good holds and go up, topping out just left of a protruding roof.

Chaos Boulder (#11)
This is the big one! Obvious from anywhere in the area, Chaos Boulder is the center of the Big Bend universe and has a plethora of great problems on all aspects. Follow the main trail from the parking for 150 yards and you will bump into it.

❏ 1. **HELL BELLY** V11
The obvious and improbable overhanging prow on the east (facing the parking lot) side of the boulder. First done as a jump start, this problem now goes from a sit start. Start sitting with a good right-hand crimp and the left on the arête, continue slapping and bumping up both sides of the prow. At the lip you can exit right or left. The left uses the arête and a small crack edge on the slab above. The right moves up to a sharp horn in a scoop near the mantel on #2.
Variation: V8 start with the left hand on the undercling pinch, and the right on the arête. Finish up either top out, as for the sit down.

❏ 2. **CHAOS** V8
Ten feet right of #1. Start matched on a big sloper and move up and left, topping out in an obvious scoop. To truly top out after mantling into the scoop, move up and right to a crack and the top.
Variation: Sit start 10 feet right in funky huecos and move left on slopers to join the normal start.

❏ 3. **THE GRIM REACHER** V5
Five feet right of #2. Start with a left-hand sloper and a right-hand pinch. Move up making the reach to a small edge above then go right to the huge keyed-in block. Go straight up, careful to avoid any fragile holds, and finally mantel (summit!) at about 20 feet.

❏ 4 **THE REACHER DIRECT** V8
Start as for #3, but proceed straight up from the crimp rail, using an undercling for the right hand, topping out straight up.

❏ 5. **HEARTSAFLUTTER** V3
Eponymously named for how one feels summiting this problem and not recommended for the V3/4/5 acolyte! Start left of the death-flakes and right of the *Reacher* and go straight up.

❏ 6. **DEATH FLAKES** V0
The problem is now a lot safer and much easier, as flakes that once leaned against it are now scattered along the base. Start ten feet right of #3 and traverse the face topping out on #5.

❏ 7. **DESCENT RAMP** V0
Five feet left of the overhanging arête on the west (facing away from the parking) side of the boulder. Start on sloping feet with any holds you like and go up and a bit right. Beware as this is also the descent!

❏ 8. **CIRCUS TRICK** V3 or V4
On the overhanging arête of the west face, start sitting (V4) and go up and right to a great dyno (the circus trick) to the top. Start standing (V3) with two good holds and finish as for the original.
Variation: Start standing with two good holds and dyno with one or two hands for the lip.

River Road

❐ 9. **CIRCUS TRICK RIGHT** V5
Five feet right of #6. Start with a vertical right-hand sloper and a high left sloper. Heel and toe hooks help to establish a dyno for the lip about five feet right of where #6 does.

❐ 10. **THE ORIGINAL CIRCUS TRICK** V5
Sit-start as for #8 and finish on #9.

❐ 11. **GOOD DAY, BAD DAY** V11
Start sitting with the left hand in a road crew shot hole and the right on a sloper. Slap, hook and grunt into the stand-up problem.

❐ 11. **PHANTOM FIGHTER** V10 or V11
For the V11, start low with a sloping left-hand crimp and a sharp gaston for the right. Go straight up to a good hold at ten feet, and either dyno to the lip or use the crack for the left hand. Originally done at V10 from a standing start, hands matched on the left-facing rail. Variation V9: Start on the in-cut jugs and climb or huck for the lip.

❐ 12. **HANGING TIGHT** V1
Five feet right of #8 on the overhanging right arête. Start standing on the back-breaking boulder and go up the arête on good jugs to an interesting mantel.

❐ 13. **PRESS TIGHT** V3
Start left of #9, with the left hand pressing the left-angling ramp and the right hand on a tiny edge. Head up and left.

❐ 14. **RAMPAGE** V5
Ten feet right of #9 is an obvious right-leaning ramp above a pile of sharp boulders. Start at the bottom of the ramp and go up to a loose keyed-in flake with a scary mantel at the top.

❐ 15.. **THE REAL RAMPAGE** V7
Start as for #10, but follow the ramp to the summit. Landing is treacherous. Best done as a TR.

Flat Top aka Roadside (#12)
If you get tired of bouldering, just set up camp on top of this wide flat boulder and soak up the sunshine. Or for a nice warm-up, try traversing around the whole thing using the lip. The Flat Top Boulder sits between Chaos Boulder and the road.

❐ 1. **THE NAZI TRAVERSE** V7
(Aka *Shot Hole Traverse*) On the west (facing away from the parking) side of the boulder is a roof with two obvious drilled holes (courtesy of the Utah Department of Transportation). Start to the left on good slopers and traverse right through the holes until your right hand is on a small gaston crimper and your left is in the rightmost shot hole, then dyno to the lip.
Variation V5: Just do the dyno at the end of #1.
Variation V5: Start with the right hand in the rightmost shot hole and go up.
Variation V4: Start with the left hand in the leftmost shot hole and go up.

❐ 2. **SKINLESS DYNO** V10
Start with the left hand on the crimper three feet right of the rightmost shot hole, and the right hand on a tiny high crimp. Dyno for the lip!

Chris Schulte on Hell Belly V11
Photo: Eric Odenthal

❐ 3. **ARÊTE** V6
This once obscure problem is now considered a Big Bend, compression 101, staple. Start with the left hand on a small edge below the gaston on #2 and the right hand on a good side-pull. Paste the feet and slap and windmill up the blunt prow.

❐ 4. **THE PREGNANCY ARÊTE** V2
Just around the corner from the above problems, start matched on the obvious big edge, high-step the right foot and press straight up to small edges to attain the lip.

❐ 5. **LEFTOVER LOVER** V0
Five feet right of #2. Start sitting with both hands on a good sidepull and go straight up through cool pockets to the top. Variation: Sit-start for an added V.

❐ 6. **1000 LB CABOOSE** V8
The ultimate eliminate. If you think this felt too easy for a BB V8, you probably did not do this variation. Ten feet right of #3 in the middle of the face closest to the road. Start sitting with a left-hand pinch and a right-hand pocket. Go straight up using a tiny sloping crimp to a small right-finger notch, to the top.

❐ 7. **CRIMPTASTIC** V2 or V4
Just right of #4, stack pads to acess two small crimps. High-step, lock off hard and summit. Variation: Start on the lower two crimps for 2 extra Vs.

❐ 8. **KICK START** V0
Ten feet right of #4 where the face begins to angle

toward the right arête. Start with a good left-hand sidepull and a sloping crimp. Go straight up to the huge pocket and the top.

❏ 9. V2
Another previously obscure problem that has become a popular thanks to omni-present chalk. Start in between 5 and 6 with a left-hand micro-crimp and a right-hand gaston. High-step the left foot and press up and left to a good jug and head up.

❏ 10. **SILLY WABBIT** V3
On the right arête of the side closest to the road. Start with a good left-hand sloper and the right hand on a low pinch. Go straight up the arête finishing with a long reach to the top.
Variation: Start as for #6 but traverse right to finish on #7.

❏ 11. **DOUBLE CRIMP** V4
Five feet right of #6. Start on the thin horizontal crimp at four feet and go straight up.
Variation: Dyno from the crimp to the lip.

❏ 12. **MR. TRUJILLO'S BIG DAY** V2
Ten feet right of #7 and just a few feet right of where Mr. Trujillo carved his name. Start on good jugs under the roof and go straight up.

❏ 13. **DYNO FOR DOLLARS** V4
Five feet right of #8 under the right corner closest to the Chaos Boulder. Start under the roof on two sloping edges and dyno to the lip.

Hueco Traverse Boulder (#13)

It's not quite Hueco Tanks, but it's the closest we could find. From the parking lot walk the main trail 200 yards until you pass Chaos Boulder and look to the left. The Hueco Boulder is the one with a line of holes at about three feet height, and sits only 15 feet from the road at one end. Problems are described from left to right, on all the available climbing surfaces.

❏ 1. **HUECO FINISH** V1
On the narrow face closest to the road. Start on good huecos near the ground and go straight up.

❏ 2. **HUECO TRAVERSE LOW FINISH** V6
Sit-start on the big under-cling, head left and finish as for #1.

❏ 3. **HUECO TRAVERSE HIGH FINISH** V3
Sit-start as for #2, go straight up to a big hold, head up and left to the good crimp, and finish as for #1.

❏ 4. **THE REVERSE-TRAVERSE** V4
Sit-start as for #2 and #3, go straight up to a good hold, traverse left-to-right, finishing on the crack feature at the right end of the traverse. Another newly-popular classic.

❏ 5. **RANGER BOB** V1
Ten feet right of Hueco Finish. Start with both hands on a wide flat ledge and go straight up a shallow seam.

❏ 6. **UPWARDLY MOBILE** V0
Fifteen feet right of the previous route. Start on two excellent huecos and go up a vertical flake topping out on good holds.

❏ 7. **THE HUECO TRAVERSE** V7
Start on the rightmost huecos and traverse about 30 feet low to the left dropping down to the big under-cling described in #2, to the crux (a desperate under-cling match left of the big flake match) just before the problem meets up with and finishes on #1.

❏ 8. **THE HUECO TRAVERSE HIGH EXIT** V5
A great pump with a much friendlier finish. Start as for #4, but after attaining the good hold at the left arête, proceed up and then left, instead of down and left.

The Sand Traverse Boulder (#14)

This is pretty much the last good boulder along the main Big Bend trail. From the parking area, stay on the trail for about 300 yards passing the Chaos and Hueco boulders on the left. The trail pretty much runs into this 10-foot-high overhanging and heavily featured mushroom of stone. Problems are described left to right.

❏ 1. **SAND TRAVERSE** V2
Start on the side facing the road, on the furthest left holds. Traverse right on good pockets through steepening terrain. Some big moves lead to a challenging mantel.

❏ 2. V2
In the middle of the traverse face, grab two decent, but awkwardly positioned holds and dead-point for the top. Mantel straight up.

❏ 3. V1
The most obvious problem as one approaches this boulder. Start matched on a good rail and go straight up. Exit to the right for an easier finish.

❏ 4. V2
Start matched as for #1 but head up and right to two small crimp slots, then straight up.

❏ 5. V0
Start matched on a huge rail located on the right. Head left and up on pockets and ham-hocks to a crack-split finish.

❏ 6. **THE WILSON CHALLENGE** V-fun
A locals' favorite! Only one known female ascent! Start on any of the above warm-ups to attain the overhanging lip. Flip around, facing out, with legs dangling. Reverse-mantel by kicking legs up and over!

❏ 7. **ROLLOVER** V3
Five feet right of #3 is a somewhat sandy roof. Start on a good big sloper under the roof and go out on crimps to the lip then roll it on over.

Punisher Boulder (#15)

Twenty feet from Sand Traverse, in the direction of the road, are two brown boulders that lean together to form a dark bombay between them.

❏ 1. **LA DERECHA** V2
On the left arête (facing the *Sand Traverse*). Start with a left-hand crimp on the arête and a right-hand in the crack. Go straight up. Variation: Sit-start for another V.

❏ 2. **BLANKETY BLANK** V4
Five feet right of #1 on the right arête. Start with a good left-hand crimp and the right hand pinching the arête. Go straight up.
Variation V6: Sit-start. Aka: The *Mini Hell Belly*. Perfect for those who can't make the span on the *Hell Belly*.

❏ 3. V5
Sit-start as for #2, but finish left on #1. Arguably the nicest of the three sit-starts on this bloc.

River Road

☐ **4. THE PUNISHER** V2
Just right of #2 is the dark bombay formed by the two leaning boulders. Start at the back of this chimney and work your way out to an awkward and perhaps punishing exit.

☐ **5. SHORT STUFF** V1
Just right of the chimney is a series of good sidepulls. Start sitting and work your way up this short problem.

The Orange Peel Boulder (#16)
This lone boulder has only one problem, but it is worth mentioning for its classic Big Bend edge-pulling style. To get there, walk the main trail for 200 yards until you are standing near Hueco Traverse Boulder then go straight uphill for about 100 feet. The Orange Peel is a small light-tan-colored boulder with a vertical face (facing the road) and a low steep roof below that.

☐ **1.** V2
On the side facing the road. Start on the two lowest crimps and follow increasingly larger crimps to the top.

The Split Boulder (#17)
Located just up from Sand Traverse and down from the Big Horn Beaver, it is obvious by the fact it is split in two. Formerly quite chossy, this bloc has cleaned up quite well and houses a very popular moderate.

☐ **1. LEFT SIDE** V2
Use the crack for your right hand, good edges for the left and head on up, finishing as you see fit, usually to the left.
Variation 1: Sit-start for another V upgrade.
Variation 2 V3: Using primarily the crack, finish right.

☐ **2. RIGHT SIDE** V6
Not quite the newly minted classic as is its neighbor to the left. Around the right side, start on friable underclings, pull hard, then dyno for a chossy ledge.

☐ **3. SATELLITE** V5
Slightly down and left of the BHB is a satellite boulder with one fun, but still crispy, problem. The problem faces Rollover (and the road). Sit-start on sloping edges and traverse right. Exit the blunt arête.

Big Horn Beaver (#18)
The Big Horn Beaver is the dark brown boulder which sits just uphill from The Orange Peel. To get there walk to the Hueco Traverse Boulder and head uphill for about 200 feet. It is recognizable by its dark brown patina and an obvious angling sloper ramp that crosses its downhill face.

☐ **2. MIDDLE EXIT** V0
Five feet right of the finish for #1 are two similar problems. Start on any of the good jugs on the rounded right corner of the boulder and go up on jugs.

☐ **2. THE BIG HORNED BEAVER** V10
Ten feet to the right of #1. Start on the rightmost holds on the long sloping rail. Move left to a desperate move for the lip and an interesting mantel above. Can you say conditions-dependent?

☐ **3. BROWN** V1
Around the corner about 10 feet right from #2. Start on good holds anywhere on the dark brown slab and go up.

Belcer Traverse, Black Boulder, and Sloper Cave Boulders
To access these boulders, go to the back side of the Black Box and look straight up the hill for the Sloper Cave or up and slightly left for the Belcer/BB trail.

The Belcer Traverse (#19)
The lone problem is good enough to warrant a visit. From Black Box Boulder, walk uphill and a little west (away from the parking). It's the first big boulder up the hill presenting a tempting, but chossy, brown face on the road side.

☐ **1. THE BELCER TRAVERSE** V5
Start on the narrow east (toward the parking lot) side of the boulder on a series of thin horizontal pinch slopers. Traverse right on good holds and big slopers to a powerful big move on crimps at the righthand arête. Variation: Start the same but go up on the good jugs midway through the traverse.

Black Boulder (#20)
This hidden gem is just uphill and behind The Belcer Traverse Boulder. To get there, go to The Belcer Traverse Boulder and keep walking 30 feet up and right looking for a 15-foot-tall velvety chocolate-colored slab.

☐ **1. THE BLACK ANGUS** V7
This problem seemed epic until trixy beta freed it up. It is absolutely an area must-do. Start on the obvious low good holds, dead-point right to the sloping arête and climb the leaning arête all the way up.

☐ **2. AUNT J** V3
Start the same as #1 and go up the arête to two good edges then step up and onto the slab.

☐ **3. BLACK S** V4
Ten feet right of #2. Start on a huge foot ledge and a series of good holds, then traverse left topping out in the same slab scoop as #2.

☐ **4. BLACK SLAB** V4
Start the same as for #3 and go up to the right, making a hard reach (or dyno) for the lip.

The Sloper Cave (#21)
A bit tricky to find, but one can usually see the chalk from the backside of the Black Box. Head straight up from the Black Box to these well-hidden problems. Quite fun and great rock!

☐ **1.** V5
Start to the right on a crimp rail. Traverse left, following the easiest line (the high rail) out. Finish left, avoiding a dab crux presented by an adjacent rock.

☐ **2. SLOPER CITY** V8
Start all the way in the back of the cave on good (but chossy) holds. Climb up and left, then drop down ~three feet. Move left to a deadpoint pinch, then straight up to another deadpoint. Contrived, but a great fitness challenge.

THE CINEMA AND THE THEATRE

These two neighboring crags are popular warmer weather destinations, offering steeper-than-usual climbing, a short approach, and routes of all grades including spectacular calcite-crimping moderates on par in quality—if not difficulty— with *Holier Than Thou* on The Nuns.

Approach: Park 11 miles up the River Road at Take Out Beach, and pick up a good trail by a big boulder on the downstream end of the parking area. Follow this to a rock step, scramble up on the left, then back right. Above this, the trail takes you right to The Theater cliff band. To reach The Cinema follow a good trail for two more minutes. The first routes are on a west-facing wall, the last four face almost due north and hold shade till mid-afternoon. The routes are 80'–100' long and require many quickdraws, up to 15 for some.

A special thanks to Sam Lightner for the beta and the development.

Fred Knapp on *Protest Too Much* 5.11

Fred Knapp onsights *Out Damn Spot* 5.12b

River Road

Theatre ☀ NW

The Theatre shares the same type of rock as The Cinema but most of the climbing is much steeper than its Cinema neighbor. This is desert-sport—a subsport of desert and sport climbing, involving pulling on pockets and edges, but you also have to know your choss. Helmets for belayers are recommended as large stuff has broken. The rock, according to F.A. Barnes, is probably a layer in the Chinle Formation of conglomerate known as the Shinarump Conglomerate. It was likely in a river delta roughly 150 to 200 million years ago. Shinarump is uncommon throughout the Colorado plateau.

The area was dubbed The Theatre because when you are working on routes in the summer and the river is in full action with tourists, you become the big show viewed from the take-out. The routes on the lower wall (where the creek drains over) were likely toproped in the early 90s by Noah Bigwood and friends. All routes were established by Sam Lightner and Billy Shakespeare.

❑ **1. ALL THE WORLD'S A STAGE** 5.12a ★★★
Climb up the sand pile to the nasty bedding seam to find your "entrance." Work the arête from each side. Drop the rope into the anchors from the pocket UNDER them for your "exit."
Gear: 13 quickdraws

❑ **2. BOLDNESS BE MY FRIEND** 5.12a ★
Again, the bedding seam then the rotten crack. A really long stick clip helps. Climb up and trend right to meet *Cowards Die*. Pull the lip of the steepness to much easier ground. You stay engaged as there are no bolts here. There is a slot for a #3 up high if you are not armed by "audacity."
Gear: 8 quickdraws (optional 3, 3.5 friends)

❑ **3. COWARDS DIE** 5.12b ★
Start in the filthy dihedral, traverse out and left and follow the positive holds to a boulder problem at the fourth bolt. Traversing all the way to #2's third bolt is a coward's death. Be valiant and do the boulder problem to the 4th clip, then continue on *Boldness* to the top.
Gear: 9 quickdraws and hand-sized cams (2.0 optional), a couple slings

❑ **4. AN OVERFLOW OF GOOD** 5.11b
★★★★
From the corner move up and left to the arête then pull the bulge. Any further would "convert to bad."
Gear: 12 quickdraws

❑ **5. WHAT'S IN A NAME** 5.10d
Climb up to the shelf and clip the first bolt of *Life is a Banquet*, then back to the first bolt of this route. Very easy to the high bulge.
Gear: 9 quickdraws

❑ **6. LIFE IS A BANQUET** 5.10d
Climb the arête to a bulge to a ledge. The first route on the wall.
Gear: 10 quickdraws

❑ **7. BE TRUE!** 5.11a
Traverse out onto the face then up through a bulge. The crux has a large block that looks dubious but seems to hang in there. The belayer should plan accordingly. Look it over and be honest with yourself.
Gear: 11 quickdraws

❑ **8. WITH BATED BREATH** 5.12a
Do a hard start, but stay with it with "whisp'ring humbleness."
Gear: 10 quickdraws

❑ **9. PROTEST TOO MUCH** 5.11c ★★
Climb up the left side of the face with technical and powerful moves.
Gear: 9 draws

❑ **10. OUT DAMNED SPOT!** 5.12b ★★
Climb the right side to a powerful boulder problem.
Gear: 7 draws

❑ **11. MIDSUMMER NIGHT'S SEAM** 5.10a
Climb the disgusting crack to an anchor, then vomit in the flake behind the anchor.
Gear: Wide gear and a few finger to hand pieces

❑ **12. TO BOO, OR NOT TO BOO** 5.10a ★★★★
Just right of the crack, ascend the calcite plates to a large flake.
Gear: 11 draws

❑ **13. TAMING OF THE BOO** 5.10c ★★★★
Climb over bulges with fun moves. Stick with it to the top and she'll be yours ... and perhaps you'll want another.
Gear: 12 draws

Thanks Sam Lightner for the photos and descriptions!

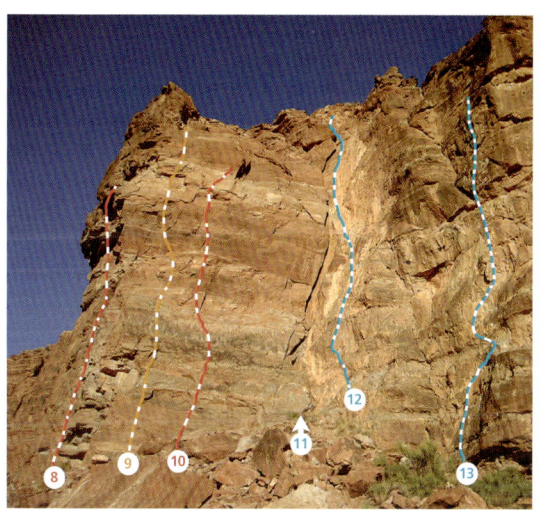

Roadside

The Cinema ☀NW

❒ 1. **SIDE SHOW** 5.11 ★
The first route in this sector. Follow the easy crack to the base of the obvious calcite-covered wall left of the arête. Tricky climbing up this leads to the anchor.
FA: Josh Gross, BJ Sbarra
Gear: Quickdraws and supplemental pro

❒ 2. **ENCORE** 5.11 ★★★★
This is the obvious soaring arête. Mellow climbing takes you to the base of the arête, where it gets real for the next 4 or 5 bolts before slabbing out higher up.
FA: Josh Gross, Lynn Sanson
Gear: draws

❒ 3. **TRUE GRIT** 5.10 ★★
Same start at *Encore*, but head right towards the middle of the face. A short but steeper crux section leads to mellower climbing to the top. Some really cool pockets on this one. Bolts.
FA: Lynn Sanson, Josh Gross
Gear: Draws

❒ 4. **BABEL** 5.10 ★★
Start off the platform of rock, and make funky moves to get established in the corner. Ascend the runout slab to the headwall and finger crack corner. Stick clip recommended, as the crux is right off the deck.
FA: Lynn Sanson, Josh Grossbb
Gear: Draws, optional finger-sized cams for start and finger crack up high.

❒ 5. **HOT YOGA STEVE, THE MOVIE** 5.10
Same start as *Babel*, then head right into the steep corner
FA: Steve Buchanan, Lynn Sanson
Gear: Draws

The next four routes are on the more north-facing wall, with excellent stone. These are all worth doing.

❒ 6. **FOOTLOOSE** 5.9 ★★
The first route in this sector, some cruxy moves past the first and second bolts leads to fun climbing to the chains.
FA: BJ Sbarra, Lynn Sanson, Josh Gross
Gear: Draws

❒ 7. **MEN IN TIGHTS** 5.10a ★★★★
This is an excellent route, long and thoughtful on great rock. Start up a tricky corner, then head up and right to a techy crux before moving back left to the final corner.
FA: Lynn Sanson, BJ Sbarra, Josh Gross
Gear: 14 draws

❒ 8. **ADVENTURES IN BABYSITTING** 5.7 ★★
An excellent outing for the grade. A long sling is helpful for the first bolt to reduce rope drag up high.
FA: BJ Sbarra, Lynn Sanson
Gear: 11 draws

❒ 9. **ONE EYED WILLY** 5.7 ★★
Same start as the previous route, then move right at the second bolt. Crux is at the last bolt.
FA: BJ Sbarra, Josh Gross
Gear: Draws

Laurel Graefe relaxing her way up *All the World's a Stage* 5.12a. Photo by Sam Lightner, Jr.

River Road .... **Castle Valley**

Holier Than Thou 5.11c on The Nuns. Photo: Andrew Burr

CASTLE VALLEY

Photo: Joe Auer

The magic is here: great summits, sunrises, and sunsets, incredible lighting, and epic rainbows, desert views to one side and mountain views on the other.

Castle Valley has long been a desirable climbing venue developed by a who's-who of venerable pioneers including Layton Kor, Huntley Ingalls, Harvey T. Carter, Jeff Achey, Chip Chace, Ed Webster, Leonard Coyne, Jim Beyer, Jay Smith, Kitty Calhoun, Jim Donini, Jack Tackle, Jim Dunn, Greg Child, Charlie Fowler, John Catto, Mark Hesse, Earl Wiggins, Keith Reynolds and, of course, Fred Beckey.

Several well-heeled and world-class climbers have chosen this place as their home (Greg Child, Jay Smith, Kitty Calhoun, Lyle Dean). Kent Wheeler (who did the first ascent of *Coyote Calling* on The Rectory) commented in a recent beta-infused email, "I've always said that Castle Valley has more residents that could climb 5.12 in the 1980s than anywhere else in the world."

Castle Valley is a climber's heaven. The word is out, as are the crowds. Hopefully this chapter will entice you to spread out and venture off the time-tested classics (*Kor-Ingalls*, *Fine Jade*, *Honeymoon Chimney*) and open up some "new classics" like *Voodoo Child* on Parriott Mesa, *Jesus Saves* on the Rectory, or even some neglected classics like *Stardust Cowboy* and *Coyote Calling*. There are some testpieces out here as well: Greg Child's *Excommunication* on The Priest, Charley Graham's *Skin Ambivalence* on Parriott Mesa, Jay Smith's *Ivory Tower*.

Like most places that are this awesome, it takes effort from us all to keep it that way. A wad of tape, a stray pop tart wrapper—please pick them up. I am sure they were not intentionally left behind and whomever spaced them would be stoked if you picked up after them. Please, please, please keep this pristine area pristine!
KARMA IS A WONDERFUL THING. DO YOUR PART. PLEASE!

To reach Castle Valley, take the River Road (Rt 128) and drive for 15.4 miles to the Castle Valley turn-off on the right. There are several areas and formations here to climb and not all are approached from the same area.

A huge thank you to Jay Smith for his hand drawn topos/beta. A true artist with his craft.

Two ropes recommended unless mentioned.

There is camping for Castle Valley in the main parking area for Castleton Tower. Toilets are located here.

Castle Valley

Parriott Mesa

Parriott Mesa is a somewhat overlooked buttress that houses some excellent climbing, albeit not super concentrated. The routes reside on all aspects of the formation and, at the time of this writing, most reach the summit. There are several approaches depending on the location of your desired climb. Two main access points are covered in this book: the NE/NW approach, and the SW approach.

Voodoo Area
1

Parriott NE Face

Crooked Arrow Spire

A really neat two-pitch feature that hangs off the northeast end of the mesa—viewed as the obvious hangnail in the photo above.

Approach: Drive on the River Road passing the Castle Valley entrance and take a right on a spur road at 16.1 miles (this is the same turn-off as for Sister Superior). Drive another 100' or so to a big parking spot, or with high clearance venture as far as you dare. I like the obvious wash until you are under the east face of the mesa. Look for a faint trail near a huge boulder and a cattle fence. This heads towards the Crooked Arrow Spire which dumps you out just left of the formation. 45 minutes.

Dylan Warren in the *Longbow Chimney* 5.8, C1

☐ 1. **LONGBOW CHIMNEY** 5.8 C1 ★★★
P1: Start on the climber's left of the tower. Climb past some pretty big, but secure, chockstones before entering the chimney (optional belay). Place pro as high as you can above the stones before entering the chimney to alleviate some rope drag. Cruise the chimney via a selection of cracks in the back (good gear the whole way). Belay from a bolted stance in the notch. From me to you, this chimney is a lot of fun.
P2: A short free-climbing section off the belay brings you to the first bolt. Climb the bolt ladder (20+ bolts) with modern gear updated by the A.S.C.A in 2010.
Rap: 1 double rope (60m) rap from new summit anchors to belay over chockstones and a single rope to the ground.
Gear: Double set of cams up to a 3.0 (optional big piece), lots of draws and/or biners. Your preferred bolt ladder ascenscion garb and jugs for the follower.

Parriott NW Face

Approach as for Crooked Arrow Spire and when you get to its base walk right (NW) around the cliffs base to the bottom of the Voodoo Area.

Voodoo Area

Located just around the corner (right) from Crooked Arrow Spire. Routes are listed left to right. ALL ROUTES RAPPEL *VOODOO CHILD*.

❒ 1. SUPER NATURAL 5.10 ★★★

A natural line all the way to the summit. NO FIXED ANCHORS—gear belays. A classic 5-pitch route to the rim. Start this route right of *Voodoo Child* and work left intersecting/crossing that route.
Gear: (2–3 each) 0.4–3.0, (2)4.0, (1)5.0
FA: Jay Smith, Jack Tackle

❒ 2. SPIRIT WORLD 5.11- ★★★

A 2-pitch variation to *Super Natural*. Shares pitches 1-3 up to the Voodoo Lounge, then continues straight up then slightly right for two more pitches.
Gear: (2–3 each) 0.4–3.0, (2)4.0, (1)5.0
FA: Jay Smith, Jim Donini

Parriott Mesa—Voodoo Area

Parriott Mesa lies just east of the River Road (Highway 120), borders the northern edge of Castle Valley, and sits across from Castleton Tower's North Face. Its western end overlooks the Colorado River and Arches National Park, sporting incredible views of the river and arches in the distance. This is the home of several of the region's great routes and some of the largest Wingate faces around. The premier route is *Voodoo Child* 5.11+. Four increasingly difficult pitches weave an incredible climb up an improbable 500-foot clean face. The route is characterized by a variety of climbing challenges with reasonably good protection and comfortable belays—it's not to be missed. How often do you find a hand crack that is nearly 200 feet long? Eight gold Camalots is barely adequate for this pitch.

Another classic is the moderate *Super Natural* 5.10-. This climb is of similar difficulty to the *Kor-Ingalls*, though longer and perhaps slightly harder. However, you won't need to wait in line or need a headlamp start to be the first on the route. Be advised, however, that there are no fixed anchors beyond where the route crosses *Voodoo Child*. It was first climbed without bolts and was the initial route on the mesa end. The original descent was made by crossing the mesa top and downclimbing *Cowboy Route*. Today, you can descend *Voodoo Child*. Please do not add bolts to this route; keep it the super-natural line that it is.

Be safe, have fun and—please—keep this area pristine.

-Jay Smith

Castle Valley

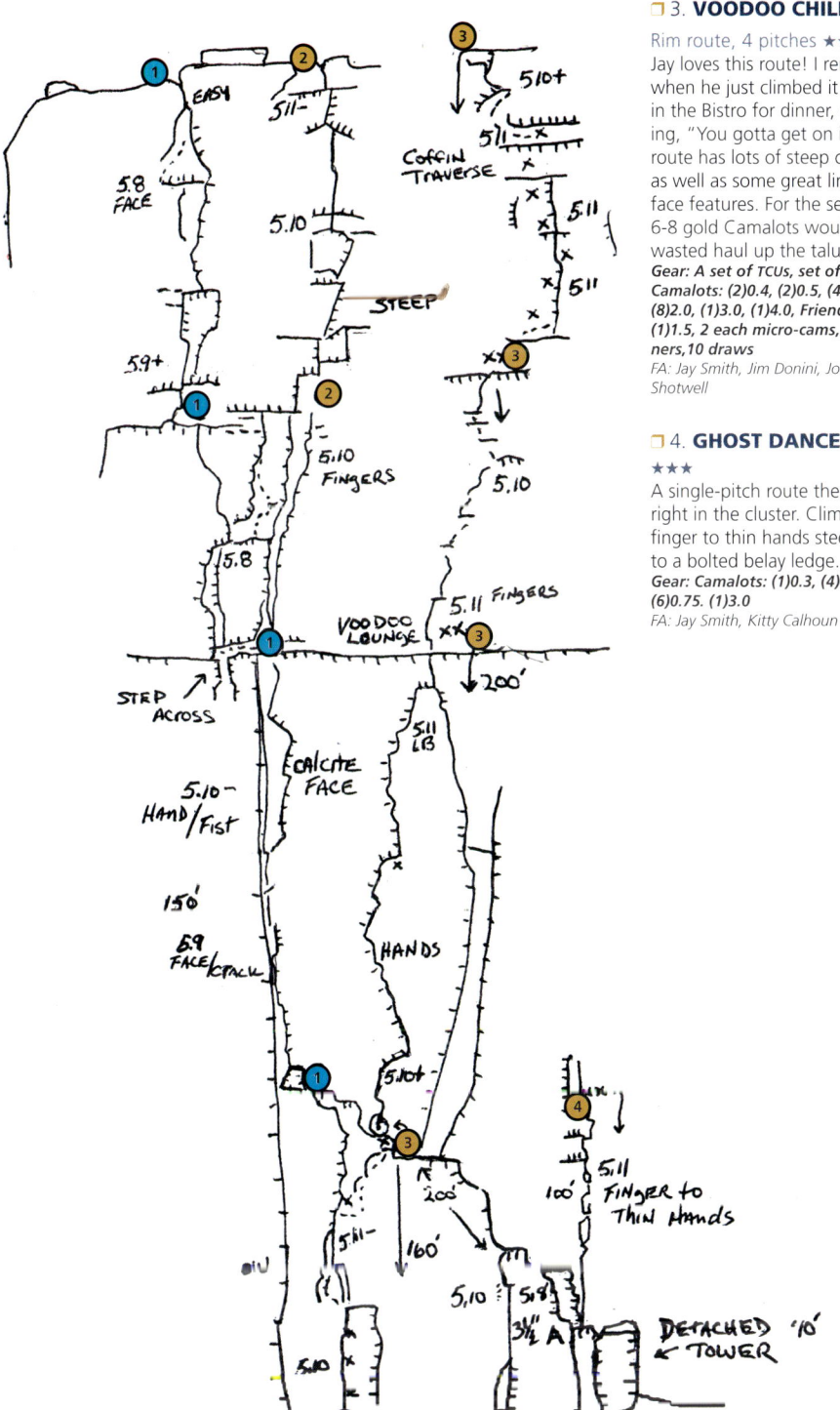

3. VOODOO CHILD 5.11+

Rim route, 4 pitches ★★★★★
Jay loves this route! I remember when he just climbed it and was in the Bistro for dinner, exclaiming, "You gotta get on it!" This route has lots of steep climbing, as well as some great link-ups on face features. For the second pitch, 6-8 gold Camalots wouldn't be a wasted haul up the talus.
Gear: A set of TCUs, set of wires, Camalots: (2)0.4, (2)0.5, (4)0.75, (3)1.0, (8)2.0, (1)3.0, (1)4.0, Friends: (1)1.0, (1)1.5, 2 each micro-cams, many runners, 10 draws
FA: Jay Smith, Jim Donini, John Catto, J Shotwell

4. GHOST DANCE 5.11 100'

★★★
A single-pitch route the farthest right in the cluster. Climbs the finger to thin hands steep splitter to a bolted belay ledge.
Gear: Camalots: (1)0.3, (4)4.0, (4)0.5, (6)0.75. (1)3.0
FA: Jay Smith, Kitty Calhoun

River Road

Southwest-Facing Section

To approach the southwest face, turn onto the Castle Valley Road at 15.4 miles from the junction with Highway 191. Reset your odometer here, drive for approximately 4.4 miles and look for a spur dirt road under a diagonaling (left to right) trail that cuts sharply across the dirt hillside. Park here and hike the angling trail then follow the obvious trail.

PARRIOTT – SW

1. FAT CRACK NAMED DESIRE 5.11- ★★★
A beautiful wide line. Man-up and go!
P1: A right-facing fists corner to double cracks. Climb the double hand cracks to a belay ledge (100+').
P2: From the belay continue past a block, gaining a left-facing corner (fists) up through an offwidth to the obvious pod and belay from gear (100').
P3: Grunt your way over a bulging ow and continue climbing with hands up to a fixed belay (100+').
P4: Climb less steep, easy ow to the top (90').
Gear: 0.75–6.0 (heavy on 3.5–4.5), long draws
FA: Keith Reynolds, Bob "Roundhead" Novellino

2. SKIN AMBIVALENCE 5.12-
Thank you Charley for the description.
Skin Ambivalence is a 0.0 TCU seam with pods and crimps that just barely link together. It does not summit.
P1: The first crux is placing a tiny cam at 15 feet. The next section has better pro and a weird move getting both your hands and feet into a small pod all at once. A sit-down ledge follows, providing a rest before powerful liebacking and a mantel above the bolt. Finally, easy climbing accesses the belay stance.
P2: Best accessed by moving the belay 40 feet right by walking along a sloping ledge. Build a natural anchor with small to medium cams and get ready for the steep tips and face climbing that awaits. This pitch is short but exciting, and very high quality.
Rap: From a two-bolt anchor with one 70m rope.
Gear: A single set of cams from 0.0 TCU to 4.0 and one quickdraw for the first pitch. The initial runout is more enjoyable with a bouldering pad. There is one protection bolt and a fixed-stopper anchor. Take one additional green and yellow Alien for the second pitch.
FA: Charley Graham

3. HAPPY ENDING 5.12
The first crack right of *Skin Ambivalence*. It doesn't not summit. There is a stance 100 feet up for a natural belay. To get down you must climb the second pitch of *Skin Ambivalence* and rappel with one 70m rope. *Happy Ending* is essentially a direct start to the second pitch of *Skin Ambivalence* but is easier and not as good.
Gear: Triple set of cams from 0.0 TCU to 1.0.
FA: Charley Graham

4. HAIL STONE 5.10 200'

A five-minute walk right of *Happy Ending* will bring you to the starting stem box (with a plaque below). Climb double cracks in the back of an elevator-shaft chimney. Exit the chimney and follow the lefthand crack up to a ledge at 180 feet. Traverse left 20 feet to a bolted rappel anchor. Does not summit.
Descent: Double 60m rope rappel.
FA: Jim Madore

5. KING KRIMSON 5.11

King Krimson is located on the southeast end of the buttress. It does not gain the summit.
P1: Climb broken corners and face (5.10-) up to a small roof with fingers (5.10), passing a few horizontals to gain a belay ledge.
P2: Move the belay up and left under the right-facing corner. Climb the sustained corner w/ mostly off-fingers.
Gear: 0.4–3.0 (heavy on 0.5 & 0.75)
FA: Jay Smith, Jo Bentley

6. ON WITH THE SHOW 5.11 ★★

This three-pitch summit route is located just right of the southeast corner of the mesa, around the corner from *King Krimson*.
P1: Begin the right-facing corner with tips laybacking that yields to fingers, ending at a belay ledge with a single-bolt rap (5.11).
P2: Off the ledge, change aspect to a steep left-facing fingers corner, then up to a splitter passing a bolt (5.10+) to another bolted belay ledge (5.11).
P3: Thin hands give way to some wide climbing above.
Descent: Rap the route with double 60m ropes
Gear: Wires, double set of TCUs, (2 each) 0.4–2.0 (1)3.0
FA: Greg Child, Jay Smith, Kitty Calhoun

Jay Smith on the FA of *Voodoo Child* 5.11+

Castleton Tower

Castleton reigns as the most iconic tower in the Moab area—famed for its pioneering *Kor-Ingalls*, picturesque in its setting backdropped by the La Sals.

Once you **turn** into Castle Valley, drive for 4.7 miles and turn left. This is the main hub for parking and camping in the Castle Valley area.

When approaching the routes on Castleton Tower, use only the established approach trail. The hike begins from the main parking area. Head east up the wash over a couple of rain-runoff scrambles. Once on top of the wash, descend left down an old road, watching for a righthand spur (maintained climber's trail). Follow this (at about the halfway point, you will need to scramble through a rock band). Continue up the trail to a fork at its top. Take the left fork towards The Rectory. Skirt around the tower. Follow a branch that heads right to the northeast face. Once you get to the flat saddle there is a short fourth-class scramble over some blocks that brings you to the base of the tower and pretty much to the base of the **North Chimney**. Going right will bring you to the **North Face** route, *Sacred Ground*, and the west face. Going left brings you to all the rest.

You can rappel Castleton Tower with a single 70m rope (must be a true 70) via the **North Face** rappel route. However it would be difficult to bail from many of the routes with a single line, as many have gear belays and rope-catching possibilities. A tag line is recommended. As of 2017, the location of the second rappel on *Kor-Ingalls* is a rope-catcher. It's best avoided by making a double rope rappel from the top anchors.

Castle Valley

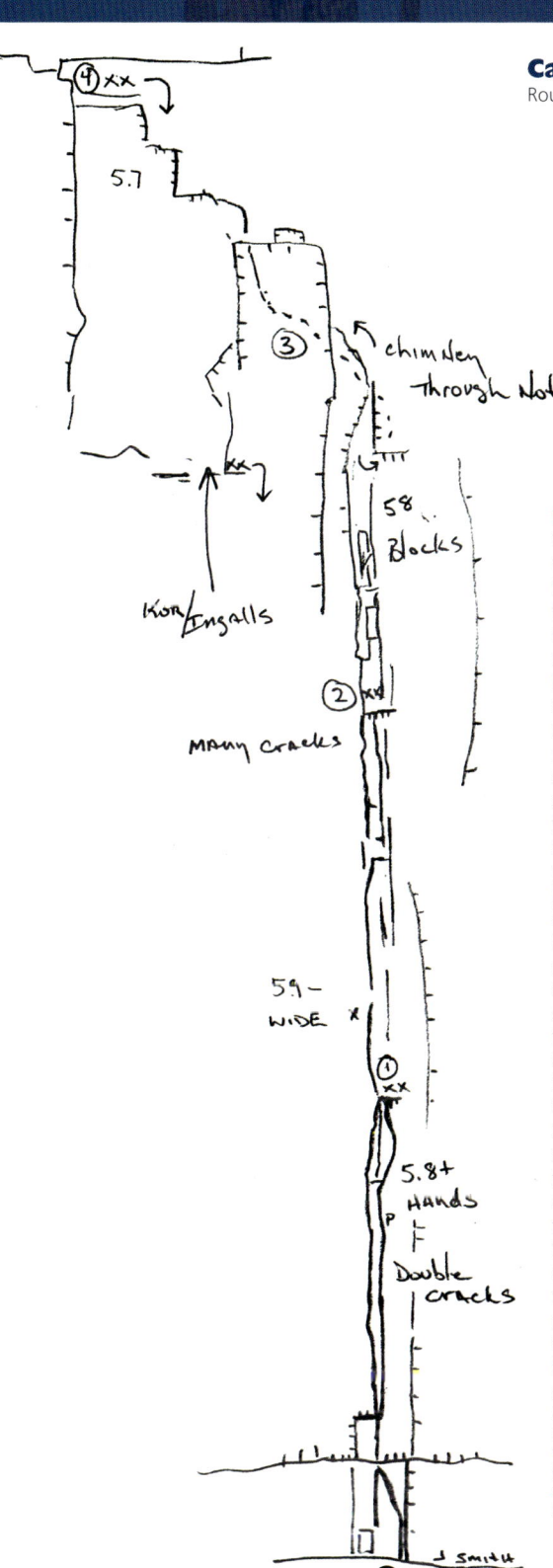

Castleton Tower—North Face
Routes are listed from left to right.

☐ 1. **NORTH CHIMNEY** 5.9 ★★★
One of Fred Beckey's 50 Favorites! The *North Chimney* is one of the finest introductions to tower climbing, offering a bit of everything from face climbing to ow. It faces a bit northeast, so the first pitch catches a few hours of morning sun.
P1: Awesome. A really quality tower pitch! Start up the small left-facing corner but traverse left after a body-length or so to the main corner system. The main left-facing corner system follows double and occasionally triple cracks of mostly hands. The crux is found up high—a few body-lengths before the bomber bolted anchor. (Bailing after this pitch is not recommended).
P2: Climb to the star drive bolt (which can be backed up by an optional large 4.5+" piece). Pass it by using face holds out left or keep off-widthing to friendlier jams above. Climb some blocky terrain in the chimney; once it starts to get steep, bust out some chimney technique. The belay is found on a ledge with a fixed bong in the left crack and fixed Tricam in the right. Some fingers cams and a gold Camalot can back these up.
P3: Ascend the left crack via hands and switch over to the right side. Climb blocky terrain until you somewhat dead-end under a roof and proceed out and right. Continue up the obvious chimney with huge chockstone/boulders to the notch that links up with the *Kor-Ingalls* (optional belay here). Continue up the righthand face on some calcite holds until reaching a ledge that offers some pro; follow this ramping ledge system to the anchors (30' from the notch). It's wise to use long slings and minimal gear to reduce drag.
Descend the North Face with (2)70m in two rappels or if the N.F. is busy rap the Kor-Ingalls route in two raps.
Gear: Set of wires (2)0.4, (2)0.5, (2)0.75, (2)2.0, (2)2.0, (2–3)3.0, optional 5.0 to back up the star drive bolt, (6)shoulder slings
FA: Dan Burgette, Allen Erickson

River Road

2. NORTH FACE WITH WEBSTER VARIATION 5.11a ★★★★★
Sweet pitch! This is the next route right of *North Chimney* beginning from a ledge system 10' higher.
P1: A right-facing corner that, from the ground, appears to be in a slot. Climb the corner/slot with hands and big hands. Pass some flake/chockstones (secure) then bust out right via an undercling/flake system. The rock here is layered with calcite and quite slick! A few more moves up the flake to juggy stone leads to the belay ledge (5.11).
P2: This short pitch starts with diagonaling fingers in calcite just left of the belay. Continue up the handcrack through the obvious pod and up to the belay ledge. Who said that dinosaurs couldn't climb? Check out the tracks! (5.10)
P3: Climb up and right to a crack varying from fist to ow/chimney, and finally to some easy ground before topping out. Some folks find this pitch easy and some don't (5.10).
Gear: Wires, triple set up to 2.0s, (4)3.0

3. SACRED GROUND 5.12b ★★★
Another awesome route from Jay. Some suggest this is the best route on the tower. A good mix of trad and sport climbing.
P1: Finger crack that switches to another finger crack via a bit of face climbing. Finish with some broken rock to a narrow belay ledge (5.11+).
P2: Shares second pitch of the *North Face* route (5.10).
P3: After moving right to a bolt, face climb left to a right-facing corner, passing another bolt and finishing on a ledge with a bolted belay (5.10c).
P4: The money pitch! In a nutshell—sport climb on calcite! Pass a bulge, look for a rest at a horizontal, and milk it! Continue on calcite face holds clipping bolts along the way. Skirt around the roof to the summit.
RAP: North Face
Gear: Wires, double set of TCUs, (3)0.4, (3)0.5, (3)0.75, (3)1.0, (6) draws
FA: Jay Smith

4. NORTH FACE ORIGINAL START 5.11b
While no longer popular, as most consider the *Webster Variation* the better start to the *North Face*, it's there if you're looking for something different. Begin just right of *Sacred Ground*.
Gear for first pitch: wires, double set of TCUs, (3)0.5, (3)0.75, (3)1.0

Rob Pizem on *North Face* 5.11a. Andrew Burr photo

Castle Valley

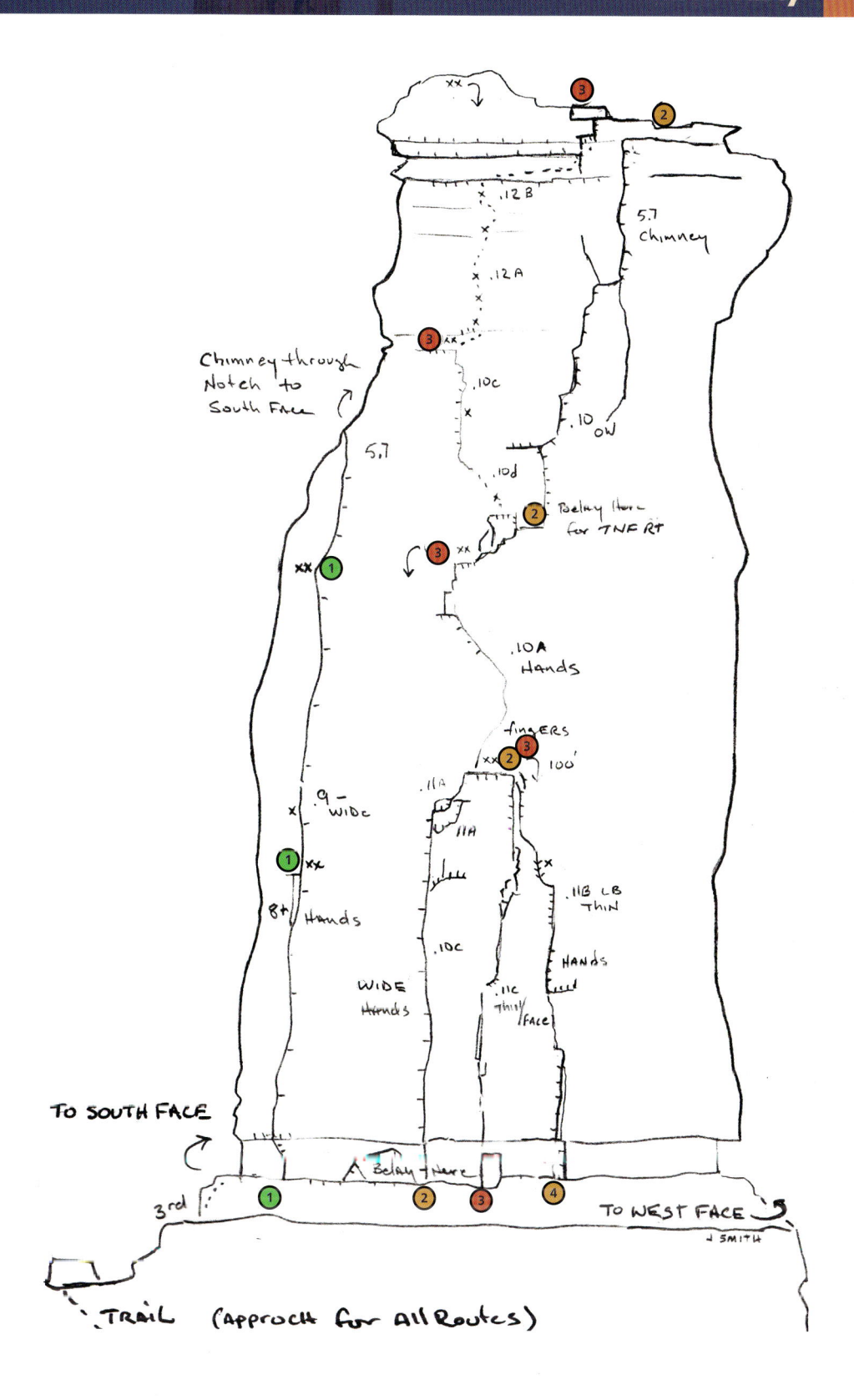

West Face

☐ **12. WEST FACE** 5.11
A worthy route that is getting more popular and, as a result, is cleaning up nicely. Walk right from the *North Face* route until you can't go any farther.
P1: The loose lead. BELAYER BEWARE ON THIS PITCH, STAND OUT OF HARM'S WAY. Start via cracks that lead over some blocks and a roof. Continue up to a good stance with a fixed belay (5.9, 110').
P2: The easier lead. Climb the V-corner (where you see the calcite from the approach) to a bolted belay on a pedestal (5.10, 85').
P3: The crux and a long lead. A squeeze chimney starts things out. Some "thank you" hand jams out the chimney yield to a short reprieve before the crux wide section. Ow or power lieback up the 4.5" crack, then a short exposed face traverse to the right leads to a hand crack. Follow the easier meandering crack to a cave belay (5.10, 150').
P4: Climb the short chimney section to the right-facing wide crack with some welcomed face holds. Traverse on a short section of less-than-stellar rock and up over the top (5.10, 55').
Rap: North Face
Gear: Set of nuts, wires, (2 each) 0.4–3.0, (1)4.0, many shoulder length slings, helmet.
FA: Jimmy Dunn, Bill Westbay, Stewart Green

There is a new-ish bolted variation off the *West Face* route. At the time of this writing I have not climbed it and have been unable to find out any sound beta. Your own private adventure awaits.

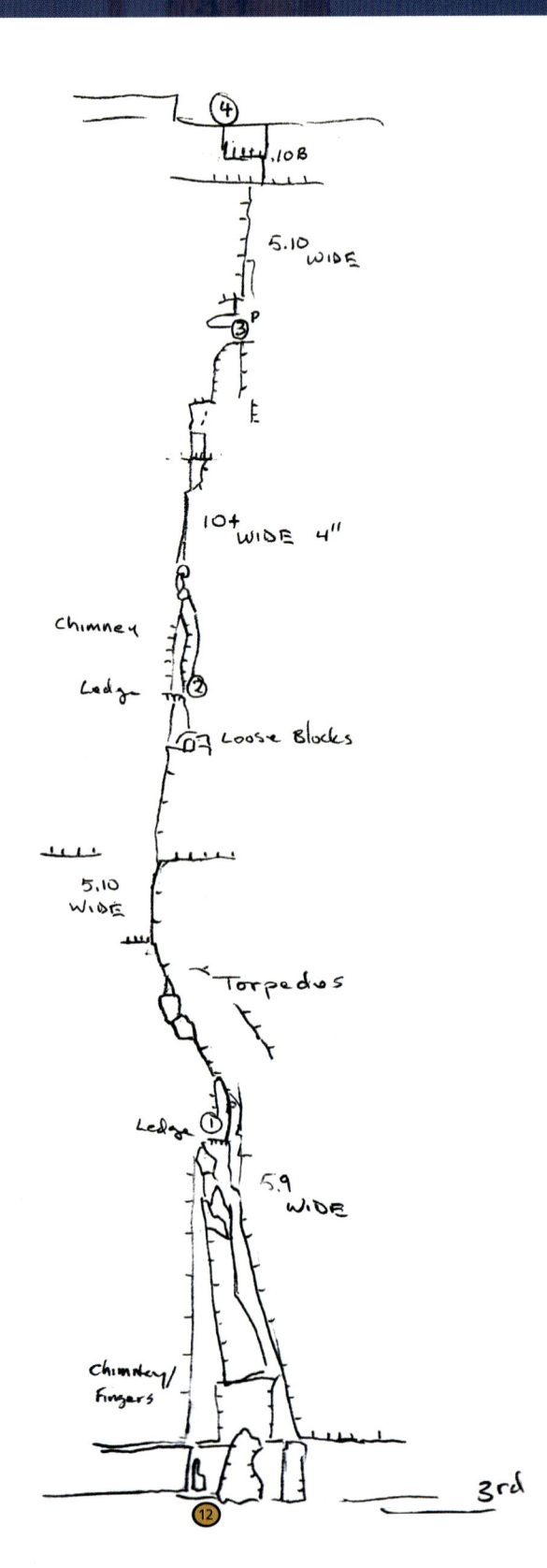

Castle Valley

South Face

1. KOR–INGALLS 5.9 ★★★★★
Listed as one of the 50 classics in the Steck & Roper book! Really a pretty moderate tower route. Though it climbs wide, you really don't need any wide gear, but carry extra slings. You can climb the route in three pitches by combining pitches 1 and 2. To approach, walk left from the start of **North Chimney** along the ledge. Squat under the roof and continue via an exposed ledge to where big blocks impede progress.
P1: Easy wide climbing leads to a big ledge a little ways up. Continue with more easy climbing in a chimney to another ledge and continue on to a third ledge with a bolted anchor. Use long slings on any gear to limit drag (5.6 130').
P2: The Junction: *Black Sun* is on the left and *Arrowhead* goes right. *Kor-Ingalls* continues straight up a double hand and fist crack past some large blocks to an awesome belay ledge with bolts (5.8, 100').
P3: The OW: Some hard moves past bolts in a heavily calcited ow make this memorable. Slick face holds outside the ow offer up some help. Place creative gear inside the wide section—long slings mandatory if you don't want to step on your rope the whole way. Finish on a nice belay ledge (5.9+, 100').
P4: The original route steps left from the belay and ascends a chimney to a large ledge with a bolted belay just under the summit.
Gear: Wires, (2)0.5, (2)0.75, (2)1.0, (2)2.0, (2)3.0, (1)4.0, (2)quickdraws, (6)shoulder slings
FA: Layton Kor, Huntley Ingalls

2. DISCRETE START TO BLACK SUN 5.9 R ★
A fairly new addition to the tower, a variation to *Black Sun* or a bypass for the crowded *Kor-Ingalls*. Start up a right-facing corner and traverse right on a horizontal towards the arête. Climb just left of the arête passing two bolts and run it out to the *Black Sun* belay.
Gear: 0.75–3.0, (2)draws
FA: Ken Trout, Wyatt Payne

3. BURNING INSIDE 5.11b ★★★
Jay Smith gives the last pitch of this route 4+ stars. The route's start is nestled in between *Kor-Ingalls* and *Arrowhead Left* and a good option to its crowded *Kor-Ingalls* neighbor.
P1: Climb the steep, left-facing fingers and hands corner left around a roof up to easy slab moves to join *Black Sun*.
P4: Break left with 5.10 climbing past four bolts; small crimping on good rock brings you to the summit.
Rappel Kor-Ingalls or North Face
Gear: Wires, double set of TCUs, (3)0.5, (3)0.75, (2)1.0, (2)2.0, (1)3.0
FA: Jay Smith, Bob Novellino, Paul Teare

4. BLACK SUN 5.10b ★★★
A three-pitch variation to the *Kor–Ingalls*.
P1: *Kor–Ingalls* (130').
P2: Take the wide crack on the left, leaving the *Kor-Ingalls*. Use some wide crack technique, pass a bolt, and keep an eye out for face holds to ease things up a bit. Belay on the ledge (65').
P3: The "Fatty" crux. Climb a fist crack that eventually goes to some ow, tunnel in and under a chockstone—suck it in and squeeze through, exhale and belay (60').
P4: Finish with the obvious crack system to the summit.
Gear: Wires, double set of TCUs, (2 each)0.5–3.0, (1)4.0,
FA: Ed Webster, Leonard Coyne, Mark Hopkins

5. ARROWHEAD LEFT 5.10+ ★★
Starts between *Burning Inside* and *Stardust Cowboy*—look for a roof a couple of body-lengths up.
P1: Climb right of the roof (easier than it looks) and continue to a hand crack which turns into a short section of ow. Set a belay on the ledge just right of *Kor-Ingalls* first pitch.
P2: Ascend the left-facing corner up to a squeeze, passing a pin. Continue with hands and big hands to the bolted belay ledge.
P3&4: Same as *Stardust Cowboy*.
Gear: wires, single set of TCUs (2–3)0.5–2.0, (2)3.0, (2)4.0
FA: Ed Webster, Chester Dreiman

Charley Graham on pitch one of Stardust Cowboy 5.11

River Road

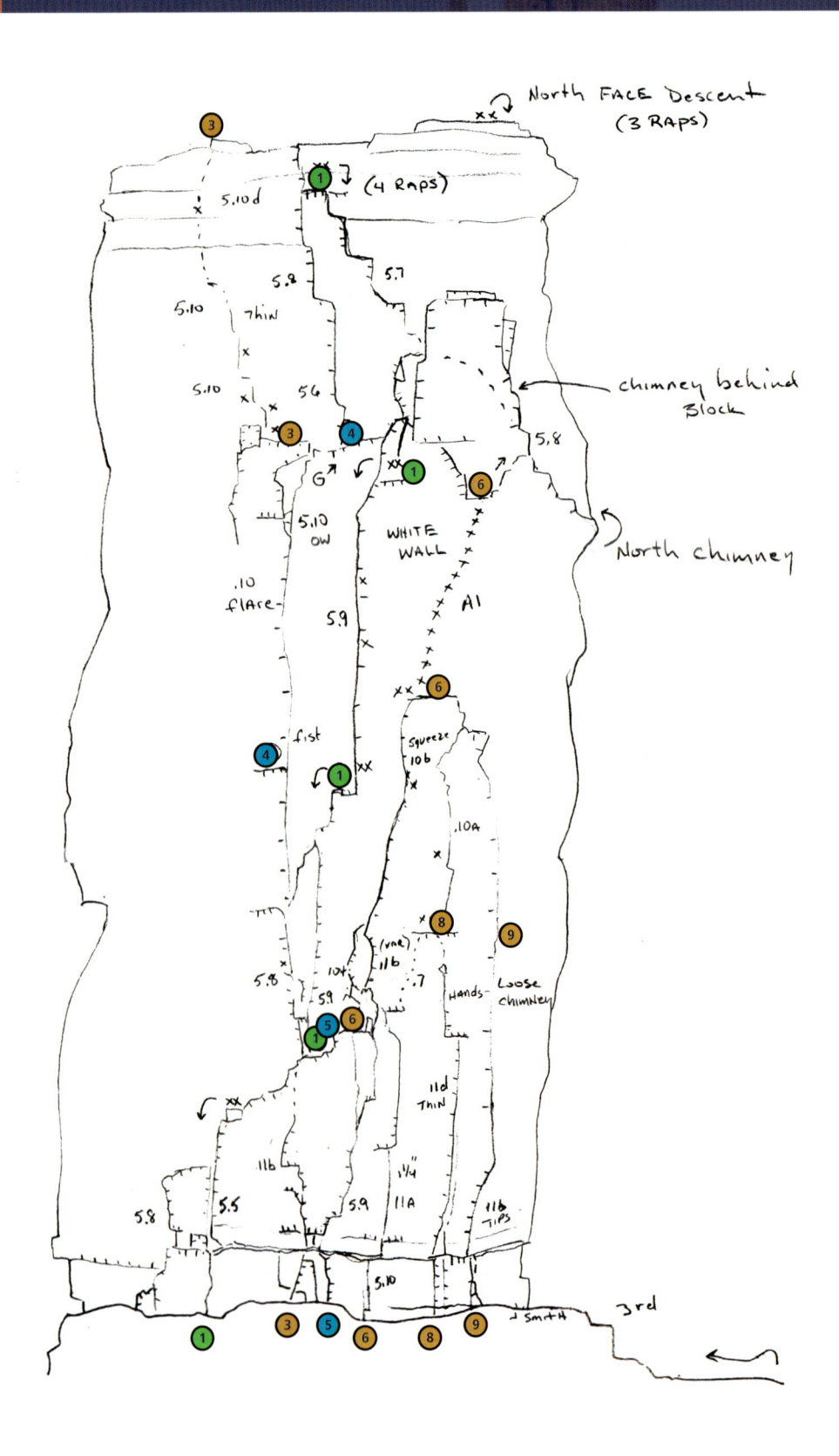

Castle Valley

6. STARDUST COWBOY 5.11a ★★★
P1: A great 4-star pitch! A fun bouldery start with an offset finger splitter leads to the horizontal break. After the horizontal, enter a steep slot with off-fingers in the back; exit the slot and traverse right under a small roof. Climb through the roof and follow a hands/tight hands splitter to the crack's end at an arête with face holds and an oddly-located bolt on the left. Move right from the bolt. Fun face climbing culminates on a ledge with a bolted belay.
P2: Move right from the belay and climb a scary flake to some scary blocks. Climb these and finish on the "thank god I made it" ledge with a bolted belay.
P3: Ascend the long bolt ladder up the white face. Build a belay on the ledge.
P4: Trend right around the corner and meet up with the last section of *North Chimney*. Double length shoulder slings are helpful.
Gear: Wires, set of TCUs, (4)0.5, (4)0.75, (3)1.0, (3)2.0, many quickdraws for the bolt ladder
FA: Ed Webster, Chester Dreiman

7. UNDERWORLD 5.11 ★★
Underworld is located on the Cutler sandstone just below *Stardust Cowboy*. It's a splitter with a roof at 2/3 height. Approach by going right at the top of the trail toward the *Kor-Ingalls*. Begin up steep stone with fingers to an off-fingers, tight hands splitter to a shelf. From the shelf take the left crack through some bubbly-looking rock (good gear) to a rest just below the roof. A hard, awkward move over the roof brings you to some hands and then the bolted anchor.
Gear: Blue TCU–2.0
FA: Jay Smith

8. HOLLOW POINT 5.11+ ★★★
The more it's climbed, the more it will clean up. Start between *Stardust Cowboy* and *Little White Lieback*. It meets up and shares the belay with the first pitch of *Stardust Cowboy*. Climb steep fingers to a big roof. Pass the roof on its left with big hands. Pass a pod with off fingers. The difficulty eases and finishes at *Stardust Cowboy's* anchors.
Rappel with double ropes
Gear: Wires, (2) tips, (2)0.3, (3)0.4, (3)0.5, (3)0.75, (2)1.0, (3)2.0, (1)3.0
FA: Jay Smith

9. LITTLE WHITE LIEBACK 5.11b ★
A seldom-done route on the far right of the south face right of *Hollow Point*. Begin up the steep right-facing corner via tip laybacking. Higher up, gain the loose chimney and eventually connect with the second pitch of *Stardust Cowboy*, finishing on that route.
Gear: Wires, TCUs, triple cams to 2"
FA: Chip Chace, Jeff Achey

Jay Smith on the FA of Underworld 5.11

River Road

THE IVORY TOWER

10. THE IVORY TOWER 5.13b ★★★
A spectacular route, requiring crack climbing from fingers to offwidth, steep face climbing, slabs, bouldering power, and the endurance to climb 35-meter pitches. All of this is packaged on a majestic arête.

P1: Start about 30 feet left of the *North Chimney*. Climb 15 feet to your first gear, then out a steep finger crack with lots of calcite. The crack turns vertical with hands, then ow higher. Use long slings on your wide gear. About 20 feet up the ow, step around the arête and clip a bolt. Climb mid-5.12 on the arête clipping 6 bolts to a hanging-stance anchor (110 feet).

P2: Climb straight to the arête. There is one technical crux and one pumpy crux (obligatory 5.12). Up high, move around to the right side of the arête and across a face to another hanging-stance belay. (5.13b, 130', 14 bolts).

P3: Climb an arête boulder problem with two bolts (5.12c) to a finger crack that diagonals across the face. Belay from a comfy ledge (50').

P4: Go up a slab to the broken arête, then up the face. Six bolts and a large-finger-size cam helps protect the arête (5.12b, 60').

Rap climbers left of the route, eventually coming down the corner you started up. A single 70m barely makes it, so watch the ends.

Gear: P1: Set of cams, including 5.0, 7 quickdraws (long draws helpful), **P2:** 16 quickdraws, **P3:** small to hand-sized cams, 3 draws, **P4:** finger-size cam, 7 draws

FA: Chris Kalous, Sam Lightner

Castle Valley

The Rectory

The Rectory, despite its bulk, is one of the more spectacular canyonlands summits. Its lofty heigh and vast summit are unique and not to be missed. Routes are listed from right to left. **Descend all summit routes via the *Fine Jade* rappels (two raps with two 70m ropes, or four raps with a single 70m cord) or the *Empirical Route* rappels (two raps with a a pair of 70m cords).**

Tom Gwinn on the first crux of Fine Jade 5.11

1. FINE JADE 5.11 ★★★★★

ULTRA CLASSIC. When you live in Moab, you start to tick away at some towers—some folks tick a LOT of towers. Most, however, log the 8-10 classic towers first. For me, *Fine Jade* took a while—not for a lack of interest or time, but crazy circumstances! My partner Dylan and I had been rained off, winded off, baked off, and even crowded off! It was one of the only classics that we hadn't done. Meanwhile Dylan had started a family and different job. We told each other we would finish this tower together! Years had gone by; it even haunted my dreams from time to time, as I am sure it did for him as well. Dylan works days; I work nights… he has weekends off, I am busy at the restaurant on weekends. It was never going to happen! We finally came to grips that this was an experience we were not going to share together.

Finally, in 2009 my wife Michelle, Fred Knapp and I finally did it. It was bittersweet to be sure. When I originally did the first pitch, I had gotten it clean, but this day I mixed up my hands and got the major flash pump trying to switch things up. TAKE! DAMMIT. I got the moves when I didn't summit and didn't do them when I summited. Bottom line is, we were on the top, amongst friends on a beautiful day. Finally I was looking at the top of Castleton instead of looking over at the top of the Rectory. It felt good! Now Dylan has moved away, but I await the time he comes for a visit and we can take care of unfinished business! That's the desert—always some unfinished business!

P1: Some folks say this is the route's crux. A steep big-hands bulge, not far from the ground (physical crux), starts things off. Continue, passing a ledge with bolts a bit to the left, up to a shallow corner followed by some thin hands and fingers splitter, eventually to a belay stance with a bolted anchor (5.10+).
P2: The technical crux pitch. Shortly after leaving the belay punch it through a bulge with splitter fingers, then the angle eases off and friendlier sizes bring you through a small roof and up to a belay ledge (5.11).
P3: Most every tower has a pitch of either wideness or poor rock. This pitch has the latter. The pitch is fairly short, and not too difficult. That being said, it may feel a bit heady and meandering—long slings are helpful. If you plan on doing the bolted finish, you could easily combine these two pitches.
P4: The original finish traverses left from the belay ledge. Follow the foot ledge with a horizontal featuring hands out to the large left-facing corner. Optional belay. Continue up the corner passing several large blocks (dicey looking but fun) to the top.
VAR. Directly above the top of the third pitch, a tricky face passes four bolts en route to to the large summit (5.11).
Follow in the steps of Bon Jovi and give it a "blaze of glory"…
Gear: Wires, 5 quickdraws (1)0.2, (2)0.3, (3)0.4, (3)0.5, (3)0.75, (3)1.0, (2)2.0, (3)3.0, (6)slings
FA: Chip Chace, Pat Ellingwood

River Road

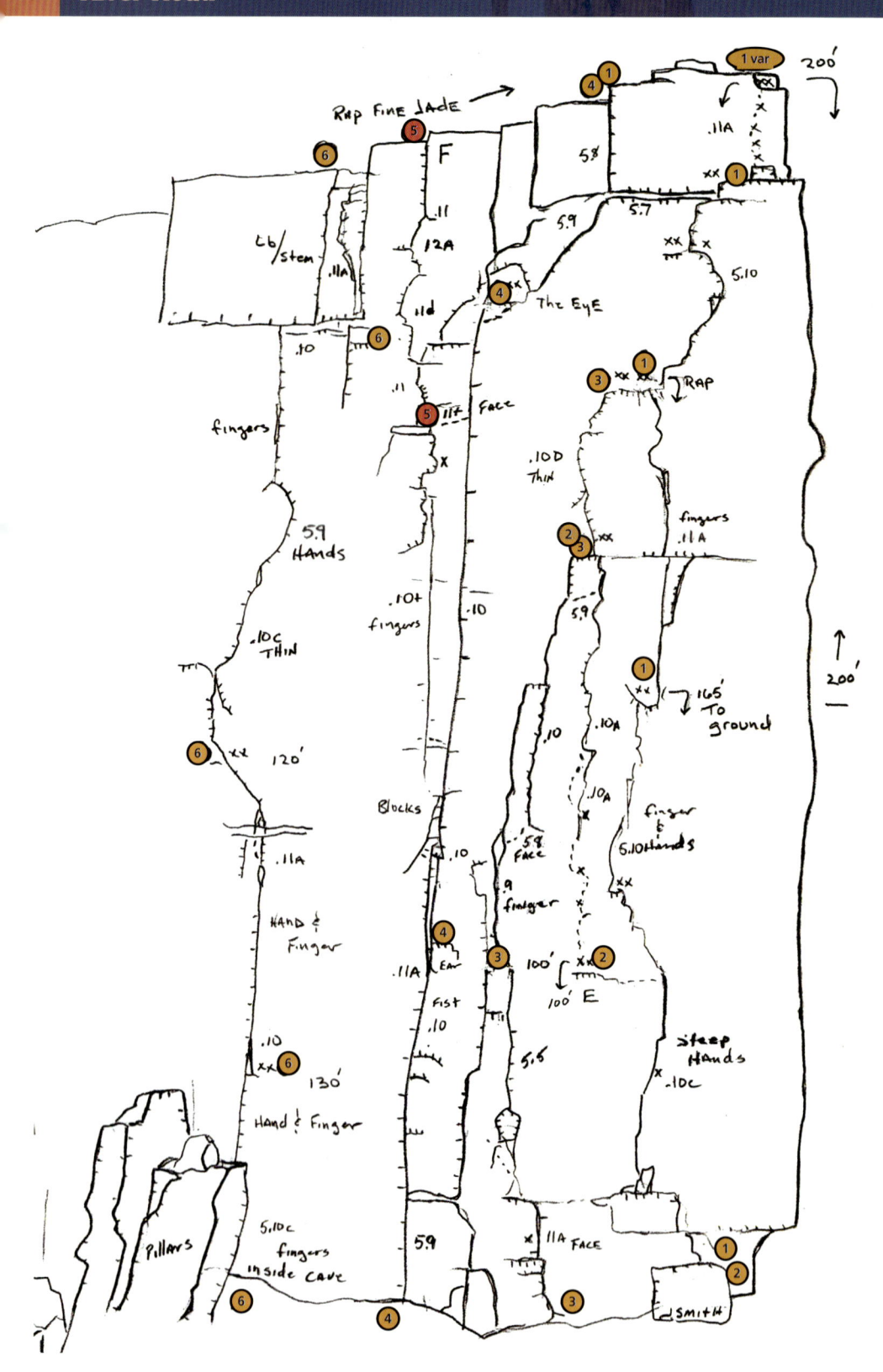

Castle Valley

2. HAIL MARY 5.10+ ★★★
P1: Climb about halfway up the first pitch of *Fine Jade* and traverse left shortly after the steep crux section to a bolted belay (5.10+).
P2: Face climb past three bolts to a right-facing corner arriving at a bolted belay ledge (5.10).
P3: Follow the steep, left-facing corner above the belay through a thin section. The angle eases off, leading to another bolted belay ledge at the top of pitch 2 on *Fine Jade* (5.10+).
P4: Continue on up pitch 3 of *Fine Jade*, linking it with the bolted variation finish of *Fine Jade*.
Gear: Same as for Fine Jade.
FA: Jay Smith, Kitty Calhoun

3. FIND SHADE 5.11a ★★★
Some hard moves near the ground give way to moderate climbing which eventually meets up with the third pitch of *Hail Mary* and finishes on *Fine Jade*.
P1: Face climb, passing a bolt (5.11a), and climb to a left-facing corner. Climb the moderate corner to a belay stance. Build a belay.
P2: Climb 5.9 fingers with some stems to some easy face climbing trending right. Follow the right-facing corner to some easier climbing above, finally reaching the belay ledge shared with *Hail Mary*.
To summit, finish by following *Hail Mary* and *Fine Jade*.
Gear: Wires, 2 sets of TCUs, (4)0.4, (3)0.5, (3)0.75, (2)1.0, (2)2.0, (1)3.0
FA: Jay Smith, Steve Quinlan

4. WEST SIDE STORY 5.11+
Commence a bit left of *Find Shade* in a right-facing corner that switches to left-facing. High on the route you can see the "eye" (a window looking through to the other side).
P1: Climb to a ledge and continue with fists and hands in the right-facing corner up to a belay ledge (the ear) and set a belay.
P2: Move off the belay and climb the roof with good fingers and feet. Climb the obvious splitter out left from the main corner up to a creepy flake with a welcomed protection bolt. Set a belay on the flake.
P3: From the belay, face traverse right (11+) to the left-facing corner. Climb the corner up to the "eye" and a bolted belay.
P4: Continue out right of the window. Easier face moves lead to a connection with the final moves of the last pitch of *Fine Jade*.
Gear: Wires, (2-3)0.3–3.0, (4)4.0
FA: Noah Bigwood, Fred Vandenberg

Jim Turner on the FA of Jesus Saves 5.12a
Jay Smith photo

5. END OF STORY 5.12
A variation of *West Side Story*. Climb the first two pitches of *West Side Story*. From the top of pitch two climb straight up over broken corners to the final right-facing corner.
FA: Greg Child, Jay Smith, Steve "Roadie" Seats

Look for a couple of pillars leaning against the wall. The next three routes start at these pillars.

6. MINISTRY 5.11a ★★★
Start behind the pillars in a left-facing corner.
P1: Climb fingers and hands to a bolted belay (5.10+).
P2: The corner switches aspects to right-facing. Climb the corner with more fingers and hands to a pod/hole. Cruxy moves exiting the hole bring you to some easier final moves and the next bolted belay ledge (5.11).
P3: Climb via hands to a stance on a ledge. Follow the steep corner with thin moves to a big-hands section then a roof. Traverse right on blocks to a belay ledge (draws and shoulder slings helpful). Set a belay.
P4: Work your way up to the stembox. Stem past some calcite to the summit.
Gear: Wires, 2 sets of TCUs, (3)0.4, (2)0.5, (2)0.75, (5)#2 Friend, (2)1.0, (2)2.0, (2)3.0, (1)4.0
FFA: Jay Smith, Jim Donini (evidence of an earlier ascent exists; bolts placed by unknown party)

River Road

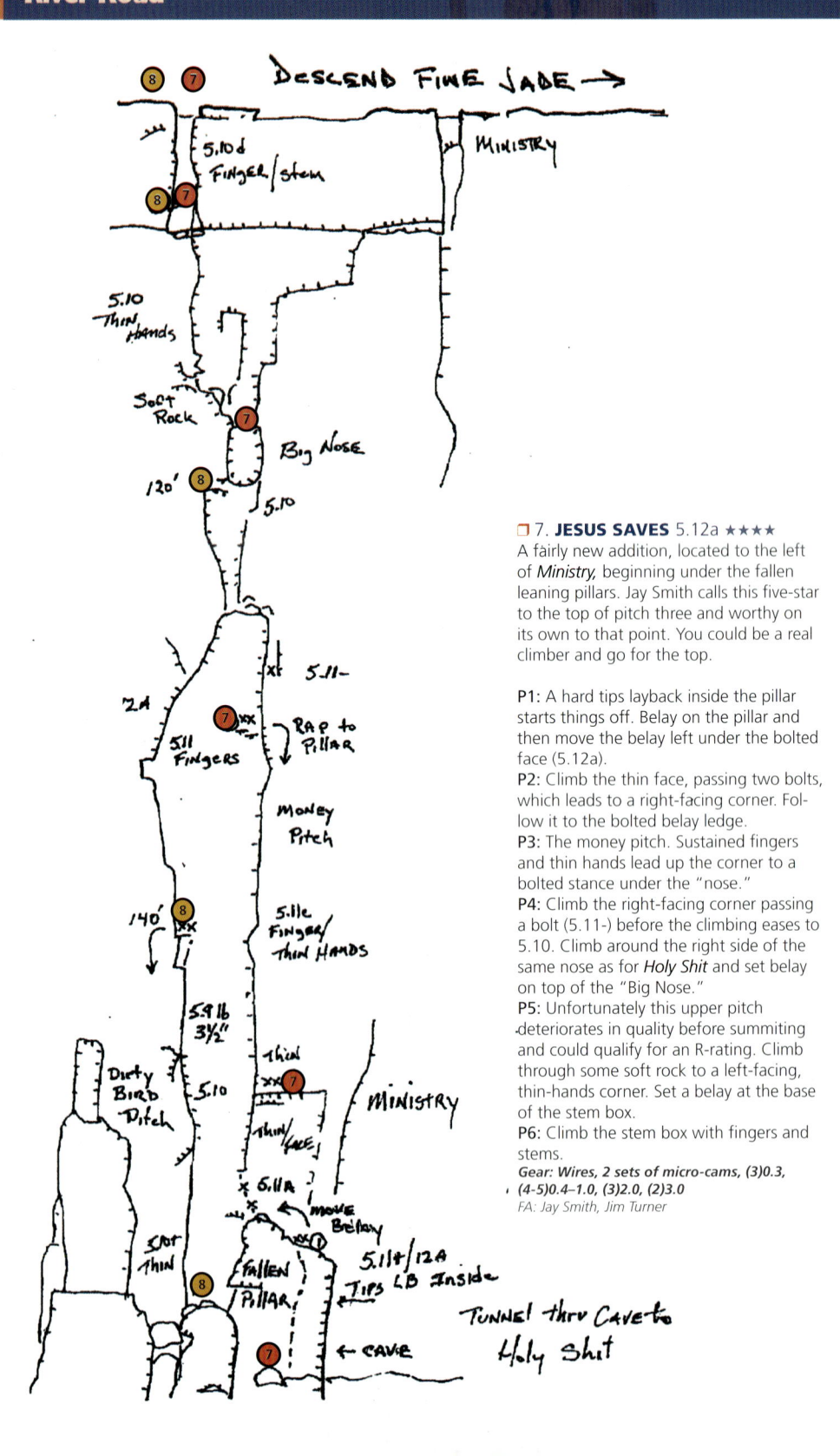

7. JESUS SAVES 5.12a ★★★★
A fairly new addition, located to the left of *Ministry*, beginning under the fallen leaning pillars. Jay Smith calls this five-star to the top of pitch three and worthy on its own to that point. You could be a real climber and go for the top.

P1: A hard tips layback inside the pillar starts things off. Belay on the pillar and then move the belay left under the bolted face (5.12a).
P2: Climb the thin face, passing two bolts, which leads to a right-facing corner. Follow it to the bolted belay ledge.
P3: The money pitch. Sustained fingers and thin hands lead up the corner to a bolted stance under the "nose."
P4: Climb the right-facing corner passing a bolt (5.11-) before the climbing eases to 5.10. Climb around the right side of the same nose as for *Holy Shit* and set belay on top of the "Big Nose."
P5: Unfortunately this upper pitch deteriorates in quality before summiting and could qualify for an R-rating. Climb through some soft rock to a left-facing, thin-hands corner. Set a belay at the base of the stem box.
P6: Climb the stem box with fingers and stems.
Gear: Wires, 2 sets of micro-cams, (3)0.3, (4–5)0.4–1.0, (3)2.0, (2)3.0
FA: Jay Smith, Jim Turner

The Priest and Nuns

PRIEST, NUNS, RECTORY

The Rectory
- 1. **FINE JADE** 5.11
- 2. **HAIL MARY** 5.10+
- 3. **FIND SHADE** 5.11a
- 4. **WEST SIDE STORY** 5.11+
- 5. **END OF STORY** 5.12
- 6. **MINISTRY** 5.11a
- 7. **JESUS SAVES** 5.12a
- 8. **HOLY SHIT** 5.11a
- 9. **SINNERS & INFIDELS** 5.10+
- 10. **OFF TO SEE ALLAH** 5.11b
- 11. **PENITENT** 5.11A, A1
- 12. **DEARLY DEPARTED** 5.11
- 13. **CRACK WARS** 5.11
- 14. **CRACK WHORES** 5.10+
- 15. **EMPIRICAL ROUTE** 5.9

The Nuns
- 1. **WHERE HAVE ALL THE WILD THINGS GONE** 5.11

The Priest
- 1. **THE HONEYMOON CHIMNEY** 5.11
- 2. **EXCOMMUNICATION** 5.13-

Castle Valley

227

River Road

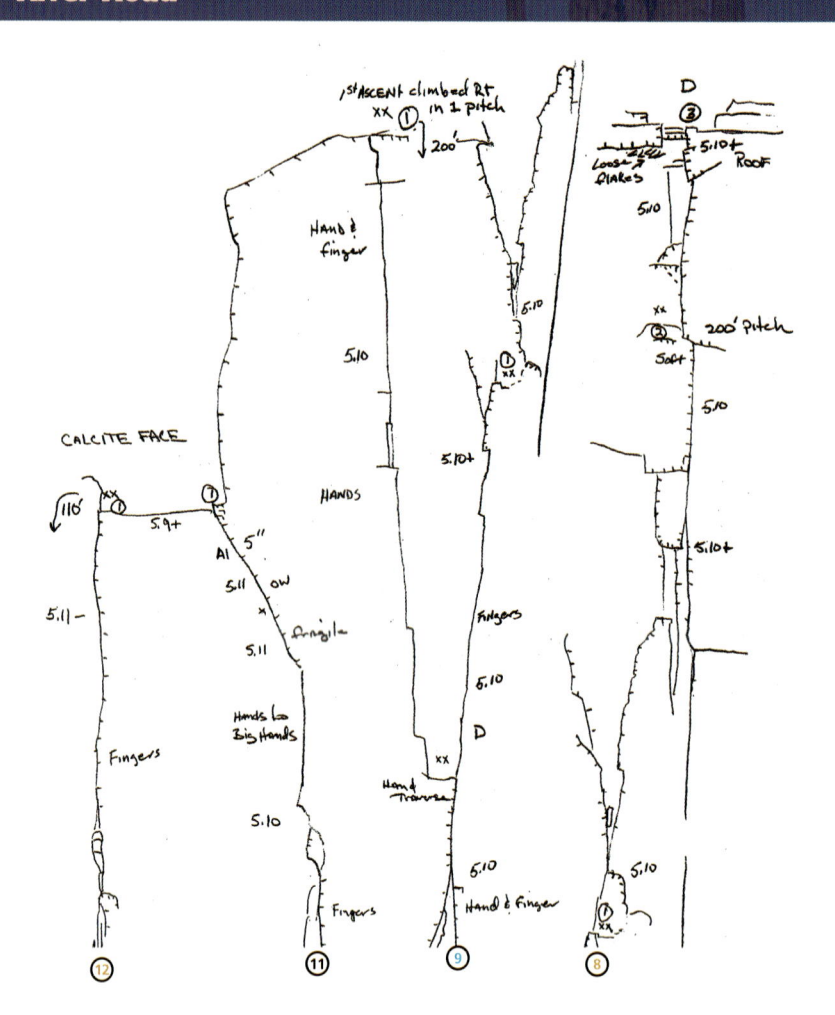

❒ 8. **HOLY SHIT** 5.11- ★
A four-pitch summit outing just left of *Jesus Saves*—sharing the last pitch of that route.
P1: A very long pitch that begins by tunneling past the start of *J.S.* deep behind the pillars. Follow a thin splitter and climb a short left-facing corner to the fist splitter. Climb the splitter to a bolted belay (140').
P2: Continue up the splitter to a steep right-facing fingers corner that switches aspects to a belay station just left and below the "nose."
P3: Work out left over some soft rock to a left-facing corner with thin hands. Belay at the bottom of the stem box.
P4: Follow the short fingery stem box to the summit.
Gear: Wires, (1)0.1, (1)0.2, (2)0.3, (3)0.4, (2)0.5, (3)0.75, (3)1.0, (3)2.0, (2)3.0, (2)4.0
FA: Jay Smth, John Catto

❒ 8a. **PRAYER BOOK** 5.11- ★★★
A couple hundred feet left of *Ministry* is another pillar leaning against the wall. *Prayer Book* is just left of this pillar.
P1: A few moves lead to a small stance; continue via fingers to a widening crack of big hands, then a roof. Traverse this via hands and underclings, turning it on the left (crux). Continue to a good ledge, climbing a thin crack with face features (5.10).
P2: Climb above the belay on cool face features (5.10 with a couple bolts). A bit of a runout on moderate ground leads to a place where it is possible to step left into a long crack system. Follow this by face and crack climbing in a chimney until it is possible to step left onto a ledge and belay. The crack above has dangerously loose, giant blocks barring the way.
Gear: Double set of Camalots to 2.0, (4)3.0, (1)4.0
FA: Jay Smth, Kitty Calhoun

Castle Valley

9. SINNERS & INFIDELS 5.10+ ★★★
A combination of great calcite and some scary sections.
P1: Start by climbing *Off to See Allah* for 100', then continue another 50' on fingers/off-fingers on a calcite face.
P2: Traverse right to a wide splitter that turns to a steeper corner. A fingers crux is encountered at a scary flake (200').
P3: A shorter scarier pitch (50').
Gear: (2)0.1, (2)0.2, (3)0.3 (4)4.0, (4)0.5, (4)0.75, (4)1.0, (3)2.0, (2)3.0, (1)4.0, set of wires
FA: Jay Smith, John Catto, Dougald McDonald

10. OFF TO SEE ALLAH 5.11b ★★
A long pitch. Climb fingers and hands to a short leftward traverse to more splitter fingers and hands. Originally climbed in one long pitch, the lower bolts were added to accommodate a descent with one rope.
Gear: (1)0.5 TCU, (2)0.75 TCU, (2)1.0 Friend, (2)1.5, (2)2.0, (3)2.5, (3)3.0 (may need more gear if climbed in one pitch).
FA: Jay Smith, Kitty Calhoun

11. PENITENT 5.11 A1
FA: John Catto, Jay Smith

12. DEARLY DEPARTED 5.11- ★★★
Gear: Wires, double set of TCUS, (double set)0.4–2.0, (1)3.0
FA Jay Smith, John Catto

13. CRACK WARS 5.11 ★★★★
P1: Start with some off-fingers/tight hands for a few body-lengths. Continue up stellar hands for 80' feet. An awesome pitch by itself!
P2: Start by climbing mostly splitter fist, then traverse left and look for the obvious ledge to build an anchor.
P3: Continue with wide climbing to a bolt under the roof. This is a good spot to build a belay using the bolt and a 3.5.
P4: Pull the roof on fist jams and continue over some looseness to a leftward traverse and a squeeze (some fingers protection would be helpful).
Gear: 0.3–# 4 Big Bro (heavy on hands and fist)
FA: Charlie Fowler, Glenn Randall

14. CRACK WHORES 5.10+ 80' ★★★
Just left of *Crack Wars*. A worthy pitch to do before or after *Crack Wars*. Too bad it doesn't continue to the top! Jay found a small, very old Hex about 25 feet lower than where he ended the climb and placed the anchor. Fingers and hands in a splitter.
Gear: Nuts up to a 3.5 (mostly hands and fingers).
FA: Jay Smith, Jack Tackle

15. EMPIRICAL ROUTE 5.9 ★★
A somewhat unattractive-looking line, *Empirical Route* was the first route to the mesa top.
P1: Climb the broken right-facing corner system with some chimneying and hand cracks for a really long pitch that brings you to the notch between the Nuns and Rectory (at a bolted belay). If you've already ticked the summit via a different route, you may want to bail here. The upper pitches may have value in a historical way, but for sure not in a quality way.
P2: Goes up the north face via a hand crack to a "real dirty" chimney and on to the summit.
Gear: Nuts, slings, 0.5–3.0 (double set)
FA: Harvey Carter, Cleve McCarty, Annie Carter

East Face

Three routes grace the east face and have two distinctly different approaches. The talus on this side of the formation is rather loose and dangerous. For *Coyote Calling*, *Scriptures*, and *Shadow of the Wind*, approach as for *Fine Jade* but keep working right. To reach *Satan's Slave*, approach past The Nuns.

❏ 17. **COYOTE CALLING** 5.11+ ★★★★★
P1: A shallow, left-facing fingers corner leads to a ledge with a bolt. Traverse left to a right-facing fingers corner until it turns to a groove; pass the crux bulge and belay at bolts (5.11+).
P2: A short face traverse leads to a varied finger crack, then to a bulging slot with hands in the back (5.11).
P3: Climb fingers and tight hands with occasional rests before a steep section.
P4: Begin with a scary leftward face traverse to a seam/finger crack (nuts recommended). The crack gets friendlier and hand-size, terminating on the ledge just below the bolted finish to *Fine Jade*.
Rappel Fine Jade
Gear: 0.0–4.0 (heavy on tips through tight hands), set of nuts, shoulder runners.
FA: Kent Wheeler, Scott Lazar

❏ 18. **SCRIPTURES** 5.10+ ★★
A two-pitch route several cracks from *Coyote Calling*.
FA: Jay Smith, Katy Cassidy

❏ 19. **SHADOW OF THE WIND** 5.10+
Walk 100 or 200 meters from *Coyote Calling* on notorious ball bearings (or as Pennings described—"marbles on glass"). Look for a chossy ledge with a plaque gained by some 3rd class. Neither I, nor anyone I know, has climbed this mysterious route. The topo and info provided by Mike Pennings may entice some of us.
FA: Mike Pennings, Josh Boroff

❏ 20. **SATAN'S SLAVE** 5.11 ★★
This route is best accessed by continuing to walk around the Priest to the back side of The Nuns. Continue past *Holier Than Thou* and look for the striking line with a bouldery start.
P1: Starts on steep rock with a key envelope slot left of the crack. Continue via fingers and face climbing to a widening crack, pass two scary-looking blocks, then climb steep, stout, off-fingers and tight hands to the hidden anchors. A 70-meter rope will barely get you down.
P2: Continue up the awkward, thin, mostly-fingers corner to another belay ledge with bolts. The crux is the changing corners roof halfway up the pitch.
Gear: 0.3–3.0 (heavy on off–fingers and thin hands)
FA: Jay Smith, Mark Hesse

Working around the blocks on *Satan's Slave* 5.11

Castle Valley 231

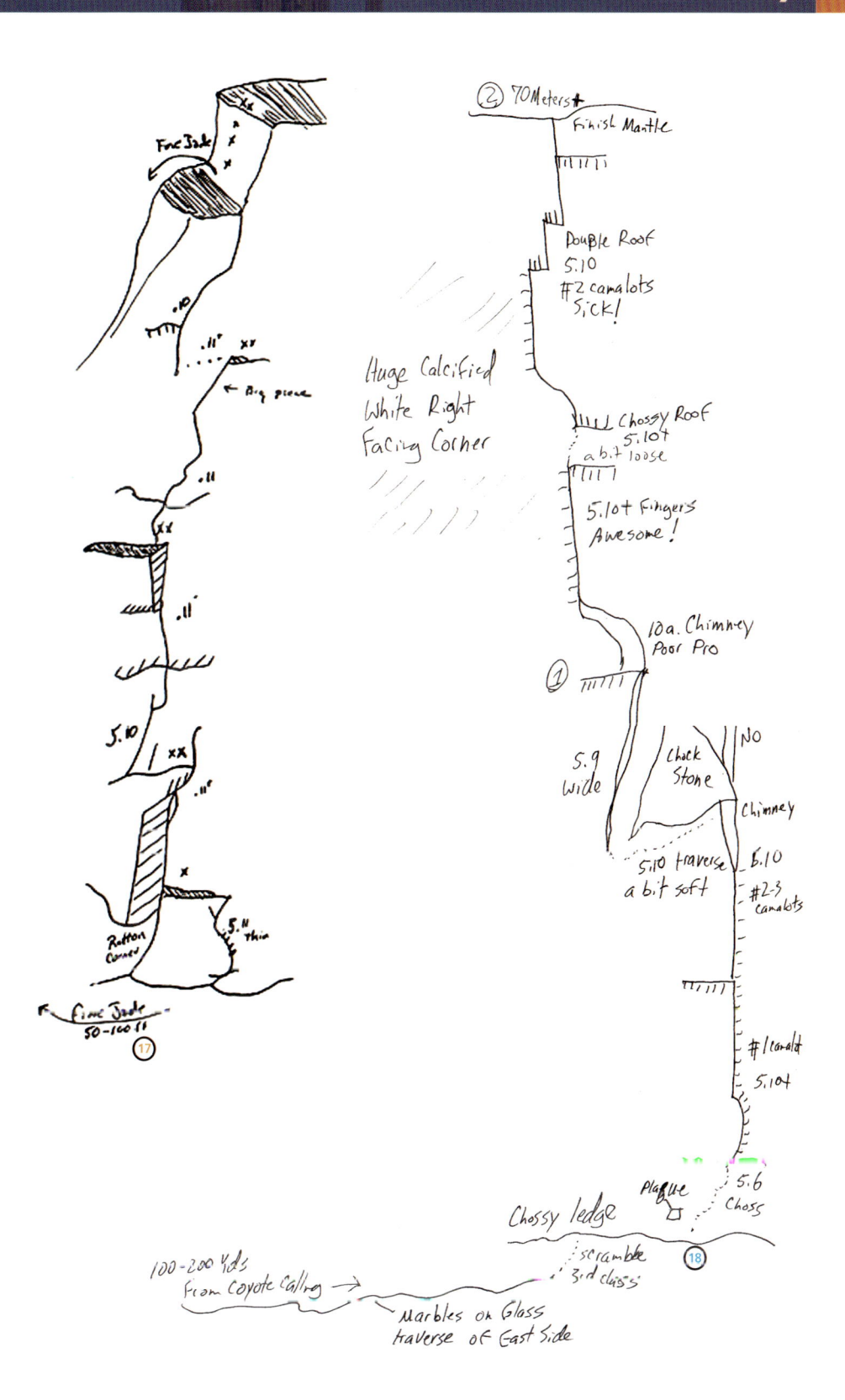

The Nuns

The next route is the only route on the west face of The Nuns. It share the last pitch of the *Empirical Route* to finish atop the Rectory.

◻ 1. **WHERE HAVE ALL THE WILD THINGS GONE** 5.11
Fun route up a right-facing corner with a calcite streak down its left side. At the beginning of the climb, look for a leaning pedestal with perfect hands on its right side.
P1: ★★★ Climb the pillar with hands, mantel to its top. Continue up the right-facing steep corner, climbing with off-fingers and tight hands. The angle lessens but the crack tightens down just a bit more. The climbing is great, but a bit sharp. A worthy pitch in itself! Two new Metolious rap hangers at the belay (5.11).
P2: Climb the various finger cracks, edges, and flakes. Nuts are a must for this pitch! Continue climbing to the notch and set a gear belay (5.11).
P3: Follow the *Empirical Route* to the summit of the Rectory.
Gear: 0.5–3.5 (heavy on off–fingers), set of nuts, shoulder length slings
FA: Romain Vogler, Christian Schwarz

Ben Riley on *Where Have All the Wild Things Gone* 5.11

# Castle Valley

North Face

Routes are listed from right to left as one walks around the Priest to the back side of the Nuns on the northeast face.

2. THE FLYING NUN 5.10 ★

The Flying Nun is the first route you encounter walking from the back of the Priest. A sharp, arcing fingers splitter.
P1: A couple of easy hands moves brings you to the calcite-lined sharp fingers splitter. Follow the splitter to its end and move left past the last couple of bolts on *Holier than Thou*.
P2: Your choice: follow either *Holier than Thou* or *Unforgiven* to the summit.
Gear: Wires, cams to 2.5 inches
FA: Mark Hesse, Jay Smith

3. HOLIER THAN THOU 5.11c ★★★★★

A route with a stout reputation.
P1: Face climb past 11 bolts to a bolted belay. Sustained 5.11c.
P2: (Black hangers) Step left and follow the bolt line at a mellower grade, but with a bit more space between bolts, to a bolted belay.
P3: Step left to a hand crack and follow to the summit.
Descent: Rap the route. A single 70m will work.
Gear: 12 draws, 0.4 TCU to hand size
FA: Jay Smith, Mark Hesse

4. UNFORGIVEN 5.11c ★★★

P1: Climb the first pitch of *Holier than Thou*.
P2: (Silver hangers) Face climb past six bolts and ascend the obvious right-to-left fingers-to-hands crack
Gear: Draws, wires, cams to 2.5 inches
FA: Greg Child

5. BAD HABIT 5.11c ★★★★

A left-facing corner that gets steeper as it trends towards the arête.
P1: Thin climbing with stems starts things off, then it goes through the sizes. Thankfully, as the route gets steeper the sizes get friendlier. When the corner ends belay at a bolted stance.
P2: Follow cracks up to a final steep hand crack before the summit.
Gear: Small wires to 2.0 Camalot, extra TCUs and #2 Friends
FA: John Catto, Jay Smith, Mark Hesse

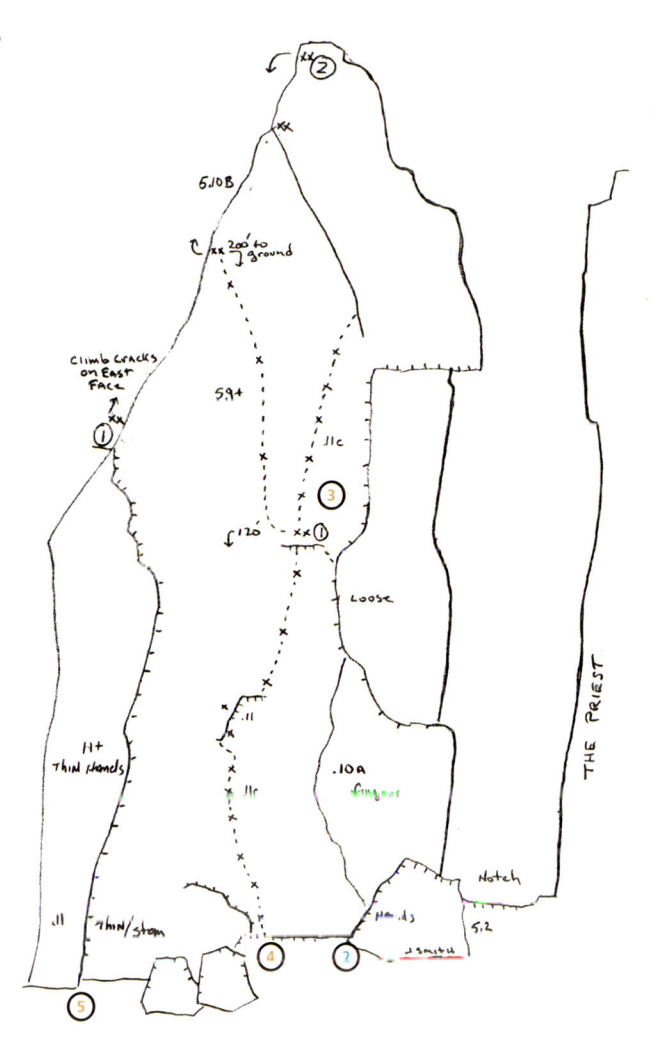

The Priest

The Priest affords some of the wildest tower climbing in Castle Valley, and boasts a stunning micro-summit.

West Face

1. THE HONEYMOON CHIMNEY 5.11 ★★★★
Starts on the west face in a right-facing wide corner.
P1: Climb the ow via off-width technique or laybacking past two relics that serve as "protection." Continue with no pro for around 40', after which there are some chockstones to sling and/or pro with nuts. There is a bolted belay tucked way back in the chimney but it is better to build a belay at the huge boulder/chockstone to alleviate drag (5.9 old school).
P2: Fun chimneying leads to a bolted ledge (5.7).
P3: Continue chimneying, passing some fixed pieces, until it gets wide enough to stem. Leave the stem and step over to the main tower and face climb (5.11) past a half dozen bolts until you can make a traverse left on a ledge to a belay.
P4: Traverse left and gain a short fingers and hands section to the summit (5.8).
FA: Layton Kor, Fred Beckey, Harvey Carter, Annie Carter

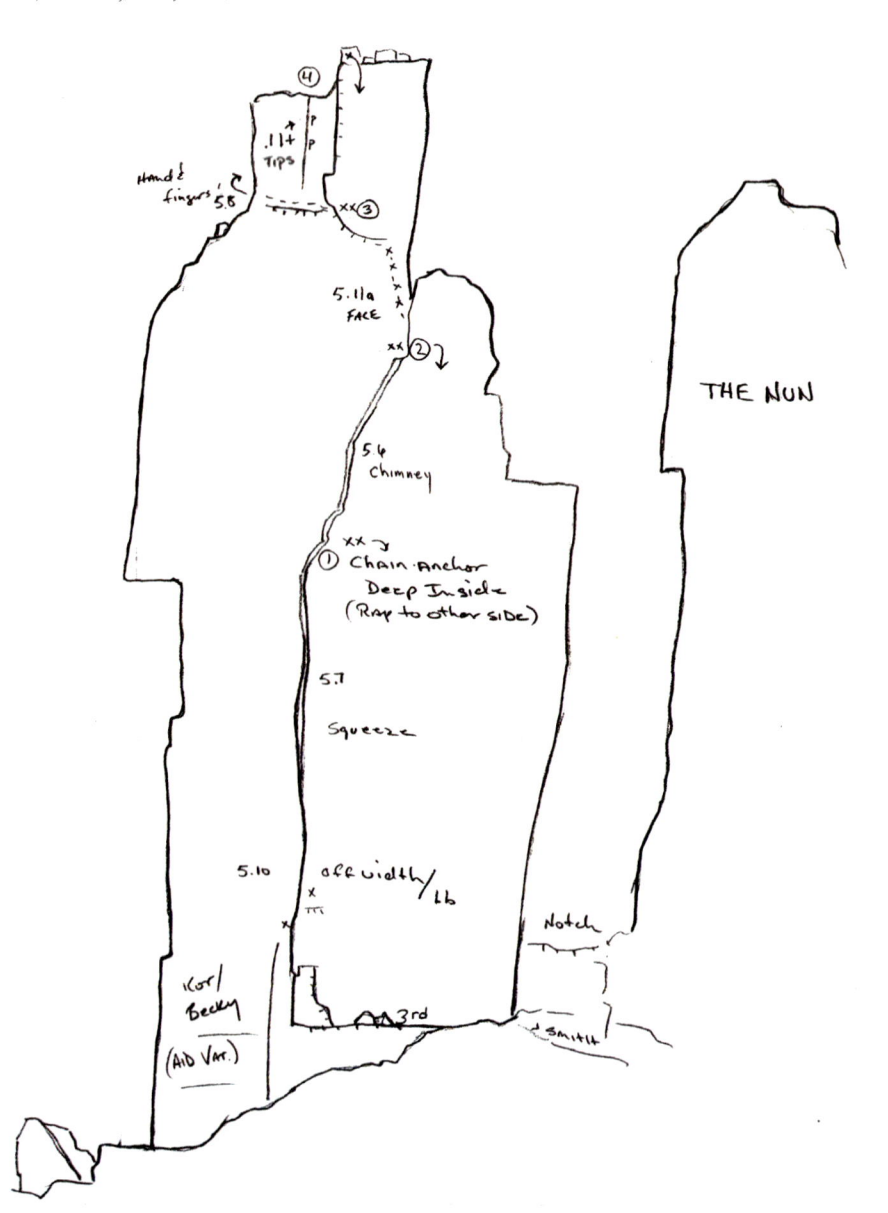

North Face

☐ 2. **EXCOMMUNICATION** 5.13- ★★★★

A reputation as the poster child of aesthetic desert bad ass climbing, but beyond my ability to give a first-hand description. A quote from Jay Smith: "I haven't done it and probably never will, but holy shit. It has got to be one of the best routes anywhere."
P1: Climb the sharp arête past nine bolts (5.12, 90').
P2: Continue up the exposed arête, passing six bolts supplemented by gear (5.12-, 75').
P3: The crux pitch begins up the arête and moves up the center of the face passing nine bolts (5.13-, 90').
P4: Continue up a short slab, passing four bolts (5.11, 40').
P5: Climb a flake and sketchy corner, protected by gear and a couple of supplemental bolts (5.10+ R, 40').
Rap the route with a single 70m
Gear: 12 draws, 0.2–2.0
FA: Greg Child

Rosie Hanek on *Honeymoon Chimney* 5.11   Andrew Burr photo.

River Road

Sister Superior

From the intersection of 191 and 128 (River Road) it is 16.1 miles to the turn-off on your right. If you see the Rocky Rapid boat launch on the left side of the road, you have gone a bit too far. From the turn off you have a couple of options:
A) The no-clearance vehicle option is to park in the pull-out just off the paved 128 road. Walk in following the dirt road/wash for close to a mile and a half. Look for a cairn and well beaten path up the steep talus to the base of the tower.
B) The high clearance vehicle option. Simply drive your vehicle as far as your comfort level allows. Beware, the road/wash changes after significant rains!
This area is well worth the effort.

There are climbs on the little spires left of the main tower, but they are not described in this book.

Sister Superior group with Sister Superior being the largest on the right

❒ 1. JAH MAN 5.10, C2? W

Once a mega classic—featuring great rock with spacious ledges—this route lost the initial climbing to recent rockfall. Two new pitches offer a path to the original line. Some aid was used, but the ascensionists believe it will go free with a 5.12 boulder-problem crux. Much of the rock at the base may still be unstable, so caution is highly recommended.
P1: Begin as for the original line, climbing blocky terrain. Follow a well-defined crack system to a ledge with a 2-bolt anchor.
P2: Enjoy a fun rightward traverse along a horizontal crack—fun and juggy with a boulder-problem crux (5.11). It might be wise to belay here. Continue up the crack, that once provided protection for the former chimney pitch. Currently this is C2, but by the time this book is printed, it may go at 5.12. It's been described as an "Eldo crack: a hybrid crack with calcite face features."
P3: Climb some finger wedges and tight hands to the obvious leftward traverse. Place a hands piece with a long draw and power up into the left-facing corner. Climb the corner with tight hands until the angle eases. From here it is a short distance of wider low-angle climbing to the belay ledge with bolts (5.10, 95').
P4: Move left to the splitter and climb tight hands to a short traverse out and left. Just above, milk a rest and continue with more tight hands and off-fingers with some *thank you* feet up to a final section of tight hands (a bit of a barn door). Place good gear at the crack's end and mantel onto a good-sized ledge. From the ledge move a touch right and climb a short section of easy but unprotected face climbing to the standard belay. Clip it with a shoulder length sling and move out right and face climb past three drilled angles to the summit (5.10, 130').
Rap: A single 70m is plenty. Rap first from summit to the top of pitch two and then to the ground. Certainly you can rap every station if you want.
Gear: 0.3–2.0 (triples on 0.75 & 1.0)
FA: Ken Trout, Kirk Miller, FA of new pitches: Gaar Laasman, Jake Warren, Mark Howe, Dave Sadoff

TRANGO

BIG BRO
ESSENTIAL GEAR FOR INDIAN CREEK

River Road

Just to the right of *Jah Man* there is a bolted arête that goes for a pitch and a half. It is my understanding that this is an open project.

❏ 2. **SAVIOR FREE VARIATION** 5.11
This less-frequented route is a worthy objective located on the east face. It enjoys morning sun. There has been much confusion over this route, as it was ascended shortly after the first ascent by another team who dubbed it *Black Sabbath*.
P1: Climb a chimney and traverse right on large ledge (5.7). Belay from gear.
P2: Follow a crack that zags left. This is left of the chimney and old bolt ladder. Belay at a bolted belay (5.11).
P3: Traverse left on face holds (5.10), and climb a crack from tight hands to hands to offwidth to chimney. Bolted belay ledge (5.10).
P4: Finish with a *Jah Man* exit of your choice.
Descent: Rappel Jah Man.
Gear: *TCUs from 0.4–0.75 (3)0.75, (3)0.5, (3)0.75, (3)1.0, (2)2.0, (2)3.0, (1)4.0*
FA: Harvey Carter, David Bentley (via chimney on right); FFA: Marco Cornacchione, Steph Davis

Todd Bogen starting up the original crux of Jah Man (now 5.10, C2)

River Road .... Onion Creek

Jake Warren on the FA of *Burn Another One Down* 5.11b/c

ONION CREEK

Onion Creek is located 20.0 miles down the River Road. While the Hideout Wall is the only "crag" covered in this region, there are other objectives, most notably The Hindu—a tall narrow spire seen from the River Road featuring quality 5.12 and 5.13 routes (or aid).

The Hindu

The Hindu is encountered along the Onion Creek Road and is a slender spire composed of what appears to be stacked slabs of rock. The tower, however, is composed of clean Cutler and offers two interesting routes.

Approach: Turn off the River Road at the Fisher Valley Ranch Road (dirt) just west of the Fisher Tower turn-off. This road takes one through Onion Creek Canyon. The tower is obvious from the road. Approach from the right side and hike up to the high point saddle.

☐ 1. **MAVERICK** 5.10 C2 or 5.13a

This south-facing route, though it has been freed, is an excellent moderate aid climb. It offers some interesting placements in old scars, a pendulum, some free climbing, and a fantastic summit. To avoid hanging belays the route is best done as two pitches.
P1: The first pitch begins up good rock on 5.9 terrain, though pin scars indicate that this section has been aided. After 15 feet a drilled angle offers protection and the aid climbing begins (for most people). A thin crack is partly fixed but requires placement of some good wires. Pendulum left from a good bolt until it becomes possible to climb an easy chimney to a comfortable belay.
P2: The next pitch climbs a groove and crack past some fixed pins to the summit (5.10c).
Rappel the route.
Gear: Two sets of cams, wires, RPs, small Tri–cams, and TCUs should prove more than adequate.
FA: Harvey Carter, Steve Miller; FFA: Stevie Haston, Laurence Gouault

☐ 2. **SHIVA** 5.12a

This route, originally described as *North Face*, offers a more moderate free grade, but can also be aided. Approach as for *Maverick* but traverse to the northwest corner via a narrow ledge. The route stays on the north side of the tower. See the topo for route description.
Gear: Wires, (3)0.00, (3)0.0, (3)0.3, (2)0.4, (2)0.5, (3)0.75, (3)1.0, (1)2.0
FA: Bill Forrest, Don Briggs; FFA: Jay Smith, Mark Hesse

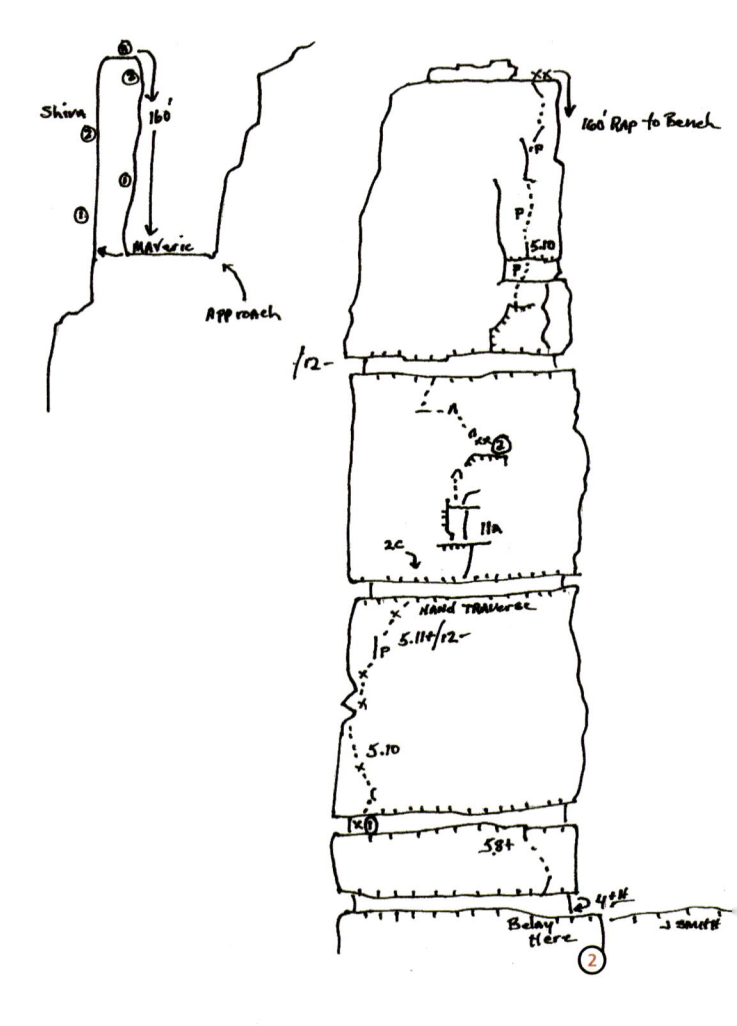

The Hideout Wall ✦W

The Hideout Wall is a bit off the beaten path but offers a broad range of grades and lengths. Wingate sandstone combined with great camping and solitude ensure a great time.

Follow the River Road until you reach 20.0 miles on your odometer. Turn right onto the Onion Creek road, aka the Fisher Valley road. In the first few miles you will cross the creek 15 times. At 2.7 miles you will get a close-up glimpse of the Hindu as you round the corner. At 3.6 miles you will cross a bridge that goes over the "Narrows." You then cross the creek seven more times before you gain some elevation. Once you are up on the hill, continue driving through the upper meadow and a cattle gate at 8.6 miles, and another at 9.7. At 10.3 miles, take a left at a junction heading to North Beaver Mesa. Ascend a bit more to 11.1 miles where you will crest a hill and pass through another fence before descending through some steep "corkscrews." Continue until the road forks again at 12.1 miles. Take a right and drive 0.1 mile to the campsite on the left.

To reach the cliff, walk straight through the campsite, cross a small drainage, and follow a faint trail marked with cairns. The trail follows a runoff drainage the majority of the way and dumps you out at the far left side of the crag just under *Bionic Chronic* (about 20 minutes).

Heather Hillier on *Paranoid* 5.10b/c photo Tom Gwinn

❏ 1. SPLIFF SPIRE 5.5 C2 65'
A small tower-esque formation on the far left (north-facing) wall.
FA: Andy Roberts

The next four routes are in close proximity to one another.

❏ 2. MAY FLY 5.12 50'
Climb broken cracks up to some face holds just before the anchor.
Gear: 0.0–0.75

❏ 3. THE CONSTRICTOR 5.10+ 150' ★★★
Start in a left-facing corner with some hands, moving into big hands. All too soon the crack widens. Run out the arching chimney, which eventually constricts, forcing the climber back out. Pass three bolts heading to the anchor.
Gear: 1.0–5.0 (heavy on 3.0–4.0)
FA: Dave Mealy

❏ 4. MOON'S UNIT 5.10 90' ★★★
Located in a left-facing corner. Start on the right wall by climbing over some secure, but loose-looking, blocks. Continue up to a hand-sized splitter, which runs into the corner. The climb steepens. Continue through off-fingers to a rest before a section of good hands which leads to a pod. Pass through the pod to a few last hands before the anchor.
Gear: 0.5–3.0
FA: Dave Mealy

❏ 5. BIONIC CHRONIC 5.10 50' ★★
Ascends a left-facing corner beginning with hands. Move to a steep flare which protects with off-fingers gear just before the chains.
Gear: 0.5–3.0
FA: Andy Roberts

❏ 6. DYNAMO HUM 5.10+ ★★★★
A two-pitch route that can be done in three. Follow splitter hands to a shallow left-facing corner with hands, fists, and a small bit of wide crack to a ledge (optional natural belay here). Continue via splitter fist and offwidth to a belay in the chimney just under a big roof.
Rappel the route with a double 70m
Gear: 1.0–5.0 (heavy on big hands and fist)
FA: Andy Roberts, Dave Mealy

❏ 7. CHICKEN LITTLE 5.10+ 55' ★★★★
Just right of *Dynamo Hum*. Start in a left-facing corner and climb a short section of steep fingers. After the bulge, move out left and follow the diagonaling hand and fist crack to the anchor.
Gear: 1 TCU–4.0 (heavy on the fist size)
FA: Dave Mealy

Onion Creek 243

❏ 8. **PABST BLUE RIBBON** 5.8 45'
Good warm-up. Climb the left-facing corner with hands and big hands to a ledge. The anchor is not easily seen from below.
Gear: 2.0–3.0
FA: Jason Repko

❏ 9. **ON THE LAMB** 5.10b 200' ★★★★
Starts just right of *PBR* and follows the large left-facing corner to a huge roof. Climb hands and fingers in a large arching flare. Move out left, passing a bolt on your way to a shallow corner. Follow the corner to a ledge with some fixed pieces. Belaying here is optional. Climb steep terrain to the anchor below the roof.
Rappel with two 70m cords
Gear: 0.4–3.0 (heavy on off–fingers)

❏ 10. **UP IN SMOKE** 5.10 30' ★★
Fun, but really short. Start by going through the roof in a right-facing corner with tight hands and big reaches. It then turns to splitter hands to the anchor. Pumpy and physical.
Gear: 2.0 Friend–2.0

❏ 11. **UNNAMED #1** 5.11 60' ★★
Start in a left-facing corner climbing with off-fingers and hands. The corner switches aspects to a right-facing corner followed by a wide roof.
Gear: 0.75–3.5

❏ 12. **UNNAMED #2** 5.11 70' ★★★
Just right of *Unnamed #1*. A left-facing corner with hands, off-fingers, and cups over a bulge.
Gear: 0.4–3.5

There is a bit of a gap between the unnamed routes and *One Hit*.

❏ 13. **ONE HIT** 5.9 ★★
A right-facing corner that starts with hands and pinches down, eventually closing up before reaching a welcome hand jam and finishing on a ledge.
Gear: 0.5–2.0
FA Andy Roberts

River Road

Hideout Center

Hideout Center is easily identifiable because the cliff skyline is much shorter. The routes here are more spread out than the Hideout. A short walk leads from *One Hit* to the start of Hideout Center.

14. **TWO MINUTES FOR ROUGHING IT** 5.9
45' ★★
Another route that would have more stars if it were only longer. Diagonaling calcite hands splitter.
Gear: Hands
FA: Andy Roberts

15. **LUNG** 5.10 ★★★★ 120'
The start of the route is on less-than-great rock but shortly turns into great rock. A right-leaning hands to fist splitter.
Gear: 2.0–4.0
FA: Lance Lemkau

The next two routes share starts and finishes.

16. **BACHELOR CRACK** 5.10 ★★
Climb easy rock to the base of the right-facing corner. Follow the corner with mostly hands to the ledge with a bolted anchor.
Gear: 0.5–2.0 (heavy on the 2.0s)
FA: Andy Roberts

17. **KISTER TWISTER** 5.10
Follow the same start as for the previous route and walk over to the left-facing corner. Mostly hands, some big and some small.
Gear: 1.0–4.0
FA: Jason Repko

Hideout Right

Walk along the cliff for 5+ minutes to an obstruction by a large block/section of the cliff. Scramble above or walk below and be on the lookout for a large right-facing corner. *Burn One Down* is a splitter on the left wall.

18. **BURN ONE DOWN** 5.10 60' ★★★
Splitter on good rock, the crack is sharp. Starts with fingers and goes up to tight hands.
FA: K3

19. **BURN ANOTHER ONE DOWN** 5.11b 100' ★★★★
Start by climbing *Burn One Down*. Clip the anchor and make a few hard boulder moves to an obvious weakness. Continue up the arching splitter with some off-fingers until it dead ends and runs into a corner and pinches down to tips. Climb the tips (small nuts are helpful here) around the ear, until you get back to the splitter. Follow the crack to a switch which leads to a large roof. Climb out the roof to the right with hands (thankfully) to the anchor.
Gear: Small nuts 1.0 TCU–3.0 (heavy on #2 Friends, 1.0s), slings are nice.
FA: Jake Warren

20. **PARANOID** 5.10+ 55' ★★
A right-facing corner that starts with fingers and widens to off-fingers. Fun climbing using some stepping features on good rock. Hopefully by the time this book goes to print two more pitches wil be added with the third being a leaning splitter on black rock. (hopefully not green Camalot size).
Gear: 0.4–#2 Friend
FA: K3

The next two routes are next to each other.

21. **KIAH CRACK** 5.10 60' ★★
Right-facing corner with big hands. Clean. A great warm up!
Gear: 3.0s
FA: Bill Kiah

22. **MOAB FLU** 5.10+ ★★★★
Sick line! Splitter forever.
P1: A splitter with a little of everything including some welcome feet up to a ledge with a bolted belay (5.10, 95').
P2: The business. Climb the splitter, sometimes offset with fingers for an eternity up to a right-facing, steep, mostly hands corner.
Gear: 0.3–4.0 (heavy on off-fingers)
FA: Andy Roberts

23. **THE STASH** 5.11 ★★★★
Great climb. Easier than it looks, you'll feel like a rock star racking up with tips gear. Good rock with a steep bulge at 2/3rds height. Just enough features to make this great fun!
Gear: 0.0–0.4 (heavy on blue TCUs and 0.3 Camalots)
FA: Andy Roberts

River Road

Fisher Towers

Fisher Towers Andrew Burr photo

FISHER TOWERS BY FRED KNAPP

In all of Canyonlands, no single grouping of towers is as grand and majestic as the Fishers; but by the same token, no other group of towers is as intimidating or outright dirty as these mud-covered giants. For the climber seeking adventure, the Fisher Towers is the place to be. Wild summits, fins, gullies, and erosion-at-work are all elements of the "mud experience." *The Finger of Fate* on the Titan is the time-tested mud classic in Steck & Roper's *Fifty Classic Climbs*.

The Fisher Towers offer the best living geology lesson possible. Twice I've been rained on in the Fishers and have witnessed erosion up close. Once, I had to rappel the entire Kingfisher in a downpour. The sandpaper action of the dirt-filled ropes wore grooves halfway through my rappel biner. When I first climbed the Titan in 1989, many old bolts were dangling on webbing, having eroded from the rock. Many other bolts on the *Finger of Fate* bolt ladder sat on raised cones—the hanger and bolt keeping the rock below from eroding while the rock surrounding it continues to deteriorate. These were replaced in 2004.

"Fisher" probably came from a nearby rancher of the same name. The unweathered Cutler rock that is found underneath the mud is quite good, but the mud casing makes placements difficult, tie-offs scary, anchors untrustworthy, and belayers miserable. Helmets and safety glasses are a must. Most routes in this area are aid routes, but several good free routes exist—Ancient Art, Lizard Rock, and The Cobra.

Each area of the desert possesses its own character. The Fisher Towers have always seemed haunted to me. My first encounter with these towers came at age sixteen when my dad brought me a copy of *Fifty Classic Climbs*. I read through the book and found myself most intimidated by the Titan.

My first climb in the Fishers was Lizard Rock, and even that route seemed scary. For a while I satisfied myself by gazing at the muddy curtains and gargoyled summits. Only once in my early years of desert climbing had I seen a party on any of the larger towers, and this emptiness reinforced the haunted-house aura of the Fishers. At night the towers felt downright terrifying. As a child, often the fear of entering a haunted house is worse than the reality. Once inside, we find the ghosts are in our minds. When I finally climbed the Titan, I felt that the ghosts had left and I began to enjoy the towers.

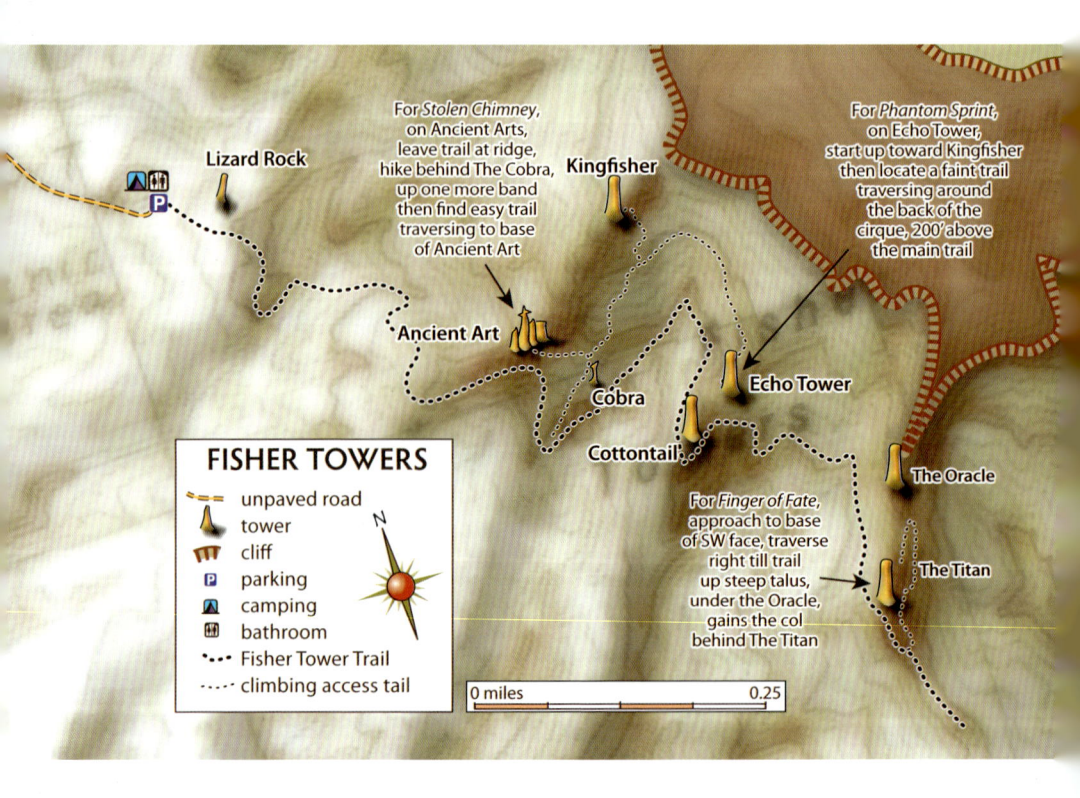

Fisher Towers

Lizard Rock

Lizard Rock is the small, cute tower clearly visible from the parking lot.

1. ENTRY FEE ROUTE
5.8 ★★★
Entry Fee is the best intro climb to the Fisher Towers. While it is a short free climb at the 5.8 level, it offers climbers a chance to experience dirt blocks and dicey gear. The route is obvious on the right side of the west face. The bolts out left are for a 5.10 variation, but you can use the upper one to protect the summit move. If traversing right, a 5.0 Camalot is useful.
FA: Harvey T. Carter, Annie S. Carter

Fred Knapp climbs Entry Fee Photo: Heidi Knapp

The Cobra (R.I.P.)

1. THE COBRA 5.11-R
★★★
The following description is for historical purposes, as the tower has tumbled, as many have speculated it would.

This 60-foot E.T.-looking tower near the Kingfisher is encountered on the approach to Ancient Art. Ascend a short crack system to a flat ledge as seen on the right of this photo. Plug in small cams and nuts, then meander to the next ledge. Tie off the tower with a long sling if you wish to be protected while clipping the drilled angle. Climb over the caprock to the freaky summit. The grade may be height-dependent.
Trivia note: Jimmy Dunn didn't have a long sling on the first ascent, so he resourcefully substituted a dog leash.

Michelle Kelley on The Cobra, before its demise.

Ancient Art (Corkscrew Summit)

Ancient Art (250 feet) is probably the second most popular "mud route" and offers very moderate climbing to the coolest of the Canyonlands summits. The tower, or rather group of towers, is the three-summited feature west of the prominent Kingfisher. The true summit is the corkscrew-shaped feature resembling a child's drip sandcastle that appears to defy gravity.

Approach: Follow the main Fisher Towers trail and walk beneath the SW face of Ancient Art, keeping to the trail around a bend. As the trail veers back towards Echo and Cottontail towers, look for a path leading up a ridge to the south face and a prominent chimney on Ancient Art. The remains of The Cobra serve as a landmark for the approximate cut-off point.

1. **STOLEN CHIMNEY** 5.10d or 5.8 A0 ★★★★
P1: Begin the route with a short 5.6 grovel that puts you at the base of a bolted trough (sling anchors visible from approach trail).
P2: Ascend via pebble climbing (5.10) or aid (A0, no aiders needed). Bolts protect this short pitch.
P3: The next pitch is, in some ways, the crux. Climb up the muddy chimney past a bolt or two (crux) and up to a fixed belay (5.8, 80').
P4: A very short A0 or 5.10 bolted pitch ascends a giant block to a belay at the beginning of "The Sidewalk."
P5: A short horizontal pitch involves walking or crawling (posture is a great indicator of fear) to the sidewalk's terminus at *The Diving Board*—a bizarre intrusion which must be surmounted with a 5.8 belly flop. Belay atop the hollow sounding diving board or continue with the next pitch.
P6: The last pitch climbs the corkscrew summit with good bolts for protection.
Rappel from slings beneath the summit or leave a toprope set up for protection on the traverse, as one must walk back across the sidewalk, then rappel the remainder of the route.
Gear: Medium and large stoppers, a set of cams through 3.0, slings, (6) quickdraws
FA: Paul Sibley, Bill Roos

Brian Edmision on the Corkscrew Summit 5.10d
Photo: Andrew Burr

Kingfisher

☐ 1. **COLORADO NORTHEAST RIDGE** 5.8 C2 ★★

The *Colorado NE Ridge* is the easiest route on the Kingfisher, involving very few technical aid placements. A good rack for the route includes a set of Friends, stoppers, Tricams, and many tie-offs or keyhole hangers. Hike up to the saddle between Ancient Art and the Kingfisher, walk past what remains of The Cobra, then follow the path of least resistance to the SE notch. The route is very obvious from the base and the action photo below will help identify it.

P1 & 2: Pitches one and two can easily be combined. Climb the obvious bolt ladder (A1) on the NE face to a belay ledge. Continue up a 5.8 chimney to a precarious stance on the ridge (150 feet total).

P3: The next pitch involves mixed aid and free climbing, and is the technical crux (C2) involving some tricky aid on gear. Belay at a three-bolt anchor.

P4: Another short C2 pitch involves aid on a couple of placements (crux) and many bolts. Belay in slings beneath a roof.

P5: The last aid pitch follows bolts and fixed pins to the left, then up to a very spacious ledge with a bolt belay.

P6: The final pitch ascends an easy chimney to a belay beneath a chockstone with slings (5.8).

P7: Boulder the summit block.

Rappel the route.

Gear: (6) rivet hangers, (2 each) 0.5 to 3.0, (1)4.0, TCUs, many biners, quickdraws, slings

FA: Harvey T. Carter, Cleve McCarty

A climber at the overhang where the rock bands change (far right)
Photo: Steve "Crusher" Bartlett

River Road

The Titan

❏ 1. **FINGER OF FATE** 5.12c or 5.9 C2+ ★★★

This is yet another fine route that attracts many by its placement in Steck and Roper's *Fifty Crowded Climbs*. The 600-foot giant isn't necessarily crowded, but it isn't uncommon to find another party on the tower on a weekend day. Still, it's not like queuing up for a clip-up at Rifle. The *Finger of Fate* ascends the east ridge of the giant spire, and holds historical significance in that it was the first of the Fishers to be climbed. The magnitude and importance of this ascent is hard to imagine.

Approach: Follow the Fisher Tower Trail via cairns until you reach the south edge of The Titan. *Finger of Fate* is reached by walking completely around The Titan to the north side. The route is normally done in seven pitches, but the first two pitches can be done as four if you don't have enough gear.

P1&2: Begin by ascending cracks which are marked by obvious pin scars and visible slings. The first two pitches are 5.8 C2 and should be climbed clean due to the radical scarring (pins can still be used without hammering).
P3: The third pitch is an exciting traverse around the west face of the Finger that leads to an C2+ roof (largely fixed).
P4: A short free pitch traverses past the descent gully and ascends a 5.8 mud chimney.
P5: The route is now quite obvious as it primarily follow bolts.
P6: The final real pitch primarily follows a bolt ladder but also involves climbing a wide 5.9 crack through the Moenkopi caprock.
P7: A short third class section puts you on the summit.
Descent: Rappel the route to the gendarme, then rappel into the gully to the west. Fixed stances take you to the base. Be cautious of loose rock when pulling your ropes.
Gear: Stoppers (2 sets), 2 sets of cams from very small–4.0, angles and sawed-off angles for hand placements, Hexes
FA: Layton Kor, George Hurley, Huntley Ingalls
FFA: Ben Bransby, Pete Robins

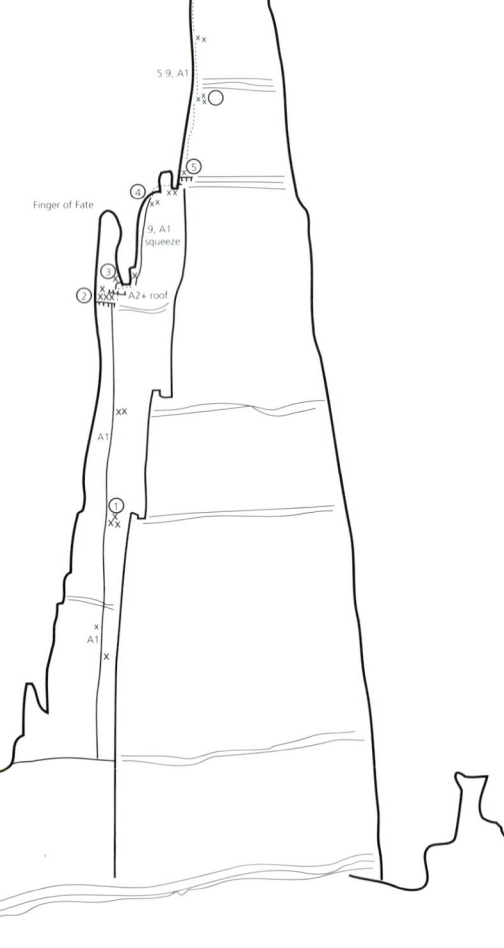

Titan the dog with his namesake in the background.

Fisher Towers   251

◘ 2. **SUNDEVIL CHIMNEY** 5.9 R/X, C3 or 5.13b
The *Sundevil Chimney* is one of the most striking lines in the Fisher Towers, ascending the obvious weakness on the south face of The Titan. Because of its southern exposure, this is an excellent line when the *Finger* is too cold.
Approach as for the *Finger of Fate*, but stop at the base of the *Sundevil Chimney*. The topo should provide all pertinent information.
Descend as for the previous route.
FA: Harvey T. Carter, Tom Merrill, Bob Sullivan, Ken Wyrick, FFA: Stevie Haston

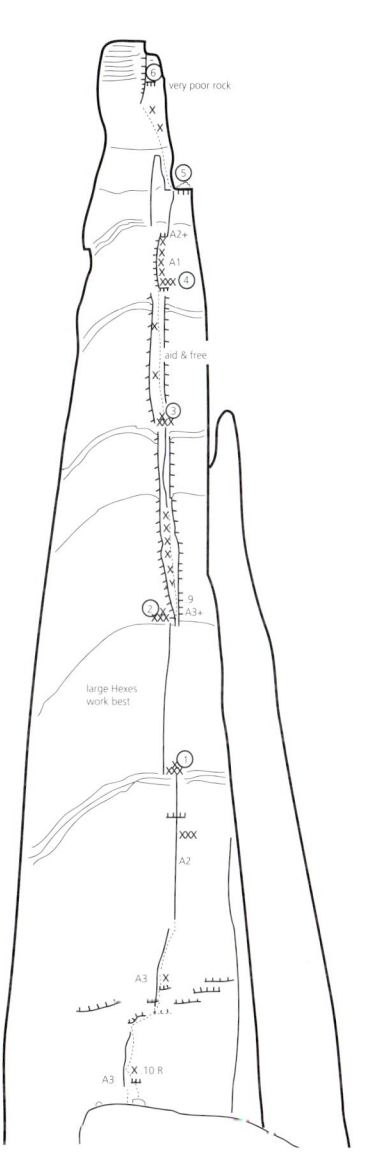

Bill Roberts on *Sundevil Chimney* 5.9 A3 or 5.13
Photo: Paul Hauser

Echo Tower

Approach as for the Kingfisher and locate a faint trail that traverses toward Echo Tower, staying above the cliff bands. Scramble across a bench which leads to the corner of Echo. Bolts have been placed so that you can fix a rope if you are doing this as a two-day climb.

◻ 1. **PHANTOM SPRINT** 5.9 C3 or 5.12b ★★★
This is certainly the most popular route on Echo Tower and one of the more popular routes in the Fishers. It ascends the northeast ridge on fairly clean rock.
P1: More of an obstacle than a climbing challenge. Get yourself and your gear up a 30-foot 5.7 chimney to where the climbing really starts.
P2: A mixed aid and free pitch that starts off thin but gets wide and flaring.
P3: Pitch three climbs a zigzagging crack on clean rock.
P4: Continue up the crack to a roof where a traverse right lands one at a sling belay.
P5: Climb up an awkward crack to a belay beneath the final bolt ladder.
P6: Bolts to the top.
Rappel the route, which requires some traverse-reversing. It also is possible to rappel the more recent Iron Chef route just to the right with two 60m ropes.
Gear: *Bring a bunch of gear from small Tricams to large Camalots, as well as some Hexes.*
FA: Jim Beyer
FFA: Stevie Haston

Mike Swanicke on *Phantom Sprint* 5.9
Photo: Steve "Crusher" Bartlett

ECHO TOWER (CENTER)
Titan (left), Cottontail (right)

Chapter 7

Kane Creek

Jay Smith on the FFA of Guinevere 5.11

KANE CREEK

The Kane Creek area's greatest attraction for climbers has been The Tombstones and Ice Cream Parlor but, truth be told, adventurous climbers will find much great cragging out here. Kane Creek is close to town and the routes provide all exposures.

Kane Creek offers an ample amount of camping, but please camp in designated areas and LEAVE NO TRACE. All climbing covered in this book in Kane Creek is on BLM land. Be careful driving on this road. It is a multi-use area and a lot of off-road vehicles access trails from Kane Creek.

Getting there:
From Center and Main, drive south 0.6 mile and turn right on Kane Creek Drive (between Burger King and McDonalds). At 0.7 miles arrive at an intersection and veer left (which is actually more like continuing straight). All mileage counts will be begin by zeroing out your odometer at the intersection.

Kane Creek

Super Chimney Area

At 1.8 miles, park on the lefthand side of the road at a parking lot.
Thank you to Crazy Joe for the beta.

❑ 1. SUPER CHIMNEY 5.10 R

Approach by walking up the Moab Rim jeep trail (about a mile) to the big flake in the shield feature (uphill of the Moab Rim Tower). Scramble to a little ledge on the left hand side of the tower, and proceed up a 15 foot section to the chimney. Walk back into the chimney. Climb straight up to a crack protected with some small and medium cams. After about 70 feet, move out right and belay from cams in a nice crack, or climb the remaining 25' to the top of the chimney (crux). Clip a drilled angle and pass by where the other pieces have been taken out. A groovy vertical feature can be challenging and it feels a ways above your pro. Bust the last few moves using "star" chimneying technique. Towards the lip of the chimney is a variation with edges on the arête. A two-bolt anchor awaits.
FA: Paul Ross and Jimmy Dunn

Paul Ross and Jim Dunn on the FA

Moab Rim Tower ✴N

❑ 2. REQUIEM 5.12+ A0

A beautifully-located steep line, *Requiem* follows dihedrals and cracks to a steep face with intense exposure. The first ascentionists expected to establish a free climb; however, the varnished Navajo proved too friable for free climbing. As it stands, the last pitch requires some free moves and some standing in slings to get from bolt to bolt.
P1: Ascend a slab then head left to a semi-loose dihedral (5.11a, 60').
P2: Climb a fairly solid but dusty crack, passing a wide move in a roof at the start of a hand and finger crack. It is best to chimney at the top (5.10, 75').
P3: Face climb up and left with a few good bolts for protection. Then ascend the steep finger crack to the right dihedral. Technical and powerful moves lead left onto the face. Reach the super-exposed ledge and clip the belay. Takes lots of finger pieces (5.12c, 110').
P4: Perhaps the most exposed pitch in the desert. A combination of free moves and aiding on good bolts (5.10+, A0) leads to mandatory free climbing on soft, sparsely-protected 5.10 terrain (80').
Descent: The route can be rapped on a single 70 meter. Be careful.

Gear: A wide selection of tight-finger pieces, with at least three or four 0.75 and 1.0 Friends. One each from 1.5 to 2.5 and a dozen quickdraws.
FA: Josh Gross, Sam Lightner

Thank you to Sam Lightner for the topo and route description.

Past the Moab Rim Tower lie several roadside climbs along the left side of the paved section. Most are short with low commitment.

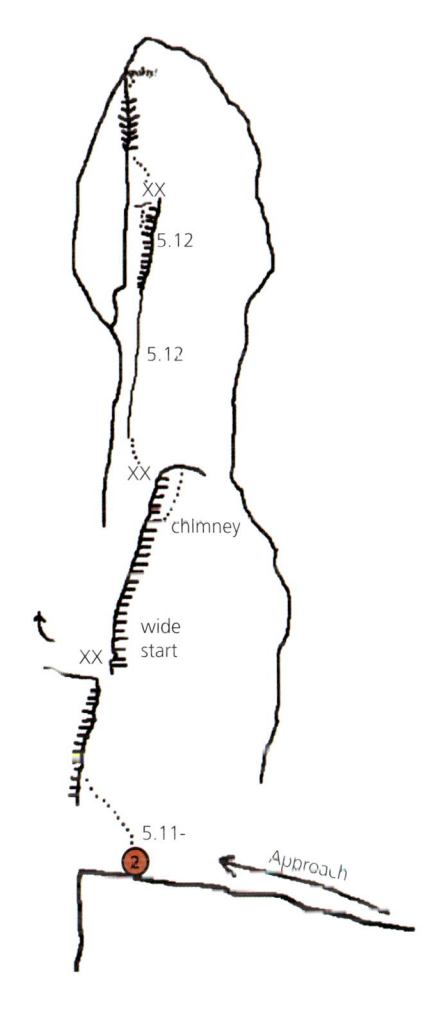

Kane Creek

Adventure

When the road turns to dirt (3.8 miles) a parking lot appears on the right. Dave Mealy has established some rim routes (east/northeast facing) across the creek at the power lines. From left to right: *The Screamin Demon* 5.10+, *Little Bunny Fu Fu* 5.10+, and *Fuzzy Bunny Crack* 5.10+

> Drive-in camp spots with toilets and dumpsters reside on the right side of the road at 1.9 miles. Also, the Moonflower camping area at 2.2 miles (on the left side of the road) offers nice camping in a cool canyon with toilets and dumpsters—park and walk in. It also features an old Indian ladder and some petroglyphs.
> More drive-in camping on private land can be found on the right side of the road.

Base jumper with climbers on *Corner Route* (left side of photo)

Mick Knurbin base jumping from the Tombstones

TOMBSTONES ⋆SSW

The Tombstones are a sweet destination for a variety of thrillseekers. Free climb, aid climb, base jump! Its all here. The approaches are short, the rock is good, and the routes span the grades. The Tombstones are located on the left side of Kane Creek shortly after the road turns to dirt and takes a left bend. Only three routes and a variation are described here.

Getting there:
Drive 4.3 miles, park in a small pullout on the lefthand side of the road. If someone is already parked there, alternate parking exists in either direction.

A SIDE NOTE: Be aware, this is a popular area for base jumpers hucking their carcasses above you.

Ben Riley onsights *Higher Reality* 5.11+

TOMBSTONES

Labels on photo:
- off-fingers 12-
- Higher Reality variation
- steep #5.0 useful
- optional belay
- thin gear (0 & 1 TCUs or small nuts) 10+
- optional belay
- 4.0s, long draws

1. CORNER ROUTE 5.12
★★★★★

A long right-facing corner to the notch between the first and second tombstones.

P1: Climb the big hands traverse using no more than three pieces with long draws on each piece. Pass the optional belay, but don't clip it. Continue up the corner via hands, pass the wide section using some face features, and arrive at a bolted stance.

P2: This is a long pitch with a bit of everything. Walk up an easy ramp to a short hands section that turns thin but offers face features where you need them. More thin climbing (protected by micro nuts) leads to an optional piton belay. Look for pro on the left wall where the very beginning of the *Higher Reality* variation becomes obvious. (The offset normal finish is nearly invisible). Climb big hands and bigger, which transitions to some tight hands, then continues via fingers up to a final wide section (5.10+).

P3: The business: head up to the corner and climb a short distance to a difficult-to-see offset arching splitter on the left wall. Stem for as long as you can, then jam the off-fingers crack to a short traverse terminating at the anchors (5.12-).

P4: An optional summit pitch exists for those not wanting to call it good at the notch. Climb the obvious ow-chimney to the summit of the Left Tombstone.

Gear: Doubles of 0.0 to 4.0, heavy on off-fingers for the last pitch, optional 4.5, shoulder and/or double shoulder-length slings.
Descent: Rappel the route with one 70m rope (be careful, it's close), though doubles get you down faster.
FA: Jim Dunn, Kevin Chase

Var: HIGHER REALITY 5.11+
★★★★

Higher Reality is the first splitter on your left at the top of the second pitch. (Many people confuse this with *Corner Route's* 5.12- finish which is just up a bit more and hard to see as it is offset.)
Follow the left-arcing splitter with fingers, off-fingers, and the occasional tight hand. Shoot for the pods to milk some awkward rests.
Gear: 0.5–2 (heavy on 0.5)
FA: Ralph Ferrara, Kevin Chase

Use caution, as ropes can get caught in the first rappel.

Kane Creek

☐ 2. EPITAPH 5.13b ★★★★
Previously *Playing Hooky* 5.10d C2
The effort from Dean and Steph was the winner of the 2002 Golden Piton award (congrats from your community).
Thank you Steph Davis for the description!
The famous beautiful thin crack line splitting the center of the Tombstone involves sections of blackened, loose, and soft rock. The free route climbs past the two-bolt hanging belay anchor below the first triangular roof and features good gear overall.

P1: Start up the center of the pillar in the obvious left-facing crack (5.10) or go around the left side into a chimney and tunnel up to the top of the big ledge (5.8). Either way, pass the bolted aid anchor on the big ledge and keep going to the very top of the pillar. Make a belay with gear and a large chockstone (50 meters) or belay from the bolted aid anchor (40 meters) and then scramble up the last 10 meters to move the belay before starting the next pitch.

P2: This pitch includes various interesting bits of crack climbing and one scary layback section on hollow rock before reaching steep, thin fingers. Continue past the aid anchor below the roof into very thin laybacking, ending in a final wide layback section up to the next ledge and a two-bolt anchor. Bouldery yet sustained. Be aware of birds and guano in the wide section (5.13, 200' or 5.12 C1—if broken into two 100' pitches by using the hanging belay).

P3: Start up a nice dihedral with good rock, then leave the crack and move right up steep, sandy rock to reach the final corner to the top (5.12, 85').

Descent: It's best to walk off the route (about 25 minutes). From the summit, head down the rock slabs away from the climb toward the La Sal Mountains, trending slightly left and down anytime you are uncertain. You will have a view of the dirt road in Pritchett Canyon down and left below while you descend the slabs (no more than five or 10 minutes). The slabs end at a very well-trodden, right-trending dirt trail through the cryptobiotic soil. Follow that for about five minutes until it ends at a small stair-step corridor going up and left for 50 feet (towards the La Sals). When it tops out, go straight for a hundred feet, then turn right into the next canyon, going down (away from the La Sals now) to regain the dirt trail which continues down and right, back to the Amasa Back parking area. Some people rappel the route with a 70 meter rope or two 60s but it requires some swinging to reach the anchors.

Gear: Doubles of black Alien to 2.0, (1)3.0, a few small nuts. A 4.0 could be placed at the top of P2 for those who are strong enough to carry it up the entire pitch.
FA: Charlie Fowler, Jimmy Dunn, Pete Verchick, Kevin Chase; FFA Dean Potter, Steph Davis, 2003

☐ 3. LINUS'S CORNER (A.K.A SURPHASE TENSION) 5.11+ 130' ★★★★ ☀ N-NW
Located just right of the third Tombstone.
A great summer route featuring shade and a short approach. Recognizable by a heavy coat of lichen on the right wall. Climb fingers and off-fingers in a right-facing corner.
Gear: 0.3–1.0, heavy on off–fingers (a bucket of endurance)
FA: Linus Platt

Steph Davis on *Epitaph* 5.13   photo Jimmy Chin

Kiosk Area E-NE

At 4.5 miles, there is a kiosk in a parking lot on your right. Park here. Look for a canyon with a trail on the left side of the road. Climbs exist on both sides, but only the climbs on the right wall as you walk in are described. The left wall features Indian writings, so please be respectful. This can be used as an alternate approach to *The Farm*—just keep following the cliff to the right for five minutes.

1. DRIVING WHILE ASIAN 5.10+ 120' ★★
A left-facing corner. Start on some blocky terrain; continue with tight hands that get steeper and a bit tighter. Finish with some fingers laybacking to the chains. A demanding lead for the grade!
Gear: 0.3–2.0

2. GLORY AND CONSEQUENCE 5.11 130' ★★
Do a short approach fourth-class scramble pitch to the start of the finger-sized flare. Climb this (extra finger-size pieces) and make a mantel to a ledge and a bolt. Continue up steep face climbing and one more bolt. Move slightly right and climb to the base of a crack. Continue up an overhanging flare with perfect hands in the back. Continue up perfect overhanging hands to big hands through a roof and a chain anchor.
Descent: Two ropes or a full 70m gets you to the start ledge. Downclimb the approach pitch.
Gear: Up to 3.5, optional 5.0
FA: James Webster

3. THE FARM 5.11 100' ★★★★★ NW
A local favorite! A right-facing corner with big hands starts things off, then continue out the steep, solid flake system with hands. Punch it out through the roof, bust up to the chains, protecting with off-fingers.
FA: Kyle Copeland
Gear: 0.75–3.0

The Farm approach: Park at the Amasa Back/cliffhanger trailhead and backtrack a few hundred feet looking for an obvious flake with anchors on the north-facing wall. Scramble off the road to a slickrock bench and follow the faint trail to the base of the climb.

Nick Oldham on *The Farm* 5.11

Abraxas Wall W-SW

The Abraxas Wall is a great little crag for cooler temperatures, as it sees sun for most of the day. To approach this crag, drive 5.0 miles to the Amasa Back trailhead (aka Cliff Hanger trail) on your right. Walk down the Cliff Hanger trail over some ledgy terrain, cut a corner via the single track on the left, and then look for a trail across the road that heads down to the sometimes-dry creek. A trail (a bit right) ascends the benches to the base of the wall.

Routes are listed right to left. Unless mentioned, one 70m rope will get you off everything.

Todd "Taco" Bogan on Xylokane 5.11+

Kane Creek

❏ 1. **ABRAXAS TOWER** 5.10
P1: Starts in a shallow left-facing corner through a slot to hands with features for footholds. A lower-off anchor exists at 50'. Reach a ledge 10' above the anchor and set a belay with gear (1.0s) in the crack straight in front of you (5.9, 60').
P2: Climb blocky cracks to a short right-facing ow that radically pinches down to fingers. Belay inside the main chimney from slung chockstones (5.9, 40').
P3: Chimney between the wall and the tower with gear placements in the wall, from fingers to tips to off-fingers (5.10).
Descend off the back side via a double-rope rappel with two 70m ropes!
Gear: (1 each) 0.1–0.4, (2)0.75, (3)0.5, (3 each) 2.0–3.0, shoulder-length runners

❏ 2. **SUGAR KANE** 5.10 45' ★★
A right-facing corner that starts with big hands then goes from fists to stacks.
Gear: 3.0–4.0
FA: Kevin Chase

❏ 3. **ABRAXAS RIGHT** 5.10+ 80' ★★★★
A left-facing corner that starts off tight hands before it eases off to some lower-angle big hands, finishing with a short offwidth. Don't let the ow scare you—it's short and does not climb like an ow. Shared anchor.
Gear: 0.75–5.0
FA: Linus Platt

❏ 4. **ABRAXAS LEFT** 5.10 80' ★★★
A great warm up! Start in a cool wedge that leads to a splitter hand crack. Go over some blocky terrain then traverse right to the chains. Shared anchor.
Gear: 0.75–3.0
FA: Linus Platt

❏ 5. **XYLOKANE** 5.11+ 70' ★★★★
Jay Smith does it again—the man has a keen eye for great lines! Right-facing corner that starts with off-fingers and fingers, then turns to tips with face features. Pull a sequential bulge for the chains. PUMPY!
Gear: Blue TCU–0.75
FA:. Jay Smith

❏ 6. **KRACK PIPE** 5.10 ★★
A double splitter. Start in the right-hand splitter using a small pillar to the right. Near the top of the pillar, switch over to the left crack (way fun) and continue up the ever-widening crack. If you're looking for the full body workout link this with the short ow second pitch.
FA: Linus Platt
Gear: Single rack from 0.4–4.0 (4.5–6.0 for the continuation)

❏ 7. **KRACK KOKANE** 5.10+ 50' ★★★
A right-facing mostly-fingers corner. I suggest going into a layback and holding your breath till the top for a great head rush. Sweet!
Gear: Blue TCUs–0.5 (heavier on 0.4)
FA: Kevin Chase

❏ 8. **DRUGSTORE COWBOY** 5.11 65' ★★
Face climb past a bolt and make a hard, scary mantel. Continue climbing the thin left-facing corner.
Gear: 1 draw, double set of TCUS–1.0, small nuts
FA: Eric Decaria

❏ 9. **NAVAJO WARRIOR** 5.11+ 160' ★★
A huge right-facing corner. Burly with a bolted crux.
Descend: Rappel with two 60m ropes to the ground
Gear: 2 draws, triple set from 0.5–3.5 lots of slings
FA: Dave Medara

❏ 10. **UNNAMED** 80'
Shallow left-facing tips corner interrupted with some overlaps. After the overlaps, splitter fingers lead to the anchors.

Jay Ackerman on Abraxas Left 5.10

Kane Creek

Along the Road

A few noteworthy climbs reside along the right side of the road between the Abraxas Wall and the Ice Cream Parlor. Park as for the Abraxas Wall.

For the next two routes use the approach for *Abraxas*, but instead of branching right, continue along the Cliff Hanger trail and cross the wash (sometimes dry, sometimes not). Shortly after this, branch right up some talus to *Shogun*.

11. SHOGUN 5.13 ★★★★★
A testpiece on the left side of the forming arch. Pass a couple of bolts through some wide, then continue via an extension called *Bushido* 5.13+.
FA: Zak Smith FFA: Noah Bigwood

Birthing Rock Area ✳W

At 5.2 miles, find a small parking area for the "Birthing Rock"—a boulder on the right side of the road peppered with petroglyphs. Walk across the road and ascend benches to the base of the cliff.

1. FACE IT 5.11+ 70' ★★★★
Originally the route went without bolts, which were added later by Charlie Fowler, unaware that it had been previously climbed. The original ascent climbed to the top and required walking off. Face climb past two bolts to a left-facing corner and continue via fingers to a rest at a small stance. Barn-door off-fingers leads to a steep tight-hands finish.
Gear: 2 draws, blue Metolius–1.0, heavy in the off–fingers.
FA: Linus Platt

PeeWee Ouellet on Bushido 5.13+
Photo: Eric Odenthal

At 6.0 miles the "Spring Site" on the right side of the road provides camping and a few slab climbs on the far side of the camping area.

Cable Arch Adventure

A great adventure, though not necessarily a rock climb, is to ascend Funnel Arch, aka Cable Arch and soak up the amazing views of the Moab Valley. Park in the large parking lot on your left at 5.5 miles. Ascend some slickrock to a bench. Walking a bit left, search for a rain run-off and scramble up this. From the top of the run-off, walk right and follow the path of least resistance to another short slickrock section. From the top of this you will be able to see the arch.

A popular cable route to the summit can be reached by walking through the arch and poceeding to the north-northwest. With outstanding views from the top, this is a great place to enjoy a sunset or full moon.

The slab of the arch can be climbed (5.6) passing some pins along the way. Once on top you can walk NE to the next fin and hand over hand down the cable route.

Kind Crag

Pass the Cable Arch parking, and park on the second switchback as you descend the corkscrews. Walk down steep talus, veering right, until you reach the valley. Follow the winding creek (sometimes a real pain after a rain) watching for two right-facing black corners on the right side. 15 minutes.

A few side notes for the area: BEWARE, DUMBASSES ABOVE YOU! You will be climbing below a popular spot for tourists throwing rocks, as well as rednecks throwing beer bottles. Yahoo! Bring a rope bag, as there's tons of broken glass on the ground where you rope up!

THIS IS A GOOD CHANCE FOR SOME KARMA POINTS… BRING SOME SORT OF CONTAINER SO YOU CAN PACK OUT SOME GLASS!

❒ 1. **KIND** 5.10 80' ★★★★
A beautiful right-facing corner. A few bouldery moves off the ground give way to off-fingers. Continue past a lower-angle hands section to a steeper big hands finish. Also known locally as *Kind Other Kind*.
Gear: 0.4–3.5
FA: Kyle Copeland, David Whidden, Marc Hirt

❒ 2. **ARCHAIC REVIVAL** 5.11- 85' ★★
May not go anymore after a dead tree, used to access the right-facing corner, disappeared. The corner starts off-fingers then trims to fingers (yellow TCU) then ends tips. A hard move and a fair amount of flakey rock (scary pro) leads to the chains.
Gear: Blue TCU–#2 Friend
FA: Kyle Copeland

Heather Hillier on Kind 5.10

Kane Creek

Stimulants Wall

The routes are just off the left side of the road at 6.6 miles—just step out the car. With a reputation as sketchy, I wasn't initially going to include these routes. Then, one day while doing some mileage recon, I ran into Jim Beyer (the first ascencionist of all the routes) bolting a new route and re-bolting some of his existing routes. There's no doubt that these are heads-up routes due to the nature of the rock. Beyer advises that these routes, though bolted, are not sport routes and that leaders supplement gear between the bolts when possible. He also utilizes fixed threads, which should be backed up as they age. All this being said, the routes are unique to the area—bouldery moves to steep huecos. Routes are listed left to right.

- 1. **VIVARIN** 5.11b ★★
- 2. **ADRENILINE** 5.11a ★★
- 3. **EARL GREY** 5.10c ★★★
- 4. **NEW ROUTE** 5.10a ★★★

At 6.8 miles, camping can be found at the Hunter Canyon entrance.

The Grave Cliff

Just after Hunter Canyon the road crosses the creek (sometimes dry) and then bends to the right. Shortly thereafter park on the side of the road. The next two Gilje routes start from the bench on the left side of the road.

- 1. **GRAVE** 5.11+ ★★★★ N

Grave climbs a right-arching fingers/off-fingers slot in black rock. It was originally lead to the the *Unleashed* anchors.
Gear: 0.3–#2 Friend
FA: Tom Gilje

- 2. **UNLEASHED** 5.11+ ★★★★ N

Face climbing leads to the left-facing, left-leaning off-fingers corner.
Gear: 0.0 TCU–0.75, heavy on 0.5–0.75
FA: Tom Gilje

Kane Creek

The Bakery ✳ S

The Bakery Crag appears just as you drive around the left bend (7.1 miles) before the Ice Cream Parlor area on the right. It sees sunlight in the morning hours. Park on the left in a spot with large boulders and walk across the road to the very black cliff. The following routes start on the same ledge and are listed left to right.

1. CHERRY ON TOP 5.10b/c 100' ★★
Climb a large flake with several wedged flakes to a bolted crux at the top.
Gear: 0.1–4.0, 2 draws
FA: Noah Bigwood, Josh Gross

2. FLOUR POWER 5.10c/d 90' ★★★
Face climb past two bolts trending right to reach the corner. Climb the tips corner to more face.
Gear: 5 draws, some tips and fingers pieces, 1.0
FA: Josh Gross, Noah Bigwood

3. FLOUR 5.12 ★★
Five bolted pitches.
Gear: Draws (all pitches are bolted)
FA: Josh Gross, Lynn Sanson, Sam Lightner

4. BAKERY ROUTE 5.11 (3 pitches) ★★
P1: Bypass the chossy ow to the right and gain a ledge. Climb a left-facing corner to a ledge then a right-facing corner to the belay ledge (5.9). A 5.10 variation continues straight.
P2: Climb the chimney (5.8) to a big ledge.
P3: Sport climb past six bolts (5.11).
Gear: 6 draws, 0.3–4.0
FA: Josh Gross, Noah Bigwood, Scott Hollander

Kane Creek

The Ice Cream Parlor Crag W-SW

The Ice Cream Parlor, one of Moab's more popular cliffs and well-rounded crags, offers something for everyone—whether a new climber, beginning leader, or veteran. With morning shade and afternoon sun, it draws climbers with such classics as the namesake 5.11 finger crack, as well as low-angle bolted climbs and some well-protected cracks on quality rock. For the bold, the Tom Gilje route *T-Rex* provides a chance to take your cojones out for a test ride.

The ICP can sometimes be crowded and it's quite popular with guides. Please be respectful as they have every right to be there. This is a high-impact area, so please, if you find other people's trash, tape, butts, etc. pick it up. Pack out human waste.

A great way to finish up the day is by walking across the road to *Hallowed Souls* on the Space Tower—sit up top and watch the sun go down!

APROACH: Drive to 7.1 and park on the left in a parking lot (with some large boulders) for access to the routes on the left side or drive to 7.2 and park off the side of the road to access the right side. The trails are well-traveled and easily followed.

The first three routes are at the far left end of the crag—a short walk from the parking area described for The Bakery.

1. PANDEMIC 5.10+ ★★
Four pitches to the rim.
P1: Start in a right-facing corner with a thin crack and finish with face moves, passing a couple bolts to a bolted belay.
P2: Climb the crack (5.9) and traverse right past a couple of bolts. Set a belay with some hand-size gear.
P3: Climb the corner/slot to some stemming, pass a bolt (crux), continue past a rap station, veering left. Pass some bolted flakes to a ledge with a bolted anchor.
P4: Climb the ow to the top (5.0 helpful)
A two-bolt variation for pitch 4 is called *Epidemic* (5.11).
Gear: 00 Metolius 5.0
FA: Josh Gross, Ralph Ferrara (Var: Josh Gross, Chris Kalous)

2. KURA BURAN 5.12 100' ★★
Pumpy! Shares a start with *Rattler*. Follow a steep bolt line over bulges where a beautiful arête awaits. The anchor is above the ledge.
Gear: 12 draws
FA: Sam Lightner

3. RATTLER 5.11 70'
A hand crack to a bulge with face moves leads to a thin finger crack.
Gear: 0.0 TCU–3.0, (heavy on the tips and fingers)
FA: Josh Gross

Kane Creek

The following routes are found 30 feet away along the path to the main area:

❏ 4. CRITICAL MASS 5.8 50' ★★
Start up a diagonaling off-fingers crack with some footholds. Move right (or continue the line with trickier gear) and climb some blocky terrain before traversing back left to the anchor.
Gear: 0.4–2.0
FA: Mike Baker

❏ 5. SPACE GHOST 5.10 ★★
Three pitches. The first pitch is a nice 5.6 and popular for new leaders (gear: 0.5–2.0). The upper two pitches are seldom done since the creation of a new variation. The original Gilje route follows the corner system to its top.
VARIATION: Wander right then left following a bolt line on some low-angle rock to a bolted belay. The third pitch follows the offwidth flake (5.10).

❏ 6. TOPROPE 5.10 45' ★★
Fun, touchy climbing on good rock. Set up a toprope by traversing a short distance right from the previous climb along a ledge to a set of anchors.

❏ 7. PARLOR GAME 5.9 50' ★★★
Just right of the previous route. Getting to the first bolt is a bit easier from the right side. The crux lies between the last bolt and the anchor. Heads up!
Gear: 4 draws

❏ 8. UNNAMED 5.7 45' ★★
Stay just right of the bolt line, switching to the left just before the chains.

❏ 9. BREWED AWAKENINGS 5.5 45'
A weakness between the two slab areas. Climb with hand-size gear.
Gear: Single rack to a 3.0
FA: Eric Odenthal

❏ 10. BLACK SLAB 5.6 50' ★★
Fun! A meandering line just right of *Brewed Awakenings*.
Gear: 6 draws

❏ 11. UNNAMED 5.7 ★★
More slab climbing.
Gear: 4 draws

For an alternate approach to the Ice Cream Parlor and easier access to the right side, park just up the road at 7.2 miles in obvious parking on the right.

The next three cracks are close to each other, and once one is ascended the anchors for the others can be reached via a sloping ledge (stay tied in!). Though of modest difficulty, they are a bit tricky to protect. The rightmost offers the easiest and safest passage.

❏ 12. CRACK 1 5.8 ★
Four bolts.

❏ 13. CRACK 2 5.8 ★
Thin crack on a less-than-vertical slab.
Gear: Nuts and small cams

❏ 14. CRACK 3 5.8 ★★★
Start by face climbing up the light colored rock to the base of the finger crack. Continue up the low-angle finger crack placing gear where available.
Gear: 0.0 TCU–0.4, a set of nuts

❏ 15. HOT CARL SUNDAY 5.10b 80' ★★★★
Begin on edges to a roof overlap. Trend left and climb a shallow right-facing corner.
Gear: 9 draws
FA: Mark Howe

❏ 16. RP CITY 5.10+ ★★
Follow easy fifth-class crack then bust left to a very thin crack system.
Gear: RPs

The next two routes share anchors.

❏ 17. VANILLA CREAM 5.10+ 75' ★
Start as for *RP City* to a confusing, upper, left-facing, bolted corner
Gear: finger units and 4 draws
FA: Eric Odenthal

❏ 18. NIGHT LIGHT 5.10- 75' ★★
Slab climb just right of *Vanilla Cream*, sharing its anchors.
Gear: 8 draws
FA: Eric Odenthal

❏ 19. FREEZER BURN 5.10a 90'
Located 20' right of *Night Light*. Pass two bolts to a crack system that finishes in "the bowl."
Gear: 2 draws, set of nuts, fist size units
FA: Eric Odenthal

❏ 20. NOT RP CITY 5.9+

❏ VARIATION: PORK SODA 5.9
Share a start with *A Good Day* but continue up the corner through the roof where *Good Day* veers right.
FA: Tom Gilje

Tom Gwinn on Hot Carl Sunday 5.10b

Kane Creek

☐ 21. A GOOD DAY TO DIE 5.9+ ★★★
Starts off the bench with some bouldery moves into a right-facing corner. When the corner gets wide, maneuver right via face moves to a bolt. Continue via face moves to a second bolt and climb a gentler angle with bigger holds to the anchor.
Gear: 0.4–4.0 (several shoulder-length slings will help alleviate rope drag)

☐ 22. ICE CREAM PARLOR CRACK 5.11 80' ★★★★
Begin with some face moves off the bench. Milk a rest with your feet on the horizontal. Work through a few tips moves, then continue with beautiful fingers up the quality right-facing corner. Gun for the hand jam. A few more moves lead to the anchor. Truly a fingery Moab treasure.
Gear: Blue TCU–0.5, heavy on 0.4 (optional: a big piece may be nice just after the bouldery start)
FA: Dan Mannix

☐ 23. PULP FRICTION 5.11 80' ★★★
Just right of the *Ice Cream Parlor Crack* (somewhat of a mirror image) climb the left-facing corner until it is possible to bust right onto the arête, face climbing past three bolts to the anchor.
FA: Tom Gilje

The next three routes climb the same leaning-pillar-like formation on the right side of the crag. They leave the same bench as for the *Ice Cream Parlor Crack*. All three share the same anchor.

☐ 24. COFFIN 5.9 ★★★
The left side of the pillar. Climb through the overhang via big hands/fist to the obvious corner. Climb the corner until it is possible to "enter the coffin" and chimney to its top.
Gear: (1 each) 0.4–6.0
FA: Tom Gilje

☐ 25. POSSESSED 5.11+ ★★
Local survey says "funky" sport climbing. From *Knee Grinder* step left and clip the first bolt. A funky move brings you around the arête. Climb the line of bolts as the holds get smaller. Good luck!
Gear: 6 draws
FA: Eric Decaria

☐ 26. KNEE GRINDER 5.9+ ★
Wide climbing on the right side of the pillar formation. It you don't fit inside, bump the grade up a solid notch. There is a bolt high on the route where it is to big for a 6.0. If you feel good about Big Bros, bring a few.
Gear: 1.0–6.0, (2 large Big Bros)
FA: John Varco

A further walk leads to two more routes.

☐ 27. DEATH TRAP 5.8
Enough said. A good route to overlook.
FA: Tom Gilje

☐ 28. T-REX 5.12 ★★★
Located at the far right side of the Ice Cream Parlor. Look at the skyline and locate the imposing horizontal roof crack, then extrapolate downward to find the start of the route. The first pitch begins from a small ledge and is the only bolt-protected line in the vicinity.
P1: Thin vertical scoops protected by bolts (5.11c, 100').
P2: Bolt-protected climbing up corners and slabs (5.10, 100').
P3: Hard-to-protect thin corner directly above the spacious belay ledge (5.11, 50').
P4: The crux. Overhanging face to horizontal crack (5.12, 100').
Thank you Charley Graham for the route description.
Descent is via rappel from an anchor to the right of the top-out.
Gear: Lots of quickdraws for all but the third pitch which requires tiny nuts and a double set of cams from tiny to off–fingers. The final roof crack takes a double set of Camalots from 0.75—3.0
FA: Tom Gilje

Jess Oldham on *Ice Cream Parlor Crack* 5.11

Kane Creek

The Space Tower N

Just across the road and a short walk from the Ice Cream Parlor lies a semi–detached tower with a sweet stemming chimney. Fledgling leaders beware, it has a reputation of being a bit runout with gear just when you need it.

Approach: Park as for the right side of ICP (7.2 miles), cross the creek and make a short walk to the tower's right side.

1. HALLOW SOULS 5.9+ ★★★
Climb carefully up to the bottom of the chimney. Follow the crack system on the right wall. Above the crack system on the main wall is a hidden bolt that protects some kick-ass stemming. Eventually move left onto the tower and follow the hand crack to the anchor.
Descent: One double-rope rap to the ground
Gear: *0.4–3.5, a set of nuts would get used, and lots of shoulder and double-length shoulder slings are a must!*
FA: Kevin Chase

Ellen Tschida on *Hallow Souls* 5.9+
photo by: Eric Odenthal

SCORCHED EARTH, WINDY RIDGE, DOG WALL, AND CAMELOT AREAS

Scorched Earth ✺ E

For the Scorched Earth Crag drive 7.5 miles, cross a cattle guard, and park just up and across the road in a small parking spot. Walk back to the roadside boulder at the cattle guard. Continue down through the weeds and tamarisk, following the fence line to the creek. Cross the creek and the fence and hike to the obvious prow. *Creeker* and *Dante* are the only climbs on the right side of the prow. The remainder are on the left. Routes are listed right to left.

❏ 1. CREEKER 5.9 45' ★★
A bouldery bombay-ish start gives way to zigzagging tips splitter. Continue on the less-than vertical wall in an offset splitter with tight hands. Clip the chains from the flake.
Gear: 0.4–3.0
FA: Kevin Chase

❏ 2. DANTE 5.9 60' ★★
A steep start with fingers to offset hands splitter to a bit of face climbing.
Gear: 0.5–3.0 (tips piece helpful at top)
FA: Kevin Chase

Rob Hess takes a break from Jackson Hole guides. Dante 5.9

Kane Creek

The next three routes are in close proximity to each other, left of the prow.

3. UNNAMED 5.11b 90' ★★
Begin by climbing a blocky section to a short chimney. Continue in the right-facing corner with off-fingers to the chains on the right wall.

4. DARK PATH 5.11b 75' ★★★★
The prize of the crag— a great route on super black rock. Start on a ledge, pass a bolt, and ascend the black face (using some tips gear) to a shallow stembox, passing two more bolts to the chains.
Gear: Mostly fingers and 3 draws
FA: Dave Medara

5. SPLIT PERSONALITY 5.11 90' ★★
A corner system that switches aspects from right to left to right. Mostly off-fingers and tight hands. Anchors are on the left wall.
TR the weakness just right from the *Split Personality* anchors at 5.11+
FA: Dave Medara

The next pair of routes are just left around the corner.

6. UNNAMED 5.10+ 60' ★★★
A left-leaning, right-facing corner that climbs with fingers and tight hands, then over some blocks to anchors on the left wall.

7. STILETTO 5.11+ 50' ★★★
A splitter tips crack with some huecos about halfway up the route on the left wall.
Gear: Tips pieces
FA: Kevin Chase

Many BLM designated camp spots exist between 7.9 and the Kane Springs/Hurrah Pass intersection.

Windy Ridge　SE

Two options exist to access this crag: 1) A short walk along the cliff line left from the Scorched Earth Crag. 2) At odometer 7.9 turn right into some camp spots and park (be mindful of the restoration in progress). Trend right to a trail, well marked by cairns. The trail dumps you out at the crag's right side. Routes are listed right to left.

1. UGLY BETTY 5.9 60'
Climb follows low-angle cracks to a corner/flake.
FA: Tom Perkins

2. FIRE FOX 5.10+ 90' ★★
Start by climbing some blocky terrain to a right-facing fingers corner then pass a few bolts to the anchors.
FA: Tom Perkins

3. BASS ACKWARDS 5.10+ 35' ★★
Starts out in a slot with tight hands and off-fingers to a tips pod exit. Awkward!
Gear: Blue Metolius–#2 Friend

4. BOY HOWDY 5.11+ 65'
Starts out fingers splitter into a pod with hands, back out to a fingers finish.
FA: Tom Perkins

5. PLUMBER'S CRACK 5.10+ 50'
Blocky face climbing with mostly tips gear.
FA: Tom Perkins

6. GONG SHOW 5.8 50'
Climb a left- to right-trending zipper-looking feature.

7. TR 5.12b
A line right of *Gong Show* has been toproped.

8. BEER RUN 5.10+ ★★
Start by passing a bolt 15' off the ground to a flake with hands. Then bust a couple of roofs with big hands. Chains are on the right.
FA: Tom Perkins

9. TOUCHÉ 5.11+ 90' ★★★
Great route. A hard ow start gives way to all sizes down to off-fingers.
Gear: 0.5–6.0
FA: Tom Perkins

10. UNNAMED 5.10+ 75' ★★★
Starts as shallow left-facing corner with hands, switching to a right-facing corner with a fingers crux before widening back to hands.
Gear: 0.4–3.0, heavier on hands

11. NAKED RUNNING "DO ME" MAN 5.11+ 80' ★★★★
The best of the cliff—a clean left facing corner. Off-fingers jamming leads to a secure, but scary-looking block. Turn a fingers roof to a sloping belay.
Gear: Fingers and off-fingers

12. UNNAMED RIGHT-FACING CORNER 5.11 80'
Starts with off-fingers, then fingers and a pod.

Heather Hillier on *Bass Ackwards* 5.10+

Tom Perkins on his *Beer Run* 5.10+
photo: Lisa Boose

The Dog Wall S-SE

Though the Dog Wall looks like it requires a burly hike, it's not that bad and well worth it—beautiful views and great routes!

At 7.9 miles, shortly after you pass a kiosk on your left, look for a right turn. This is the same road as for Windy Ridge. Drive across the wash and follow the road to the bottom of the old mining road and park. Walk up the mining road for about 10 minutes and watch for a talus-filled break allowing access through the lower cliff band. Hike up this steep talus. When you reach the top, you'll spot *Doggonit* 5.12—an obvious splitter that doglegs right; the rest of the climbs are to the left.
Routes are listed from right to left.

◻ 1. **DOGGONIT** 5.12- ★★★
Follow an offset splitter over a roof, then dogleg right—mostly fingers and hands for 100'.
FA: Paul Irby, Jason "Jayfro" Matz; FFA: Charley Graham

Charley Graham onsights the FFA of Doggonit 5.12-

◻ 2. **BIG PUSSY IN DOGTOWN** 5.11- ★★
A beautiful left-facing offwidth. Fist through body scums.
Gear: 0.75–1.0
FA: Sammy Burrell

◻ 3. **UNNAMED** 5.10 60 ★★
Climbs the right side of a pillar formation leaning against the wall. Has a little bit of wide but mostly hands. Good warm up!
Gear: 1.0–4.0
FA: Dave Mealy

◻ 4. **DOG DAYS** 5.11 100' ★★
Double splitter, fingers and hands.
Gear: 0.3–3.0
FA: Paul Irby

◻ 5. **UNNAMED** 5.10+ 90'
Left-facing corner. Plenty offwidth and chimney for the wide lovers.
FA: Dave Mealy

VERTICAL MIND

By Don McGrath & Jeff Elison

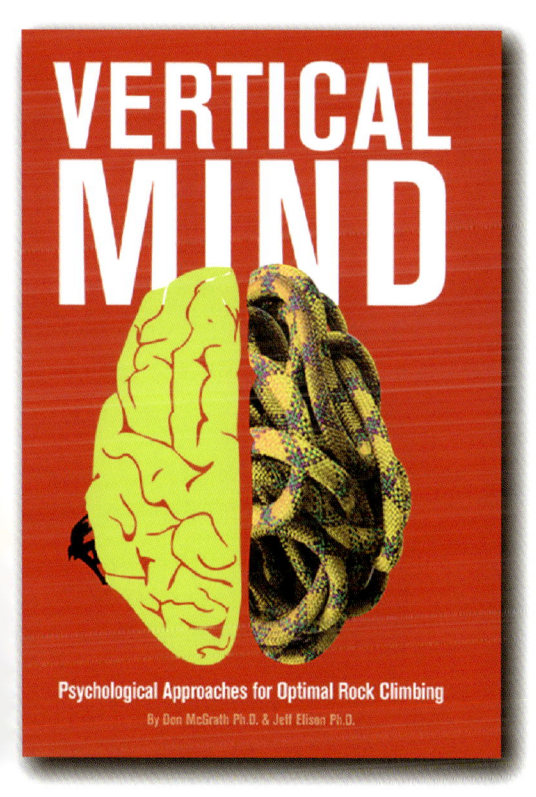

In Vertical Mind, Don McGrath and Jeff Elison teach rock climbers how to improve their mental game so they can climb better and have more fun. They teach how the latest research in brain science and psychology can help you retrain your mind and body for higher levels of rock climbing performance, while also demonstrating how to train and overcome fears and anxiety that hold you back. Finally, they teach climbing partners how to engage in co-creative coaching and help each other improve as climbers.

With numerous and practical step-by-step drills and exercises, in a simple to follow training framework, your path to harder climbing has never been clearer. If you are a climber who wants to climb harder and have more fun climbing, then Vertical Mind is required reading. Well, what's stopping you? Pick it up and get training today!

Curious about our latest books? Follow us:

◉ ▮ @sharpendpublishing

www.sharpendbooks.com

☐ 6. **UNNAMED** 65'
A left-facing corner to a splitter with anchors just under a bulge with some death flakes above. An absolutely stellar unclimbed splitter lingers above.
Gear: fingers and off-fingers
FA: Dave Mealy

☐ 7. **THE NERDGATE** 5.10 100' ★★
Negotiate the block at the bottom of the route then tackle the right-facing hands corner. Continue past a bouldery move at mid-height where it seams out. A short section of off-finger moves leads to hand pods and the chains.
Gear: 0.4– 2.0
FA: Paul Irby

☐ 8. **UNNAMED** 5.10+ 80' ★★★
A left-facing corner starts with a few hand jams. However, as the angle eases off, the size pinches. Fun climbing with just enough small pods and face features, but a little silty and a tricky move to the anchors.
Gear: 0.5–3.0

☐ 9. **DOGMATIC** 5.11 80' ★★★★★
Wavy left-facing corner, mostly tight hands to an off-fingers finish. Steep!
Gear: 0.5–2.5
FA: Paul Irby

☐ 10. **SLY DOG** 5.11 100' ★★★
Bouldery start to fingers and then mostly thin hands.
Gear: yellow TCU–3.0, a small nut may be helpful at the start.
FA: Paul Irby

"No Falls" Paul Irby on his *Dogmatic* 5.11

Camelot

This crag houses *Guinevere*—one of my favorite hand cracks in the Moab area, including Indian Creek! To access Camelot, walk the old mining road as for Dog Wall but instead of busting off the old mining road, follow it to its end. Once at cliff level, backtrack right towards the Dog Cliff area.
Routes are listed left to right

1. MERLIN 5.10 40' ★★
Steep tricky start in right-facing corner that switches aspect to a left-facing corner. Off-fingers and tight hands.
Gear: 0.5–1.0
FA: K3

2. MEDIEVAL 5.10+ 40' ★★
Fingers off the ground to left-facing off-fingers corner. Stout for the length. Good rock in the corner.
Gear: (2 each) 0.3–0.75
FA: Tom Gwinn

3. ROUND TABLE 5.10+ 60' ★
Follows a left-facing flared finger crack in the back of a flared chimney.
FA: Eric Odenthal

4. GUINEVERE 5.11c ★★★★★
A stunning, steep, swerving, splitter hand crack. Climb with gold Camalots, then, as the story goes, *Guinevere* needs a friend to fill her needs (actually #3 Friends) and then she gets the blues right at the end when things get difficult. *Guinevere* likes a good pump.
FA: K3; FFA: Jay Smith
Gear: 2.0–3.0

Chris L-W Willie on *Guinevere* 5.11c

ADVENTURE IN THE AREA

At 9.3 miles park just off the left side of the road and walk five minutes down the "now closed to vehicles" road to the formation.

Happy Turk

❏ **HAPPY TURK AKA THE DEVILS GOLF BALL** A0 40' ★★
Cool leaning hoodoo! Ascend a bolt ladder to a couple of free moves at the top. Reaching the first bolt can be tricky even with a stick-clip because of the link hangers. Patience! A really fun full-moon outing!
Gear: 6 quickdraws, stick-clip

Jeanine Saia and Michelle Kelley out for adventure on the Happy Turk A0

Kane Creek

Pensive Putterman

At the same parking, but on the right side of the road lies another formation.

❐ 1. **ALL ALONG THE PUTT TOWER** 5.8, C0 40'
After the Happy Turk you may as well knock off another summit. The route actually starts on the opposite side of the formation from the road. An easy walk around the backside brings you to the base of the route. Climb up and left following a hand crack. Then trend back right on off-fingers terrain, passing a bulge with a couple of fixed pieces. Fun in a creepy way.
FA: Cameron Burns
Gear: 2 draws, 0.5–2.0

Predator Tower

The Predator Tower is a small tower (but bigger than the previous two) that is quite close to town with a fairly easy approach. There are two routes on either end of the tower. The rock is not super inspiring, but once you start climbing it proves to be worthy. Fun climbing, low commitment and a cool setting make for a worthwhile outing. Approach: Drive 8.7 miles to the new Ledge A campground, passing the I.C.P. area, a kiosk, and a cattle guard along the way. Park at the campground. Adjust your eyes and look west across the desert for the Cutler sandstone tower. It really blends in with its surroundings, so look carefully. Walk from the campground to the tower for 5–10 minutes. Look for the best pasage, likely on the far east of the campground, as during some months the creek can become swampy.

❐ 1. **REIGN OF TERROR** 5.11 ★★
As you walk toward the tower, the route is on the left (NW) side. Start up some less-than stellar rock for a couple of body-lengths to a steep, wide overhang then work your way into the right-facing corner with tight hands/hands to a short left-facing corner offering more of the same. At the top of the left-facing corner you can set a belay (best), or with careful placements and long runners you can pass the belay, clip the pin and continue trending right on slabby ground to a crack leading to the summit.
Gear: 0.75–3.0 (optional 5.0 or 6.0), long runners
FA: Jimmy Dunn, Kyle Copeland, Eric Johnson

❐ 2. **REIGN OF DUST** 5.11+ ★
Climb the opposite side of the tower on lesser quality rock.
FA: Jimmy Dunn, Keith Reynolds

Eric Odenthal and Chris Hill on *Reign of Terror* 5.11

The intersection of Kane Springs and Hurrah pass arrives at mile 10.4. There are some quality routes down in Kane Springs (the left fork) but they aren't covered in this book. It is helpful to have a burly 4-wheel-drive or a dirt bike to venture to those climbs.

SELECT

Take a right at the Kane/Hurrah Pass intersection and park at a small pullout on your left. The cliff is on the same side as the parking lot. From the parking, the cliff is identified as the second second south-facing buttress, heading towards Kane Springs, rather than Hurrah Pass. To approach, walk along an old restored road into Kane Springs. Hike to the first drainage on the right marked by some big boulders at the bottom of the talus. Hike steep terrain from those boulders straight up to the cliff and you will arrive at the base of the pitch.

1. INCREDIBLY BRUSHED WALKING KANE
5.10 ★★★★
Sweet route and worth the walk. Steep hands like *Incredible Hand Crack* on a feature like *Brush Painted Datsun*.
Gear: #2 Friend–3.5
FA: K3

The author on FA of Incredibly Brushed Walking Kane 5.10   photo: Tom Gwinn

Chapter 8

La Sal Mountains

Joe Smith on Yeyo 5.11b

LA SAL MOUNTAINS

Covered in this chapter:
The lower Brumley crag off the Loop Road, North Dakota crag on the Geyser Pass Road.

The La Sal Mountains, a Shangri La for desert living, is a small range offering climbing in cooler environs. The Loop Road—a scenic drive and a stellar 65-mile road bicycle ride—serves as the main access. A pair of hiking boots go a long way here. You can be at an elevation of almost 13,000' looking down on the vastness of the high desert in no time. The single-track mountain biking here is awesome as well, offering some great link-ups of the mountainous single track and the unforgiving desert rides below.

TO ACCESS THE CRAGS
From the center of town (Main and Center) drive south for 7.8 miles and turn left at the La Sal Loop Road (home of the Le Grand Johnson company). RESET YOUR ODOMETER and drive 0.5 miles to a stop sign and take a right. Follow the road, passing Ken's Lake (a manmade reservoir on your left), continue past the Pack Creek turn-off further down the road on your right. The road will start to get steep going through a section of sharp corners. Continue until your odometer reads 9.1—here you will see a dirt road on your right. This is the access for the Lower Brumley Crag. Continue on the Loop Road until your odometer reading is 12.1 and you arrive at the Geyser Pass intersection. Take a right heading up the winding dirt Geyser Pass Road, passing several camp spots, as well as the Trans-La Sal trail. After the trailhead the road will wind a few more times, eventually curving left at 16.3 miles. This is where the North Dakota crag begins.

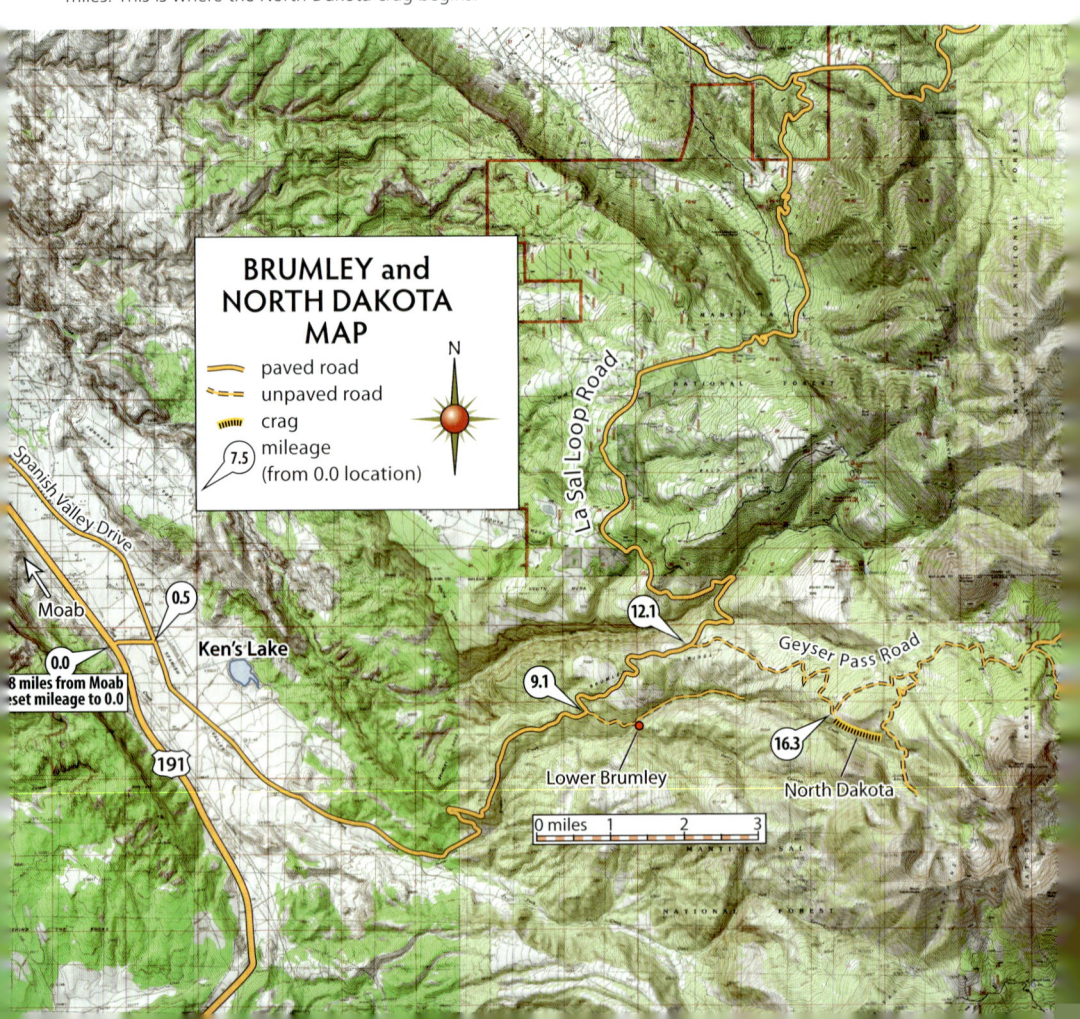

Lower Brumley Crag

The Brumley Crag (affectionately known as the Brumhole) resides in a narrow canyon with steep Dakota sandstone lining both sides of a flowing creek. High quality sport and trad climbs grace the area. Approach by locating the dirt road on the right side at about 9.1 miles. The parking varies based on your vehicle, but there are options for all models. In a nutshell, the crag is located about 0.7 mile from the main road, and autos with clearance can make it all the way to the crag. Those driving Porches will want to stop at the cattle guard. After driving or walking the three-quarters of a mile, the road bends left and the canyon wall (pictured below) comes into view. Look for a trail on the right that heads down to the canyon base. Once at the bottom hike up-canyon. It is also possible to rap in from various anchors. *Thank you Zack Smith for the beta!*

This side of the creek:
Routes are listed left to right from just right of the approach trail.

❏ 1. HAND CRACK 5.10 ★★
Hand Crack is the first climb you come to when walking into the canyon. Climb a broken right-facing corner to a few face moves to an obvious hands splitter and a ramp. Use the tree as an anchor.
Gear: Mostly hand sized units.

❏ 2. THE SNATCH 5.11c ★★★
A headpoint. Great climbing with creative gear. Starts with thin cracks up to a roof. Climb over the roof, trending right, to a thin crack and follow it to the top. Belay from a tree.
Gear: Nuts, tips, and finger cams.
FA: Zack Smith, Josh Gross

❏ 3. UNNAMED 5.12 ★★★
Follow a sharp arête to the diving board.
Gear: Draws
FA: Kevin Chase

❏ 4. THE MEXICAN 5.10 ★★
Begin in a splitter with off-fingers and tight hands; make a short traverse left to an arching splitter with fingers.
Gear: Nuts, 0.4–2.0
FA: Zack Smith, Josh Gross

❏ 5. 12 MONKEYS 5.12c R ★★★★
Climb off-fingers in a left-facing corner to two bolts next to each other. Continue out a big roof with a bolt next to the crack.
Gear: Draws, nuts, thin pieces
FA: Zack Smith

❏ 6. WARM-UP LEFT 5.11 45' ★★★
This right-facing corner starts with tight hands followed by a sharp steep flake with rattly fists. Continue via fingers to the difficult-to-clip anchors.
Gear: 1.0 TCU–3.5

❏ 7. WARM-UP RIGHT 5.10b 45' ★★★
A left-facing corner that starts with some hand jams, then works past some off-fingers to a few moves of big hands. Finish over a boulder bulge to a guano-covered ledge and the anchors.
Gear: 0.4–3.0

❏ 8. OPEN PROJECT
The bolted arête features protection on both sides.

❏ 9. UNNAMED 5.11a ★★★★
A left-facing corner to a sweet roof crack concluding in shallow switching corners.
Gear: 0.5–4.0

❏ 10. UNNAMED SPORT 5.10b ★★★★
Around the corner from previous route lies a beautiful, crimpy, black face. A great route to end the day by climbing out rather than hiking.

❏ 11. BEN'S CRACK 5.10
A short left-facing corner into a shallow stem-box, featuring mostly hands to a two-bolt ring anchor.
Gear: #2 Friend–3.5

❏ 12. UNNAMED
Climb the face past a single bolt to a right-facing corner. At around half height, the corner changes to left-facing.

❏ 13. EL CAHONE (AKA EL CULCHILLO) 5.12d
★★★★★
Steep, desperate arête climbing, dubbed by Zack Smith "the best route in the canyon."
Gear: Draws
FA: Mark Howe

❏ 14. FIGHT CLUB 5.12c ★★★★
Trend left passing two bolts to a shallow right-facing corner. Some wideness brings you to the top. Zack Smith: "Technical, perplexing, chicken-winging."
FA: Justin Cassels

❏ 15. OPEN PROJECT
Climbs lichen-covered overlaps.

❏ 16. OPEN PROJECT
The left of two splitters. Features thin climbing past a fixed nut.
Gear: Nuts, tips and fingers

❏ 17. JELLO AND TRAMPOLINES 5.10
The righthand more friendly splitter.
Gear: 0.5–1.0
FA: Zack Smith

Across the Creek

❏ 1. SENTENCE TO BURN 5.12d ★★★★
A Gilje testpiece with a hard clip at the the fourth bolt. A 0.75 Friend in a pocket near the top may help calm your nerves.
FA: Tom Gilje

❏ 2. GILJE SOLO 5.9 ★★★★
Arching hand crack. Good fun!

❏ 3. BUMPING UGLIES 5.11b
A steep crack out a cave that leads to the top of the cliff.
Gear: Bring some wide
FA: Justin Cassels

La Sal Mountains | 285

Tom Gwinn on *Warm-Up Right* 5.10b

North Dakota Crags ✳ S

The North Dakota Crag resides between 9,000–10,000 feet and faces west. Routes range from 5.6 to 5.12 with most requiring around a dozen draws and a 70 meter rope. The few gear lines are of great quality, and a few routes require a mix of gear and bolts. **Fifteen draws should be adequate for most sport routes.** This is a national forest area, camp and recreate accordingly.

My friend Linus Platt told me that Kyle Copeland, back in the day, referred to this area as North Dakota because the rock is primarily Dakota sandstone. When I arrived, the only evidence of climbing was the Outward Bound toprope anchors at the Kentucky Fried Chicken crag and a single bolt with a bail biner high on the cliff—thought to be Kyle's.

In 2004 Dylan Warren and Joe Slansky put up the first two lead routes at the Good Times Wall. The thought was with Mill Creek (famed for its bold leads and harder lines) just down the road, the rock in this area would lend itself more towards mid-grade routes and would be bolted for leaders of that grade. At the time of this writing there are roughly 55 routes, and though some bold leads have arrived, hopefully this crag will remain a place to go without concern for ground-fall and ledge-fall potential—a place where you can push yourself with better chances of hurting your pride than your body, a place you can bring your friends and family to get them jazzed on something you love so much. My kids grew up at this crag and it was the site of my son's first lead. I was so grateful that such a place exists in the Moab area. This is a great spot to escape the summer heat, to climb in the fall amid the cottonwood foliage, and look down on the vastness of the desert. The camping is awesome! Add a can of Deet to your gear list.

The crag is about a mile in length. For description purposes it is broken into three sections (Left, Middle and Right—each with its own approach). It is possible to walk the entire cliff along the bottom with some bushwhacking from time to time.

For the first approach (Left Section) park at the big lefthand corner at around 16.3 miles. Walk 100' or so into the woods and cut back right, making a few switchbacks and descending to the base. The first area is the Outward Bound toprope area referred to as the KFC area. Continuing right on a faint trail along the bottom of the cliff for 3–5 minutes will bring you to the Good Times Wall, Exam Wall, and Times Wall.

For the Middle Sector park in the same spot but instead of walking to the bottom of the crag, continue 100' or so above the edge of the cliff until you reach two lone pine trees; veer right and look for a recess in the wall and find a rope ladder leading down for 30'. This is an easy way to access the middle of the cliff. At the bottom (climbers left) resides the Ghost Buster area, while at climbers right is the Mighty Re-arranger and Great Roof area.

Finally **the third section** is accessed from the Gold Basin area. Instead of parking at 16.3, continue driving, passing the kiosk and bathrooms, to the Gold Basin turn-off at 17.6 miles. Take a right and continue to 18.7 miles where the road cranks a hard left. Park here and walk right along the edge of the cottonwood tree-line until you reach the cliff's edge (5 min) and continue on a zigzag trail down to areas known as Trench Town and North Trench Town.

IMPORTANT: IF YOU APPROACH TRENCH TOWN FROM GOLD BASIN, THE ORDER OF CLIMBS FOR THAT SECTION WILL BE IN REVERSE. THE ENTIRE CLIFF IS FROM LEFT TO RIGHT

Approaching from the Gold Basin side in the fall foliage

Overview Map with Routes

18.7 miles 🅿

Til the Sun Goes Down 5.10+/5.11
Roofus 5.12a/b
Cockblocker 5.9+
Up in Smoke 5.8
Hot Chicks on Wet Bikes 5.10+
Unnamed 5.11c/d
Sky Dog 5.10b
Time Will Tell 5.10a
Get Up, Stand Up 5.10
Jamming 5.8
Guava Jelly 5.9+
Exodus 5.11d
Nothing Circumstantial 5.12b
No More Trouble 5.11
Is this Love? 5.11
Alpha Blondy 5.12-
Screwface 5.10b
Sweet Thing 5.10
Grimmis 5.10
Fuggin Fun 5.10
Jungle Corner 5.10
10 to 8 5.10
Drag Queen 5.11
Room with a View 5.11

Trench Town

Yeyo 5.11b
Hydroponics 5.10d
Dope 5.10a
Chillum 5.8
Sweet Cheeba 5.7
Pinched Sack 5.10d
Herbaceous 5.11a
Mantel for Herb 5.11b

Ganja Wall
Mighty Re-arranger
big pines
Ghost Buster
Times Wall

Generations 5.8
Hand Prints 5.10c
Lawn Dart 5.10d
Story of My Life 5.10c
Sequential Line 5.11c
Time Line 5.11c
Dog on a Stone Roof 5.12
Dinner Mondue 5.10
PFG 5.10

6.3 miles 🅿

Exam Wall

Prostate Exam 5.11
Papsmear 5.10b
Turn Your Head... 5.11
Lichen the Exam 5.10

Good Times Wall

Czech Vag 5.10b
Salad Days 5.9
Good Times 5.7

KFC Toprope Area

Good Times Wall

Walk past the KFC toprope area and look for a faint trail below the cliffs that initially veers away from the cliff but then climbs steeply back up to the cliff bottom.

☐ 1. **CZECHOSLOVAKIAN VAG** 5.10b ★
Start from stepping across from block trend left to a crux in the black streak.
Gear: 10 draws
FA: K3

☐ 2. **SALAD DAYS** 5.9 ★
Start just right of *CV* by stepping off the same block and going straight up. A bit contrived.
FA: Dylan Warren

☐ 3. **GOOD TIMES** 5.7 ★★★★★
Low-angle climbing with plentiful holds with the crux over a bulge. The first route at the North Dakota Crags
FA: Dylan Warren

The following route sits by inself between Good Times Wall and Exam Wall

☐ 4. **BONE DOCTOR** 5.10b ★★★
Climb over a bulge and cruise a finger crack up to some balancy moves. Easier ground leads to anchors.
FA: K3

Exam Wall

To reach the Exam Wall, walk right from the Good Times Wall a short distance along the bottom of the cliff.

☐ 1. **PROSTATE EXAM** 5.11 ★★★
Start in a left-facing corner (optional gear placements) passing a bolt on the right wall. Make an off-fingers traverse with gear, pull the roof and continue up a beautiful bolted arête.
Gear: 0.75, 6 draws
FA: K3

☐ 2. **PAP SMEAR** 5.10b ★★★
An alternate bouldery start to *Prostate* joins the latter at the stellar arête.
Gear: 3 draws
FA: K3

The next two routes share a start.

☐ 3. **TURN YOUR HEAD AND COUGH** 5.11 ★★
A bit shorter but super fun with a steep upper face. Start as for *Lichen* but break left over a fun flake/arête, then follow bolts up the gold face with powerful moves on pockets and crimps.
Gear: draws
FA: K3

☐ 4. **LICHEN THE EXAM** 5.10 ★★
A long route with a technical crux in the middle and steep, licheny stems at the top.
Gear: draws

Pete (the skirt) Rensing onsighting the *Lawn Dart* 5.10d on Times Wall (next page)

Times Wall

Continue walking along the base just around the corner and up the hill. Generations is easily identifiable.

☐ 1. **GENERATIONS** 5.8 ★★★
Right-facing hand crack and a great first trad lead.
Gear: 1.0–2.0
FA: K3

☐ 2. **HAND PRINTS** 5.10c ★★★
Climbs a quality arête with some funky clips. Shares anchors with *Generations*.
Gear: 5 draws
FA: K3

☐ 3. **LAWN DART** 5.10d ★★
Thought provoking climbing and a bit runout. Balancy and sequential. Check out the rock sticking in the ground at the bottom—it came off on the first ascent from halfway up, never touching the cliff on the way down and creating a really neat thud sound as it buried itself in the ground (hence the *Lawn Dart*).
Gear: 6 bolts
FA: K3

☐ 4. **STORY OF MY LIFE** 5.10c ★★
Climbs near the black streak up to a ledge. The mental crux occurs leaving the ledge. Continue up small crimps to the anchor.
Gear: draws
FA: Dylan Warren

☐ 5 . **SEQUENTIAL LINE** 5.11c ★★★★
Just left of *Time Line*. A short, stout and sequential right-trending route.
Gear: 7 draws
FA: K3

☐ 6. **TIME LINE** 5.11c ★★★
Dylan and I both eyed this unique line when we first walked the wall. We split the lead in half. This is a girdle traverse under a huge roof featuring sparse feet and protected mostly by 0.75 Camelots. After 50' or so of traversing, pull the roof and clip a few bolts to the anchor.
Gear: 0.5–0.75 & 2 draws
FA: K3, Dylan Warren

☐ 7. **DOG ON A STONE ROOF** 5.12
Located on the far right end of the *Time Line* girdle. Start between the wall and a huge boulder, traverse left under the roof with hand jams, pull the barn-doory roof, and face climb to the anchors.
Gear: 5 bolts

☐ 8. **DINNER MONDUE** 5.10 ★★★★
A nice right-facing corner with fingers, off-fingers and tight hands.
Gear: Yellow TCU–0.75 (heavy on the off-fingers)
FA: Jay Ackerman

☐ 9. **P.F.G.** 5.10 ★★
Just around the corner from *Dinner Mondue* lies this right-facing corner with mostly hands.
Gear: Hand sized cams
FA: K3

Charley Graham on *Sequintial Line* 5.11c

La Sal Mountains

NORTH DAKOTA CENTER

ND Center can be approached from either end of the crag but is most easily approached via the rope ladder in the center of the cliff.

Ghost Buster Crag

The Ghost Buster Crag is most easily accessed from the top via the rope ladder in the center of the cliff. Once at the bottom walk a short distance (climbers left). You can also approach from the Times Wall with a bit of trudging through some pricker bushes.
The next three routes are short, powerful and share the same anchors. Routes are listed from left to right.

❏ 1. **GATE KEEPER** 5.10d
Gear: 4 draws
FA: K3

❏ 2. **ZOOL** 5.10/d
Roof crack variation to *Gate Keeper*.
Gear: 1.0 & 3 draws
FA: K3

❏ 3. **KEY MASTER** 5.10d
Gear: 3 bolts
FA: K3

Mighty Re-arranger

This climb resides by itself and is located immediately climbers right of the rope ladder.

❏ 1. **MIGHTY RE-ARRANGER** 5.10b/c ★★★★
Great quality rock with very delicate climbing up a beautiful dark face. Only one sequence connects the puzzle pieces.
Gear: 5 draws
FA: K3

Ganja Wall

The Ganja Wall is a great addition to the North Dakota Crag, featuring really fun routes on really good rock with a variety of grades and lengths.

The Ganja Wall is in the middle of the cliff, climbers right of the rope ladder. Using the rope ladder is the easiest access if this is your destination. If you are cragging at Trench Town or Good Times, you can access it by walking the cliff line for 5 to 10 minutes.

❏ 1. **YEYO** 5.11b ★★★★★
Pull a steep move off the ground at the crack/seam then make a traverse left for 45' staying just above the roof all the way out to the arête. Follow a few more bolts up the arête on friendlier holds to the spacious belay ledge (Stoners Ledge) with outstanding views!
Gear: 11 draws
FA: K3; FFA: Joe Smith

❏ 2. **HYDROPONICS** 5.10d ★★★★
Start by pulling a bulge, sharing the first bolt with *Yeyo*. Continue climbing just left of the seam. Punch it up the steep water groove on pockets and crimps to a ledge. Pumpy! Finish on a friendlier angle and better holds.
Gear: 8 draws
FA: K3

Tim Naylor on the *Mighty Re-arranger* 5.10b/c

Joe Smith crimps up *Hydroponics* 5.10d

3. DOPE 5.10a ★★★★
A bouldery start to the first clip, then some sequential climbing on edges with hidden pockets from time to time. Rest on the ledge and get ready for some edgy climbing. You can bust left to share anchors on *Hydroponics* or head right to share anchors with *Chillum*.
Gear: 6 draws
FA: K3

4. CHILLUM 5.8 ★★★★
Start to the right of the first bolt and continue up the bolt line on plentiful edges and pockets. At the time of this writing, the route is a bit "crispy" but with more ascent should clean up nicely. Super fun and a good warm-up.
Gear: 5 draws
FA: K3

5. SWEET CHEEBA 5.7
★★★★
A route that diagonals from right to left on big holds (sometimes hidden—be patient and you'll find them).
Gear: 4 draws
FA: T.J. Stephans

The following three routes are a bit right and up the hill.

6. PINCHED SACK 5.10d
★★★★
Really good rock with some reachy clips. Steep.
Gear: 5 draws
FA: Tim Naylor

7. HERBACEOUS 5.11a
★★★★
Short and stout! Steep pinches and edges.
Gear: 4 draws
FA: Tim Naylor

8. MANTEL FOR HERB
5.11b ★★★★
Fun climbing on good rock. A climb that makes you think—great climbing with a really hard mantel just before the anchors.
FA: K3

Like father, like son!! Joeseph Smith (age 5) cruising *Chillum* 5.8

NORTH DAKOTA RIGHT
Trenchtown North

❑ 1. **GRIMMIS** 5.10 ★★
Begins on a sharp arête, climbs broken rock to a slabby shelf, and continues to some balancy clips (careful for ledge falls) with a crux up high.
FA: Dave Sadoff

❑ 2. **FUGGIN FUN** 5.10 ★★★
Climbs a black face to smooth brown rock to a more featured face.
FA: Dave Sadoff

❑ 3. **JUNGLE CORNER** 5.10
Climb a right-facing corner with fingers and hands through a pricker bush crux.
FA: Charley Graham

❑ 4. **10 TO 8** 5.10 ★★
Great face climbing with a low crux and then eases to 5.8 climbing.
FA: K3

❑ 5. **DRAG QUEEN** 5.11 ★★★
Start off of a rock ledge in a right-facing corner through a bulge, passing three bolts to a horizontal bolt line then an arête with three more bolts.
FA: Dave Sadoff

❑ 6. **ROOM WITH A VIEW** 5.11 ★★
Left-trending climbing leads to a ledge, then more face climbing. Just left of the bolt line is an obvious left to right overlap.
FA: Erin Labelle

Trenchtown

❑ 1. **TIL THE SUN GOES DOWN** 5.10+/5.11- ★
Left to right green ramping feature to the rim. Most of the route is fun cruising with the crux near its top.
FA: Eric Odenthal

❑ 2. **ROOFUS** 5.12a/b ★★
Starts on a featured arête to some slabbier rock, then to a blocky roof before continuing on some face. An optional 3.0 Camelot may be nice.
Gear: 3.0
FA: Paul Irby

❑ 3. **COCKBLOCKER** 5.9+ ★★★
Really fun! Climbs opposing flakes (double Gastons) to a hidden anchor behind a huge block. The small picture is Dylan Warren on the route.
FA: Eric Odenthal

❑ 4. **UP IN SMOKE** 5.8 ★★
Fun climbing. The start goes between some outcrops.
FA: Larry Harpe
Gear: Single bolt

❑ 5. **HOT CHICKS ON WET BIKES** 5.10+ ★★★
Starts just right of a detached pillar and climbs a featured face.
FA: Dave Sadoff, Aaron, Paul Irby

❑ 6. **UNNAMED** 5.11c/d ★★★
Starts just right of previous route.
FA: Nathan Martin

❑ 7. **SKY DOG** 5.10b ★
Mixed gear and bolts up a shallow, right-facing dihedral then continue up the face. (Loved having you around Linus!)
Gear: Set of nuts and a selection of small cams along with draws
FA: Linus Platt

❑ 8. **TIME WILL TELL** 5.10a ★★★
Fun, featured climbing to a slabby crux, then over a bulge.
FA: Dylan Warren

❑ 9. **GET UP, STAND UP** 5.10 ★★★
Steep bouldery start to an arête.
Gear: 6 draws
FA: K3

Rusty Rigg on Get Up Stand Up 5.10

La Sal Mountains

Tahnee Torres on Guava Jelly 5.9+

Pete Rensing off balance on the touchy Exodus 5.11d

10. JAMMING 5.8 ★
Face and crack requiring some thin gear (an unknown second pitch up a lichen-covered arête is rumored to be a Nathan Martin 5.12).
FA: K3

11. GUAVA JELLY 5.9+ ★★★★
Stemming and palming up a natural rain runnel leads to a crack finish!
Gear: 6 draws
FA: K3

12. EXODUS 5.11d ★★★
Meandering bolts up some duotone rock to the rim. Thin edges and balancy.
Gear: Draws
FA: K3

13. NOTHING CIRCUMSTANTIAL 5.12b
Just right of *Exodus*.
FA: Dave Sadoff

14. NO MORE TROUBLE 5.11 ★★★
A thin start leads to a traverse left around and over a roof.
Gear: 4 draws
FA: K3

15. IS THIS LOVE? 5.11 ★★
Weird climbing in a chimney slot to face climbing over a roof. It is cruxy exiting the chimney. Shares anchors with *No More Trouble*.
Gear: 5 bolts
FA: K3

16. ALPHA BLONDY 5.12- ★★★
Climbs the face that starts over the shantytown.
FA: Paul Irby

17. SCREWFACE 5.10b ★★★★
Start just right of the shantytown crux, low to the ground with stacks of fun climbing above.
Gear: 12 draws
FA: K3

18. SWEET THING 5.10 ★★★
The last climb on the cliff or the first if you approached from Gold Basin. Balancy arête climbing with a reachy first clip.
Gear: 5 draws
FA: K3

Chapter 9
191 South

Adam Serro on the *Hidden Gem* 5.13

191 SOUTH ✦E

While most climbers think of Highway 191 as the path to Indian Creek, this section of the book will describe a crag, a select route, and a few adventures. All but the crag could easily be a worthy stop to or from the Creek. Areas are described traveling south from Main and Center.

Town Wall

The BLM-managed Town Wall is an east-facing crag receiving morning sun and afternoon/evening shade. The Wingate crag offers great views of the La Sal Mountains to the southeast and birds-eye views of Spanish Valley. With a nearly nearly non-existent drive, this is a prime crag for Moab locals.

If you want a real genuine gem, get on the Hidden Gem—free it, French it, hang dog, get a rope gun, make a deal with the devil, but "get ur dun." Don't miss it!

Two approaches exist, with the Hidden Gem being pretty much in the middle. Unless you're just gunning for the aforementioned route, my suggestion is to access the crag from the south (left) where there is a heavier concentration of pitches reached by a half-hour approach. You can approach from the right with an overall time to the Hidden Gem of about 50 minutes.

The left approach: From the center of town drive to the south for 4.7 miles to Lemon Lane. Turn right, reset your odometer, travel 0.1 mile to a left on a dirt road before the dead end sign. Follow this until your odometer reads 0.4 (where the dirt road turns right). Park in the spur on the left, looking for a saddle to a sub-knoll left of the main drainage. Hiking the main drainage looks easy but is "no bueno." Park and head for the sub-knoll and hike on a well-beaten path to the knoll's summit. From here, the trail gets faint; look for cairns marking the easiest way through a small cliff band above. After reaching the top you will descend 100 or so feet to the Wingate cliff straight in front of you. A dominant prow/arête contains routes on both sides. About 100' left of these are the routes of the Town Wall, listed left to right. This is hard to see from Hwy 191.

The right approach: I recommend this for the Hidden Angel. Drive 4.6 miles to Angel Rock Road; follow to its end and turn right and continue to the Hidden Valley trailhead. Start up the Hidden Valley trail until it takes a hard right across a dry waterway. Just after crossing this, ascend the steep talus flute, headed towards a large boulder resembling a sail. After reaching the sail, veer left until you reach a field with pleasant walking, passing a few climbs on your right and the Disappearing Angel down on the left under a sub-rim.

The routes are listed left to right.

191 South

❑ 1. UNNAMED RIGHT-FACING CORNER 5.10+ 70' ★★★
Sweet off-fingers to fingers in a right-facing corner.
Gear: Yellow TCUs to 2.0 Friends

❑ 2. RAMBLIN' MAN 5.10+ 80' ★★★
Great fun! Hands in a left-facing corner. Pull past a fun hand-sized roof into a short wide section. Continue on great hand jams to a second roof, pull the sharp tight hands roof then up onto a small belay ledge in a slot.
Gear: 1.0–4.0 (heavy on hands)
FA: Jay Ackerman

❑ 3. UNNAMED 5.10 90' ★★★
Just right of the prominent prow, an aesthetic left-facing corner begins with hands and moves through the sizes up to a bit of off-width before the chains.
Gear: 1.0–5.0, heavy on the big hands

❑ 4. TOWN HOE 5.9 40' ★
Easy left-facing corner to a ledge with anchors. A good warm-up.
Gear: 2.0–3.0
FA: K3

Rumsfeld's Head

❑ 5. TIGER'S TALE 5.10 C2 800'
This is one of the bigger routes in the Moab area, climbing through three different sandstone layers. Wingate, Kayenta, and Navajo. No pins are needed but bring lots of cams. Approach from Lemon Lane to upper Hidden Valley. Locate a Wingate pillar below Rumsfeld's Head. The route is six pitches plus scrambling. Route details are shown on the topo.
FA: Dave Madera, M. Ruth

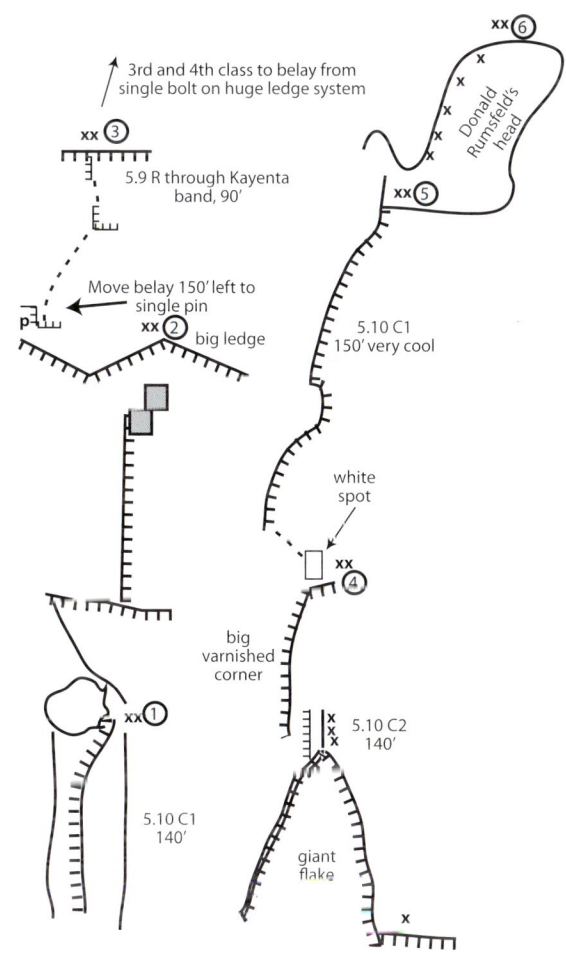

191 South

❏ 6. **TOWN FULL OF FINGERS** 5.12 55' ★★★★
Really good rock! Begin with a bouldering move to a stance followed by more bouldering off the stance (tips and face holds). Bust up the shallow right-facing corner via "chisel tip" fingers to a hard mantel and a rest. Continue via more generous-sized fingers to a wedge and the anchor.
Gear: 0.0 TCU–0.4
FA: K3

❏ 7. **GOING TO HOLLYWOOD** 5.13- ★★★★
Starts just right of *Town Full*. Begin up the corner and pull a small roof to a beautiful fingers splitter on stellar rock. Eventually the splitter pinches down to nothing. Finish with face climbing to the anchor.
Gear: 0.0 TCU to 0.4
FA: Mason Earle

❏ 8. **LOVE AND A 45** 5.10+ 60'
Reminiscent of *Mexican Crack* in Little Cottonwood Canyon. Starts off-fingers/tight hands then crooks right and finishes with hands. Located above the drainage. The original line went to the top. An unknown party added the anchors.
Gear: Lots of fingers and tips pieces.
FA: Bob Novellino

❏ 9. **UNNAMED SPLITTER** 5.10+ 45' ★★
Climb splitter big hands/fist to a short ow section and a reachy anchor clip. Shares anchors with #10.
Gear: 3.0–5.0

❏ 10. **UNNAMED RIGHT-FACING CORNER**
5.10 45' ★★
Good clean rock. Starts out fingers and turns to tight hands. A flake on the right wall offers some footholds.
Gear: yellow TCU–1.0

❏ 11. **UNNAMED FACE TO SLOT** 35' ★
Some unprotected face climbing to an off-fingers slot.

If you're looking up from the Spanish trail area you can see a prominent talus cone up and right from the "No Bueno" drainage. The hidden gem is on the right side of the cone.

❏ 12. **HIDDEN GEM** 5.13 60' ★★★★★
A very aesthetic climb on great rock. The splitter starts right from the ground in the center of a shield. Straight in diagonaling fingers to plumb off-fingers, and deceptively steep!
Gear: 0.3–0.75 (heavy on the 0.5 and 0.75)
FA: K3; FFA: Adam Serro

The next three routes are close to each other and directly over the Beeman drilling area off Highway 191.

❏ 13. **UNNAMED RIGHT-FACING CORNER**
5.10 50' ★★
Starts with tighter hands then goes over some blocky terrain protected by a bolt to a hidden anchor.
Gear: 1.0s and a quickdraw

❏ 14. **UNNAMED SPLITTER WITH CORNER**
5.10 65' ★★
Climb a sweet cups to hands splitter with stems to the corner. Meet up with the corner just before the anchor. Can be silty after a rain.
Gear: 0.5–3.5 heavier on 3.0s

❏ 15. **UNNAMED FLAKE** 5.10 60' ★★
Climb delicate fingers past a bolt. Continue in a wide flake to the anchor
Gear: Fingers to wide

The next route is above storage units and Nations Towing

❏ 14. **UNNAMED** 5.11 100' ★★★
This is the left of three splitters and the only one with anchors. Sweet route despite some wideness at the top! Start with off-fingers up to an offwidth with a bolt. Continue wide to the anchor.
Gear: 0.4–5.0 (heavy on off-fingers)

The next route is 350' to the right and almost directly behind Hidden Angel.

❏ 15. **UNNAMED OFFSET** 5.11 60' ★★
Start with off-fingers in a wedge formed by a huge piece of rock leaning against the wall. Continue splitter offset with fingers into tips.
Gear: 0.0–1.0

Flanking both sides of the Town Wall are many good quality pitches with ample solitude. I urge you to explore.

Jay Ackerman on the FA of *Ramblin' Man* 5.10+

The Disappearing Angel

The Disappearing Angel is the formation you see when coming from the south or north, but as you drive into town it disappears. There are a few routes on it. Approach by following the right-side approach to the Town Wall.

1. THE ORIGINAL BJØRNSTAD ROUTE 5.8 A0
Gear: Mostly draws, bolts without hangers, and a double set from blue TCU–4.0

2. SATAN'S REVENGE 5.12 ★★★★
A route with a stout reputation. Climb this when you're feeling scrappy and fresh.
P1: Begin in a crack system on the right side of the tower's north face, on the right side. Ever-widening, it abruptly ends as it leads into a short finger splitter, which then changes into slightly loose face climbing before continuing as a thin hands splitter. Clip a bolt and traverse on poor hands and feet to a good bolt. From here, the route arcs up and right, passing about six bolts. Belay from a double bolt anchor at a good ledge.
P2: Traverse right and wrap around the arête, making a few moves before a funky 5.11 move takes you back to the north face. Traverse the ledge treading through crumbly rock to another comfy bolted belay.
P3: Walk around to the south side of the tower along the ledge and ascend easy 5th class to the summit.
RAP: Two single 60m rappels get you down.
Gear: *0.0 TCU–3.0, 10 quickdraws, 6 runners, double ropes can help with the first pitch.*
FA: Tom Gilje

Jake Warren and Geoff Unger on *Satan's Revenge* 5.12

Roadside Select

☐ 1. **NOSE DIVE** 5.12 ★★★★ 🌱 SW
Super steep and super quality Entrada. Burly! A Steve Hong contribution just off the road with no approach. A left-facing ow to overhanging cups and fist.
Gear: 3.0–4.0, very heavy on the 3.5, long draw, optional 6.0

Charley Graham on *Nose Dive* 5.12

ADVENTURE CLIMBING IN THE AREA

Looking Glass Rock

This is a great outing for beginner climbers, offering bolt protected face and friction pitches and bolted belays. Climbers, however, must be able to rappel. For added fun, a pendulum (King Swing) can be set up from the back of the forming arch at the bottom of the rappel—oh yeah!

❏ 1. **COWBOY ROUTE** 5.6 ★★★
P1: Start on the south face, ascending a short left-facing corner, clip a fixed piece with a double shoulder-length sling, and proceed up the slabby SE-facing fin. Pass a bolt and proceed to a bolted belay (5.6).
P2: Follow the slabby fin past three more bolts to a shallow right-facing corner to another nice bolted belay stance.
P3: Stand up next to the bolts and follow a low-angle slab to a single-bolt belay. Clip this with a long sling and continue leftward past it to another set of belay anchors. From here you can access the top of the formation.
RAP: From the last belay, look to the south and find a slot/hole with some rappel anchors. A single 70m will make it to the ground.
ADDED FUN & ADVENTURE: With all parties on the ground, keep the rope hanging. One person can tie in, and another put him on belay. The belayer walks to the tree, while the "climber/swinger" walks to the terminus of the giant cave, towards the aid route. The belayer takes up the slack and stretch and the swinger hucks his carcass into the King Swing!

Rusty Rigg on the King Swing

302 191 South

Inverted King Swing

Kastle Kelley on Looking Glass

The author and kids (now adults—not the author)

Kastle lowering off Looking Glass

2. WILSON ARCH 5.5 ★★★ ☀ SW
This is a legal arch climb. No fixed belays or anchors, but a rap anchor is located on the side opposite the road. Please do not simul-rap, as this damages the rock. Wilson Arch is reached by driving 25.6 miles south from Main & Center on Highway 191. The arch is obvious just off the left side of the highway. A short walk brings you to the base. Climb the southwest facing (looker's right) side.

Chapter 10

Appendices

Tom Gwinn on *Unnamed* 5.11- (p.139) Day Canyon

HIGHLINING BY LARRY HARPE

Slacklining is the art of dynamic balance. For many, it has become a great way to pass the time on rest days. Highlining, with a nearly self-explanatory name, is the next step in rigging and mastering the art of slackline. The desert canyons, towers, and beautiful vistas makes Moab one of the best places for highlining. The potential is virtually unlimited.

As with any desert activity it is important that we keep a low profile and our impact to a minimum. Highlines should not be left unattended and should be broken down when done for the day. If there is no trail, follow washes and slickrock—don't bust the crust! Highline rigging is complex and dangerous. If you don't know how to do it find someone who does. Please never add bolts near a climbing route!

Here are some great lines to get you started:

GEMINI BRIDGES is one of the original highlining spots in this area. To get there drive north on 191 to the Canyonlands turn off on 313. Follow this road 12.5 miles and turn left onto Gemini Bridges Road. Follow this for 6.2 miles and park at the Gemini Bridges parking lot.

THE DOG HOLE is the obvious hole next to the bridges. It has bolts for rigging and is 80 ft long.

THE BIRTHDAY GAP is a few fins north of the Dog Hole. It has bolts and a crack on the rigging side (30 ft).

THE TWINS are two lines—95 ft and 105 ft—right next to each other. They are just up over the hill, east of the *Dog Hole*. Four bolts on each side for each line and a sick view.

THE MEXICAN CAULK GUN is one of the most scenic highlines out there. Head up Sand Flats road for about 9.9 mi from the kiosk. Park just past the wash. Follow washes and slickrock up and around to the tower. (The tower will be out of view up and right behind a large rock outcrop. Climb the NW arête at 5.10+R A2. You can hike to the other side of the gap. Bolts and gear for the rigging side (38 ft).

CINCO DE FROGO AKA THE POINT OF MOAB is 55 ft long and quite the odyssey. Hike up The Portal trail to the base of the Point of Moab. Climb the route of your choice. To get to the other side hike up and around the portal trail and scramble up the slickrock buttress to just above the tower, rappel down to anchors.

THE MOPHO GAP is a fun little line (30 ft) just below the Moab Rim Trail. Park at pullout 1/4 mile before the Moab Rim trail head and head up a faint trail there. Hike up and past a large tower. The gap is right of and just past the tower. Scramble up and behind the gap to access it. Bolts for anchors.

MEDIEVAL TURD TICKLER is located at Sands Flats above Morning Glory Arch rappels. Approach via the Fins and Things trail (40 ft).

THE FRUIT BOWL is the only "official" highline spot in Moab. Located 10 miles down Mineral Bottom Road at the second right turn after the cattle guard. Look for a parking lot with a sign that explains how to reach the highline.

Dean Potter highlining the Mexican Caulk Gun

Larry Harpe on The Birthday Gap   photo: Wayne Bowers

Single Pitch Routes Not to Be Missed!

ARCHES NATIONAL PARK
☐ **OWL ROCK** 5.8 (GARDEN OF EDEN)
☐ **HEART OF THE DESERT** 5.10
☐ **MR. SOMBRERO** 5.11+ (GREAT WALL)

WALL STREET
☐ **30 SECONDS OVER POTASH** 5.8
☐ **NERVOUS IN SUBURBIA** 5.9
☐ **STEEL YOUR FACE** 5.10
☐ **ASTRO LAD** 5.11
☐ **BABY BLUE** 5.11
☐ **KNAPPING WITH THE ALIEN** 5.11B/C
☐ **MOTHER TRUCKER** 5.11C
☐ **STATIC CLING** 5.11
☐ **DARK HORSE** 5.12
☐ **UNDER THE BOARD WALK** 5.12B/C

DAY CANYON
☐ **BRUSH PAINTED DATSUN** 5.10
☐ **POCKET ROCKET** 5.10C
☐ **KISS OF THE SPIDER WOMAN** 5.12

POTASH ROADSIDE
☐ **SKINWALKER** 5.11

LONG CANYON
☐ **CHOPPER** 5.10 (DEAD MANS BUTTRESS)
☐ **PROGRAM DIRECTOR** 5.10 (DEAD MANS BUTTRESS)
☐ **TEQUILA SUNRISE** 5.10 (MAVERICK BUTTRESS)
☐ **DAWN OF AN ERROR** 5.11 (DEAD MANS BUTTRESS)
☐ **FINGER BANG** 5.11 (SHADY CRAG)
☐ **GUNSMOKE** 5.11 (MAVERICK BUTTRESS)
☐ **HAND DELIVERY** 5.11 (DELIVERY AREA)
☐ **MISS KITTY LIKES IT THAT WAY** 5.11+ (MAVERICK BUTTRESS)
☐ **PECCADILLO** 5.11 (GIN & TECTONICS AREA)
☐ **RALPH** 5.12 (OFFWIDTH CITY)
☐ **WEAK BOSONS** 5.11+ (PHYSICS DEPARTMENT)
☐ **5/15/37** 5.12 (SHADY CRAG)
☐ **BOOT HILL** 5.12 (MAVERICK BUTTRESS)

☐ **CARNIVORE** 5.12 (CARNOVORE AREA)
☐ **OCTOPUSSY** 5.12 (BOND BUTTRESS)
☐ **SEVENTH SERPENT AND EXTENSION** 5.12R (REPTILIAN WALL)
☐ **TORPEDO BAY** 5.12 (SHIPYARD)
☐ **WICKED** 5.13

MINERAL BOTTOM/CANYONLANDS
☐ **SEOUL GAMES** 5.10+ (TRAD WALL)
☐ **CIRCLE OF QUIET** 5.11 (BOUNDARY WALL)
☐ **B.F.E.** 5.11 (MINERAL BOTTOM)
☐ **GLAD TO BE TRAD** 5.13 (TRAD WALL)

KANE CREEK
☐ **DOGMATIC** 5.10+ (DOG WALL)
☐ **THE FARM** 5.10 (KANE CREEK)
☐ **GUINEVERE** 5.11 (CAMELOT)
☐ **ICE CREAM PARLOR CRACK** 5.11 (ICE CREAM PARLOR)
☐ **XYLOKANE** 5.11+ (ABRAXES WALL)
☐ **DARK PATH** 5.11 (SCORCHED EARTH CRAG)
☐ **DOGGONIT** 5.12 (DOG WALL)
☐ **BUSHIDO** 5.13

NORTH DAKOTA
☐ **GOOD TIMES** 5.7 (GOOD TIMES WALL)
☐ **GENERATIONS** 5.8 (TIMES WALL)
☐ **GUAVA JELLY** 5.9 (TRENCHTOWN)
☐ **HOT CHICKS ON WET BIKES** 5.10+ (TRENCHTOWN)
☐ **HYDROPONICS** 5.10D (GANJA WALL)
☐ **SCREW FACE** 5.10B (TRENCHTOWN)
☐ **HERBACEOUS** 5.11A (GANJA WALL)
☐ **YEYO** 5.11 (GANJA WALL)

LOWER BRUMLEY
☐ **EL CAHONE** 5.12D
☐ **FIGHT CLUB** 5.12C
☐ **SENTENCE TO BURN** 5.12D

191 SOUTH
☐ **NOSE DIVE** 5.12 (191 SOUTH)
☐ **HIDDEN GEM** 5.13 (TOWN WALL)

Multi-pitch and Rim Routes Not to Be Missed!

POTASH ROADSIDE
☐ **FRENCHIES NIGHTMARE** 5.10

DAY CANYON
☐ **ANDROIDS WAFFLE HOT LINE** 5.10
☐ **AEROBICIDE** 5.11+
☐ **CONCEPCION** 5.13

LONG CANYON
☐ **GIN & TECTONICS** 5.11+ (GIN & TECTONICS AREA)
☐ **MAYOR** 5.11+ (OFFWIDTH CITY)
☐ **MINI SKIRTS AND HALTER TOPS** 5.11 (SHADY CRAG)
☐ **TWO PLUMB** 5.11+ (FORMING ARCH AREA)
☐ **UNNAMED AKA RUCKMAN ROUTE** (BOND BUTTRESS)
☐ **GET OVER IT** 5.12 (DEADMANS BUTTRESS)
☐ **JINX** 5.12 (BOND BUTTRESS)
☐ **QUANTUM OF SOLACE** 5.12 (BOND BUTTRESS)
☐ **RADIOACTIVE PORKSICKLE 5.13** (PHYSICS DEPARTMENT)

313 ROAD
☐ **CLASS ACT** 5.11 (313 ROADSIDE)

MINERAL BOTTOM/CANYONLANDS
☐ **GRAND PLAN** 5.11 (ISLAND IN THE SKY)
☐ **NO BOUNDARIES** 5.11 (DEAD HORSE AREA)
☐ **TWO FRIENDS GETTIN RED** 5.11 (BOUNDARY WALL)
☐ **WORD TO THE BIRD** 5.12 (DEAD HORSE AREA)

TUSHER VALLEY
☐ **ALBATROSS** 5.12 (MERRIMAC)
☐ **PLUNGE** 5.12 (MONITOR)

RIVER ROAD
☐ **CLEARLIGHT** 5.11 (BIG BEND BUTTE)
☐ **SCORCERERS APPRENTICE** 5.11+ (ROADSIDE)
☐ **TRAIL OF THE NAVAJO 5.11+** (ARCHES NATIONAL PARK–RIVER ROAD ACCESS)
☐ **INFRARED** 5.12 (BIG BEND BUTTE)
☐ **O'GRADY** 5.12 (BIG BEND BUTTE)

CASTLE VALLEY
☐ **SINNERS AND INFIDELS** 5.10+ (RECTORY)
☐ **SUPER NATURAL** 5.10 (PARRIOTT MESA)
☐ **FINE JADE** 5.11 (RECTORY)
☐ **VOODOO CHILD** 5.11+ (PARRIOTT MESA)
☐ **JESUS SAVES** 5.12 (RECTORY)

191 SOUTH
☐ **LOOKING GLASS** 5.6

KANE CREEK
☐ **CORNER ROUTE** 5.12 (TOMBSTONE)
☐ **FLOUR** 5.12 (BAKERY)
☐ **T-REX** 5.12 (ICE CREAM PARLOR)

Tower Highlights

You could say that every tower should not be missed! They are special—they are towers. What follows is a list of highlights for the towers in this book:

ANCIENT ART: Just a crazy formation featuring the smallest summit in this book. When I moved here I remember introducing myself to Brian Jonas, the owner of Pagan. He asked, "Have you done Ancient Art yet? You're the man if you do a handstand on the summit." Welcome to Moab!

KINGFISHER: The easiest of the big ones. You can pull out bolts and baby angles with your bare hands on this extended bolt ladder, but it won't much matter as there's seemingly hundreds. Exquisite views.

TITAN: The biggest. Its historic context is, perhaps, more important than any other tower. The uber-exposed *Finger of Fate* is a *50 Classic*.

HINDU: A slender spire in a lonesome, yet roadside, locale. Good stone allows for free climbing, albeit not at a modest grade.

SISTER SUPERIOR: Some say *Jah Man* is the perfect tower route, offering chimneying, splitter crack climbing, as well as nice face moves to summit the slender spire (with the added bonus of comfortable belay ledges and stellar views of the Castleton group).

THE PRIEST: Greg Child's *Excommunication* offers the most demanding free climbing on a tower in this book! The historic *Honeymoon Chimney* offers some wild stemming up high that leads to some demanding face moves before the top.

THE NUNS: *Holier Than Thou* offers two pitches of unreal, unrelenting, calcite-gripping face climbing before summiting via a final crack pitch.

RECTORY: Some would argue that the Rectory is a butte and not a tower. The simple truth is that it's a summit worthy enough for Bon Jovi to want to be on top! There are many routes to the top with one, *Fine Jade*, being the ultra-classic and for good reason.

CASTLETON TOWER: Ultra-historic, ultra-iconic, and ultra-good. There are many fine routes to the top on all parts of the compass. The *Kor-Ingalls* offers up a fine route with much historic value on the south face while the north face has two 5-star routes (*North Face* and *Sacred Ground*) which offer up ample shade for warm-weather ascents to the iconic summit.

DOLOMITE: A beautiful slender spire along the Colorado River. Climbing the *Dolofright* route is an excellent way to summit a tower primarily clipping bolts (beware, however, as it has a reputation for being a bold lead).

LIGHTHOUSE TOWER: With good routes on both the sunny and shady sides of the tower, it can comfortably be climbed in all times of the year. It also has a unique summit block that has no anchors on it—forcing a legendary downclimb.

PODUNK TOWER: Known for being a mostly moderate route with a wildly exposed finale.

ECHO TOWER: This tower has two separate unique windows. The window on top of the first pitch allows you to walk straight through to the opposite side. It also has a window up higher that offers, perhaps, some of the wildest/craziest and weirdest climbing in the book! To top it off, it also sports a girdle traverse circumnavigating the tower at the top of the first pitch.

TOMBSTONE (DUBINKEY WELL): The free route up this formation is often sandy and offers a crux literally off the ground.

THE WITCH: As you can read in Sam's account on page 42, this route is known for the second *business* pitch. Hard climbing with gear that umbrellas.

CAULDRONS: Nestled between its larger big brother (Warlock) and sister (Witch), the Cauldrons offer a remote feel as well as a mammoth roof on one of the upper pitches.

WARLOCK: Both routes on this secluded tower offer up wide cruxes!

CHARLIE HORSE NEEDLE: A great hot weather destination. This tower offers a great shaded route and a really cool window looking to the Green River. And great photo ops!

MOSES: Perhaps my personal favorite tower! Fantastic climbing on both the sunny side and the shady side. Give the famed ear on *Primrose* a try! Or Jimmy Dunn's overhanging fist crack, perhaps clip the "relics" on the Pale Fire route. However you choose to summit, hang out for the always outstanding sunsets offered in one of the most magnificent settings in Canyonlands!

ZEUS: *Sisyphus* offers lots of face climbing over small gear with very few jams required. A short hike, small rack, and the ability to descend with one rope are all advantages to enjoy a small summit in a location with outstanding views. If you are a fast and strong party, linking Zeus with Moses makes for a fantastic day in Canyonlands.

STANDING ROCK: A very remote tower in the heart of Canyonlands described by many as a "tall stack of sandstone pancakes." Layton Kor declared, "We climbed it not because it's there, but because it won't always be there." Hope for no seismic activity, as it appears to be brittle as well as leaning! The summit has to be one of the top places to stand.

Appendices

WASHER WOMAN: The *Search of Suds* route is an outstanding moderate route to a stellar Canyonlands summit. It has the added bonus of a legendary free hanging rappel over an arch, as well as fantastic views of its big brother neighbor, the Monster Tower.

MONSTER TOWER: A huge summer tower hosting plenty of shade. Most people will remember the off-fingers crux as well as a bold summit finish.

PINKY TOWER: A visionary route from Keith Reynolds. The tower's second pitch starts with face climbing, passing just enough bolts, while spiraling around the tower to a cool traverse finishing on a series of cracks. A short hike from the roadside as well a single rope rappel rounds out a great climb.

GOONEY BIRD: Another spiraling route from Keith Reynolds. This tower enjoys a "Wall Street approach." The route wraps the tower in three pitches (I am dying to know if Keith has a spiral staircase in his house).

THREE PENGUINS: The tower offers a quality Entrada route to the top of the center summit with great views of the Moab Valley. It's a spectators route! Expect to be on display with many of the park's visitors taking photos or giving celebratory honks from their vehicles.

ARGON TOWER: Heads up with a gritty feel!

THREE GOSSIPS: Featuring multiple summits, great Entrada climbing on the the center and south towers. Go with another party and enjoy an exposed game of frisbee (tied in of course)!

OWL ROCK: You know it is an awesome 5.8 when a climber like Steph Davis lists it as one of her Top 5! An easy approach with great and unique climbing brings you to a summit with a surreal setting.

EVE: Sometimes referred to as "Devil's Golf Ball." Spicy climbing that leads to a bolt ladder. Being in Arches Park it offers up some fantastic photo ops.

DEVILS DOG SPIRE: Beside residing in the park, it features hard offwidth climbing with a prize handcrack roof before reaching its summit.

DARK ANGEL: A world class hike in Arches which brings you past Landscape Arch and Double O Arch. Two pitches of moderate climbing bring you to a summit at the far reaches of the park. The rappel offers some wonderful photo opps.

BOOTLEG TOWER: Known for being a short, burly, bolted arête tower route.

RAPTOR TOWER: When living in Moab, you hear of certain people with legendary reputations of being very bold. Keith Reynolds is one of those souls. His route up this tower is known for some burly offwidth climbing combined with some sturdy face climbing between bolts on the summit pitch.

MISSION TOWER: The route has a fantastic hands splitter on it as well as a burly offwidth section.

HEISENBERG TOWER: Perhaps Moab's newest tower! Might become addictive.

HIDDEN ANGEL: This tower seems to be magical. While driving closer to Moab from the north or the south it disappears in front of your eyes. As mentioned earlier, some people are known for their boldness. Tom Gilje, no doubt, is at the top of the list. His *Satan's Revenge* is known for hard, bold climbing.

SPACE TOWER: This tower can be done in one long pitch. Though an easier grade it is known for being a bit *heady* with a protection bolt just where you need it. It is a wonderful way to wrap up your day at the Ice Cream Parlor.

PREDATOR TOWER: A small but worthy tower with an easy approach allowing you to punch out both of its routes in a quick visit. Both lines have the reputation for bouldery cruxes on Cutler sandstone featuring trippy colors and a gritty feel.

Locals' Favorites

I've asked some Moab locals to list their favorite routes, excluding towers (because all towers are cool and should be climbed).

Jay Smith
Voodoo Child 5.11+ (Parriott Mesa)
Sacred Ground 5.12b (Castleton Tower—I know you said no towers, right?)
Infrared 5.12a (Big Bend Butte)
Fine Jade 5.11a (Rectory)
Corner Route 5.12a (Tombstone)
Jay Smith on Greg Child's *Excommunication* 5.13b on the Priest: "I haven't done it and probably never will, but holy shit—it has got to be one of the best routes anywhere."

Dave Medara
Dave founded Moab Desert Adventures, and has guided here for years, and has been a big presence behind route development. He was also our local avalanche forecaster for the La Sal Mountains.
Under the Boardwalk 5.12b/c (Wall Street)
Boot Hill 5.12b (Maverick Buttress, Long Canyon)
30 Seconds Over Potash 5.8 (Wall Street)
Skinwalker 5.11c (Potash Road, mile 12)

Steph Davis
No introduction necessary. This woman just flat out sends! She may be the only vegan I know that I still like to cook for!
Concepciòn 5.13 (Day Canyon)
Corner Route 5.12 (Tombstones)
North Face 5.11 (Castleton Tower)
Epitaph 5.13 (Tombstones)
Owl Rock 5.8 (Arches Park)

Dylan Warren
Dylan was my partner for years (on a temporary hold for fatherhood and life), my right-hand man at work, my slab mentor (with his "just let out a bunch of rope, I'm just going to run" technique), and a dear friend. He has contributed stacks of new routes to the area.
Seventh Serpent 5.11 (Reptilian Left, Long Canyon)
Class Act 5.11 (313 Road)
Gunsmoke 5.11 (Maverick Buttress)
Peccadillo, 5.11 (Gin & Tectonics Area, Long Canyon)
Aerobicide 5.11 (Day Canyon)

Linus Platt
Linus concerning desert climbing: "It's all choss; some is five-star; some is no star; but its all choss!"

Larry Harpe
Lawrence has been around Moab for years, working as a guide for Moab Desert Adventures. He is our resident slacker (a.k.a. slackliner). He even named his dog Slack.
Working Class Hero 5.9+ (Day Canyon)
Brush Painted Datsun 5.10 (Day Canyon)
The Farm 5.10+ (Kane Creek)
Kane Walker (Kane Creek)
A Good Day to Die 5.9 (Kane Creek)

Zack Smith
Zack is bad ass! It may be that Zack has a different gravitational aura than most. He climbs harder than anyone I've met in real life. And he's pleasantly humble, which—in my opinion—makes for an all-around great person to talk/go climbing with. Zak on locals: "Moab climbers are a lot like the landscape: hard, dry, and a little prickly at times."
Infrared 5.12 (River Road)
Trail of the Navajo 5.11+ (Arches)

Todd Bogen (aka Taco)
Skinwalker 5.11c (Potash Road, mile 12)
Peccadillo 5.11 (Long Canyon)
Frogs of a Feather (Wall Street)
Brush Painted Datsun 5.10 (Day Canyon)
Corner Route 5.12 (Tombstones)

Paul Irby
People around here refer to him as "No Falls Paul." He has lived in the area for years and has added some quality routes (go check out the Dog Wall). By the way, I have seen him fall!
Under the Boardwalk 5.12b/c (Wall Street)
Infrared 5.12 (River Road)
Program Director 5.10 (Long Canyon)
The Plunge 5.12 (Monitor)
Dogmatic 5.11 (Kane Creek)

Charley Graham
I like to call him "Flash." What a maniac. He seems to have super human finger strength. If his appetite for food matched his appetite for climbing (actually it does) he should be big as a house!
Miss Kitty Likes It Raw 5.11+ (Long Canyon)
5-15-37 5.12 (Long Canyon)
Skin Ambivalence 5.12- (Parriott Mesa)
Octopussy 5.12 (Long Canyon)
Torpedo Bay 5.12 (Long Canyon)

K3
A wanna-be dirt bag.
No Boundaries 5.11 (Dead Horse Point Area)
Jinx 5.12- (Bond Buttress, Long Canyon)
Finger Bang 5.11 (Shady Crag, Long Canyon)
Guinevere 5.11 (Camelot, Kane Creek)
Yeyo 5.11b (Ganja wall, North Dakota)

Michelle Kelley
Watch out, she's on the sharp end! What an amazing athlete. If she puts her mind to it, she can do anything. She is a passionate (and humble) marathoner, an excellent skier, mountaineer, and best of all, a kick-ass baker! Oh, and my wife.
Where Egos Dare , 5.10+,
Chopper 5.10+
Brush Painted Datsun 5.10
Gunsmoke 5.10+
Seventh Serpent 5.11

Appendices

Amy Barnes

Amy guides for Jackson Hole Mountain Guides, dividing her time between here and Jackson. She is super skilled at her craft and a great neighbor!

Gunsmoke 5.11 (Long Canyon)
Miss Kitty Likes It That Way 5.11 (Long Canyon)
Chopper 5.10+ (Long Canyon)
Astrolad 5.11 (Wall Street)
Infrared 5.12 (River Road)
Baby Blue 5.11 (Wall Street)

Jeanine Saia

Jeanine has lived in Moab since 2000. She's been involved in the climbing community for all those years, and has worked at one of the local climbing shops and sat on the board of Friends of Indian Creek.

Steal Your Face 5.10+ (Wall Street)
The Farm 5.10+ (Kane Creek)
Tequila Sunrise 5.10c (Maverick Buttress, Long Canyon)
Scarpelli's Finger Crack 5.10 (Kane Creek)
Electronic Battleship 5.10 (Shipyard, Long Canyon)

Sam Lightner

Sam is another driving force behind route development in the area as well as our local anchor replacement rep for the ASCA (thanks Sam for keeping us all safe!). He is also active with Friends of Indian Creek.

Heart of the Desert 5.10c (Park Avenue, Arches Park)
Xylokane 5.11+ (Abraxas Wall, Kane Creek)
Fernando 5.11b (Wall Street)
Skinwalker 5.11c (mile 12 on Potash)
Program Director 5.10 (Long Canyon, right)

Lisa Hathaway

What to say, Lisa is hardcore! She spends most of her time sport climbing in the mountains. She has been here for years. She is active with the Chicks on Crack program here, as well as being active in route development. A skilled writer who has written articles (that I am sure we have all read) for R&I, Climbing and Alpinist. Also, I understand, she's an amazing ice skater!

Sorcerer's Apprentice 5.10+ or 5.11+ (River Road)
Chasin' Skirt 5.10+ (Long Canyon)
Full Moon Apology 5.11 (Long Canyon)
El Segundo 5.9+ (Arches)

Josh Gross

Josh has been guiding here for years.
Ice Cream Parlor Crack 5.11 (I.C.P.)
Fernando 5.11b (Wall Street)
Last Tango on Potash 5.11d (Wall Street)
Butterfly 5.13 (The Scar)
Trail of the Navajo 5.11+ (River Road)

Herb Crimp

Herb, in addition to a perfect climbing name, has worked for Desert Highlights for about a decade.
Mr. Sombrero 5.11+ (Arches)
Kiss of the Spider Women 5.12 (Day Canyon)
Ice Cream Parlor Crack 5.11 (I.C.P)
Frogs of a Feather 5.10c (Wall Street)
Skinwalker 5.11 (Potash Road)

Joe Slansky

Joe is a great friend who becomes a greater friend when it comes time to climb something wide or chossy (or both). Joe lived in the area for years, and is now studying physics in Logan. He's a source of constant entertainment. He goes from "bell to bell" and gives it a "full can of corn." He also did the pre-press for this book.

Super Chimney 5.10+ (Kane Creek)
Frenchie's Nightmare 5.10 (Potash Road)
Driving while Asian 5.10+ (Kane Creek)
A Good Day to Die (Kane Creek)
Gunsmoke 5.11 (Maverick Buttress, Long Canyon)

Kiefer Kelley

Kiefer has climbed in Moab since he was 9-years-old. His first lead climb was *Good Times* on the Good Times Wall.

Finger Bang 5.11 (Shady Crag)
Potash Bong Hit 5.10 (Wall Street)
A Good Day to Die 5.9 (I.C.P.)
Hydroponics 5.10d (Ganja Wall)
Encore 5.11 (The Cinema)

Tim Noonan

Known affectionately as "the prez." If you have climbed on Wall Street, you have met Tim. NOBODY CLIMBS SMARTER THAN THE PREZ, PERIOD! His foot work is unmatched. He both likes and dislikes everything on Wall Street.

Appendices

Route Index by Grade

5.3
CHOCOLATE CHUNK 5.3 127

5.4
GUMBY GULLY 5.4 124

5.5
BREWED AWAKENINGS 5.5 268
HIDDEN MESSAGE 5.5 127
HOLY MOLEY 5.5 127
PRACTICAL RELIGION 5.5 127
WILSON ARCH 5.5 302

5.6
BLACK SLAB 5.6 268
COWBOY ROUTE 5.6 301
KOR ROUTE 5.6 36
UNNAMED (WALL STREET) 5.6 116
VAN GO 5.6 156
WILLOW WHIP 5.6 120

5.7
SLAB ROUTE 5.7 127
SWEET CHEEBA 5.7 292
YOGINI 5.7 127

5.8
30 SECONDS OVER POTASH 5.8 121
CHILLUM 5.8 292
CRACK 1 5.8 268
CRACK 2 5.8 268
CRACK 3 5.8 268
CRITICAL MASS 5.8 268
DEATH TRAP 5.8 269
ENTRY FEE ROUTE 5.8 247
FUNNEL CAKE 5.8 148
GENERATIONS 5.8 290
GONG SHOW 5.8 273
HIGH DESERT DRIFTER 5.8 120
JAMMING 5.8 294
MANUS LEFT 5.8 159
OWL ROCK 5.8 96
PABST BLUE RIBBON 5.8 243
ROOT CANAL 5.8 182
SEIBERNETICS 5.8 110
SLAB 5.8 124
TOP 40 5.8 124
UNNAMED HANG NAIL (GOLD BAR TOWER AREA) 5.8 134
UP IN SMOKE 5.8 293

5.9
BAD MOKI ROOF 5.9 116
BEYER FRICTION 5.9 36
BLOODY KNEES 5.9 182
BROWN BANANA 5.9 126
CHRISTINE'S WAY BUFF SAAB 5.9 137
COFFIN 5.9 269
CREEKER 5.9 271
DANTE 5.9 271
DISCRETE START TO BLACK SUN 5.9 217
BLOODY ELBOWS 5.9 182
EAST OF WRATH 5.9 116
EL NACHO 5.9 131
EL SEGUNDO 5.9+ 88
EMPIRICAL ROUTE 5.9 229
EYES OF FALINA 5.9 116
FINGER FOOD 5.9 131
FOOTLOOSE 5.9 203
GILJE SOLO 5.9 284
KER-THUD 5.9 182
KOR-INGALLS 5.9 217
LK & KC 5.9 131
LOOMING 5.9 153
MANUS RIGHT 5.9 159
MINI ME 5.9 114
MOCHA CHOCOLATE YAYA 5.9 149
NORTH CHIMNEY (CASTLETON) 5.9 213
ONE HIT 5.9 243
PARLOR GAME 5.9 268
POPPED CHERRIES 5.9 165
PORK SODA 5.9 268
PRICKLY PEAR 5.9 153
PUTTERMAN'S BIG TOE 5.9 28
RADON DAUGHTERS 5.9 88
RIGHT SIDE IN 5.9 121
RING PIN BOULDER 5.9 120
SALAD DAYS 5.9 289
SHE-LA THE PEELER 5.9 127
STEGO SLAB 5.9 114
SUMMIT CHIMNEY 5.9 121
TOMATO BASIL APPETIZER 5.9 173
TOWN HOE 5.9 297
TWO BUCK CHUCK 5.9 156
TWO MINUTES FOR ROUGHING IT 5.9 244
UGLY BETTY 5.9 273
UNNAMED (DAY CANYON) 5.9 136
UNNAMED (WALL STREET) 5.9 121
WORKING CLASS HERO 5.9 136

5.10-
MIGHT AS WELL 5.10- 48
NIGHT LIGHT 5.10- 268
SEMI-SWEET 5.10- 174
TRICERATOPS RIGHT 5.10- 157
UNNAMED #2 (PINKY TOWER BUTTRESS) 5.10- 81

5.10A
FREEZER BURN 5.10A 268
MEN IN TIGHTS 5.10A 203
MIDSUMMER NIGHT'S SEAM 5.10A 202
NEW ROUTE (STIMULANTS WALL) 5.10A 265
TIME WILL TELL 5.10A 293

5.10B
ANOTHER ROADSIDE DISTRACTION 5.10B 115
BANANA PEEL 5.10B 126
BEGINNING 5.10B 153
BLACK SUN 5.10B 217
BONE DOCTOR 5.10B 289
CZECHOSLOVAKIAN VAG 5.10B 289
HOT CARL SUNDAY 5.10B 268
LACTO MANGULATION 5.10B 126
LITTLE TUFAS 5.10B 126
LIZARD'S HEX 5.10B 159
ON THE LAMB 5.10B 243
PAP SMEAR 5.10B 289
PINHEAD 5.10B 114
POUNDING THE FROG 5.10B 119
SCREWFACE 5.10B 294
SKY DOG 5.10B 293
TUNE IN 5.10B 120
UNNAMED SPORT 5.10B 284
WARM-UP RIGHT 5.10B 284

5.10
10 TO 8 5.10 293
A3B 5.10 48
ABRAXAS LEFT 5.10 262
ANDROIDS 5.10B/C 106
ALL ALONG THE PUTT TOWER 5.10 279
ANOTHER FINE DAY 5.10 138
ARC ANGEL 5.10 127
BABEL 5.10 203
BACHELOR CRACK 5.10 244
BEN'S CRACK 5.10 284
BIHEDRAL 5.10 138
BIONIC CHRONIC 5.10 242
BIRTH CANAL 5.10 176
BITTERSWEET 5.10 174
BOOGNISH TOWER 5.10 137
BRUSH-PAINTED DATSUN 5.10 137
BURN ONE DOWN 5.10 244
CHEF'S SPECIAL 5.10 173
CHERRY ON TOP 5.10B/C 266
CHIMNEY SWEEP 5.10 120
CHINESE EYES 5.10 95
DINNER MONDUE 5.10 290
DON JUAN 5.10 65
DON SMURFO 5.10 128
DOS MO-MOS 5.10 141
EL CRACKO DIABLO 5.10 111
ELECTRONIC BATTLESHIP 5.10 147
EWE WHAT 5.10 81
FISTFUL OF POTASH 5.10 114
FLAKES OF BONGO 5.10 128
FLYING THE 5.10 233
FOODBORNE ILLNESS 5.10 172
FOREPLAY FOR A SERPENT 5.10 159
FOR JOEY 5.10 164
FOUR GUITARS AND A PIANO 5.10 156
FOURTH OF JULY 5.10 138
FUGGIN FUN 5.10 293
GECKO 5.10 159
GRIMMIS 5.10 293
HAIL STONE 5.10 211
HAND CRACK 5.10 284
HANDY MAN SPLITS 5.10 138
HOT TODDY 5.10 161
HOT YOGA STEVE THE MOVIE 5.10 203
INCREDIBLY BRUSHED WALKING KANE 5.10 280
JAHMAN 5.10 236
JELLO AND TRAMPOLINES 5.10 284
JUG ROOF 5.10 120
JUNE'S BOX 5.10 136
JUNGLE CORNER 5.10 293
JUST ANOTHER PRETTY FACE 5.10 128
KIAH CRACK 5.10 244
KIND 5.10 264
KISTER TWISTER 5.10 244
KRACK PIPE 5.10 262
LICHEN THE EXAM 5.10 289
LONELY VIGIL 5.10 189
LUCY IN THE SKY WITH POTASH 5.10 121
LUNG 5.10 244
MAV 1 5.10 162
MERLIN 5.10 277
METASOMA 5.10 159
MEXICAN 5.10 284
MIGHTY RE-ARRANGER 5.10B/C 291
MOAB'S SUPER CRACK 5.10 33
MOON'S UNIT 5.10 242
NERDGATE 5.10 276
NERVOUS IN SUBURBIA 5.10 121
OFFWIDTHS ARE BEAUTIFUL 5.10 141
ONATOPP 5.10 167
PASTA WORLD 5.10 173
P.F.G. 5.10 290
PIGASUS 5.10 36
PLUMB AND PIT 5.10 173
POOR MOTA 5.10 80
PORK CHOPS AND KETCHUP 5.10 173
POTASH BONG HIT 5.10 124
PREMIER 5.10 79
PRIVATE MYSTERY 5.10 81
PROGRAM DIRECTOR 5.10 150
PUSSY GALORE 5.10 169
PUTTERMAN'S PINKIES 5.10 28

Index

REACH IN 5.10 173
RING SIZER 5.10 82
ROAD NOT TAKEN 5.10 39
ROSEMARY AND THYME 5.10 174
ROUGH START TO A GOOD DAY 5.10 139
ROUNDHEAD RUCKUS 5.10 131
ROUTE WITH A VIEW 5.10 80
SADDLE SORES 5.10 162
SHEEP IN WOLF'S CLOTHING 5.10 94
SHIPWRECKED 5.10 145
SMOKIN' DEAL 5.10 47
SOLAR FLARE 5.10 168
SPACE GHOST 5.10 268
STEALTH BELLY 5.10 158
STEEL YOUR FACE 5.10 128
SUGAR KANE 5.10 262
SUPER CHIMNEY 5.10 255
SUPER NATURAL 5.10 208
SWEET THING 5.10 294
TEXAS TWO STEP 5.10 162
T.L.R. 5.10 139
TOPROPE (ICP) 5.10 268
TRICERATOPS LEFT 5.10 157
TRUE GRIT 5.10 203
TWO SIDES OF PURPLE 5.10 114
TWO THUMBS UP 5.10 106
UNNAMED (ALCOVE LEFT) 5.10 80
UNNAMED CORNER (BUTTRESS 2) 5.10 169
UNNAMED (COVE) 5.10 35
UNNAMED (DEADMAN'S BUTTRESS) 5.10 148
UNNAMED (DOG WALL) 5.10 274
UNNAMED FLAKE (TOWN WALL) 5.10 298
UNNAMED (MAVERICK CENTER) 5.10 162
UNNAMED (MAVERICK LEFT) 5.10 162
UNNAMED RIGHT-FACING CORNER (TOWN WALL) 5.10 298
UNNAMED (SHADY CRAG) 5.10 164
UNNAMED SPLITTER WITH CORNER (TOWN WALL) 5.10 298
UNNAMED (TOWN WALL) 5.10 297
UP IN SMOKE 5.10 243
VISIBLE PANTY LINE 5.10 119
WALDEN'S ROOM 5.10 27
WALK ON THE WIDE SIDE 5.10 129
WITH A SOUTHWEST FLARE 5.10 173
YESTERDAY'S NEWS 5.10 65
ZIGZAG 5.10 118

5.10C

EARL GREY 5.10C 265
EAT THE RICH 5.10C 124
FIST A LIZARD 5.10B/C 159
FROGS OF A FEATHER 5.10C 118
HAND PRINTS 5.10C 290
HEART OF THE DESERT 5.10C 91
POCKET ROCKET 5.10C 136
RIGHT CHIMNEY 5.10C 89
STORY OF MY LIFE 5.10C 290
TAMING OF THE BOO 5.10C 202
TAX FREE 5.10C 106
WAKE OF THE FLOOD 5.10C 119

5.10D

FLOUR POWER 5.10C/D 266
GATE KEEPER 5.10D 291
HYDROPONIC 5.10D 291
KEY MASTER 5.10D 291
LAWN DART 5.10D 290
LIFE IS BANQUET 5.10D 202
PINCHED SACK 5.10D 292
STOLEN CHIMNEY 5.10D 248

WHAT'S IN A NAME 5.10D 202
ZOOL 5.10D 291

5.10+

ABRAXAS RIGHT 5.10+ 262
ADRENALINE CIRCUS 5.10+ 186
AFTER THE RAIN 5.10+ 28
ANDROIDS WAFFLE HOT LINE 5.10+ 137
APE INDEX 5.10+ 147
ARROWHEAD LEFT 5.10+ 217
BASS ACKWARDS 5.10+ 273
BEE LINE 5.10+ 136
BEER RUN 5.10+ 273
BENSON AND LEDGES 5.10+ 47
BIG SKY MUD FLAPS 5.10+ 129
BLACK AND STACKS 5.10+ 176
BROADS HATE PODS 5.10+ 145
CHASIN' SKIRT 5.10+ 150
CHICKEN LITTLE 5.10+ 242
CHOPPER 5.10+ 149
CLANTONS IN THE DUST 5.10+ 161
CONSTRICTOR 5.10+ 242
CRACK WHORES 5.10+ 229
DON IGUANA 5.10+ 158
DR. GOODHEAD 5.10+ 169
DRIVING WHILE ASIAN 5.10+ 260
DYNAMO HUM 5.10+ 242
ENERGY DECAY 5.10+ 178
EPITAPH 5.10+ 38
EYE OF THE NEWT 5.10+ 43
FIRE FOX 5.10+ 273
FREE WINDOW ROUTE 5.10+ 29
GRAND PLAN 5.10+ 76
GREAT AMERICAN SQUIGGLER 5.10+ 67
HAIL MARY 5.10+ 223
HALF PIPE 5.10+ 116
HALF SNAKE HALF CHICKEN 5.10+ 159
HOT CHICKS ON WET BIKES 5.10+ 293
IN SEARCH OF SUDS 5.10+ 69
JACOB'S LADDER 5.10+ 129
JAG 5.10+ 35
KID'S DAY OFF 5.10+ 153
KRACK KOKANE 5.10+ 262
KUNDA 5.10+ 174
LIZARD ACTION 5.10+ 65
LOVE AND A 45 5.10+ 298
MARCO MY WORD 5.10+ 49
MEDIEVAL 5.10+ 277
MEDIUM RARE 5.10+ A0 173
MICHELLE'S BITCHEN' BLUE SUBARU 5.10+ 137
MOAB FLU 5.10+ 244
MOONSHINE 5.10+ 137
MUTTON FOR PUNISHMENT 5.10+ 173
NECRO DANCER 5.10+ 148
NINA 5.10+ 147
PANDEMIC 5.10+ 267
PARANOID 5.10+ 244
PILLAR ROUTE 5.10+ 176
PLUMBER'S CRACK 5.10+ 273
POWDER MY LIZARD 5.10+ 159
RAIN CATCHER 5.10+ 111
RAMBLIN' MAN 5.10+ 297
RARE 5.10+ 173
ROUND TABLE 5.10+ 277
RP CITY 5.10+ 268
SCRIPTURES 5.10+ 230
SEOUL GAMES 5.10+ 48
SHADOW CHASER 5.10+ 49
SHADOW OF THE WIND 5.10+ 230
SHED YOUR SKIN 5.10+ 158
SIDE STREET 5.10+ 176
SINNERS & INFIDELS 5.10+ 229
SMASHED FRUIT 5.10+ 172
TEA PARTY 5.10+ 83
TEQUILA SUNRISE 5.10+ 161

TIL THE SUN GOES DOWN 5.10+/5.11- 293
TRAD BADGER 5.10+ 48
UNEMPLOYMENT LINE 5.10+ 110
UNNAMED #1 (PINKY TOWER BUTTRESS) 5.10+ 81
UNNAMED (BUTTRESS 3) 5.10+ 169
UNNAMED (CARNIVORE AREA) 5.10+ 167
UNNAMED (COOLER WALL) 5.10+ 172
UNNAMED (DOG WALL) 5.10+ 274
UNNAMED (MAVERICK LEFT) 5.10+ 162
UNNAMED RIGHT-FACING CORNER 5.10+ 297
UNNAMED (SCORCHED EARTH) 5.10+ 272
UNNAMED SPLITTER (REPTILIAN WALL RIGHT) 5.10+ 157
UNNAMED SPLITTER (TOWN WALL) 5.10+ 298
UNNAMED (WALL STREET) 5.10+ 118
VANILLA CREAM 5.10+ 268
VERTICAL FLU 5.10+ 157
WEST FACE 5.10+ 97
WHERE EGOS DARE 5.10+ 130
ZIPPY 5.10+ 47
HABANERO 5.10+ 174

5.11-

2 FRIENDS GETTING RED 5.11- 50
ARCHAIC REVIVAL 5.11- 264
BIG PUSSY IN DOGTOWN 5.11- 274
DEARLY DEPARTED 5.11- 229
FAT CRACK NAMED DESIRE 5.11- 210
GRAND BLAST 5.11- 74
HIDDEN DOOR 5.11- 159
KINDER AND GENTLER 5.11- 49
PEANUT DELIVERY 5.11- 166
PECCADILLO 5.11- 151
PUPPIES AND TAILS 5.11- 148
SHADOWFAX 5.11- 129
SPIRIT WORLD 5.11- 208

5.11A

ADRENALINE 5.11A 265
BE TRUE! 5.11A 202
CHRISCROSS 5.11A 128
FAITH FLAKE 5.11A 111
FIND SHADE 5.11A 223
HERBACEOUS 5.11A 292
HOLY SHIT 5.11A 229
MINISTRY 5.11A 223
NORTH FACE WEBSTER VARIATION 5.11A 214
SHOOT UP OR SHUT UP CORNER 5.11A 119
STARDUST COWBOY 5.11A 219
STATIC CLING 5.11A 124
TENDER TO THE TOUCH 5.11A 107
UNNAMED (BRUMLEY) 5.11A 284
UNNAMED CORNER 2 (BUTTRESS 2) 5.11A 169

5.11B

BLOWIN' CHUNKS 5.11B 121
BUMPING UGLIES 5.11B 284
BURN ANOTHER ONE DOWN 5.11B 244
BURNING INSIDE 5.11B 217
DARK PATH 5.11B 272
FIST TO CUFFS 5.11B 148
LAST TANGO IN POTASH 5.11B 114
LITTLE WHITE LIEBACK 5.11B 219
MANTEL FOR HERB 5.11B 292
NORTH FACE ORIGINAL START (CASTLETON) 5.11B 214
OFF TO SEE ALLAH 5.11B 229
OVERFLOW OF GOOD 5.11B 202

Appendices

SAND AND STEEL 5.11B 121
SEAM AS IT EVER WAS 5.11B 110
SHOOT OUT 5.11B 163
TRIPLE SHAFT DRIVEN 5.11B 167
TWITIN' SHINKIES 5.11B 121
UNNAMED (WALL STREET) 5.11B 111
VIVARIN 5.11B 265
YEYO 5.11B 291

5.11
100TH MONKEY 5.11 147
2012 5.11 163
ABOVE A FISTFUL 5.11 114
ALBATROSS 5.11 29
ANACONDA 5.11 158
APOLOGY 5.11 176
ASTROLAD 5.11 115
B4WARNED 5.11 48
BABY BLUE 5.11 123
BAKERY ROUTE 5.11 266
BEACH PARTY 5.11 36
BEAR BONES 5.11 153
BEEF TIPS 5.11 173
BE THERE OR BE TALKED ABOUT 5.11 C0 93
BFE 5.11 51
BOLTS TO BUMPY LAND 5.11 120
BUTT PYGMIES 5.11 145
CAPTAIN HOOK 5.11 156
CHAMELEON 5.11 157
CHARLIE HORSE NEEDLE 5.11 52
CHICKEN TEJERO 5.11 136
CLEARLIGHT 5.11 190
CRACK WARS 5.11 229
CYCLOPS 5.11 80
DAWN OF AN ERROR 5.11 148
DELIVERANCE 5.11 166
DESERT GLOW 5.11 106
DESTINATION 1 5.11 174
DIRECT START (WALDEN'S ROOM) 5.11 27
DOG DAYS 5.11 274
DOGMATIC 5.11 276
DONE LUBIN' 5.11 164
DOUBLE CRACKS 5.11 164
DRAGON'S LAIR 5.11 148
DRAG QUEEN 5.11 293
DRUGSTORE COWBOY 5.11 262
DR. YU 5.11 156
DUNN ROUTE 5.11 54
ENCORE 5.11 203
EXTRA LEAN 5.11 172
FADED MIDGET 5.11 157
FERNANDO 5.11 123
FINE JADE 5.11 221
FINGER BANG 5.11 164
FLASH FLOOD 5.11 119
FRENCH COOKING 5.11 173
FRICTION 5.11 36
FUCK IF I KNOW 5.11 48
GHOST DANCE 5.11 209
GLORY AND CONSEQUENCE 5.11 260
GUNSMOKE 5.11 161
HANG ON 5.11 153
HANG OVER 5.11 153
HAPPY FACE 5.11 67
HERBIVORE 5.11 167
HIGH NOON 5.11 161
HONEYMOON CHIMNEY 5.11 234
HYPERCRACK ON THE ANCHOR CHAIN 5.11 29
ICE CREAM PARLOR CRACK 5.11 269
INCREDIBLE POOH 5.11 176
IS THIS LOVE? 5.11 294
KING KRIMSON 5.11 211
KNIGHT MOVES 5.11 124
LEANIE MEANIE OF THE DESERT 5.11 35
LEAN LIZARD 5.11 159
LIZARD LUST 5.11 158
MINI SKIRTS & HALTER TOPS 5.11 164
MONSTER 5.11 151
MOTHER SHIP 5.11 156
NEANDERTHAL 5.11 153
NO BOUNDARIES 5.11 62
NO MORE TROUBLE 5.11 294
NO NAME (WALL STREET) 5.11 121
NORTH FACE 5.11 69
NORTH-NORTHEAST ARÊTE 5.11 92
ON WITH THE SHOW 5.11 211
ROOM WITH A VIEW 5.11 293
5.11 124
POTASH SANCTION 5.11 114
POUNDING THE FROG DIRECT 5.11 119
PROSTATE EXAM 5.11 289
PULP FRICTION 5.11 269
PUSS IN BOOTS 5.11 106
QUICKDRAW 5.11 163
AT 5.11 114
RATTLER 5.11 267
REIGN OF TERROR 5.11 279
ROUND-ABOUT 5.11 29
ROUND UP 5.11 162
SATAN'S SLAVE 5.11 230
SAVIOR FREE VARIATION 5.11 237
SCRATCH AND SNIFF 5.11 110
SEVENTH SERPENT 5.11 159
SHAKE AND BAKE 5.11 36
SHOOT UP OR SHUT UP 5.11 119
SHOWDOWN 5.11 163
SIDE SHOW 5.11 203
SIDEWINDER 5.11 159
SLAP CHOP 5.11 106
SLY DOG 5.11 276
SMELL OF DEAD EURO-PEONS 5.11 120
SMOKE-FILLED ROOMS 5.11 111
SNAKES AND SNAILS 5.11 148
SOUTHEAST FACE 5.11 131
SPELUNKING SPANKY 5.11 173
SPICY MEATBALL 5.11 151
SPLIT PERSONALITY 5.11 272
STANDING ROCK 5.11 71
STASH, THE 5.11 244
STICK TO THE MISSION 5.11 140
SUNDAWG 5.11 169
SUPER NINJA CHIPMUNK 5.11 48
THREE SHEEPS TO THE WIND 5.11 124
TIRED OF TALUS 5.11 124
TITANIC CORNER 5.11 61
TOASTED SEEDS 5.11 174
TRAGEDY OF THE COMMONS 5.11 A1 27
TURN YOUR HEAD AND COUGH 5.11 289
TWICE BAKED 5.11 172
UNCERTAINTY PRINCIPLE 5.11 178
UNDERWORLD 5.11 219
UNEMPLOYMENT LINE 5.11 66
UNNAMED #1 (HIDEOUT) 5.11 243
UNNAMED #2 (HIDEOUT) 5.11 243
UNNAMED (ALCOVE RIGHT) 5.11 79
UNNAMED (BUTTRESS 1) 5.11 167
UNNAMED CORNER (BLOCK TOWER AREA) 5.11 131
UNNAMED (DEADMAN'S BUTTRESS) 5.11 148, 150
UNNAMED (MAVERICK CENTER) 5.11 162
UNNAMED (MAVERICK LEFT) 5.11 163
UNNAMED OFFSET (TOWN WALL) 5.11 298
UNNAMED (RAPTOR TOWER) 5.11 138
UNNAMED (SHADY CRAG) 5.11 164
UNNAMED (TOWN WALL) 5.11 298
UNNAMED (WALL STREET) 5.11 114
WALDEN'S ROOM DIRECT START 5.11 27
WARM-UP LEFT 5.11 284
WARSTEINER 5.11 111
WEAPONS GRADE 5.11 83
WEST FACE 5.11 93
WEST FACE (CASTLETON) 5.11 216
WHERE HAVE ALL THE WILD THINGS GONE 5.11 232
WHITE WAY 5.11 129
WHY DOES IT HURT WHEN I PEE 5.11 156
WINGS OF LEATHER 5.11 44

5.11C
BAD HABIT 5.11C 233
FLAPPER 5.11C 107
FREE BEER 5.11C 106
GOOD, THE BAD, THE POTASH 5.11B/C 124
GUINEVERE 5.11C 277
HOLIER THAN THOU 5.11C 233
MOTHER TRUCKER 5.11C 116
PROTEST TOO MUCH 5.11C 202
SEQUENTIAL LINE 5.11C 290
SNATCH 5.11C 284
TIME LINE 5.11C 290
UNFORGIVEN 5.11C 233
WEST FACE 5.11C 92

5.11D
EXODUS 5.11D 294
DEAD RINGER 5.11D 149
HUBBLE 5.11D 106
KNAPPING WITH THE ALIEN 5.11C/D 116
SPRING FLING 5.11D 151
SUNKIST 5.11D 107
UNNAMED (TRENCHTOWN) 5.11C/D 293
UNNAMED ROUTE (WALL STREET) 5.11D 121
PLANET CARAVAN 5.11D 82

5.11+
BIRTH CANAL 5.11+ 84
BOY HOWDY 5.11+ 273
CIRCLE OF QUIET 5.11+ 49
COUP D'ETAT 5.11+ 111
COYOTE CALLING 5.11+ 230
DOLOFRIGHT 5.11+ 190
EL CRACKO DIABLO DIRECT 5.11+ 111
FACE IT 5.11+ 263
FLAKES OF WRATH DIRECT 5.11+ 116
FULL SPECTRUM 5.11+ 115
GIN AND TECTONICS 5.11+ 151
GRAVE 5.11+ 265
HAND DELIVERY 5.11+ 166
HIGH OVER DATURA 5.11+ 119
HOLLOW POINT 5.11+ 219
HOT LIPS 5.11+ 151
I LOVE LOOSEY 5.11+ 123
INDUSTRIAL DISEASE 5.11+ 97
JOCK STRAPS AND BANANA HAMMOCKS 5.11+ 164
LINUS'S CORNER 5.11+ 259
MAIN STREET 5.11+ 176
MAYOR 5.11+ 176
MIDNIGHT RIDER 5.11+ 41
MIRAGE CRACK 5.11+ 39
MISS KITTY LIKES IT RAW 5.11+ 161
MISS KITTY LIKES IT THAT WAY 5.11+ 161
MR. SOMBRERO 5.11+ 95

Index 317

DESP-ARÊTE 5.12B 123
DESTINATION 1 5.11 174
DESTINATION 2 174
DESTINATION CRAG 174
DEVIL DOG SPIRE 97
DEVILS GOLF BALL A0 278
DINNER MONDUE 5.10 290
DIRECT START (WALDEN'S ROOM) 5.11 27
DISAPPEARING ANGEL 299
DISCRETE START TO BLACK SUN 5.9R 217
DOG DAYS 5.11 274
DOGMATIC 5.11 276
DOG ON A STONE ROOF 5.12 290
DOG WALL 274
DOLOFRIGHT 5.11+ R 190
DOLOMITE TOWER 190
DONE LUBIN' 5.11 164
DON IGUANA 5.10+ 158
DON JUAN 5.10R 65
DON JUAN SPIRE 65
DON SMURFO 5.10 128
DOPE 5.10A 292
DOS MO-MOS 5.10 141
DOUBLE CRACKS 5.11 164
DOUBLE CRIMP V4 199
DRAGON'S BREATH 5.12 134
DRAGON'S LAIR 5.11 148
DRAG QUEEN 5.11 293
DR. GOODHEAD 5.10+ 169
DRIVING WHILE ASIAN 5.10+ 260
DR. NO 5.9 A0 168
DRUGSTORE COWBOY 5.11 262
DR. YU 5.11 156
DUBINKY WELL AREA 37
DUDE, THAT'S NOT FUNNY 5.12B 44
DUNN ROUTE 5.11 54
DYNAMO HUM 5.10+ 242

E

EARL GREY 5.10C 265
EAST DIHEDRAL AKA BLOODY ELBOWS 5.9 182
EAST OF WRATH 5.9 116
EAT THE RICH 5.10C 124
ECHO TOWER 252
ECHO TOWER 29
EL CAHONE 5.12D 284
EL CRACKO DIABLO 5.10 111
EL CRACKO DIABLO DIRECT 5.11+ 111
EL CUCHILLO 5.12D 284
EL SEGUNDO 5.9+ 88
ELECTRONIC BATTLESHIP 5.10 147
EL NACHO 5.9 131
ELVIS MEMORIAL 5.12 35
EMPIRICAL ROUTE 5.9 229
ENCORE 5.11 203
END OF STORY 5.12 223
ENERGY DECAY 5.10+ 178
ENTRY FEE ROUTE 5.8 247
EPITAPH 5.10+ 38
EPITAPH 5.13R 259
EVE AKA DEVIL'S GOLF BALL 5.10 C1 OR 5.12 96
EVISCERATE 5.12A 107
EWE WHAT 5.10 81
EXAM WALL 289
EXCOMMUNICATION 5.13 235
EXODUS 5.11D 294
EXTENDED CARE 5.13A 107
EXTRA LEAN 5.11 172
EYE OF THE NEWT 5.10+ 43
EYES OF FALINA 5.9 116

F

FACE IT 5.11+ 263
FADED MIDGET 5.11 157
FAITH FLAKE 5.11A 111
FAMILY PLOT 5.9 C1 38
FARM 5.11 260
FAT CRACK NAMED DESIRE 5.11- 210
FELIX DREAM 5.12+? 167
FERNANDO 5.11 123
FESTUS 5.12 162
FIGHT CLUB 5.12C 284
FIND SHADE 5.11A 223
FINE JADE 5.11 221
FINGER BANDIT 5.12 137
FINGER BANG 5.11 164
FINGER FOOD 5.9 131
FINGER OF FATE 5.12C OR 5.9 C2+ 250
FIRE FOX 5.10+ 273
FIRST SWITCHBACK 156
FISHER TOWERS 245
FIST A LIZARD 5.10B/C 159
FISTFUL OF POTASH 5.10 114
FIST TO CUFFS 5.11B 148
FIVE FINGER DISCOUNT V9 196
FLAKES OF BONGO 5.10 128
FLAKES OF WRATH 5.9+ 116
FLAKES OF WRATH DIRECT 5.11+ 116
FLAPPER 5.11C 107
FLASH FLOOD 5.11 119
FLAT TOP BOULDER (#9) 198
FLOUR 5.12 266
FLOUR POWER 5.10C/D 266
FLYING GUILLOTINE V8 134
FLYING, THE 5.10 233
FOODBORNE ILLNESS 5.10 172
FOOTLOOSE 5.9 203
FOREPLAY FOR A SERPENT 5.10 159
FOR JOEY 5.10 164
FORMING ARCH AREA 153
FOUR GUITARS AND A PIANO 5.10 156
FOURTH OF JULY 5.10 138
FREE BEER 5.11C 106
FREE WINDOW ROUTE 5.10+ 29
FREEZER BURN 5.10A 268
FRENCH COOKING 5.11 173
FRICTION 5.11 36
FROGS OF A FEATHER 5.10C 118
FUCK IF I KNOW 5.11 48
FUGGIN FUN 5.10 293
FULL SPECTRUM 5.11+ 121
FUNNEL CAKE 5.8 148

G

GANJA WALL 291
GARDEN OF EDEN 96
GATE KEEPER 5.10D 291
GECKO 5.10 159
GENERATIONS 5.8 290
GET OVER IT 5.12,C1 149
GET UP, STAND UP 5.10 293
GHOST BUSTER CRAG 291
GHOST DANCE 5.11 209
GILJE SOLO 5.9 284
GIN AND TECTONICS 5.11+ 151
GIN AND TECTONICS AREA 151
GLAD TO BE TRAD 5.12 19
GLORY AND CONSEQUENCE 5.11 260
GOING TO HOLLYWOOD 5.13- 298
GOLD BAR TOWER 134
GOLD BAR TOWER AREA 134
GONG SHOW 5.8 273
GOOD DAY TO DIE 5.9+ 269
GOOD, THE BAD, THE POTASH 5.11B/C 124
GOOD TIMES 5.7 289

GOOD TIMES WALL 289
GOONEY BIRD 83
GOOSE ISLAND AREA 182
GRAMA & THE GREEN SUEDE SHOES 5.7 126
GRAND BLAST 5.11- 74
GRAND PLAN 5.10+ 76
GRAVE 5.11+ 265
GRAVE CLIFF 265
GREAT AMERICAN SQUIGGLER 5.10+ 67
GREAT WALL 95
GRIMMIS 5.10 293
GRIM REACHER V5 198
GUAVA JELLY 5.9+ 294
GUINEVERE 5.11C 277
GUMBY GULLY 5.4 124
GUNSMOKE 5.11 161

H

HABANERO 10+ 174
HAIL MARY 5.10+ 223
HAIL STONE 5.10 211
HALF PIPE 5.10+ 116
HALF SNAKE, HALF CHICKEN 5.10+ 159
HALLOW SOULS 5.9+ 270
HAND CRACK 5.10 284
HAND DELIVERY 5.11+ 166
HAND DELIVERY AREA 166
HAND PRINTS 5.10C 290
HANDY MAN SPLITS 5.10 138
HANG ON 5.11 153
HANG OVER 5.11 153
HAPPY ENDING 5.12 210
HAPPY FACE 5.11 67
HAPPY HUNTING GROUND 5.12- 171
HAPPY TURK 278
HAPPY TURK A0 278
HEADSTACK 5.12 151
HEART OF THE DESERT 5.10C 91
HEISENBERG TOWER 178
HELL BELLY V11 197
HELL ROARING CANYON 40
HERBACEOUS 5.11A 292
HERBIVORE 5.11 167
HIDDEN DOOR 5.11- 159
HIDDEN GEM 5.13 298
HIDDEN MESSAGE 5.5 127
HIDEOUT WALL 241
HIGH BALLS BOULDER (#4) 196
HIGH BALLS V7 196
HIGH DESERT DRIFTER 5.8 120
HIGH NOON 5.11 161
HIGH OVER DATURA 5.11+ 119
HIGHWAY 191 NORTH 25
HINDU 240
HOE DOWN 5.12 161
HOLIER THAN THOU 5.11C 233
HOLLOW POINT 5.11+ 219
HOLY MOLEY 5.5 127
HOLY SHIT 5.11A 229
HONEYMOON CHIMNEY 5.11 234
HORIZONTAL MAMBO 5.12D 116
HOT CARL SUNDAY 5.10B 268
HOT CHICKS ON WET BIKES 5.10+ 293
HOT LIPS 5.11+ 151
HOT TODDY 5.10 161
HOT YOGA STEVE, THE MOVIE 5.10 203
HOUSE OF PUTTERMAN FORMATION 27
HUBBLE 5.11D 106
HUECO FINISH V1 199
HUECO TRAVERSE BOULDER (#10) 199
HYDROPONIC 5.10D 291
HYPERCRACK ON THE ANCHOR CHAIN 5.11 29

Appendices

I
ICE CREAM PARLOR CRACK 5.11 269
ICE CREAM PARLOR CRAG 267
I LOVE LOOSEY 5.11+ 123
IMPASSE 5.12+ 129
INCREDIBLE POOH 5.11 176
INCREDIBLY BRUSHED WALKING KANE 5.10 280
INDUSTRIAL DISEASE 5.11+ 97
INFRARED 5.12 190
IN SEARCH OF SUDS 5.10+ 69
IRON MAIDEN 5.12 189
ISLAND IN THE SKY 74
IS THIS LOVE? 5.11 294
IVORY TOWER 5.13B 220

J
JACOB'S LADDER 5.10+ 129
JAG 5.10+ 35
JAH MAN 5.10 236
JAMMING 5.8 294
JAWS 5.11 169
JELLO AND TRAMPOLINES 5.10 284
JESUS SAVES 5.12A 224
JINGUS LAUNCH 5.12R/X 121
JINX 5.12- 169
JOCK STRAPS AND BANANA HAMMOCKS 5.11+ 164
JUG ROOF 5.10 120
JUNE'S BOX 5.10 136
JUNGLE CORNER 5.10 293
JUNK IN THE TRUNK 5.12 111
JUST ANOTHER PRETTY FACE 5.10 128
JUST WHISTLING DIXIE 5.11 168

K
KANE CREEK 253
KENTUCKY BROWN WATER A2 136
KER-THUD 5.9 182
KEY MASTER 5.10D 291
KIAH CRACK 5.10 244
KID'S DAY OFF 5.10+ 153
KINDER AND GENTLER 5.11- 49
KIND 5.10 264
KING FISHER 249
KING KRIMSON 5.11 211
KIOSK AREA 260
KISS OF THE SPIDER WOMEN 5.12 136
KISTER TWISTER 5.10 244
KITCHEN WALL 173
KNAPPING WITH THE ALIEN 5.11C/D 116
KNEE GRINDER 5.9+ 269
KNIGHT MOVES 5.11 124
KOR-INGALLS 5.9 217
KOR ROUTE 5.6 36
KRACK KOKANE 5.10+ 262
KRACK PIPE 5.10 262
KUNDA 5.10+ 174
KURA BURAN 5.12 267

L
LACTO MANGULATION 5.10B 126
LAMB 94
LA SAL MOUNTAINS 281
LASER CRACK 5.11 C1 61
LAST TANGO IN POTASH 5.11B 114
LAWN DART 5.10D 290
LEANIE MEANIE OF THE DESERT 5.11 35
LEAN LIZARD 5.11 159
LICHEN THE EXAM 5.10 289
LIFE IS BANQUET 5.10D 202
LIGHTHOUSE, DOLOMITE, AND BIG BEND BUTTE AREA 187
LIGHT HOUSE TOWER 189
LINUS'S CORNER 5.11+ 259
LITTLE BIG MAN 5.12 48

LITTLE TUFAS 5.10B 126
LITTLE VALLEY 77
LITTLE WHITE LIEBACK 5.11B 219
LIZARD ACTION 5.10+ 65
LIZARD LUST 5.11 158
LIZARD ROCK 247
LIZARD'S HEX 5.10B 159
LK & KC 5.9 131
LONELY VIGIL 5.10 189
LONGBOW CHIMNEY 5.8 C1 207
LONG CANYON 143
LONG CANYON LEFT SIDE 164
LONG CANYON RIGHT SIDE 145
LONG CANYON TO THE POTASH PLANT 176
LOOKING GLASS ROCK 301
LOOMING 5.9 153
LOST WORLD BUTTE 38
LOVE AND A 45 5.10+ 298
LOVERIDGE 5.12 C2 130
LOWER BRUMLEY CRAG 283
LUCY IN THE SKY WITH POTASH 5.10 121
LUMINOUS BEING SPIRE 65
LUNG 5.10 244

M
MADE IN THE SHADE 5.12 167
MAIN STREET 5.11+ 176
MAN AFTER MIDNIGHT 5.12- 123
MANTEL FOR HERB 5.11B 292
MANUS LEFT 5.8 159
MANUS RIGHT 5.9 159
MARCO MY WORD 5.10+ 49
MARLBORO CIG 5.9+ 47
MARS 106
MAV 1 5.10 162
MAVERICK 5.9 C2 OR 5.13A 240
MAVERICK BUTTRESS 161
MAVERICK CENTER 161
MAVERICK LEFT 162
MAVERICK RIGHT 163
MAY FLY 5.12 242
MAYOR 5.11+ 176
MEDIEVAL 5.10+ 277
MEDIUM RARE 5.10+,A0 173
MEN IN TIGHTS 5.10A 203
MERLIN 5.10 277
MERRIMAC 29
METASOMA 5.10 159
MEXICAN 5.10 284
MICHELLE'S BITCHEN' BLUE SUBARU 5.10+ 137
MIDNIGHT FRIGHTENING 5.12B 111
MIDNIGHT RIDER 5.11+ R 41
MIDSUMMER NIGHT'S SEAM 5.10A 202
MIGHT AS WELL 5.10- 48
MIGHTY RE-ARRANGER 291
MIGHTY RE-ARRANGER 5.10B/C 291
MINI ME 5.9 114
MINI SKIRTS & HALTER TOPS 5.11 164
MINISTRY 5.11A 223
MIRAGE CRACK 5.11+ 39
MISSION TOWER 140
MISSISSIPPI HIGH STEP 5.12- 116
MISS KITTY LIKES IT RAW 5.11+ 161
MISS KITTY LIKES IT THAT WAY 5.11+ 161
MOAB FLU 5.10+ 244
MOAB RIM TOWER 255
MOAB'S SUPER CRACK 5.10 33
MOCHA CHOCOLATE YAYA 5.9 149
MONITOR 29
MONSTER 5.11 151
MONSTER TOWER 69
MOONSHINE 5.10+ 137

MOON'S UNIT 5.10 242
MOSES 54
MOTHER SHIP 5.11 156
MOTHER TRUCKER 5.11C 116
MR. SOMBRERO 5.11+ 95
MUSTANG MAN 5.11+ 162
MUTTON FOR PUNISHMENT 5.10+ 173

N
NAKED RUNNING "DO ME" MAN 5.11+ 273
NAVAJO WARRIOR 5.11+ 262
NAZI TRAVERSE A.K.A. SHOT HOLE TRAVERSE V7 198
NEANDERTHAL 5.11 153
NECRO DANCER 5.10+ 148
NEIGHBOR OF PUTTERMAN 28
NEOPOLITAN 5.7 127
NERDGATE 5.10 276
NERVE NET 5.12B 108
NERVOUS IN SUBURBIA 5.10 121
NEW ROUTE (STIMULANTS WALL) 5.10A 265
NIGHT LIGHT 5.10- 268
NIGHT VISION 5.11+ 145
NINA 5.10+ 147
NINJA TRAINING CENTER 134
NO BOUNDARIES 5.11 62
NO BOUNDARIES WALL 62, 64
NO FLY ZONE 5.12C 114
NO MORE TROUBLE 5.11 294
NO NAME (WALL STREET) 5.11 121
NORTH CHIMNEY 5.9 213
NORTH DAKOTA CRAGS 287
NORTH FACE 5.11 69
NORTH FACE ORIGINAL START (CASTLETON) 5.11B 214
NORTH FACE WEBSTER VARIATION 5.11A 214
NORTH-NORTHEAST ARÊTE 5.11 92
NOTHING CIRCUMSTANTIAL 5.12B 294
NOT RP CITY 5.9+ 268
NUNS 232

O
OCTOPUSSY 5.12- 169
OFF TO SEE ALLAH 5.11B 229
OFFWIDTH CITY 176
OFFWIDTHS ARE BEAUTIFUL 5.10 141
O'GRADY 5.12+ 187
ONATOPP 5.10 167
ONE EYED WILLY 5.7 203
ONE HIT 5.9 243
ONION CREEK 239
ON THE LAMB 5.10B 243
ON WITH THE SHOW 5.11 211
ORANGE PEEL BOULDER (#13) 200
ORIGINAL BJØRNSTAD ROUTE 5.8 A0 299
OUT DAMNED SPOT! 5.12B 202
OUTLYING ARCHES CLIMBS 88
OVERFLOW OF GOOD 5.11B 202
OWL ROCK 5.8 96
OXYGEN DEBT 5.11+ 182

P
PABST BLUE RIBBON 5.8 243
PALE FIRE 5.12C 54
PANDEMIC 5.10+ 267
PANTRY 173
PAP SMEAR 5.10B 289
PARANOID 5.10+ 244
PARK AVENUE 91
PARLOR GAME 5.9 268
PARRIOTT MESA 207
PARRIOTT NE FACE 207
PASTA WORLD 5.10 173

Index

PEANUT DELIVERY 5.11- 166
PEARLY GATES 5.5 A0 39
PECCADILLO 5.11- 151
PENITENT 5.11 A1 229
PENSIVE PUTTERMAN 279
PERVERSE TRAVERSE 5.11 124
P.F.G. 5.10 290
PHANTOM FIGHTER V11 198
PHANTOM SPRINT 5.9 C3 OR 5.12B 252
PHYSICS DEPARTMENT 178
PICKLE 89
PICKLE 5.7 A0 89
PIGASUS 5.10 36
PILLAR ROUTE 5.10+ 176
PINCHED SACK 5.10D 292
PINHEAD 5.10B 114
PINKY TOWER BUTTRESS 81
PLANET CARAVAN 5.11D 82
PLUMB AND PIT 5.10 173
PLUMBER'S CRACK 5.10+ 273
PLUNGE 5.12 29
POCKET ROCKET 5.10C 136
POCKMARKS 5.12A 107
PODUNK MESA TOWER 186
POOR MOTA 5.10 80
POPPED CHERRIES 5.9 165
PORK CHOPS AND KETCHUP 5.10 173
PORK SODA 5.9 268
POSSESSED 5.11+ 269
POTASH BONG HIT 5.10 124
POTASH ROAD 101
POTASH SANCTION 5.11 114
POTSTASH 5.9+ 129
POUNDING THE FROG 5.10B 119
POUNDING THE FROG DIRECT 5.11 119
POWDER MY LIZARD 5.10+ 159
PRACTICAL RELIGION 5.5 127
PREDATOR TOWER 279
PREMIER 5.10 79
PRICKLY PEAR 5.9 153
PRIEST 234
PRIMROSE DIHEDRALS 5.11+ 56
PRIVATE MYSTERY 5.10 81
PROGRAM DIRECTOR 5.10 150
PROHIBITION CRACK 5.11+ 137
PROSTATE EXAM 5.11 289
PROTEST TOO MUCH 5.11C 202
PROUDEST MONKEY 5.12 147
PULP FRICTION 5.11 269
PUNISHER V2 199
PUPPIES AND TAILS 5.11- 148
PUPPY LOVE 5.9X 128
PUSS IN BOOTS 5.11 106
PUSSY GALORE 5.10 169
PUTTERMAN'S BIG TOE 5.9 28
PUTTERMANS PINKIES 28

Q
QUANTUM OF SOLACE 5.12- 169
QUICKDRAW 5.11 163

R
RADIOACTIVE PORKSICKLE 5.13 178
RADON DAUGHTERS 5.9 88
RAIN CATCHER 5.10+ 111
RALPH 5.12 178
RALPH THE RAT 5.11 114
RAMBLIN' MAN 5.10+ 297
RAPTOR TOWER 137
RARE 5.10+ 173
RATTLER 5.11 267
RAVENS DELIGHT 5.9+ 100
RAWHIDE 5.11+ 161
REACH IN 5.10 173
RECTORY 221
REIGN OF DUST 5.11+ 279

REIGN OF TERROR 5.11 279
REPTILIAN WALL LEFT 159
REPTILIAN WALL RIGHT 157
REPTILIAN WALLS 157
REQUIEM 5.12+ A0 255
RETURN OF THE JEDI V10 196
RIGHT CHIMNEY 5.10C 89
RIGHT SIDE IN 5.9 121
RIM DESCENT WALL 61
RING PIN BOULDER 5.9 120
RING SIZER 5.10 82
RIVER ROAD 179
RIVER ROAD DIHEDRALS 182
ROAD NOT TAKEN 5.10 39
ROADSIDE CRAG 33
ROADSIDE SELECT-DAY CANYON TO LONG CANYON 141
ROOFUS 5.12A/B 293
ROOK WITH A VIEW 5.11 293
ROOM WITH A VIEW 5.11+ 116
ROOT CANAL 5.8 182
ROSEMARY AND THYME 5.10 174
ROUGH START TO A GOOD DAY 5.10 139
ROUND-ABOUT 5.11 29
ROUNDHEAD RUCKUS 5.10 131
ROUND TABLE 5.10+ 277
ROUND UP 5.11 162
ROUTE WITH A VIEW 5.10 80
RP CITY 5.10+ 268
RUDE OLD MEN 5.12 110
RUMSFELD'S HEAD 297

S
SACRED GROUND 5.12B 214
SADDLE SORES 5.10 162
SALAD DAYS 5.9 289
SAND AND STEEL 5.11B 121
SATAN'S REVENGE 5.12 299
SATAN'S SLAVE 5.11 230
SAVIOR FREE VARIATION 5.11 237
SAY YOUR PRAYERS 5.13? 141
SCAR 107
SCHOOL MASTER 5.11+ 154
SCHOOL ROOM 1 5.4-5.8 114
SCOOPULA BOULDER (#5) 197
SCORCHED EARTH 271
SCRATCH AND SNIFF 5.11 110
SCREWFACE 5.10B 294
SCRIPTURES 5.10+ 230
SEAM AS IT EVER WAS 5.11B 110
SEIBERNETICS 5.8 110
SEMI-SWEET 5.10- 174
SENTENCE TO BURN 5.12D 284
SEOUL GAMES 5.10+ 48
SEQUENTIAL LINE 5.11C 290
SEVENTH SERPENT 5.11 159
SEVENTH SERPENT EXTENSION 5.12- 159
SHADOW CHASER 5.10+ 49
SHADOWFAX 5.11- 129
SHADOW OF THE WIND 5.10+ 230
SHADY CRAG 164
SHAKE AND BAKE 5.11 36
SHAKEN, NOT STIRRED 5.10 167
SHAOLIN FINGER JAB V7 134
SHED YOUR SKIN 5.10+ 158
SHEEP IN WOLF'S CLOTHING 5.10 94
SHF-I A THE PEELER 5.9 127
SHIPWRECKED 5.10 145
SHIPYARD 145
SHIPYARD LEFT SIDE 147
SHIPYARD RIGHT SIDE 145
SHIT EATIN' GRIN 5.12 150
SHIVA 5.12A 240
SHOGUN 5.13 263

SHOOT OUT 5.11B 163
SHOOT UP OR SHUT UP 5.11 119
SHOOT UP OR SHUT UP CORNER 5.11A 119
SHORT CRACK 5.11+ 163
SHOWDOWN 5.11 163
SIDE SHOW 5.11 203
SIDE STREET 5.10+ 176
SIDEWINDER 5.11 159
SINNERS & INFIDELS 5.10+ 229
SISTER SUPERIOR 236
SISYPHUS 5.11+ R 59
SKELETONIC 5.11+ 124
SKIN AMBIVALENCE 5.12- 210
SKINLESS DYNO V10 199
SKINWALKER 5.11+ 141
SKY DOG 5.10B 293
SLAB 5.8 124
SLAB ROUTE 5.7 127
SLAP CHOP 5.11 106
SLY DOG 5.11 276
SMASHED FRUIT 5.10+ 172
SMELL OF DEAD EURO-PEONS 5.11 120
SMOKE-FILLED ROOMS 5.11 111
SMOKE ON THE WATER 5.12+ 116
SMOKIN' DEAL 5.10 47
SNAKES AND SNAILS 5.11 148
SNATCH 5.11C 284
SOLAR FLARE 5.10 168
SOMETHING NASTY 5.12 123
SOUTHEAST FACE 5.11 131
SPACE GHOST 5.10 268
SPACE TOWER 270
SPELUNKING SPANKY 5.11 173
SPICY MEATBALL 5.11 151
SPIRIT WORLD 5.11- 208
SPLIFF SPIRE 5.5 C2 242
SPLIT PERSONALITY 5.11 272
SPRING FLING 5.11D 151
SPUR OF THE MOMENT TOWER 130
STANDING ROCK 71
STANDING ROCK 5.11 71
STAPH 5.12C/D 107
STARDUST COWBOY 5.11A 219
STASH, THE 5.11 244
STATIC CLING 5.11A 124
STEALTH BELLY 5.10 158
STEEL YOUR FACE 5.10 128
STEGO SLAB 5.9 114
STEWING OVER ART 5.12- 147
STICK TO THE MISSION 5.11 140
STILETTO 5.11+ 272
STIMULANTS WALL 265
STINGRAY 5.11+ 153
STOLEN CHIMNEY 5.10D 248
STORY OF MY LIFE 5.10C 290
STRONG MOONS 5.12 178
SUB LUX 5.12B 107
SUGAR KANE 5.10 262
SUMMIT CHIMNEY 5.9 121
SUNDAWG 5.11 169
SUNDEVIL CHIMNEY 5.9 R, A3 OR 5.13B 251
SUNKIST 5.11D 107
SUNSET TOWER 5.8 C3 OR 5.13 33
SUPER CHIMNEY 5.10 PG13 255
SUPER CHIMNEY AREA 255
SUPER NATURAL 5.10 208
SUPER NINJA CHIPMUNK 5.11 48
SURFACE TENSION 5.11+ 259
SWEET CHEEBA 5.7 292
SWEET THING 5.10 294

T
TAKE A CHANCE ON ME 5.12B 116
TAMING OF THE BOO 5.10C 202

Appendices

TANK BRAIN 5.12 148
TAX FREE 5.10C 106
TAYLOR CANYON 54
TEA PARTY 5.10+ 83
TENDER TO THE TOUCH 5.11A 107
TEQUILA SUNRISE 5.10+ 161
TEXAS TWO STEP 5.10 162
THEATRE 202
THE BIG HORNED BEAVER V10 200
THINK YA SHOULD 5.11+ 61
THREE GOSSIPS 93
THREE PENGUINS 89
THREE SHEEPS TO THE WIND 5.11 124
TIGER'S TALE 5.10 C2 297
TIL THE SUN GOES DOWN 5.10+/5.11- 293
TIME LINE 5.11C 290
TIMES WALL 290
TIME WILL TELL 5.10A 293
TIRED OF TALUS 5.11 124
TITANIC CORNER 5.11 61
T.L.R. 5.10 139
TOASTED SEEDS 5.11 174
TO BOO, OR NOT TO BOO 5.10A 202
TOMATO BASIL APPETIZER 5.9 173
TOMBSTONE 38
TOMBSTONES 257
TOP 40 5.8 124
TOPROPE (ICP) 5.10 268
TORPEDO BAY 5.12 147
TOUCHÉ 5.11+ 273
TOWER OF BABEL 94
TOWN FULL OF FINGERS 5.12 298
TOWN HOE 5.9 297
TOWN WALL 296
TRAD BADGER 5.10+ 48
TRAD WALL 47
TRAGEDY OF COMMONS 5.11, A1 27
TRAIL BOULDER (#6) 197
TRAIL OF THE NAVAJO 5.11+ 98
T-REX 5.12 269
TRICERATOPS LEFT 5.10 157
TRICERATOPS MIDDLE 5.12- 157
TRICERATOPS RIGHT 5.10- 157
TRIPLE BUTTRESS AREA 167
TRIPLE SHAFT DRIVEN 5.11B 167
TRUE GRIT 5.10 203
TR (WINDY RIDGE) 5.12B 273
TUNE IN 5.10B 120
TURN YOUR HEAD AND COUGH 5.11 289
TUSHER WASH AREA 27
TWICE BAKED 5.11 172
TWITIN' SHINKIES 5.11B 121
TWO BUCK CHUCK 5.9 156
TWO HEATHENS & THE PROPHET 5.12 150
TWO MINUTES FOR ROUGHING IT 5.9 244
TWO PLUMB 5.11+ 153
TWO SCORPION TELSONS 5.12- 159
TWO SIDES OF PURPLE 5.10 114
TWO THUMBS UP 5.10 106

U

UGLY BETTY 5.9 273
UNCERTAINTY PRINCIPLE 5.11 178
UNDER THE BOARDWALK 5.12B/C 121
UNDERWORLD 5.11 219
UNEMPLOYMENT LINE 5.10+ 110
UNEMPLOYMENT LINE 5.11 66
UNFORGIVEN 5.11C 233
UNKNOWN (SHIPYARD LEFT SIDE) 5.13 147
UNLEASHED 5.11+ 265
UNNAMED #1 (HIDEOUT) 5.11 243
UNNAMED #1 (PINKY TOWER BUTTRESS) 5.10+ 81

UNNAMED #2 (HIDEOUT) 5.11 243
UNNAMED #2 (PINKY TOWER BUTTRESS) 5.10- 81
UNNAMED (ABRAXAS) 5.9+ 262
UNNAMED AID ROUTE (MAVERICK CENTER) 162
UNNAMED (ALCOVE LEFT) 5.10 80
UNNAMED (ALCOVE RIGHT) 5.11 79
UNNAMED (BRUMLEY) 5.11A 284
UNNAMED (BRUMLEY)5.12 284
UNNAMED (BUTTRESS 1) 5.11 167
UNNAMED (BUTTRESS 3) 5.10+ 169
UNNAMED (CARNIVORE AREA) 5.10+ 167
UNNAMED (COOLER WALL) 5.10+ 172
UNNAMED CORNER 2 (BUTTRESS 2) 5.11A 169
UNNAMED CORNER (BLOCK TOWER AREA) 5.11 131
UNNAMED CORNER (BUTTRESS 2) 5.10 169
UNNAMED (COVE) 5.10 35
UNNAMED (COVE) 5.11+ 35
UNNAMED (DAY CANYON) 5.9 136
UNNAMED (DEADMAN'S BUTTRESS) 5.10 148
UNNAMED (DEADMAN'S BUTTRESS) 5.11 148
UNNAMED (DEADMAN'S BUTTRESS) 5.11 150
UNNAMED (DOG WALL) 5.10 274
UNNAMED (DOG WALL) 5.10+ 274
UNNAMED FLAKE (TOWN WALL) 5.10 298
UNNAMED (GIN AND TECTONICS AREA) 5.? 151
UNNAMED HANG NAIL (GOLD BAR TOWER AREA) 5.8 134
UNNAMED (ICP) 5.7 268
UNNAMED (MAVERICK CENTER) 5.10 162
UNNAMED (MAVERICK CENTER) 5.11 162
UNNAMED (MAVERICK LEFT) 5.10 162
UNNAMED (MAVERICK LEFT) 5.10+ 162
UNNAMED (MAVERICK LEFT) 5.11 163
UNNAMED (MAVERICK LEFT) 5.XXX 163
UNNAMED OFFSET (TOWN WALL) 5.11 298
UNNAMED (RAPTOR TOWER) 5.11 138
UNNAMED RIGHT-FACING CORNER (TOWN WALL) 5.10 298
UNNAMED ROUTE (WALL STREET) 5.11D 121
UNNAMED (SCORCHED EARTH) 5.10+ 272
UNNAMED (SHADY CRAG) 5.10 164
UNNAMED (SHADY CRAG) 5.11 164
UNNAMED (SHIPYARD LEFT SIDE) 5.12D A0 147
UNNAMED SPLITTER (REPTILIAN WALL RIGHT) 5.10+ 157
UNNAMED SPLITTER (TOWN WALL) 5.10+ 298
UNNAMED SPLITTER WITH CORNER (TOWN WALL) 5.10 298
UNNAMED SPORT 5.10B 284
UNNAMED (TOWN WALL) 5.10 297
UNNAMED (TOWN WALL) 5.11 298
UNNAMED (TRAD WALL) 5.11+ 48
UNNAMED (TRENCHTOWN) 5.11C/D 293
UNNAMED (WALL STREET) 5.6 116
UNNAMED (WALL STREET) 5.9 121
UNNAMED (WALL STREET) 5.10+ 118
UNNAMED (WALL STREET) 5.11 114
UNNAMED (WALL STREET) 5.11B 111
UNNAMED (WALL STREET) 5.12 114, 118
UNNAMED (WALL STREET) 5.12+ 124
UNNAMED (WALL STREET) 5.12B 121
UP IN SMOKE 5.8 293
UP IN SMOKE 5.10 243
USS TOLEDO (SSN-769) 5.11+ 145

V

VAN GO 5.6 156
VANILLA CREAM 5.10+ 268
VERTICAL FLU 5.10+ 157
VIETCONG DOUBLE CLUTCH V7 134
VISIBLE PANTY LINE 5.10 119
VIVARIN 5.11B 265
VOODOO AREA 208
VOODOO CHILD 5.11+ 209

W

WAKE OF THE FLOOD 5.10C 119
WALDEN'S ROOM 5.10 27
WALK ON THE WIDE SIDE 5.10 129
WALL STREET 105, 110
WARLOCK 44
WARM-UP LEFT 5.11 284
WARM-UP RIGHT 5.10B 284
WARRIOR TOWER 171
WARSTEINER 5.11 111
WASH BOULDER (#3) 196
WASHER WOMAN TOWER 69
WATER STREAK 108
WAY OF IGNORANCE 5.12- 65
WEAK BOSONS 5.11+ 178
WEAPONS GRADE 5.11 83
WELCOME TO ANEXIA 5.12 116
WEST FACE 5.10+ 97
WEST FACE 5.11 93
WEST FACE 5.11C 92
WEST FACE (CASTLETON) 5.11 216
WEST SIDE STORY 5.11+ 223
WHAT'S IN A NAME 5.10D 202
WHERE EGOS DARE 5.10+ 130
WHERE HAVE ALL THE WILD THINGS GONE 5.11 232
WHITE RIM-RIGHT 47
WHITE WAY 5.11 129
WHY DOES IT HURT WHEN I PEE 5.11 156
WICKED 5.13 153
WILD-EYED DEAR 5.12 121
WILLOW WHIP 5.6 120
WILSON ARCH 5.5 302
WINDY RIDGE 273
WINGS OF LEATHER 5.11 PG-13 44
WITCH 41
WITH A SOUTHWEST FLARE 5.10 173
WITH BATED BREATH 5.12A 202
WORD TO THE BIRD 5.12- 61
WORKING CLASS HERO 5.9 136

X

XYLOKANE 5.11+ 262

Y

YESTERDAY'S NEWS 5.10 65
YEYO 5.11B 291
YOGINI 5.7 127

Z

ZEN GARDEN V10 134
ZENYATTA ENTRADA 5.8 C3- 94
ZEUS 59
ZIGZAG 5.10 118
ZIPPER 5.12C 107
ZIPPY 5.10+ 47
ZOOL 5.10D 291

Appendices

Index of Routes and Crags

SYMBOLS
2 FRIENDS GETTING RED 5.11- 50
313 SLABS 36
5/15/37 5.12 165
10 TO 8 5.10 293
12 MONKEYS 5.12C R 284
30 SECONDS OVER POTASH 5.8 121
100TH MONKEY 5.11 147
191 SOUTH 295
313 ROAD 31
2012 5.11 163

A
A3B 5.10 48
ABOVE A FISTFUL 5.11 114
ABRAXAS LEFT 5.10 262
ABRAXAS RIGHT 5.10+ 262
ABRAXAS WALL 261
ADRENALINE CIRCUS 5.10+ 186
ADRENILINE 5.11A 265
ADVENTURE 183
ADVENTURES IN BABYSITTING 5.7 203
AEROBICIDE 5.11+ 138
AFTER THE RAIN 5.10+ 28
ALBATROSS 5.11 29
ALBERTS-WEBSTER 5.12+ 147
ALCOVE 79
ALCOVE LEFT 80
ALCOVE RIGHT 79
ALIEN ABDUCTION 5.12A 106
ALL ALONG THE PUTT TOWER 5.10 279
ALL THE WORLD'S A STAGE 5.12A 202
ALPHA BLONDY 5.12- 294
ANACONDA 5.11 158
ANCIENT ART 248
ANDROIDS 5.10B/C 106
ANDROIDS WAFFLE HOT LINE 5.10+ 137
ANGLE RUNNER A2 148
ANOTHER FINE DAY 5.10 138
ANOTHER ROADSIDE DISTRACTION 5.10B 115
APE INDEX 5.10+ 147
APOLOGY 5.11 176
ARC ANGEL 5.10 127
ARCHAIC REVIVAL 5.11- 264
ARCHES NATIONAL PARK 85
ARGON TOWER 92
ARMAGEDDON 5.12A/B 129
ARMY OF DARKNESS (#2) 196
ARROWHEAD LEFT 5.10+ 217
ARTIST TEARS 5.8 C3 183
ASTROLAD 5.11 115

B
B4WARNED 5.11 48
BABEL 5.10 203
BABY BLUE 5.11 123
BACHELOR CRACK 5.10 244
BAD HABIT 5.11C 233
BAD MOKI ROOF 5.9 116
BAKERY 266
BAKERY ROUTE 5.11 266
BANANA PEEL 5.10B 126
BARNEY RUMBLE TOWER 100
BASKETBALL DIARIES V5 196
BASS ACKWARDS 5.10+ 273
BEACH PARTY 5.11 36
BEAR BONES 5.11 153
BEEF TIPS 5.11 173
BEE LINE 5.10+ 136
BEER RUN 5.10+ 273
BEGINNING 5.10B 153

BELCER TRAVERSE (#15) 200
BELCER TRAVERSE V6 200
BEN'S CRACK 5.10 284
BENSON AND LEDGES 5.10+ 47
BE THERE OR BE TALKED ABOUT 5.11 C0 93
BE TRUE! 5.11A 202
BEYER FRICTION 5.9 36
BEYER OFFWIDTH 5.9+ 124
B.F.E. 51
BFE 5.11 51
BIG BEND BOULDERS 193
BIG BEND BUTTE 190
BIG HORN BEAVER (#14) 200
BIG HORNY SHEEP 5.12A 106
BIG HUCK V7 197
BIG MAN WALL 48
BIG PUSSY IN DOGTOWN 5.11- 274
BIG SKY MUD FLAPS 5.10+ 129
BIHEDRAL 5.10 138
BIONIC CHRONIC 5.10 242
BIRDS VIEW BUTTE 66
BIRTH CANAL 5.10 176
BIRTH CANAL 5.11+ 84
BIRTHING ROCK AREA 263
BISTRO CRAGS 171
BITTERSWEET 5.10 174
BLACK BOX BOULDER (#7) 197
BLACK BOULDER (#16) 200
BLACK AND STACKS 5.10+ 176
BLACK SLAB 5.6 268
BLACK SUN 5.10B 217
BLACK WIDOW 5.12- 138
BLOCK TOP BOULDER (#1) 196
BLOCK TOWER AREA 131
BLOOD HUSH 5.12 178
BLOODY KNEES 5.9 182
BLOWIN' CHUNKS 5.11B 121
BLUE LIGHT SPECIAL V9 197
BOLDNESS BE MY FRIEND 5.12A 202
BOLTS TO BUMPY LAND 5.11 120
BOMBAY MARTINI 5.12- 169
BONE DOCTOR 5.10B 289
BOOGNISH TOWER 5.10 137
BOOT HILL 5.12 161
BOOTLEG TOWER 137
BOUNDARY WALL 49
BUY HOWDY 5.11+ 273
BREWED AWAKENINGS 5.5 268
BROADS HATE PODS 5.10+ 145
BROKEN ENGAGEMENTS 5.10 A3 126
BROWN BANANA 5.9 126
BRUSH-PAINTED DATSUN 5.10 137
BUMPING UGLIES 5.11D 284
BURN ANOTHER ONE DOWN 5.11B 244
BURNING INSIDE 5.11B 217
BURN ONE DOWN 5.10 244
BUSHIDO 5.13+ 263
BUTTERFLY 5.13A 107
BUTT PYGMIES 5.11 145
BUTTRESS 1 167
BUTTRESS 2 (BOND BUTTRESS) 167
BUTTRESS 3 169
BUY OR FLY 5.12 36
BUZZ LUST 5.12 137

C
CAMELOT 277
CAMEO 5.9+ 106
CANYONLANDS 45
CANYONLANDS/WHITE RIM LEFT 68
CAPTAIN HOOK 5.11 156
CARNIVORE 5.12B 107
CARNIVORE AREA 167
CASTLETON TOWER 212
CASTLE VALLEY 205

CAULDRONS 43
CHALK IS CHEAP 5.12 149
CHAMELEON 5.11 157
CHAOS BOULDER (#8) 197
CHAOS V8 197
CHARLIE HORSE NEEDLE 52
CHARLIE HORSE NEEDLE 5.11 52
CHASIN' SKIRT 5.10+ 150
CHEF'S SPECIAL 5.10 173
CHEMISTRY 5.12 115
CHERRY ON TOP 5.10B/C 266
CHICKEN LITTLE 5.10+ 242
CHICKEN TEJERO 5.11 136
CHILLUM 5.8 292
CHIMNEY SWEEP 5.10 120
CHINESE EYES 5.10 95
CHOCOLATE CHUNK 5.3 127
CHOPPER 5.10+ 149
CHRISCROSS 5.11A 128
CHRISTINE'S WAY BUFF SAAB 5.9 137
CINEMA 203
CINEMA AND THE THEATRE 201
CIRCLE OF QUIET 5.11+ 49
CIRCUS TRICK LEFT V4 198
CIRCUS TRICK RIGHT V5 198
CLANTONS IN THE DUST 5.10+ 161
CLEARLIGHT 5.11 190
COBRA 5.11 R 247
COBRA 5.12 158
COCKBLOCKER 5.9+ 293
COFFIN 5.9 269
CONCEPCION 5.13- 136
CONSTRICTOR 5.10+ 242
COOLER WALL 172
CORNER ROUTE (TOMBSTONES) 5.12 258
COUP D'ETAT 5.11+ 111
COVE 35
COWARDS DIE 5.12B 202
COWBOY ROUTE 5.6 301
COYOTE CALLING 5.11+ 230
CRACK 1 5.8 268
CRACK 2 5.8 268
CRACK 3 5.8 268
CRACK HOUSE 84
CRACK HOUSE 5.13 84
CRACK V3 (HIGH BALLS BOULDER #4) 196
CRACK WARS 5.11 229
CRACK WHORES 5.10+ 229
CREEKER 5.9 271
CRITICAL MASS 5.8 268
CROOKED ARROW SPIRE 207
CROW'S HEAD SPIRE/BIRD'S EYE BUTTE 65
CULVERT CANYON 131
CYCLOPS 5.11 80
CZECHOSLOVAKIAN VAG 5.10B 289

D
DANTE 5.9 271
DARK ANGEL 97
DARK PATH 5.11B 272
DAVID 5.?? 165
DAWN OF AN ERROR 5.11 148
DAY CANYON 136
DEAD END AREA 27
DEAD HORSE POINT AREA 60
DEADMAN'S BUTTRESS 148
DEAD RINGER 5.11D 149
DEARLY DEPARTED 5.11- 229
DEATH FLAKES TRAVERSE V0 198
DEATH TRAP 5.8 269
DELIVERANCE 5.11 166
DESCENT RAMP V0 198
DESERT GLOW 5.11 106

Index

MUSTANG MAN 5.11+ 162
NAKED RUNNING "DO ME" MAN 5.11+ 273
NAVAJO WARRIOR 5.11+ 262
NIGHT VISION 5.11+ 145
OXYGEN DEBT 5.11+ 182
POSSESSED 5.11+ 269
PRIMROSE DIHEDRALS 5.11+ 56
PROHIBITION CRACK 5.11+ 137
RAWHIDE 5.11+ 161
REIGN OF DUST 5.11+ 279
ROOM WITH A VIEW 5.11+ 116
SCHOOL MASTER 5.11+ 154
SHORT CRACK 5.11+ 163
SISYPHUS 5.11+ 59
SKELETONIC 5.11+ 124
SKINWALKER 5.11+ 141
STILETTO 5.11+ 272
STINGRAY 5.11+ 153
SURFACE TENSION 5.11+ 259
THINK YA SHOULD 5.11+ 61
TOUCHÉ 5.11+ 273
TRAIL OF THE NAVAJO 5.11+ 98
TWO PLUMB 5.11+ 153
UNLEASHED 5.11+ 265
UNNAMED (COVE) 5.11+ 35
UNNAMED (TRAD WALL) 5.11+ 48
USS TOLEDO (SSN-769) 5.11+ 145
VOODOO CHILD 5.11+ 209
WEAK BOSONS 5.11+ 178
WEST SIDE STORY 5.11+ 223
XYLOKANE 5.11+ 262

5.12-

ALPHA BLONDY 5.12- 294
BLACK WIDOW 5.12- 138
BOMBAY MARTINI 5.12- 169
HAPPY HUNTING GROUND 5.12- 171
JINX 5.12- 169
MAN AFTER MIDNIGHT 5.12- 123
MISSISSIPPI HIGH STEP 5.12- 116
OCTOPUSSY 5.12- 169
QUANTUM OF SOLACE 5.12- 169
SEVENTH SERPENT EXTENSION 5.12- 159
SKIN AMBIVALENCE 5.12- 210
STEWING OVER ART 5.12- 147
TRICERATOPS MIDDLE 5.12- 157
TWO SCORPION TELSONS 5.12- 159
WAY OF IGNORANCE 5.12- 65
WORD TO THE BIRD 5.12- 61

5.12A

ALIEN ABDUCTION 5.12A 106
ALL THE WORLD'S A STAGE 5.12A 202
BIG HORNY SHEEP 5.12A 106
BOLDNESS BE MY FRIEND 5.12A 202
EVISCERATE 5.12A 107
JESUS SAVES 5.12A 224
POCKMARKS 5.12A 107
SHIVA 5.12A 240
WITH BATED BREATH 5.12A 202

5.12B

ARMAGEDDON 5.12A/B 129
CARNIVORE 5.12B 167
COWARDS DIE 5.12B 202
DESP-ARÊTE 5.12B 123
MIDNIGHT FRIGHTENING 5.12B 111
NERVE NET 5.12B 108
NOTHING CIRCUMSTANTIAL 5.12B 294
OUT DAMNED SPOT! 5.12B 202
ROOFUS 5.12A/B 293
SACRED GROUND 5.12B 214
SUB LUX 5.12B 107
TAKE A CHANCE ON ME 5.12B 116
TR (WINDY RIDGE) 5.12B 273
UNNAMED (WALL STREET) 5.12B 121
UNDER THE BOARDWALK 5.12B/C 121

5.12

BLOOD HUSH 5.12 178
BOOT HILL 5.12 161
BUY OR FLY 5.12 36
BUZZ LUST 5.12 137
CHALK IS CHEAP 5.12 149
CHEMISTRY 5.12 115
COBRA 5.12 158
CORNER ROUTE (TOMBSTONES) 5.12 258
DOG ON A STONE ROOF 5.12 290
DRAGON'S BREATH 5.12 134
ELVIS MEMORIAL 5.12 35
END OF STORY 5.12 223
FESTUS 5.12 162
FINGER BANDIT 5.12 137
FLOUR 5.12 266
HAPPY ENDING 5.12 210
HEADSTACK 5.12 151
HOE DOWN 5.12 161
INFRARED 5.12 190
IRON MAIDEN 5.12 189
JUNK IN THE TRUNK 5.12 111
KISS OF THE SPIDER WOMEN 5.12 136
KURA BURAN 5.12 267
LITTLE BIG MAN 5.12 48
MADE IN THE SHADE 5.12 167
MAY FLY 5.12 242
PLUNGE 5.12 29
PROUDEST MONKEY 5.12 147
RALPH 5.12 176
RUDE OLD MEN 5.12 110
SATAN'S REVENGE 5.12 299
SHIT EATIN' GRIN 5.12 150
SOMETHING NASTY 5.12 123
STRONG MUONS 5.12 178
TANK BRAIN 5.12 148
TORPEDO BAY 5.12 147
TOWN FULL OF FINGERS 5.12 298
T-REX 5.12 269
TWO HEATHENS & THE PROPHET 5.12 150
UNNAMED (BRUMLEY) 5.12 284
UNNAMED (WALL STREET) 5.12 114
WELCOME TO ANEXIA 5.12 116
WILD-EYED DEAR 5.12 121
5/15/37 5.12 165

5.12C

FIGHT CLUB 5.12C 284
FINGER OF FATE 5.12C 250
JINGUS LAUNCH 5.12 121
PALE FIRE 5.12C 54
ZIPPER 5.12C 107
NO FLY ZONE 5.12C 114
12 MONKEYS 5.12C 284

5.12D

STAPH 5.12C/D 107
EL CUCHILLO 5.12D 284
EL CAHONE 5.12D 284
SENTENCE TO BURN 5.12D 284
HORIZONTAL MAMBO 5.12D 116

5.13

CRACK HOUSE 5.13 84
EXCOMMUNICATION 5.13 235
GLAD TO BE TRAD 5.13 48
HIDDEN GEM 5.13 298
RADIOACTIVE PORKSICKLE 5.13 178
SHOGUN 5.13 263
SUNSET TOWER 5.13 33
UNKNOWN (SHIPYARD LEFT SIDE) 5.13 147
WICKED 5.13 153

5.14

CENTURY CRACK 5.14B 73